Rebuilding Leviathan

Why do some governing parties limit their opportunistic behavior and constrain the extraction of private gains from the state? The analysis of post-communist state reconstruction provides surprising answers to this fundamental question of party politics. Across the post-communist democracies, governing parties have opportunistically reconstructed the state – simultaneously exploiting it by extracting state resources and building new institutions that further such extraction. They enfeebled or delayed formal state institutions of monitoring and oversight, established new discretionary structures of state administration, and extracted enormous informal profits from the privatization of the communist economy.

Yet there is also enormous variation in these processes across the post-communist democracies of Bulgaria, the Czech Republic, Estonia, Hungary, Latvia, Lithuania, Poland, Slovakia, and Slovenia. Party competition is responsible – specifically, the more robust the competition, the more the governing parties faced a credible threat of replacement and the more they curbed exploitation by building formal barriers, moderating their own behavior and sharing power with the opposition.

Anna Grzymała-Busse is Associate Professor of Political Science at the University of Michigan, Ann Arbor. She previously taught at Yale University. Her first book, *Redeeming the Communist Past*, was published by Cambridge University Press in 2002. She has also published articles in *Comparative Political Studies*, *Comparative Politics*, *East European Politics and Societies*, *Party Politics*, *Politics and Society*, and other journals.

Cambridge Studies in Comparative Politics

General Editor
Margaret Levi   *University of Washington, Seattle*

Assistant General Editor
Stephen Hanson   *University of Washington, Seattle*

Associate Editors
Robert H. Bates   *Harvard University*
Helen Milner   *Princeton University*
Frances Rosenbluth   *Yale University*
Susan Stokes   *Yale University*
Sidney Tarrow   *Cornell University*
Kathleen Thelen   *Northwestern University*
Erik Wibbels   *University of Washington, Seattle*

Other Books in the Series

Lisa Baldez, *Why Women Protest: Women's Movements in Chile*
Stefano Bartolini, *The Political Mobilization of the European Left,
     1860–1980: The Class Cleavage*
Mark R. Beissinger, *Nationalist Mobilization and the Collapse of the Soviet
     State*
Nancy Bermeo, ed., *Unemployment in the New Europe*
Carles Boix, *Democracy and Redistribution*
Carles Boix, *Political Parties, Growth, and Equality: Conservative and Social
     Democratic Economic Strategies in the World Economy*
Catherine Boone, *Merchant Capital and the Roots of State Power in Senegal,
     1930–1985*
Catherine Boone, *Political Topographies of the African State: Territorial
     Authority and Institutional Change*
Michael Bratton and Nicolas van de Walle, *Democratic Experiments in
     Africa: Regime Transitions in Comparative Perspective*

Continued after the Index

Rebuilding Leviathan

PARTY COMPETITION AND STATE EXPLOITATION IN POST-COMMUNIST DEMOCRACIES

ANNA GRZYMAŁA-BUSSE

University of Michigan, Ann Arbor

CAMBRIDGE
UNIVERSITY PRESS

CAMBRIDGE UNIVERSITY PRESS
Cambridge, New York, Melbourne, Madrid, Cape Town, Singapore, São Paulo

Cambridge University Press
32 Avenue of the Americas, New York, NY 10013-2473, USA

www.cambridge.org
Information on this title: www.cambridge.org/9780521873963

First published 2007

Printed in the United States of America

A catalog record for this publication is available from the British Library.

Library of Congress Cataloging in Publication Data
Grzymała-Busse, Anna Maria, 1970–
Rebuilding Leviathan : party competition and state exploitation in post-communist
democracies / Anna Grzymała-Busse.
    p.   cm. – (Cambridge studies in comparative politics)
Includes bibliographical references and index.
ISBN-13: 978-0-521-87396-3 (hardback)
ISBN-13: 978-0-521-69615-9 (pbk.)
ISBN-10: 0-521-87396-7 (hardback)
ISBN-10: 0-521-69615-1 (pbk.)
1. Political parties – Europe, Eastern.   2. Post-communism – Europe, Eastern.
3. Europe, Eastern – Politics and government – 1989–   I. Title.
JN96.A979G78   2007
324.20947–dc22   2006026397

ISBN   978-0-521-87396-3 hardback
ISBN   978-0-521-69615-9 paperback

For Conrad

Contents

Acknowledgments

This book could not have been written without the kindness and generosity of friends, colleagues, and family.

Much of the primary research for this book was made possible with the help of, among others, Jacek Czaputowicz, Dace Dance, Urszula Krassowska, Tomasz Krause, Jacek Kwieciński, Maria Laatspera, Monika Saarman, Adéla Seidlová, and Martin Slosiarik.

I am extremely grateful to those who read the manuscript in its entirety: Jessica Allina-Pisano, Umut Aydin, Joshua Berke, Jim Caporaso, Erica Johnson, Steve Hanson, Yoshiko Herrera, Pauline Jones Luong, Margaret Levi, Vicky Murillo, Işik Özel, Lucan Way, and Erik Wibbels. Val Bunce, Bill Clark, Keith Darden, Abby Innes, Orit Kedar, Kelly McMann, Rob Mickey, Grigo Pop-Eleches, Cindy Skach, Barry Weingast, Rebecca Weitz-Shapiro, and Daniel Ziblatt read chapters of the book, improving them immensely.

Along the way, Jake Bowers, Tim Colton, Grzegorz Ekiert, Venelin Ganev, Don Green, Peter Hall, Allen Hicken, Gary King, Orit Kedar, Ken Kollman, Kaz Poznanski, Jim Vreeland, and Barry Weingast all provided very helpful criticism and advice. Gary Bass, Heather Gerken, and Jennifer Pitts greatly helped in the final stages. Daniel Hopkins analyzed public opinion data, and Ben Lawless, Jesse Shook, and Shubra Sohri provided research assistance.

Lew Bateman was the pluperfect editor, encouraging and exacting. I am especially grateful to Margaret Levi, not only for editing the series and arranging a manuscript workshop at the University of Washington, Seattle, but for her terrific mentoring. I am one of the many scholars who have benefited from her generosity and support.

The University of Michigan, the Center for European Studies at Harvard University, the Harvard Academy, and Yale University were congenial settings in which to research, think, and write. For their financial and intellectual support, I am grateful to IREX, NCEEER, the Institution for Social and Policy Studies at Yale University, the Yale Center for International and Area Studies, and the International Institute at the University of Michigan.

The ideas for this book first sprouted at the "Rethinking the Post-Communist State" conference Pauline Jones Luong and I organized at Yale University in 2001. They grew as parts of this manuscript were presented at the University of California-Berkeley, the University of Chicago, Cornell University, Harvard University, McGill University, the Massachusetts Institute of Technology (MIT), the University of Michigan, the University of Wisconsin-Madison, the World Bank, and Yale University. The careful readers and listeners at these institutions helped me to sharpen the argument and clarify my thinking.

My wonderful parents and brothers, as always, provided inspiration, love, and perspective. My final and greatest thanks go to Joshua Berke, for his intelligence, sense of humor, and passion. As I was finishing this book, our first formal collaboration arrived. This book is dedicated to him, with his parents' love.

List of Political Party Abbreviations and Acronyms

Acronym	Organization	Translation	Country
AWS	Akcja Wyborcza Solidarność	Election Action Solidarity	Poland
BSP	Balgarska Socialisticheska Partija	Bulgarian Socialist Party	Bulgaria
ČSSD	Česká strana sociálně demokratická	Social Democratic Party of the Czech Republic	Czech Republic
DemOS	Demokratska Opozicija Slovenije	Democratic Opposition of Slovenia	Slovenia
DP	Darbo Partija	Labor Party	Lithuania
DU	Demokratická Únia	Democratic Union	Slovakia
EK	Eesti Keskerakond	Center Party	Estonia
Fidesz-MPP	Fiatal Demokraták Szövetsége–Magyar Polgári Szövetség	Alliance of Young Democrats–Hungarian Civic Party	Hungary
FKgP	Független Kisgazda, Földmunkás és Polgári Párt	Smallholders' Party	Hungary
HZDS	Hnutie za Demokratické Slovensko	Movement for a Democratic Slovakia	Slovakia
JL	Jaunais Laiks	New Era	Latvia
KDU-ČSL	Křesťanská a demokratická unie–Česká strana lidová	Christian Democrats	Czech Republic
LC	Latvijas Ceļš	Latvia's Way	Latvia
LDDP	Lietuvos Demokratinė Darbo Partija	Lithuanian Democratic Labor Party	Lithuania
LDS	Liberalna Demokracija Slovenije	Liberal Democratic Party of Slovenia	Slovenia
MDF	Magyar Demokrata Fórum	Hungarian Democratic Forum	Hungary

Acronym	Organization	Translation	Country
MIEP	Magyar Igazság és Élet Pártja	Justice and Life Party	Hungary
MSzP	Magyar Szocialista Párt	Hungarian Socialist Party	Hungary
NDSV	Nacionalno Dvizhenie Simeon Vtori	National Movement Simeon II	Bulgaria
PC	Porozumienie Centrum	Center Alliance	Poland
PCTVL	Par Cilvēka Tiesībām Vienotā Latvijā	For Human Rights in a United Latvia	Latvia
PiS	Prawo i Sprawiedliwosc	Law and Justice	Poland
PO	Platforma Obywatelska	Civic Platform	Poland
PSL	Polskie Stronnictwo Ludowe	Polish Peasants' Party	Poland
PZPR	Polska Zjednoczona Partia Robotnicza	Polish United Workers' Party	Poland
NS	Naujoji sajunga	New Union Party	Lithuania
ODA	Občanská Democratická Aliance	Civic Democratic Alliance	Czech Republic
ODS	Občanská Demokratická Strana	Civil Democratic Party	Czech Republic
OF	Občanské Forum	Civic Forum	Czech Republic
SDK	Slovenska Demokraticka Koalície	Democratic Coalition of Slovakia	Slovakia
SDS	Sajuz na demokratichnite sili	Union of Democratic Forces	Bulgaria
SdRP	Socjaldemokracja Rzeczpospolitej Polskiej	Social Democracy of the Republic of Poland	Poland
SLD	Sojusz Lewicy Demokratycznej	Democratic Left Alliance	Poland
SLS	Slovenska Ljudska Stranka	Slovenian People's Party	Slovenia
SzDSz	Szabad Demokraták Szövetsége	Alliance of Free Democrats	Hungary
TS/LK	Tėvynės Sajunga/Lietuvos Konservatoriai	Homeland Union/Lithuanian Conservatives	Lithuania
UD	Unia Demokratyczna	Democratic Union	Poland
US	Unie Svobody	Freedom Union	Czech Republic
UW	Unia Wolności	Freedom Union	Poland
VPN	Verejnost' proti násiliu	Public Against Violence	Slovakia
ZRS	Združenie robotníkov Slovenska	Association of Slovak Workers	Slovakia

1

Introduction

> All happy families are alike; each unhappy family is unhappy in its own way.
> Leo Tolstoy, *Anna Karenina*

Why can some political parties freely reap private gains from the state while others constrain such extraction? The proliferation of sovereign states after the communist collapse in Eastern Europe and the Soviet Union in 1989–91 provides surprising answers that recast the relationship among political parties, party competition, and the state. It demonstrates that the degree to which governing parties can obtain private benefits from public state assets is constrained by *robust competition*: opposition parties that offer a clear, plausible, and critical governing alternative that threatens the governing coalition with replacement. This prospect induces anxious governments to moderate their behavior, create formal state institutions, and share power – in short, to construct safeguards against the extraction of state resources. Opposition can thus limit discretion – and inadvertently build the state.

Such competition is critical in new democracies, as the development of post-communist states shows. As democratic governing parties established the institutions of market and democracy after the communist collapse, they also opportunistically reconstructed the state: the set of formal institutions that implement policy and enforce legal sanctions.[1] Democratic

---

[1] These institutions comprise the formal rules and structures that administer citizen obligations (taxes, military service, and so on) and public provisions (infrastructure, rule of law, welfare, defense, and so on). The political control of the state may change (as governments do), but the state administrative apparatus endures as the executive framework. See Lawson, Stephanie. 1993. "Conceptual Issues in the Comparative Study of Regime Change and Democratization," *Comparative Politics*, 25, 2 (January): 183–205.

parties that earlier sought to eliminate authoritarian abuses of the state[2] were all too happy to benefit themselves subsequently while rebuilding state institutions, and to build in continued access to state resources. The result was an exploitative reconstruction of state institutions, or simply put, *state exploitation*: the direct extraction of state resources and the building of new channels for such extraction. Across the post-communist countries, democratic parties shared the motives, means, and opportunities to exploit the state. However, differences in political competition explain why democracy alone could not stop state exploitation, and why some parties were more constrained than others. Rebuilding the post-communist Leviathan – the structures of the state – thus comprised both competition and exploitation.

Post-Communist Democratic Parties and the State

While the majority of post-communist states remained authoritarian (if no longer communist),[3] full-fledged parliamentary democracies arose in Bulgaria, the Czech Republic, Estonia, Hungary, Latvia, Lithuania, Poland, Slovakia, and Slovenia. They joined the "happy family" of democracies with functioning free markets, pluralist party politics, and democratic parliaments. Yet even as these countries navigated the treacherous terrain of economic and democratic transition, they also embarked on a path of reconstructing state administration, institutions, and agencies. As important as state development was to prove, however, few domestic political observers or international organizations paid heed to this transformation, in contrast to the close attention paid to economic and democratic transitions.

Away from the spotlight, democratic parties strove to ensure their own survival – the long-term ability to contest elections and enter office. Defying Tolstoy, political parties in post-communist democracies differed a great deal from other democratic parties in their relationship to the state. They did not use strategies of survival widely observed in earlier West European or Latin American democracies, such as the building of clientelist networks that exchange club goods for voter support or the "encapsulation" of voters through extensive mass party organizations that build loyal constituencies. Post-communist parties did make programmatic appeals – but

---

[2] Many of the post-1989 democratic parties had initially arisen out of the opposition to the communist regime.

[3] Freedom House identifies fifteen of the twenty-seven states as either authoritarian or "hybrid," combining some democratic practices with undemocratic outcomes. Freedom House. 2004. *Nations in Transit, 2004*. Washington: Freedom House.

did not rely on them to ensure their ability to contest elections in the long term. Nor did they simply prey on the state, extracting as much as possible without building new state institutions of public good provision. They also explicitly rejected their communist predecessors' strategy of eliminating political competition and fusing the state with the ruling party.

Instead, post-communist democratic parties relied on opportunistic state reconstruction, establishing longer-term access to state resources where possible. Such reconstruction meant renovating outdated and porous communist-era state institutions and creating the new legal and regulatory frameworks for market and democratic competition. New institutions were frequently established on the basis of existing communist state structures: Civil service laws, for example, augmented existing labor codes. Governing parties also built entirely new state institutions of public good provision: creating new agencies and ministries, defining the domains of state oversight and regulation of markets, and enforcing new economic and political rules. State rebuilding thus resembled bricolage: using both new institutional bricks and materials leftover from the communist state structures.[4]

Where they could, political parties also exploited the state.[5] Parties politicized the privatization and distribution of state assets for their own benefit and skimmed directly, as part of a larger system of an unregulated and unrestricted party funding. They delayed or enfeebled formal state institutions of oversight and regulation, and expanded the discretionary (uncontrolled and unmonitored) sector of state administration (such as extrabudgetary funds or state institutions removed from public oversight). Most of these new institutions were established in the wake of economic and political reforms. As a result, the ostensible building of democracies and markets was inextricably linked to state exploitation and side benefits for the political actors in charge. The prizes included public contracts, financial transfers, and built-in channels that allowed future gains.[6]

The key constraint on such exploitation was robust party competition. Where the opposition parties were clear and plausible governing alternatives and powerful critics, governing parties did not take advantage of

---

[4] Grzymała-Busse, Anna, and Jones Luong, Pauline. 2002. "Reconceptualizing the Post-Communist State," *Politics and Society*, 30, 4 (December): 529–54.

[5] Kopecký, Petr. 2006. "Political Parties and the State in Post-Communist Europe: The Nature of the Symbiosis." *Journal of Communist Studies and Transition Politics*, 22, 3 (September): 251–73.

[6] Suleiman, Ezra N. 2003. *Dismantling Democratic States*. Princeton: Princeton University Press, p. 245.

the full opportunities for private gain in state reconstruction. Instead, they gained less from privatization processes, rapidly built formal institutions of monitoring and oversight, and controlled the growth of state administration. Where the opposition was vague, implausible, and uncritical, governing parties more freely exploited the state, both by directly obtaining resources and by building in enormous discretion to extract in the future.

We thus see distinct patterns of state exploitation across the consolidated post-communist democracies and free markets of Bulgaria, the Czech Republic, Estonia, Hungary, Latvia, Lithuania, Poland, Slovakia, and Slovenia. There is pronounced variation across three key state domains that fell under the direct control of governing coalitions: a) the creation of formal state institutions of oversight and monitoring; b) the discretionary (unmonitored and unregulated) expansion of state administration employment, such as the growth of extrabudgetary agencies and funds; and c) the appropriation of privatization profits and unregulated public subsidies. Public opinion polls and World Bank governance rankings reveal a similar pattern.[7] A simple additive index summarizes the variation across these three domains, shown in Table 1.1.

As Table 1.1 indicates, two clusters arose as early as 1993. In one, including Bulgaria, the former Czechoslovakia, and Latvia, governing parties extracted material gains, and deliberately delayed the introduction of oversight and regulation of state assets, with little effort to transform the state into a more rational-bureaucratic organization.[8] Accusations surfaced of deliberate sabotage of state effectiveness and transparency.[9] These same parties expanded state administration employment through discretionary hiring and the creation of numerous extrabudgetary funds and agencies. They also skimmed profits from privatization revenues and deliberately

---

[7] For example, public opinion polls reveal that parliaments were seen as corrupt by 58 percent of the respondents in Slovakia, 74 percent in Romania, 49 percent in Bulgaria and the Czech Republic, 48 percent in Hungary, and 40 percent in Poland (USAID public opinion poll, Radio Free Europe/Radio Liberty broadcast, 10 November 1999, Slovakia). See Kaufman, Daniel, Kraay, A., and Mastruzzi, M. 2005. *Governance Matters IV: Governance Indicators 1996–2004*. Washington: World Bank. The *Governance Matters* dataset reveal a consistent pattern with Estonia, Hungary, and Slovenia receiving highest rankings in categories such as Rule of Law, Regulatory Quality, Control of Corruption, Government Effectiveness, and so on. Bulgaria, Latvia, and Slovakia tend to receive considerably lower rankings, with the Czech Republic and Poland in the middle, changing places from year to year (the dataset aggregated think tank and expert surveys in 1996, 1998, 2000, 2002, and 2004).

[8] Rice, Eric. 1992. "Public Administration in Post-Socialist Eastern Europe," *Public Administration Review*, 52, 2 (March/April): 116–24.

[9] See the scandals that broke out in the Czech press in 1996–8 and in Slovakia in 1998–9.

Table 1.1. *Summary of State Exploitation, 1990–2002*

Country	Formal State Institutions (EU Conditionality Begins 1998)	Growth in State Admin Employment, 1990–2002 (%)	Party Funding Rules	Summary Index of Exploitation
Hungary	In place by 1997	138	Limited donors, highly regulated	1.4
Estonia	In place by 1996	158	Limited donors, highly regulated	1.6
Slovenia	In place by 1997	214	Limited donors, highly regulated	2.1
Lithuania	In place by 1996	239	Limited donors, highly regulated	2.4
Poland	In place by 1998	244	Limited donors, increasingly regulated	4.4
Czech Rep.	Begun in 1998	400	Sources unrestricted, unregulated	7.0
Slovakia	Begun in 2001	300	Sources unrestricted, regulation after 2000	6.0
Bulgaria	Begun in 2000	431	Sources unrestricted, unregulated	8.3
Latvia	Begun in 2000	467	Sources unrestricted, unregulated	8.7

Note: Index: additive and unweighted. Scoring: 2 points for formal state institutional building beginning after EU conditionality set in 1998 + % increase in state administration employment/100 (avg: 287%) + 2 points for party funding (1 for unrestricted sources, 1 for lack of regulation). Mean: 4.61. Standard deviation: 2.93. Variance: 8.62.

built lax party financing regimes that were neither transparent nor regulated – state firms often contributed to party coffers, as did local governments, while state-owned banks offered preferential credits. All four countries did little to reform the state until 1998, after the European Union (EU) made improved state administration a condition of accession.

The other cluster is led by Estonia, Hungary, and Slovenia, and includes Lithuania and Poland. Here, political parties rapidly built state institutions of monitoring and oversight, constraining discretionary access to state resources. Even if they were not always entirely successful (as in Lithuania or Poland), these countries embarked on far earlier and more ambitious reforms of formal state institutions and regional devolution, showing smaller increases in state administration employment and extensive regulation of party financing. They were the first to introduce formal institutions of monitoring and oversight, limit the discretionary expansion of the state administration, and make party finances more transparent and regulated.[10] In short, despite roughly similar levels of political and economic reform, political parties were able to exploit the state far more in Bulgaria, the Czech Republic, Latvia, and Slovakia than in Estonia, Hungary, Lithuania, Poland, or Slovenia.

We thus observe both a shared pattern in post-communist democracies of self-serving state reconstruction – and considerable variation in the extent to which the state was exploited. This variance in the willingness of post-communist democratic parties to place limits on their own exploitation of the state suggests that it is not democracy per se that matters.

Shared Motives, Means, and Opportunities

For the new democratic parties that came to power after the communist collapse, the challenges of building new markets, democracies, and states and at the same time ensuring their own survival as guarantors of the new democratic order were formidable. As Stefano Bartolini notes, these "differing demands of party building, competition for votes and regime founding or defending are, to a large extent, incompatible."[11] The transition to democracy created motives, means, and opportunities for these parties to exploit the state as they balanced these roles.

The chief *motives* for state exploitation consisted both of short-term survival and long-term commitments to democracy. New democratic parties faced enormous uncertainty and had few guarantees of material or electoral support. As we will see in the next chapter, these nascent parties were extremely fragile, possessed few members or local organizations, and had to contend with high electoral volatility. In an age of expensive media campaigns, they had few material resources and no certain sources of income. Nor did they have the ability to form extensive organizational networks, which could have allowed them to pursue other strategies of survival, such

---

[10] Poland was less successful at constraining state exploitation, as we will see in Chapter 2, but is still in the cluster of early adopters of formal institutions, slow-growing state administrations, and transparent party financing.

[11] Bartolini, Stefano. 1999–2000. "Collusion, Competition, and Democracy," *Journal of Theoretical Politics*, 11, 4: 435–70; 12, 1: 33–65.

as clientelism. Meanwhile, the resources of the state were the most stable source of funds needed for election campaigns and party maintenance.

At the same time, these new democratic parties' greatest fear and biggest challenge was avoiding a relapse into an authoritarian monopoly over both the economy and the polity. They faced "the nightmare of elimination altogether: the return to power of a communist apparatus that would snuff out not only privatization, but democracy as well."[12] As a result, the dilemma for budding democratic parties was that they had to commit themselves to fierce new political competition – and to survive it. The temptation to raid the states they governed, and to build in future discretionary access to these resources, was clear – but so was the imperative to preserve democratic institutions.

The *means* at the parties' disposal consisted of their enormous policy-making role. Political parties were responsible for leading these countries out of the communist morass and through difficult and enormous institutional and political transformations.[13] They played the central role in policy making and state building after the collapse of communism, with access both to the reconstruction of formal state institutions and to the distribution of the states resources. Given the weakness of civil society, presidents,[14] and existing legal institutions *and* the enormous power given to political parties in parliamentary systems, governing parties freely decided how to liberalize the economy, privatize state holdings, and reform state structures – and what form these institutions would take. In short, the very democratic actors who could extract from the state were in charge of rebuilding it.

The *opportunity* for exploitation arose from both the hereditary weakness of the communist state and the lack of external restraints on party actions. Where rulers elsewhere inherited constraining institutions, post-communist political actors first had to dismantle an economic and political monopoly. During the nearly five decades of its rule, the communist party ran the state administration as its personal fiefdom: The state was the chief bank account and political tool of the party, a source of public largesse and private benefits. Formal laws and parallel organizational hierarchies

---

[12] Frydman, Roman, Murphy, Kenneth, and Rapaczynski, Andrzej. 1998. *Capitalism with a Comrade's Face*. Budapest: Central European University Press, p. 34.

[13] Beginnings mattered a great deal; however, they did not imply path dependence, since few reinforcement or lock-in mechanisms existed. Early competition thus set, but did not determine, the trajectories of state emergence.

[14] The one country where a president played a more powerful role was Poland – but his powers were severely circumscribed, and the position made largely ceremonial, by 1995.

upheld the party control of the state.[15] Party apparatchiks ran most state institutions, so that few "real" bureaucrats existed, while the planned economy made most workers into state employees.[16] While the degree of direct party control over the economy and state varied,[17] the generally low differentiation of state and party functions made "political clout the foundation for economic control."[18] The era of communist abuse "hollowed out" the state, leaving its institutions both vulnerable and unable to prevent extractive incursions.[19]

The fall of communism in 1989–91 formally abolished this long-standing fusion of the ruling authoritarian party and the state. The communist parties themselves were forced to exit from power and began the arduous process of adaptation to multiparty democracy.[20] Their monopoly over state resources ended. In embarking on ambitious programs of abolishing state control of the economy and the polity, new democratic governments committed themselves to privatizing state holdings, selling off state enterprises, and eliminating laborious economic planning. The hope was that without an authoritarian monopolist to abuse it, the state could become a more apolitical and effective administrative force and a buffer against a slide into authoritarianism.[21]

At the same time, however, both international advisers and domestic policy makers focused on the challenges of democratic and economic transformations rather than on the state.[22] Many reformers, international advisers,

[15] For example, all state hiring above a certain level was vetted by regional and central party committees. See Kaminski, Antoni. 1992. *An Institutional Theory of Communist Regimes*. San Francisco: ICS Press, p. 164.

[16] The party also controlled the *nomenklatura* system: an extensive list of positions vetted by the party.

[17] In Hungary, the separation of political power and legal authority by the 1980s meant that as long as state officials were acting within legal limits, party officials had less influence on their everyday decisions.

[18] Comisso, Ellen. 1986. "State Structures, Political Processes, and Collective Choice in CMEA States," in Comisso, Ellen, and Tyson, Laura D'Andrea, eds. *Power, Purpose, and Collective Choice: Economic Strategy in Socialist States*. Ithaca: Cornell University Press, p. 32.

[19] For an account of elite predation on the state, see Ganev, Venelin. 2005. *Preying on the State: State Formation in Post-Communist Bulgaria (1989–1997)*. Unpublished book mss.

[20] See Grzymała-Busse, Anna. 2002. *Redeeming the Communist Past*. New York: Cambridge University Press.

[21] Schamis, Hector E. 2002. *Re-Forming the State: The Politics of Privatization in Latin America and Europe*. Ann Arbor: University of Michigan Press, p. 169.

[22] See also Elster, Jon, Offe, Claus, and Preuss, Ulrich K. 1998. *Institutional Design in Post-Communist Societies*. Cambridge: Cambridge University Press; Zielonka, Jan. 1994. "New

and international organizations saw the economy as a separate problem from institutional development, and the state itself as a source of inefficiency and corruption.[23] While a considerable literature addressed the development of representative and constitutional institutions, it neglected the (re)building of the state,[24] and "the dominant view among reformers and their advisors during the early transition period was that because [state] institutions would necessarily take time to develop, it was best to focus first on liberalization and privatization."[25] If anything, the prevalent but vague assumption was that the state would now shed employees and functions,[26] encouraging both democracy and markets to flourish.[27] For all their

Institutions in the Old East Bloc," *Journal of Democracy*, 5: 87–104. Notable exceptions include Bunce, Valerie. 2001. "Democratization and Economic Reform," *Annual Review of Political Science*, 4: 43–65; Cirtautas, Arista. 1995. "The Post-Leninist State: A Conceptual and Empirical Examination," *Communist and Post-Communist Studies*, 28, 4: 379–92; Ekiert, Grzegorz. 2001. *The State After State Socialism: Poland in Comparative Perspective*. Manuscript, Harvard University, 2001; McFaul, M. 1995. "State Power, Institutional Change, and the Politics of Privatization in Russia," *World Politics*, 47, 2: 210–43; Staniszkis, Jadwiga. 1999. *Post-Socialism*. Warsaw: PAN.

[23] Herrera, Yoshiko. 2001. "Russian Economic Reform, 1991–1998," in *Russian Politics*, Barany, Zoltan, and Moser, Robert, eds. Cambridge: Cambridge University Press, 135–73.

[24] See Stepan, Alfred, and Skach, Cindy. 1993. "Constitutional Frameworks and Democratic Consolidation: Parliamentarianism Versus Presidentialism," *World Politics*, 46, 1: 1–22; Benoit, Kenneth, and Hayden, Jacqueline. 2004. "Institutional Change and Persistence: The Evolution of Poland's Electoral System, 1989–2001," *Journal of Politics*, 66, 2 :396–427; Mainwaring, Scott. 1993, July "Presidentialism, Multipartism, and Democracy: The Difficult Combination." *Comparative Political Studies*, 26, 2 (July): 198–228; Frye, Timothy. 1997. "A Politics of Institutional Choice: Post-Communist Presidencies," *Comparative Political Studies*, 30: 523–52; Elster et al. 1998.

[25] Raiser, Martin, Di Tommaso, Maria, and Weeks, Melvyn. 2000. "The Measurement and Determinants of Institutional Change: Evidence from Transition Economies." European Bank for Reconstruction and Development (EBRD) Working Paper No. 60. For an excellent analysis of the neglect of state institutions in the debates over market privatization and reform, see Herrera 2001.

[26] See Kochanowicz, Jacek. 1994. "Reforming Weak States and Deficient Bureaucracies," in Nelson, Joan M., Kochanowicz, Jacek, Mizsei, Kalman, and Munoz, Oscar, eds. *Intricate Links: Democratization and Market Reforms in Latin America and Eastern Europe*. New Brunswick: Transaction, pp. 194–206.

[27] Roland, Gerard. 2001. "Ten Years After … Transition and Economics." IMF Staff Papers, No. 48. Washington: International Monetary Fund, p. 34; Przeworski, Adam. 1997. "The State in a Market Economy," in Nelson, Joan, Tilly, Charles, and Walker, Lee, eds. *Transforming Post-Communist Political Economies*. Washington: National Academy Press, pp. 411–31; Shleifer, Andrei, and Vishny, Robert W. 1998. *The Grabbing Hand: Government Pathologies and Their Cures*. Cambridge, MA: Harvard University Press; Holmes, Stephen. 1996. "Cultural Legacies or State Collapse: Probing the Postcommunist Dilemma," in

assistance in consolidating markets and democracies, neither the financial organizations involved, such as the International Monetary Fund (IMF) or the World Bank, nor the regional powerhouses, such as the EU, paid attention to state administration until 1996–7, well into the post-communist era. In short, the huge project of dismantling the extant communist state offered little resistance to incursion by political actors, and few external constraints prevented its exploitation.

Explaining the Variation: Robust Competition

In the absence of existing institutional safeguards, international attention, or domestic watchdogs, the main constraint would have to come from the political parties themselves and their interactions – specifically, party competition. Yet since such competition often leads parties to grasp for state resources to gain a competitive edge, how can it prompt political actors to protect the state? This question is at the heart of both theoretical discussions and empirical analyses of democratic competition.[28]

To constrain exploitation, competition had to threaten the parties in power with replacement. It had to present a credible alternative both to coalition partners and the electorate without acting as a threat to the system of competition itself. The more vigorous the opposition, the more likely it was to lead the governing parties to moderate their rent seeking, anticipate an exit from office by building formal constraints, and coopt the opposition through power-sharing measures that limited any one party's ability to gain private benefits from the state.[29] In short, such an opposition limited the

Mandelbaum, Michael, ed. *Postcommunism: Four Perspectives.* New York: Council on Foreign Relations; Przeworski, Adam, et al. 1995. *Sustainable Democracy.* Cambridge: Cambridge University Press, p. 37. Earlier scholarship had pointed out the association between large states and rent-seeking opportunities. See Habermas, Jürgen. 1975. *Legitimation Crisis.* Boston: Beacon; Stigler, George. 1975. *The Citizen and the State.* Chicago: University of Chicago Press.

[28] Wittman, Donald. 1995. *The Myth of Democratic Failure.* Chicago: University of Chicago Press; Schumpeter, Joseph. 1948. *Capitalism, Socialism, and Democracy.* Chicago: University of Chicago Press; Rose-Ackerman, Susan. 1978. *Corruption.* New York: Academic Press; idem. 1999. *Corruption and Government: Causes, Consequences, and Reform.* Cambridge: Cambridge University Press; Demsetz, Harold. 1982. *Economic, Legal, and Political Dimensions of Competition.* Amsterdam: North-Holland; Stigler, George. 1972. "Economic Competition and Political Competition," *Public Choice,* 13: 91–106.

[29] As the next chapter shows, the threat of replacement shows a curvilinear relationship to state exploitation: If it threatens to eliminate the governing parties entirely, they will prey upon the state. If there is no competition, the party can fuse itself with the state entirely.

exploitation of the state by raising the costs of doing so for governing parties and lowering the potential benefits.

Such *robust competition* is characterized by an opposition that is clearly identifiable, plausible as a governing alternative, and vociferously critical, constantly monitoring and censuring government action.[30] Together, these three aspects of competition comprise a daunting threat of replacement to the government.

The *clarity* of competition consists of easily identifiable opposing camps. In developed democracies, regional, religious, and class-based historical cleavages of the sort identified by Seymour Lipset and Stein Rokkan can produce clear party camps. One potential measure is voter evaluation of the extent of the differences among political parties. This indicator, however, tends to rely on decades of democratic experience and well-developed historical cleavages that are missing in the post-communist context. Instead, in these new democracies, the regime divide between the former communist rulers and their opposition was the key electoral cleavage. The more the communist parties reinvented themselves – shedding their organizational, ideological, and symbolic attachments to the authoritarian *ancien régime* to return as democratic victors – the clearer the competition. The communist successors were the instant lightning rods of post-communist politics, as we will see in the next chapter. They both instantly attracted the hostility of the other parties and served as a clear alternative to them. Therefore, in this book, the clarity of competition is measured by the extent of the reinvention of the communist successor parties.

Robust competition parties are also *plausible* as governing parties. Such parties can enter coalitions with at least one other party and are not ostracized in parliament or excluded a priori from all potential coalitions.[31] Where there are few plausible competitors, governing parties rest easier, knowing that neither elections nor defections can easily produce an alternative governing coalition. Therefore, the more seats held by plausible

---

[30] See Grzymała-Busse, Anna. 2004. "Political Competition and the Post-Communist State: Rethinking the Determinants of State Corruption." Annual Meeting of the American Political Science Association, Chicago, 2–5 September 2004, and "Informal Institutions and the Post-Communist State." Conference on "The Role of Ideas in Postcommunist Politics: a Re-Evaluation," Havighurst Center, Luxembourg, 5–9 July 2004. Others have used "robust competition" to denote bimodal, nonfragmented party competition. See O'Dwyer, Conor. 2004. "Runaway State Building," *World Politics*, 56, 4: 520–53.

[31] Such ostracism also limits coalition diversity, which tends to delay reforms. See Hellman, Joel. 1998. "Winners Take All: The Politics of Partial Reform," *World Politics*, 50, 2 (January): 203–34.

opponents, the greater the number of potential alternative coalitions.[32] Plausibility is measured by the share of parliamentary seats held by parties that have not been excluded *by all other parliamentary parties* as potential coalition partners. The greater the seat share held by such ostracized parties, the safer the governing parties in their office.[33]

Finally, robust competition also features vociferous critics. By monitoring and criticizing the governing parties in the media and in parliamentary committees, opposition parties change voter perceptions of the governing parties. Governing parties then fear that their electoral performance will suffer as a result of their transgressions. Incumbents thus have incentives both to moderate their own expropriation and to build state institutions more rapidly and sincerely, to prevent their successors from exploiting the state.[34]

The direct measure of opposition criticism used in this analysis is the average annual number of formal parliamentary questions asked by each party representative in parliament. Such questions require extensive preparation to address government policies and policy proposals. The opposition asked the vast majority of these questions (around 80 percent). The topics ranged from specific inquiries on behalf of constituents to pointed questioning of privatization decisions, government bills, ministerial actions, or inconsistencies in budgeting and policy. Both party electoral campaigns and media evaluations repeatedly referred to these questions. Parties documented the number of questions their representatives had asked and how they forced the governments to account for themselves.[35] Further, interpellations were frequently reported in the media – journalists ridiculed trivial ones or those focused too much on strictly local concerns. In short, parliamentary questions were both an indicator of the vigor of the opposition and

---

[32] Ferejohn, John. 1986. "Incumbent Performance and Electoral Control," *Public Choice*, 30: 5–25. The impact of plausibility on alternative governing coalitions is independent of considerations of both ideology and the minimum size of the winning coalition.

[33] One counterargument is that since neither government nor opposition can rely on nonplausible parties, they make no difference to government stability. However, precisely because they limit the range of potential *alternative* governments, they limit the opposition's ability to form a countercoalition and thus increase the government's certainty of remaining in office.

[34] Laver, Michael, and Shepsle, Kenneth. 1999. "Government Accountability in Parliamentary Democracy," in Stokes, Susan, Przeworski, Adam, and Manin, Bernard, eds. *Democracy, Accountability, and Representation*. Cambridge: Cambridge University Press, pp. 279–96. See also Diermeier, Daniel, and Merlo, Antonio. 2000. "Government Turnover in Parliamentary Democracies," *Journal of Economic Theory*, 94: 46–79.

[35] See, for example, *Gazeta Wyborcza*, 9 October 1993, 11 July 2002; *Respekt*, 22 January 1996.

its readiness to assume national power. Not surprisingly, they were seen as "fundamental instruments" of the opposition.[36] These inquiries held the government accountable and demonstrated that the opposition was constantly monitoring the government. The more questions were asked, the more they suggest a critical opposition.

Added together, these attributes indicate the extent to which governing parties are monitored and threatened with replacement. The resulting index of robust competition shown in Table 1.2 summarizes the variation. We see the emergence of two clusters that correspond to the two groupings of higher and lower state exploitation. In one, voters have clear alternatives on offer, all parties can be potential coalition members with some other party, and parliamentarians avidly criticize each other in parliament. In the other, the clarity of alternative party offers is lower, numerous parties are excluded from consideration as coalition partners, and parliamentary criticism is far more muted.

Where competition was less robust, as in the Czech Republic, Bulgaria, Latvia, and Slovakia, incumbent political parties could more freely extract resources and create new formal institutions that would allow further exploitation. Where the opposition was more robust, as in Estonia, Hungary, Lithuania, Poland, and Slovenia, governing parties could take less advantage of the opportunities inherent in reconstructing the state.

Robust competition correlates strongly and negatively with state exploitation (–.85) and less so with indicators of democratic and market progress.[37] Other specifications of the index also conclude that where the opposition was weak, even the champions of democratic and economic reform could have highly exploited states.[38]

In principle, the concept of robust competition is continuous, but the cases examined here form two distinct groupings. Each attribute is independent of each other: Plausible parties may not be critical, clearly profiled

---

[36] *Gazeta Wyborcza*, 9 October 1993.

[37] Robust competition correlates with Freedom House democracy rankings in 2004 at –.51, and with 2000 democracy and market rankings at –.50 and –.65, respectively.

[38] The necessary condition for robust competition, the communist exit, is present in all cases but Bulgaria, where the communist party held on to power through the regime collapse and won the first elections. Adding the components and multiplying by the value on the communist exit (a necessary condition) produces the same ranking, as does normalizing the "questions asked" variable from 0 to 1. For the conceptual issues involved in the creation of such indices, see especially Munck, Gerardo, and Verkuilen, Jay. 2002. "Conceptualizing and Measuring Democracy: Evaluating Alternative Indices," *Comparative Political Studies*, 35, 1: 5–34.

Table 1.2. *Robust Competition Summary*

	Clear? Communist Regeneration: (0: None, 1: Partial, 2: Full)	Plausible? Avg Seat Share of Plausible Parties	Critical? Avg # Questions/MP	Summary Index of Competition
Hungary	2: MSzP immediately and rapidly reinvents itself, wins 2nd election	.99	2.30	3/3
Estonia	0: Rump communist party disappears	1.00	3.54	2/3
Slovenia	2: LDS immediately and rapidly reinvents itself, wins 2nd election	1.00	4.42	3/3
Lithuania	2: LDDP immediately and rapidly reinvents itself, wins 2nd election	1.00	3.00	3/3
Poland	2: SdRP immediately and rapidly reinvents itself, wins 2nd election	.97	3.78	3/3
Czech R.	0: KSČM does not reinvent itself	.79	.97	1/3
Slovakia	1: SDL' reinvents itself, no electoral win	.81	.94	1/3
Bulgaria	1: BPS wins first election, delayed and gradual reinvention	.99	1.54	1/3
Latvia	0: Rump communist party disappears	.82	.84	0/3
Diff of means test*	n/a	P = .014 T = 3.14	P = .001 T = 5.43	n/a

Notes: Coding: 1 point for more than 2 questions/MP/year (mean: 2.37; mean for countries with robust competition: 3.41; for countries without robust competition: 1.07), 1 point for less than 5 percent ostracized parties, 1 point for partial communist regeneration, and 2 for full. Plausibility was measured by party declarations prior to elections: If a party was publicly excluded from coalition considerations by all other parties, it was coded as implausible. Communist parties were coded as having reinvented themselves if they fulfilled all of the following conditions: a) name and symbol change, b) organizational dissolution and refounding, c) return of assets to the state, and d) ideological and programmatic disavowal of Marxism, the communist regime, and state ownership of the economy.

*Two-tailed t-test, null hypothesis (H0): difference between means = 0. Hypothesis tested (Ha): difference between means # 0. Pr ($|T| > |t|$) = P.

Sources: Foreign Broadcasting Information Service, *Gazeta Wyborcza, Rzeczpospolita, Mlad Fronta Dnes, Lidové Noviny, Sme, Hospodarské Noviny.* Parliamentary databases and institutes for the average number of questions asked by each representative. All formal questions posed as official interpellations and queries were included. Informal questions asked during debates were not included.

parties may not be plausible, and so on.[39] However, each of the three aspects of robust competition reinforced the constraint on governing parties, without any one being sufficient. If the opposition is not clear, it cannot be a credible substitute for governing parties. If it is ostracized, it cannot join a government and therefore poses no threat of replacement. If it is not critical, there is no basis to its claims as a governing alternative. Finally, individual opposition parties may be clear, critical, and plausible, but for competition to be robust, they have to occupy the requisite parliamentary seats to constitute a credible coalition threat. In most multiparty parliamentary regimes, therefore, the robustness of competition is an aspect of the party system rather than of individual parties.

Sources of Robust Competition

At the heart of robust competition lie the mutual suspicions of democratic political parties. With the few noble exceptions of countries where all parties obey norms and the codes of conduct place public officials beyond reproach, most polities have to rely on political parties' mutual exposure of each other's wrongdoings to curb rent seeking. No matter how committed to democracy all involved actors might be, competing political parties must be willing and able to investigate and publicize each other's actions.

The bases for such party competition are diverse, ranging from ethnic and cultural pluralism, to industrial production profiles and economic inequalities, to configurations of social organization such as unionization or religious membership.[40] These cleavages both allow parties to develop distinct profiles and sharpen their incentives to criticize. They may also provide the channels through which parties can publicize their criticism, such as party-owned media or mass organizations. These often take decades, if not centuries, of democratic experience to develop.

In most post-communist countries, however, where robust competition existed, it did so thanks largely to the reinvented communist successor parties: former authoritarian rulers who successfully transformed themselves into moderate and professional democratic competitors. Reinvented

---

[39] As a final caveat, the values reported here are averages over the first fifteen years of democracy. The robustness of competition changed over time, however, with immediate effects on state exploitation, as the substantive chapters demonstrate. Thus, it increased in Slovakia after 1998 and in the Czech Republic after 2002, and decreased in Hungary in 1998–2002.

[40] For a review of these, see Strøm, Kaare. 2000. "Delegation and Accountability in Parliamentary Democracies." *European Journal of Political Research*, 37: 261–89.

1989: Communist Party in crisis

CP stays in office   CP exits office

No robust opposition   Multiparty rule

CP fails to reinvent itself   CP reinvents itself

Weaker opposition   Robust opposition

Figure 1.1. The impact of the Communist exit on party competition

communist parties were formidable opponents – clear, plausible, and critical, as the next chapter shows in detail. They are both the most suspect, and the most skeptical, of the post-communist political formations. They are not the only force around which robust competition emerges, as Estonia shows – but they were able to spur the other parties as few could.

As a result, one of the grand ironies is that the authoritarian regime could produce successful democratic competitors who then act as powerful protectors of the very state institutions these same elites had exploited earlier. The logic is simple: Until the communist party exits office, no democratic competition can take place. Unless it rapidly and extensively transforms itself, an enormous swath of the political spectrum (roughly described as the "Left") is left vacant until new social democratic parties consolidate. After decades of communist rule, the Left was discredited as a political alternative, and it could take years for noncommunist Left parties to emerge, as in the Czech Republic. Figure 1.1. summarizes this relationship between the communist exit, reinvention, and robust competition.

The Mechanisms of Constraint

Robust competition operates through three mechanisms of constraint on state exploitation, which can be summarized as *moderation, anticipation,* and *cooptation,* elaborated in the next chapter. First, criticism leads to a moderation of governing party behavior – or, at the very least, greater subterfuge. As we will see, this informal mechanism was especially influential in curbing the expansion of state agencies and administration. Fearing exposure and subsequent punishment in both parliament and in elections, government parties curb their opportunistic extraction of state resources.

Second, the incentives for formal constraints grow all the more compelling when governing parties fear that their successors will use existing discretion against them. As a result, robust competition both limits the *capacity* of governing parties to exploit the state and generates the incentives to create formal state institutions that limit discretion even before exploitation takes place. This anticipatory mechanism arose very early in Hungary, Poland, and Slovenia: During the negotiations in the last days of communism, pragmatic communist parties and determined opposition representatives developed numerous institutional channels for parliamentary participation.

Third, robust competition induces governing parties to share power, and to coopt their critics as much as possible. As informal rules evolved in parliaments, the opposition gained further power, including representation on and leadership of important legislative committees and party financing laws that benefited all parties, rather than just the incumbents. Robust competition also prevented a government monopoly on resources by leading potential donors to "insure" themselves by donating to multiple parties.

This is not to say that all these constraints were deliberate or carefully thought-out strategies. Political parties were the inadvertent architects of the state, driven by the desire to survive as organizations and to ensure a stable order in which they would continue to thrive (that is, democracy) rather than by an explicit perception that they needed to build the state. For example, party programs barely mentioned the state and administration.[41]

If robust competition is responsible for the variation we observe, we should first see a correlation between levels of robust competition and the extent of state exploitation, irrespective of other explanatory factors such as the differences in existing state shortcomings, communist regime legacies,

---

[41] For example, party questions of government and administrative efficiency took up 3.1 percent of party programs in Poland. See Bukowska, Xymena, and Cześnik, Mikołaj. 2002. "Analiza Treści Programów Wyborczych," in Markowski, Radosław, ed. *System Partyjny i Zachowania Wyborcze*. Warsaw: ISP PAN.

or the demands of international institutions. More importantly, we should see more avid criticism of the governing parties. Governments respond to this criticism – and to the threat of replacement it represents – by moderating their own behavior, building more formal constraints that bind all parties, and attempting to share power with the opposition. If governing parties respond to this threat, we should see them attempt to lower discretion by introducing formal institutions, regardless of their ideology or external pressures. Because they involve lengthy legislative procedures, the processes of institutional creation may be slower to respond to changes in competition than more informal domains such as party financing. And, competition ought to have its strongest effects where parties are present: on the national, parliamentary level, rather than on the local, where there is far less party presence.

Implications

The role of robust competition in containing state exploitation is surprising in three ways. First, it challenges our understanding of post-communist pathways. After the collapse of communism, economic, political, and social reforms have tended to go hand in hand. Several scholars have noted the remarkable correlation between economic and democratic reforms.[42] As Table 1.3 and the covariance matrix show, the development of markets and democracies are very closely correlated (as high as .91 for the 2000 market and democracy rankings). However, state reconstruction shows a far weaker correlation to market and democratic accomplishments (−.48 to −.65). Some countries that implemented extensive market and democratic reforms, such as the Czech Republic or Latvia, have highly exploited states. Why, then, do we not see a stronger correlation among state, market, and democracy?

We need to disaggregate the "great transformation" that followed the collapse of communism: Despite the high correlation between democratic and economic reforms, state reforms do not necessarily follow the same trajectory. Not all good things go together: Free market leaders could exploit the state as easily as liberalization laggards, and democracy itself proved a weak constraint. Public demands, international pressures, and

---

[42] Fish, M. Steven. 1998. "The Determinants of Economic Reform in the Postcommunist World," *East European Politics and Societies*, 12: 31–78; Bunce, Valerie. 1999. "The Political Economy of Postsocialism," *Slavic Review*, 58, 4: 756–93.

Table 1.3. *Post-Communist Democracies*

Country	FH 2004 Democracy Score	FH 2000 Democracy Score	FH 2000 Market Reform Score	EU Entry
Poland	1.75	1.44	1.67	1 May 2004
Slovenia	1.75	1.94	2.08	1 May 2004
Estonia	1.92	2.06	1.92	1 May 2004
Hungary	1.96	1.75	1.75	1 May 2004
Slovakia	2.08	2.5	3.25	1 May 2004
Lithuania	2.13	2.0	2.83	1 May 2004
Latvia	2.17	2.06	2.5	1 May 2004
Czech Rep.	2.33	1.75	1.92	1 May 2004
Bulgaria	3.25	3.31	3.75	Anticipated
Romania	3.58	3.19	4.17	Anticipated
Croatia	3.83	4.19	3.67	Anticipated
Montenegro	3.83	5.5	5.33	Anticipated
Serbia	3.83	5.5	5.33	Possible
Macedonia	4.0	3.44	4.58	Possible
Albania	4.13	4.38	4.5	Possible
Bosnia	4.29	5.13	5.58	Possible
Georgia	4.83	4.0	3.67	Unlikely
Moldova	4.88	3.88	4.0	Unlikely
Ukraine	4.88	4.31	4.58	Unlikely
Armenia	5.0	4.5	3.58	Unlikely
Russia	5.25	4.25	4.33	Unlikely
Kosovo	5.5	5.5	5.33	Possible
Azerbaijan	5.63	5.5	5.0	Unlikely
Kyrgyzstan	5.67	5.88	3.83	Unlikely
Tajikistan	5.71	5.69	6.0	Unlikely
Kazakhstan	6.25	5.38	4.5	Unlikely
Uzbekistan	6.46	6.44	6.25	Unlikely
Belarus	6.54	6.44	6.25	Unlikely
Turkmenistan	6.88	6.94	6.42	Unlikely

Source: Freedom House, 2004; Freedom House. 2000. *Nations in Transit, 1999–2000.* Washington: Freedom House. Market reforms were no longer scored in 2004.

Covariance Matrix for Table 1.3

	State Exploitation	Robust Competition	2004 Democracy	2000 Democracy	2000 Market
State exploitation	1.0				
Robust competition	−.85	1.0			
2004 democracy	.65	−.51	1.0		
2000 democracy	.48	−.50	.83	1.0	
2000 market	.52	−.65	.75	.91	1.0

a broad elite consensus all backed economic and democratic reforms but neglected the state. Only robust party competition itself hampered state exploitation.

Post-communist state exploitation also requires a rethinking of the *mechanisms* of political competition. Not only did committed post-communist democrats use the state, but their behavior defies our existing understanding of how competition among political parties constrains exploitation. As we will see, even where traditional indicators of party competition, such as turnover or fragmentation, indicate vigorous political competition, we still see considerable exploitation. These powerful indicators do not capture the threat that opposition can pose to the incumbents or the moderating effects thereof. To go beyond tradition in social science that argues that competition can limit rent seeking, we need to identify what *kind* of competition matters, and explain *how* it does so. Only certain types of competition limit rent seeking and expropriation. Therefore, rather than measuring the share of parties' seats in parliament, their incumbency, or their ideological distance, this book suggests we measure how parties actually behave in parliament, and the ways in which they criticize, cooperate, and coopt each other.

This study further explains the strategic choices made by political parties to ensure their survival. While existing studies of clientelism and predation have tended to focus on long-term economic and political conditions, this book focuses on the more immediate and direct constraints on party strategies. A key point is that both democratic commitments and organizational characteristics can influence party strategic choices as much (and often more than) ideological traditions or electoral cleavages. Given their fear of an authoritarian backslide, post-communist parties neither preyed on the state nor did they attempt to fuse it again with a governing party. And, with their scarce members and meager resources, these new parties could not hope to survive by encapsulating electorates, á la mass parties, or by disbursing selective incentives via clientelism. As a result, post-communist parties did not follow the strategies of the Christian Democrats in Italy, the Liberal Democratic Party in Japan, or the Institutional Revolutionary Party in Mexico.[43] Nor could they credibly commit to collusion or

---

[43] Even relatively short-lived absence of a robust opposition can have deleterious effects: Both the Socialists in Spain under Felipe Gonzalez, governing from 1982 to 1996, and the Conservatives in the UK, in power for eight years from 1979–97, were accused of exploiting the state.

concession swapping, since high initial instability precluded the long-term contracts required. Instead, they gained state resources by exploiting their institution-building role in the transition to the market and to democracy.

More fundamentally, the notion of political parties as state builders diverges considerably from the analysis of political parties simply as elite teams of office seekers.[44] Political parties are the formal teams that field competitors for office, but their strategies of remaining in office are not purely (or even mostly) electoral. Moreover, where the current literature analyzes political parties as competitors, it assumes existing rules of competition, linkage strategies, and the parties' policy roles. But post-communist political parties could not take any of these for granted. After the fall of communism, barely constituted democratic political parties simultaneously had to establish electoral rules, constituency relationships, and functioning markets and democracies.

Finally, the variation in post-communist state exploitation defied both predictions that the new state would become a more efficient and neutral administrator once the communist party no longer colonized it and that the communist legacy of a bloated and ineffective state could not be overcome.[45] As the state withdrew and its function in the economy and polity radically changed, it did not become more resistant to exploitation. Governing parties continued to extract private benefits from the state and to reconfigure state institutions to promote this extraction further.[46] Moreover, where an "accommodative" communist regime type was expected to produce highly politicized states, we instead see less exploitation (as in Hungary and Poland).[47] Historical legacies of state development mattered less than the immediate competitive context.

---

[44] Schumpeter 1948; Downs, Anthony. 1957. *An Economic Theory of Democracy.* New York, Harper and Row; Aldrich, John. 1995. *Why Parties?* Chicago: University of Chicago Press.

[45] Albats, Yevgenia. 2003. *The State Within a State: The KGB and Its Hold on Russia.* Ph.D. Dissertation, Harvard University.

[46] To be sure, there are differences with the communist regime, where the unchallenged communist rulers were the de facto owners of most state resources and had discretion in their distribution. In contrast, new democratic political parties fought for access to state resources, such as control over privatization processes or the founding of new state agencies, and to new networks of elite and electoral supporters. Ganev, Venelin. 2000. "Postcommunism as a Historical Episode of State Building, or Explaining the Weakness of the Postcommunist State." Paper presented at the Twelfth International Conference of Europeanists, Chicago; 28–30 March. McFaul 1995.

[47] An "national-accommodative" communist regime was characterized by a greater willingness to respond to society and bargain with the opposition, often buying off society with consumer goods and rarely building an autonomous bureaucracy. Kitschelt, Herbert,

More broadly, the literature on state-building has focused on the external conflicts that lead to state building, such as war and the demand it creates for state institutions of taxation, conscription, and constitution building.[48] The result of this West European pattern has been largely the gradual development, expansion, and accretion of state institutions.[49] Yet the era of post-communist state building was marked by remarkably little external conflict that forced the building of state institutions.[50] There were few external pressures or constraints on state formation: The institutions inherited from the communist era were weak and neglected, little domestic pressure existed for prioritizing the reforms of the state, international actors were largely uninterested in state reform, and scholarship focused on economic and democratic changes. Instead, the conflicts that determined state outcomes were internal, consisting of competing political parties, not warring monarchs.

The culprits and beneficiaries of opportunistic state reconstruction in post-communist democracies also differ from the protagonists of analyses focusing on state autonomy and capacity.[51] These prominent works focused on the state as a unitary actor in its own right, able to formulate and implement its preferences when these differed from society's. The analysis of opportunistic reconstruction in this book, however, focuses on how the forces that protect the state from incursions of *elite* actors, rather than from *societal* representatives. And, it makes no assumptions about either the unitary nature of the state or its ability to "act" – rather, it focuses on the determinants of elite extraction from the state, and argues that this extraction occurred at different rates in distinct state sectors.

Mansfeldová, Zdenka, Markowski, Radoslaw, and Toka, Gábor. 1999. *Post-Communist Party Systems*. Cambridge: Cambridge University Press.

[48] Some classic works here include Tilly, Charles. 1990. *Coercion, Capital, and European States*. Cambridge: Blackwell; Spruyt, Hendrik. 1992. *The Sovereign State and Its Competitors*. Princeton: Princeton University Press; Levi, Margaret. 1988. *Of Rule and Revenue*. Berkeley: University of California Press; North, Douglass, and Weingast, Barry. 1989. "Constitutions and Commitment: The Evolution of Institutional Governing Public Choice in Seventeenth-Century England," *Journal of Economic History*, 4 (December): 803–32.

[49] There have been notable exceptions of revolutionary episodes.

[50] See Grzymała-Busse and Luong 2002.

[51] Krasner, Stephen. 1984. "Approaches to the State: Alternative Conceptions and Historical Dynamics," *Comparative Politics*, 16, 2 (January): 223–46; Evans, Peter, Rueschemeyer, Dietrich, and Skocpol, Theda, eds. 1985. *Bringing the State Back In*. Cambridge: Cambridge University Press.

Case Selection

To explain the variation in state exploitation, this book examines the consolidated post-communist democracies – Bulgaria, the Czech Republic, Estonia, Hungary, Latvia, Lithuania, Poland, Slovakia, and Slovenia – in the fifteen years from the collapse of communism (1989) to their entry into the European Union (2004),[52] a moment that for many observers marked the consolidation of democracy and markets. These cases were chosen on the basis of variation in existing indicators of competition, which ought to have correlated with state exploitation. All nine countries under consideration were subject to considerable pressure from the European Union to reform their state administration. All are parliamentary democracies, allowing political parties to compete and to seize the critical role in policy making.[53] They share roughly equal levels of economic development, a correlate of corruption.[54] With the exception of Bulgaria, the communist parties were forced to exit from power in 1989 and thus could not entrench themselves and block reform. The cases share similar electoral institutions, a factor that might influence state exploitation.[55] Yet despite the similar favor (and pressure) shown by the EU, levels of democratic and economic

---

[52] Only Bulgaria has yet to enter to EU.

[53] In presidential regimes, such as Russia and Ukraine, presidents and oligarchs extract public goods for private benefit. Albania, Croatia, Macedonia, Moldova, and Serbia were not democratic during their state building.

[54] Montinola, Gabriella, and Jackman, Robert. 2002. "Source of Corruption: A Cross-Country Study," *British Journal of Political Science*, 32, 1 (January): 147–70, p. 149. Country-specific regressions show that the Czech Republic and Slovakia are significantly worse off than their gross domestic product (GDP) would predict. Gros, Daniel, and Suhcrke, Marc. 2000, August. "Ten Years After: What Is Special About Transition Countries?" EBRD Working Paper No. 56.

[55] All are parliamentary systems, and most have proportional representation (PR); Lithuania and Hungary have systems that mix single-member districting with PR. Debates focus on the propensity of PR and SMD systems to promote rent seeking, with the power of presidents, party leaders, monitoring costs, and district magnitude as intervening variables. See Kunicová, Jana, and Rose-Ackerman, Susan. 2005. "Electoral Rules and Constitutional Structures as Constraints on Corruption," *British Journal of Political Sciences*, 35: 573–606; Lijphart, Arendt. 1999. *Patterns of Democracy: Government Forms and Performance in Thirty Six Countries.* New Haven: Yale University Press; Myerson, Roger. 1993. Effectiveness of Electoral Systems for Reducing Government Corruption," *Games and Economic Behavior*, 5: 118–32. Persson, Torsten, and Tabellini, Guido. 1999. "The Size and Scope of Government: Comparative Politics with Rational Politicians," *European Economic Review*, 43: 699–735; Persson, Torsten, Tabellini, Guido, and Trebbi, Francesco. 2001. "Electoral Rules and Corruption." National Bureau of Economic Research (NBER) Working Paper No. 8154.

development, and type of electoral institutions, the patterns of domestic competition and state exploitation differ considerably.

The causal propositions were developed on the basis of four countries: the Czech Republic, Hungary, Poland, and Slovakia, and tested further on data from Bulgaria, Estonia, Latvia, Lithuania, and Slovenia. These are the "difficult" cases, where standard measures of competition would lead us to predict opposite outcomes. Such cases further isolate the causal mechanisms by which robust competition constrains state exploitation. Thus, Slovenia shows far less exploitation than we would expect, despite years of low turnover (the same party governed throughout the 1992–2000 period). Bulgarian turnover is high, yet its state was heavily exploited and no real reforms began until 1997. Latvia shows both high rates of party competition, as measured by turnover and fragmentation, and high levels of exploitation. Finally, the Estonian communist party disappeared, rather than reinventing itself, yet competition was robust. By including all of these post-communist consolidated democracies, the analysis affords us a perspective that provides the comparative context and the explanatory leverage that are missing from single-country studies, as valuable as they are.[56]

To be sure, there are numerous polities whose states have been far more exploited (and barely reconstructed), such as Serbia and many of the former Soviet republics, including Russia. However, these are not democracies, or instead are "democracies with adjectives"[57] – regimes where free competition does not take place. Similarly, the nondemocratic detours taken by Romania, Moldova, and Ukraine do not allow us to examine the mechanisms by which democratic competition continuously affects state development. The predicted correlation still exists, but these cases do not allow us to examine *how* competition constrains exploitation.

In short, the conclusions of this study should apply directly to other cases of *democratic* state reconstruction, where the same political parties compete for power – and build the very state institutions that can ensure their survival in the political arena.

---

[56] See, for example, Meyer-Sahling, Jan-Hinrik. 2006. "The Rise of the Partisan State? Parties, Patronage, and the Ministerial Bureaucracy in Hungary." *Journal of Communist Studies and Transition Politics*, 22, 3 (September): 274–97. Meyer-Sahling argues the Hungarian state is exploited – a conclusion that is both true and incomplete, since it is far less exploited than the state in most post-communist democracies.

[57] Collier, David, and Levitsky, Steven. 1997. "Research Note: Democracy with Adjectives: Conceptual Innovation in Comparative Research," *World Politics*, 49, 3: 430–51.

Measurement and Data

There is no single and direct measure of the extent to which political parties build and benefit from the state, especially since political actors *informally* exploit state structures, making use of covert agreements, resources, and networks rather than formal procedures.[58] To examine the state exploitation, this book focuses on its three key domains: the creation of formal institutions of state monitoring and oversight; the expansion of state administration employment, funds, agencies, and institutions; and the channeling of privatization profits and other subsidies.[59]

1. The *introduction of formal state institutions* of oversight, such as security and exchange commissions, civil rights ombudsmen, and independent national audit agencies, can act as a formal barrier against exploitation.[60] To exploit the state, parties can build in discretion and/or delay the formal institutions of monitoring and oversight. In contrast, the introduction of such institutions is a self-imposed brake on exploitation, as it reduces access of private actors to state resources and helps to establish both universal and transparent distribution of state resources.[61] Such institutions were implemented immediately in some cases and greatly delayed in others.[62]

2. The *expansion of state administration*, as measured by the number of central state administration agencies and the rate of increase in administration hiring, increases the share of public resources under party control. By itself, state administration growth may be a response to functional deficits or

---

[58] Such informal practices include covert party financing, informal staffing of the state administration, and the use of party networks. See Hellman, Joel, Jones, Geraint, and Kaufmann, Daniel. 2000. "Seize the State, Seize the Day." Paper presented at the World Bank Annual Conference on Development Economics, 18–20 April 2000; Geddes, Barbara, and Neto, Artur Ribeiro. 1992. "Institutional Sources of Corruption in Brazil," *Third World Quarterly*, 4: 641–2. Della Porta, Donatella, and Vannucci, Alberto. 1997. "The 'Perverse Effects' of Political Corruption," *Political Studies*, 45, 3: 516–38.

[59] Of course, international actors and domestic economic elites can also exploit state resources – but they have far less influence on state construction. Moreover, the focus here is on party strategies of survival and how the state provides parties with resources necessary for their long-term livelihood.

[60] Winiecki, Jan. 1996. "Impediments to Institutional Change in the Former Soviet System," in Lee Alston et al., eds. *Empirical Studies in Institutional Change*. Cambridge: Cambridge University Press; Olson, Mancur. 1993. "Dictatorship, Democracy and Development," *American Political Science Review*, 87 (3 September): 567–76.

[61] Thus, this is not a direct indicator of exploitation but a measure of the controls against it.

[62] The focus is thus on the state's "infrastructural" capacity, as opposed to its "despotic" power. Mann, Michael. 1988. *States, War, and Capitalism*. Oxford: Basil Blackwell; idem. 1986. "The Autonomous Power of the State," in John Hall, ed. *States in History*. Oxford: Basil Blackwell.

new demands. It should then correlate with state independence or extensive market regulations. However, if it does not, and if parties multiply new institutions and nominate officials to hire at will in the absence of civil service regulations or other constraints, growth in state administration employment indicates discretion to exploit the state. Expanding the state administration is then a strategy of extending the scope of party control over state resources. Opinion surveys further examine individual experiences of respondents in obtaining state jobs.

3. The *patterns of party financing* consist both of how the party was formally controlled and its informal sources. Unlike other institutions of monitoring or oversight, party financing regulations are a direct constraint on the parties themselves. Lax regulations of party financing promote exploitation: They allow *state* agents, such as state-owned firms and banks, to fund parties, let parties leave their finances opaque, and offer few sanctions. Just as important were the indirect and informal sources of party funding: The differences in privatization processes translated into distinct opportunities for "informal payments."

These are the main forms that state exploitation took in the post-communist cases. Unlike tax collection or military protection, these are not the constitutive elements of the state[63]; rather, they are arenas where parties could ensure their survival. Party strategies in these three domains reinforced each other; for example, party financing through lucrative privatization deals and kickbacks was made even easier by the absence of formal institutions of monitoring and oversight. Discretion in state hiring converted various quasistate agencies and supervisory councils of state firms into another source of party financing. The absence of formal civil service laws and fiscal oversight institutions allowed state agencies and discretionary hiring to expand.

The exploitation of state institutions is analytically distinct from corruption: the use of public goods for private benefit.[64] The concept of corruption

---

[63] Levi 1988; Levi, Margaret. 1997. *Consent, Dissent, and Patriotism*. Cambridge: Cambridge University Press.

[64] Rose-Ackerman 1978; Montinola and Jackman 2002; Della Porta, Donatella. 2000. "Political Parties and Corruption: 17 Hypotheses on the Interactions Between Parties and Corruption." European University Institute (EUI) Working Paper No. 2000/60; Della Porta, Donatella, and Meny, Yves, eds. 1997. *Democracy and Corruption in Europe*. London: Pinter; Heidenheimer, Arnold J., Johnston, Michael, and Levine, Victor, eds. 1989. *Political Corruption*. New Brunswick: Transaction; Scott, James. 1972. *Comparative Political Corruption*. Englewood Cliffs: Prentice Hall; Waterbury, John. 1973, July. "Endemic and Planned Corruption in a Monarchical Regime," *World Politics*, 25, 4 (July): 533–55; Miller, William,

presupposes the delineation of public and private – and in a setting where state resources were officially owned by the people, such distinctions are not always clear. State exploitation, however, has a direct impact on the *opportunities* for subsequent corruption, since state formation and reconstruction establish both the distinction between private and public domains and the access to the latter. Exploitation is also distinct from individual interactions between economic and state agents, such as petty corruption or state capture.[65] As we will see in the next chapter, exploitation also differs from predation, clientelism, and authoritarian fusion of party and state.

Both qualitative and quantitative data substantiate the central argument that robust competition constrains state exploitation. To establish the patterns of opposition, the mechanisms of state exploitation, and its constraints, this book relies on archival records, parliamentary transcripts, government documents and statistics, extensive elite interviews, party programs, and coalition event histories. Documentary sources comprise transcripts of party congresses, parliamentary committee meetings (where available), and parliamentary sessions. Coalition event histories and media reports detail the extent of the criticism among parliamentary parties. Finally, since both exploitation and its constraints often rely on informal networks and instruments, extensive interviews with party and state administration representatives help to establish their role.

To examine the emergence of state institutions, I constructed a new database of over sixty-five formal state institutions of monitoring and oversight, the dates of their founding, the key policy pressures that led to their emergence, and their regulatory powers. I gathered the data on establishment and functioning of each of these institutions from the parliamentary records of laws proposed and passed, as well as from domestic media reports. To supplement these findings, I conducted public opinion surveys in the Czech Republic, Poland, and Slovakia to measure individual experiences with the state and party discretion. The surveys use "anchoring vignettes," which enable valid interpersonal comparisons across countries as detailed in Appendix C.

Grødeland, Ase, and Koshechkina, Tatyana. 2001. *A Culture of Corruption? Coping with Government in Post-Communist Europe.* Budapest: CEU Press; Treisman, Daniel. 2000. "The Causes of Corruption: A Cross-National Study," *Journal of Public Economics,* 76: 399–457.

[65] State capture consists of firms bribing officials to obtain advantages. Hellman et al., 2000, also examine influence (firms affect the formation of laws without bribes) and administrative corruption (officials regulate firms to derive rents for themselves).

A Roadmap

To develop the argument that robust competition constrains state exploitation, Chapter 2 examines configurations of party competition and their impact on party strategies, showing how existing measures of party competition are inadequate. Chapter 3 analyzes the rise of formal state oversight and control institutions and how domestic competition trumped external pressures to introduce these institutions. These institutions provided the critical formal framework within which political parties would subsequently govern and attempt to exploit the state. Chapter 4 argues that parties staffed and stuffed the state administration in a bid to increase the fiscal resources under their control. Governing parties expanded the state through the creation of informal and extrabudgetary state institutions, building the state and ensuring their own future gains. Chapter 5 shows how privatization and the creation of state agencies became a major source of party financing – a form of direct extraction of state assets made easier where governing parties had earlier created porous formal institutional frameworks. Finally, the conclusion examines the implications for the relationship between political parties and the construction and transformation of the state.

2

Competing for the State

Everyone is trying to get ahead of his competitors, which some claim is the common ill of all democratic countries.

Nakae Chōmin, *A Discourse by Three Drunkards on Government*

Why did post-communist parties pursue state exploitation? And why do we see variation in its subsequent levels? To answer the first question, this chapter analyzes how democratic commitments and organizational resources lead parties to adopt specific strategies of survival through the state. In other contexts, these lead some parties to choose clientelism as a way of extracting state resources, while other parties prey on the state or control it by fusing the state administration with party organization.

To explain why we see variation in exploitation, this chapter looks to political competition, reconceptualized as parliamentary *behavior* rather than as shares of seats or turnover in office. The impact of competition on rent seeking is controversial. On the one hand, intense competition creates incentives for parties to grab resources to ensure their future success.[1] The more intense the competition, therefore, the more exploitation we would expect to observe. On the other hand, a long tradition in both economics and politics argues that competition hinders opportunism and the seeking of excess profits or private benefits.[2] In some analyses, the third-party benefits of competition are even its chief legitimation. We would therefore expect party competition to constrain political party opportunism. This

---

[1] Rose-Ackerman 1978; Golden, Miriam, and Chang, Eric. 2001. "Competitive Corruption: Factional Conflict and Political Malfeasance in Postwar Italian Christian Democracy," *World Politics*, 53: 588–622.

[2] Rose-Ackerman 1978; North, Douglass. 1981. *Structure and Change in Economic History.* New York: W. W. Norton, p. 35.

dispute begs two questions: What *kind* of party competition can curb state exploitation? And, *how* does it do so – what are the mechanisms by which competition reduces rent seeking?

This chapter first examines the determinants of party strategies of survival and then analyzes why and how post-communist parties chose exploitation. The organizational resources and democratic commitments of post-communist parties precluded other strategies. Several explanations could account for the subsequent variation in exploitation, but these do not adequately explain the observed differences. Similarly, existing indicators of party competition show neither correlation nor causal links to state exploitation. Instead, *robust competition*, as measured by party behavior, both covaries with levels exploitation and shows clear causal connections. The chapter concludes by examining the configurations of competition in post-communist democracies.

Party Strategies of Survival

The state is an inevitable target of governing parties seeking material assets. Other sources exist: firms and wealthy entrepreneurs; party members and supporters; international actors, including international political party organizations such as Socialist International; and civil society representatives, such as trade unions, churches, or other nongovernmental associations. Yet even parties that rely on nonstate support tend to seek benefits from the state, such as a redistribution of state resources that favors their constituents. As a result, although this chapter is concerned with *direct* forms of extraction of state resources, the state is the indirect target and supporter of almost all political parties. And for post-communist parties, it was the most lucrative and readily available wellspring of material resources.

At the same time, the strategies of survival through the state vary considerably. The strategic choices of political parties are fundamentally shaped by two forces: the degree of their commitment to democratic rules of competition, and the local organizational resources at their disposal. *Democratic commitment* is defined as the parties' willingness to constitute and to perpetuate the democratic rules of the game: respecting the opposition's right to exist, engaging in democratic elections and abiding by their results, and not using their role in government to eliminate opponents. This is not to say that parties do not wish to win elections and dominate the electoral arena; rather, they are unwilling to subvert the rules of the game to do so. Such democratic commitments are not necessarily accompanied by a similar devotion to clean governance in the post-communist context.

Local organizational resources comprise not so much party membership or a strongly institutionalized vertical hierarchy as local party presence – that is, the concentration of local party organizations, activists, and affiliated party brokers, and the subsequent possibilities they offer for direct mobilization of voters, or a thorough takeover of the state. Members themselves are less important than the party's ability to reach individual voters through the organizational networks they command.

The sources of democratic commitments and organizational resources are diverse. The fear of backsliding into a system that would eliminate democratic competition, and thus the new political parties, was the main motivation for democratic commitment among political parties in post-communist settings. The continued activity of the communist parties, the economic power of former communist elite networks, and the occasional Soviet (and then Russian) reassertion of influence over the "near abroad" made the return to authoritarian rule all too viable a possibility. In other settings, the sources of democratic commitments may include existing traditions of democratic competition or the equating of nationhood with democratic competition.

Similarly, the determinants of organizational resources range from the parties' ideology (for example, communist and social democratic parties have traditionally emphasized extensive local presence) to the availability of campaign techniques (for instance, nineteenth-century mass parties sought to mobilize swathes of voters for elections). In the post-communist context, the parties' very genealogy – their rapid rise and the enormity of the electoral and parliamentary challenges they faced – precluded extensive organizational investments. Subsequently, the dominance of national media campaigns made gaining funds far more attractive than attempting to encapsulate loyal electorates through mass organizations. Building mass organizations, moreover, would take time – and most of these parties faced the first free elections within months of their formation.

Democratic commitments and organizational resources are not the only influences on party strategies; economic modernization, the extent and kind of state ownership, and patterns of ethnic heterogeneity have been found to influence the *levels* of clientelism, for example.[3] Powerful forces such as

---

[3] Kitschelt, Herbert, and Wilkinson, Steven, eds. Forthcoming. *Patrons, Clients, and Linkages*. Manuscript, Duke University.

Table 2.1. *Party Strategies of Extracting Resources from the State*

	High Commitment to Democracy	Low Commitment to Democracy
Extensive organizational resources	Clientelism/patronage	State fusion
Scarce organizational resources	Opportunistic reconstruction: exploitation	Predation

ideology, social inequalities, or party traditions can influence the particulars of party electoral and parliamentary strategies. Existing state structures and different international contexts also offer different opportunities for political parties.

However, democratic commitments and organizational resources fundamentally define what the parties would *want* to do and what they *could* do, respectively. They represent constraints on the choice of party strategies of resource extraction in a variety of political and economic contexts. Table 2.1 summarizes their impact. Where parties have no democratic commitments, their organizational resources influence whether they will prey on the state directly or fuse the extensive organizations of party and state together. Where they are committed to democracy, party organizational resources affect whether they will pursue clientelism or exploitation.

All of these strategies are compatible with programmatic or other electoral appeals. Programmatic and personalistic appeals are strategies directed at *voter*; they may go hand in hand with clientelism, predation, fusion, or exploitation, all of which are strategies of deriving material benefits from the *state*. (In the case of fusion and predation, such compatibility, of course, may be very short-lived.) Despite a posited trade-off between the organizational investments necessary for the provision of clientelistic goods and programmatic competition,[4] these strategies frequently coexist in practice.[5] Parties may seek to capture one electorate's loyalty with the provision of narrow goods but also hope to gain voters on the margin with programmatic

---

[4] Kitschelt, Herbert. 2000. "Linkages Between Citizens and Politicians in Democratic Polities," *Comparative Political Studies*, 33, 617: 845–79. But see Kitschelt and Wilkinson forthcoming.

[5] Coppedge, Michael. 2001. "Political Darwinism in Latin America's Lost Decade," in Larry Diamond and Richard Gunther, eds. *Political Parties and Democracy*. Baltimore: Johns Hopkins Press: 173–205, p. 177.

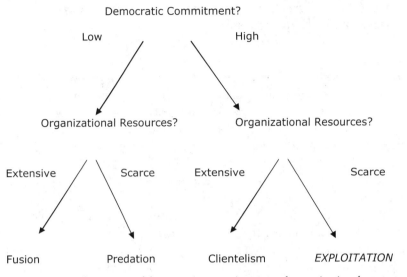

Figure 2.1. The impact of democratic commitment and organizational resources

appeals.[6] Even parties that explicitly turn to clientelism, such as the Argentinian Partido Justicialista (PJ), retain programmatic appeals.[7]

How, then, do democratic commitments and local organizational presence translate into political party strategies of survival? The first and fundamental choice is of a commitment to democracy: the rules of the game by which politics will be played. The second choice is that of the "equipment" with which this game will be played: whether or not parties will build the extensive organizational networks that allow them to pursue labor-intensive mobilization in either democratic or nondemocratic settings. Figure 2.1 illustrates the sequence of these decisions.

Two resulting strategies of party survival do not rely on democratic commitments. The wholesale takeover by political parties of the state administration, or the *fusion of party and state*, is already familiar to students of communist and fascist parties. Precisely because this strategy precludes pluralism or competition among political actors, it is not compatible with

---

[6] See Greene, Kenneth. 2004. *Defeating Dominance: Opposition Party Building and Mexico's Democratization in Comparative Perspective*. Ph.D. Dissertation, University of California at Berkeley.
[7] Levitsky, Steven. 2003. *Transforming Labor-Based Parties in Latin America*. Cambridge: Cambridge University Press.

democratic commitments. However, it requires building an extensive local presence to colonize and to control all state agencies, and to ensure their subjugation to party interests and control. Parties pursuing fusion developed dense networks of local organizations and activists who could reach all the way first to the level of local governments and then to workplaces and residential units. These party organizations then issued directives and monitored local government agencies; named officials at all levels; and delivered (or withheld) welfare state services such as housing, education, vacations, and health care to individual workers; and ensured the party's primacy over the agencies of the state administration.[8] Examples of fusion in the post-communist world include the authoritarian states of Turkmenistan and Uzbekistan.[9]

Elite *predation* relies neither on extensive party organizations nor on democratic commitments. It consists of extracting resources directly for the rulers' benefit, with neither the redistribution of goods to supporters nor the construction of building long-lasting political or economic institutions. Rather, it is a unilateral elite extraction of assets, á la Nigeria in the 1980s and 1990s or Zimbabwe in the 1990s. As an elite strategy, it does not rely on an extensive local presence, though predatory elites may activate temporary alliances with local power brokers. Thus, the modal party organization in Africa is a "one-person operation,"[10] with few regional-national linkages other than ad hoc coalitions with local leaders who deliver voters and intimidation in varying proportions.[11] Parties buy off supporters locally but rely on siphoning off resources through national-level predation. Similarly, in the Philippines, predatory elites have extracted privileges from a patrimonial state, relying on oligarchic family conglomerates.[12] Nor does predation presuppose democratic commitments; instead, parties and other actors can more readily prey on the state if they do not expect to enter electoral competition and its cycles of incumbency and opposition:

---

[8] See Kaplan, Karel. 1987. *The Short March: The Communist Takeover of Power in Czechoslovakia, 1945–1948.* New York: St. Martin's Press; idem. 1993. *Aparát ÚV KSČ v letech 1948–1968.* Sešity Ústavu pro Soudobé Dějiny AV ČR, Sv. 10.

[9] Jones Luong, Pauline. 2002. *Institutional Change and Political Continuity in Post-Soviet Central Asia: Power, Perceptions, and Pacts.* Cambridge: Cambridge University Press. Without a commitment to democracy, these countries maintained a fused party-state.

[10] Lindberg, Staffan. 2004. *The Power of Elections: Democratic Participation, Competition, and Legitimacy in Africa.* Lund: Lund University.

[11] Ichino, Nahomi. 2006. *Thugs and Voters: Political Tournaments in Nigeria.* Ph.D. Thesis, Stanford University.

[12] Hutchcroft, Paul. 1998. *Booty Capitalism.* Ithaca: Cornell University Press, p. 7.

"[M]yopic legislators have little incentive to turn down bribes in exchange for votes since they will leave politics at the end of their terms in any event."[13]

Yet in the nascent post-communist democracies, neither fusion nor predation was compatible with the new democratic parties' commitment to the one system that could guarantee their survival: democratic pluralism. Having just emerged from decades of authoritarian rule, which was established and maintained through the systematic elimination of potential competitors, new post-communist parties had little interest in pursuing strategies that could easily turn against them and give rise to another one-party hegemony. Under such a system, they expected to face prosecution, as democratic parties had when communists took over power after World War II and dissidents had subsequently. At the very least, any gains they had accumulated would be expropriated by the new authoritarian rulers. Thus, democratic post-communist parties preferred long-term "stationary banditry" to short-term predation, even if they expected to lose office in the next elections. For the same reasons, they denounced the fusion of party and state, even if they had few qualms about obtaining resources from the state. The European Union's firm stance that only democratic countries could enter the EU further reinforced such commitments.

Among the political party strategies compatible with democracy, *clientelism* consists of exchanging electoral support for the provision of private goods to select constituencies or individuals. It relies on an extensive local presence, yet is compatible with democratic commitments and pluralist competition. Clientelism is a familiar and widespread strategy of obtaining state resources necessary for party survival. For example, "virtually all electorally successful parties in Latin America, even the more ideological ones, have learned to cultivate clientelistic ties at the grassroots."[14] As a strategy of political survival, clientelism provides a self-enforcing solution to the twin problems of administrative loyalty and popular support.[15]

Clientelism demands a well-developed party organization – an established organizational network that can act as a mechanism for delivering goods from office to party to constituency and for monitoring of the voters'

---

[13] Rose-Ackerman 1978, pp. 18–58. Note that if elites believe they cannot be removed from office, they are likely to prey as well but redistribute their extraction over time.

[14] Coppedge 2001, p. 176.

[15] Crenson, Matthew, and Ginsberg, Benjamin. 2004. *Downsizing Democracy*. Baltimore: Johns Hopkins Press, p. 24.

support – in short, for enforcing the exchange "contract."[16] This local organizational presence can rely on the classic hierarchical mass party organization: "highly effective group devices for surveillance and mobilization, in
which local party bosses closely monitor individuals' conduct."[17] Such mass
party clientelism was the hallmark of the Austrian *proporz* system, which
neatly divided jobs and contracts between the two main parties at all levels
of public administration, the educational system, and the vast state-owned
industrial sector.[18]

Clientelist exchanges can also rely on much more loosely organized networks of local activists and brokers who mobilize the vote. For example, the
Argentine Peronistas, Bolivian MNR, Mexican PRI, and Peruvian APRA
functioned as populist parties with extensive but very flexible organizations, no stable bureaucratic structures, and extensive organizational networks that relied on informal, activist-led neighborhood networks to deliver
particularist provisions.[19] Similarly, the Italian Christian Democrats after
World War II had weak membership structures, with ordinary members
having little contact with the party organization. Instead, the "burden rested
mostly on party activists, with five or six in each local branch. Many of them
held salaried public offices, allowing them to work almost full-time for the
party and thus greatly reducing the party's need for permanent staff."[20]
Finally, the clientelistic structures of the Japanese Liberal Democrats Party
(LDP) did not rely on enormous and committed members, but on local candidate constituency organizations, the *koenkai*, which disbursed donations
for various local festivals and special events.[21] Each politician was obliged
to create one, and so five or six LDP organizations in each electoral district

---

16 Piattoni, Simona. 2001. "Introduction," in Piattoni, Simona, ed. *Clientelism, Interests,
and Democratic Representation*. Cambridge: Cambridge University Press, p. 6. See also
Chandra, Kanchan. 2004. *Why Ethnic Parties Succeed*. Cambridge: Cambridge University
Press.

17 Kitschelt, Herbert, and Wilkinson, Steven. Forthcoming. "Citizen-Politician Linkages: An
Introduction," in Kitschelt and Wilkinson forthcoming.

18 Plasser, Fritz, Ulram, Peter, and Grausgruber, Alfred. 1992. "The Decline of 'Lager Mentality' and the New Model of Electoral Competition in Austria," in Luther, Kurt Richard,
and Müller, Wolfgang, eds. *Politics in Austria: Still a Case of Consociationalism?* London: Frank
Cass, p. 18.

19 Levitsky, 2003, p. 194.

20 Morlino, Leonardo. 2001. "The Three Phases of Italian Parties," in Diamond, Larry, and
Gunther, Richard, eds. *Political Parties and Democracy*. Baltimore: Johns Hopkins Press, pp.
109–42, p. 118.

21 Richardson, Bradley. 2001. "Japan's '1995 System' and Beyond," in Diamond and Gunther.
Political Parties and Democracy. pp. 143–69, p. 147.

delivered services and created the social networks (women's clubs, community activities) that would translate into LDP support.[22] Thus, in contrast to Martin Shefter's powerful account of mass parties mobilizing outside of parliament and never relying on patronage, such parties can be well placed to succeed as clientelist forces thanks to their extensive organization.[23]

Clientelistic strategies are entirely compatible with both democratic competition and a commitment to democracy. In fact, competition can enhance clientelistic exchanges, intensifying ethnic and class mobilization and leading politicians to "employ every imaginable strategy of attracting constituents."[24] Voters auction off their support in exchange for the highest bid from politicians organizing rival clientelist networks. More generally, clientelism may buttress popular support for democracy and its daily functioning. For example, the Austrian turn to *proporz* was a consequence of new, postwar democratic commitments (enforced by the Allied occupation until 1955).[25] This system of dividing patronage between the SPÖ and the ÖVP, the two main ruling parties, was established partly to avoid the antidemocratic fractioning and conflict of the Weimar era. Similarly, in Italy, clientelist exchanges cemented the new democratic system: Popular support for democracy immediately after World War II was not based on the Christian Democrats' commitments and "democratic sturdiness" but on "concrete benefits the party provided to its social bases."[26]

For all its successes in keeping parties in office in several postwar democracies, pursuing clientelism would do little to ensure the political futures of post-communist parties. First, both party membership and party organizations were scarce and difficult to construct.[27] Thanks to their rapid development, minimal election registration requirements, and modern campaign techniques, parties have not established a local presence or mass

---

[22] Thayer, Nathaniel. 1969. *How the Conservatives Rule Japan*. Princeton: Princeton University Press.

[23] Shefter, Martin. 1994. *Political Parties and the State: The American Experience*. Princeton: Princeton University Press.

[24] Kitschelt and Wilkinson forthcoming, pp. 29–30.

[25] Luther and Müller 1992, p. 9.

[26] Tarrow, Sidney. 1990. "Maintaining Hegemony in Italy: 'The Softer They Rise, the Slower They Fall!'" in Pempel, T. J., ed. *Uncommon Democracies: The One-Party Dominant Regimes*. Ithaca: Cornell University Press, pp. 306–32, p. 312.

[27] See Appendix A for detailed figures. The Bulgarian BSP and the Romanian PDSR were two communist party successors who tried to keep their organizations from dissolving. The peasant party in Poland (PSL) also tried to funnel resources to local party organizations, but was constrained both by the opposition, and by its coalition partner, the SLD.

memberships.[28] In fact, the rates of post-communist organizational presence are a fraction of West European parties', as Figure 2.2 shows.[29] Party membership rates were below 3.0 percent, less than half of the West European average of 8.2 percent, and only a tenth of the membership rates of countries such as Austria or Sweden. In another example, the Argentine PJ's dense organizational networks covered each square kilometer with an average of 1.8 base units, and its membership alone comprised 18 percent of the electorate.[30] In contrast, the densest organizational network in the post-communist democracies, that of the Czech Republic's Communist Party, Komunistická Strana Čech a Moravy (KSČM), counted an average of .09 units per square kilometer and comprised less than 3 percent of the electorate. Even if we add up *all* party organizations per square kilometer in the post-communist democracies, they are still less than the PJ's alone.[31]

Thus, post-communist parties did not develop the organizational resources for clientelist strategies. It was not the case that clientelism failed to arise in post-communist democracies because the elected officials were weak, public sector budgets were shrinking, or elites converted their former communist party positions into local government strength.[32] Post-communist elected officials were powerful policy makers (especially when not constrained by strong formal institutions) and public sector budgets did not decrease (see Figure 4.2). Elites, for their part, dispersed into a variety of economic and political millieu rather than concentrating in the local administration. As we will see in Chapter 4, delivering jobs to party elites was a strategy of expanding party control over the state rather than

[28] Ost, David. 1991. "Shaping a New Politics in Poland." Program on Central and Eastern Europe Working Paper Series, Center for European Studies (CES), Harvard University, No. 8; Szelenyi, Ivan, and Szelenyi, Sonya. 1991. "The Vacuum in Hungarian Politics: Classes and Parties," *New Left Review* (May–June): 121–37; Panków, Irena. 1991. "Przemiany środowiska społecznego Polaków w latach osiemdziesiatych," *Kultura i Spoŀeczenstwo* 1: 53–65; Lewis, Paul, and Gortat, Radzisława. 1995. "Models of Party Development and Questions of State Dependence in Poland," *Party Politics*, 4: 599–608.

[29] Post-communist party organizations per municipality ranged from .01 in Slovenia and .05 in Latvia to .64 in Poland and .68 in Slovakia. In 1989, West European parties averaged 2.5 party organizations per municipality. Scarrow, Susan. 2002. "Parties Without Members?" in Dalton, Russell, and Wattenberg, Martin, eds. *Parties Without Partisans: Political Change in Advanced Industrial Democracies.* Oxford: Oxford University Press.

[30] Levitsky 2003, p. 30.

[31] The rates of all party units per square kilometer are .19 (Czech Republic), .09 (Slovakia), .07 (Hungary), .05 (Slovenia and Lithuania), .018 (Poland), .010 (Bulgaria), .009 (Estonia), and .008 (Latvia).

[32] Perkins, Doug. 1996. "Structure and Choice: The Role of Organizations, Patronage, and the Media in Party Formation," *Party Politics*, 2, 3: 355–75.

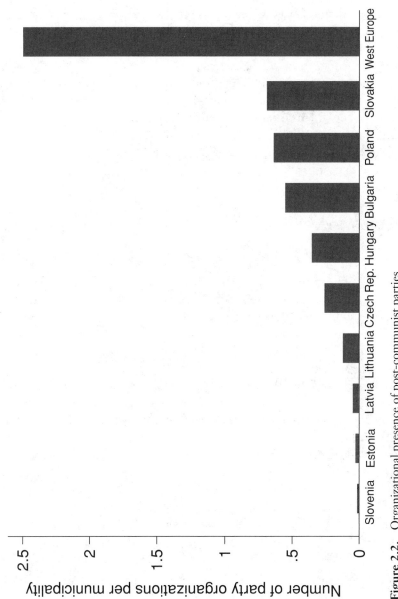

Figure 2.2. Organizational presence of post-communist parties

building party organizations or rewarding voters. Even if post-communist political parties wanted to develop clientelist networks (and certainly had incentive to do so, given their precarious electoral and material position), they had neither the time nor the personnel to do so.

In short, the democratic commitments of post-communist parties precluded both predation and fusion, and their low organizational resources did not allow them to pursue clientelism. Instead, in reconstructing the state, post-communist parties turned to exploitation: They extracted state resources while building democracy, a free market – and configurations of state institutions that would allow further extraction.

Choosing Exploitation?

With their democratic commitments and scarce organizations, post-communist political parties could more readily follow exploitation rather than the other strategies of survival through the state. The shortcomings of the communist state, the parties' huge new policy-making discretion, and the lack of external monitoring or oversight all made exploitation more profitable. Post-communist political parties reconstructed the institutions of market, state, and democracy – and built in the discretion and loopholes that ensured further gain.

Why and how did state reconstruction result in exploitation? The new democratic parties that arose from the former communist parties and their opposition scrabbled to survive after communism's collapse. Elections were held within months of the communist collapse, which meant that these nascent political parties had to position themselves to gain the material and electoral support necessary to enter parliaments soon after their founding. Parties needed resources, and needed them quickly: Post-communist elections, held within months of the communist collapse, were largely fought through expensive national media campaigns. The future remained uncertain even for parties who entered parliament. Political groupings continued to fissure and to fragment: The Czechoslovak federal assembly went from six to twenty parties in under two years.[33] Nearly thirty parties entered Poland's first freely elected parliament in 1991, eleven of whom only had one seat. In Hungary, the post-communist MSzP (Magyar Szocialista Párt), the post-opposition Hungarian Democratic Forum (Magyar Demokrata Fórum,

---

[33] Elster et al. 1998, p. 136.

MDF), and the Smallholders' Party (Független Kisgazda, Földmunkás és Polgári Párt, FKgP) saw splits as well.

Not only were organizations weak, but the modal party was "electoral-professional": comprised a group of elites and their staff, centered in parliament, with few local organizations or outreach.[34] Party members were not only scarce, but poor, given the general economic downturn and fall in real incomes after 1989. Similarly, there was minimal support initially from the fledgling entrepreneurs. Party identification remained low: Up to a third of those surveyed could not name a party they would support,[35] and over 80 percent felt that representatives lose touch with their constituents.[36] Nor were these electorates loyal: Electoral volatility averaged 18.3 percent and much higher in the first few years after 1989.[37] Average voter turnout in the region was 68 percent from 1990–2003,[38] compared to over 80 percent in Western Europe in the 1990s.[39]

In a situation where support was as scarce as it was unstable, organizations were barely founded, and few business ties existed, state resources were the most secure source of party support.[40] Some scholars argue that parties with strong organizations do not need to rely on the private benefits of office to survive and therefore are less likely to exploit the state.[41] Yet the only parties with an extensive resource base, stable voter support, and established organizations were the unreconstructed communist parties that held onto

---

[34] Exceptions ranged from the unreconstructed Bulgarian post-communist party to the Hungarian Christian Democrats and their aim to "socialize members." See Enyedi, Zsolt. 1996. "Organizing a Sub-Cultural Party in Eastern Europe," *Party Politics*, 2, 3: 377–96.

[35] Ilonszki, Gabriella. 1998. "Representation Deficit in a New Democracy: Theoretical Considerations and the Hungarian Case," *Communist and Post-Communist Studies*, 14: 157–70; Turner, Arthur. 1993. "Postauthoritarian Elections: Testing Expectations About 'First' Elections," *Comparative Political Studies*, 26, 3 (October): 330–49.

[36] "Party Systems and Electoral Alignments in East Central Europe" database, available in machine-readable data form from Gábor Toka, Central European University.

[37] Bartolini, Stefano, and Mair, Peter. 1990. *Identity, Competition, and Electoral Availability*. Cambridge: Cambridge University Press; Lewis, Paul. 2000. *Political Parties in Post-Communist Eastern Europe*. London: Routledge. West European rates averaged 9 percent.

[38] International Institute for Democracy and Electoral Assistance. 2005. "Voter Turnout Report." Available at http://www.idea.int/vt. Accessed 20 January 2005.

[39] Mair, Peter. 1995. "Political Parties, Popular Legitimacy, and Public Privilege," *West European Politics*, 18, 2 (July): 40–57, p. 45.

[40] See Dyson, Kenneth. 1970. "Party, State, and Bureaucracy in Western Germany." Sage Professional Papers in Comparative Politics No. 01–063. Beverly Hills: Sage.

[41] Della Porta, Donatella. 2000, "Political Parties and Corruption: 17 Hypotheses on the Interactions Between Parties and Corruption." EUI Working Papers RSC 2000/6; O'Dwyer 2004.

power in 1989 – which personified state exploitation. As we will see, it is instead the case that exploitation strengthens party organizations.

How, then, did post-communist political parties pursue exploitation? In reconstructing the institutions of the state – patching holes in existing laws and agencies and establishing new institutions of market and democracy – several tactics allowed governing parties both to extract benefits immediately and to obtain longer-term gains from discretionary access to state resources. These moves included building new institutional configurations, maintaining communist-era discretion, implementing specific reforms such as privatization, and relying on existing informal sources of information and alliances.

First, governing parties were the key architects of free competition in both the marketplace and the polity. Since policy demands were so huge and the state itself so weak, parliamentary parties initially assumed much of the legislative administrative work after 1989. Parliaments expanded to fill the vacuum created by cabinet and state inadequacy.[42] The sheer volume of laws to be drafted and the unresolved debates about powers and functions led to political parties dominating policy making and implementation. It also meant that political parties in parliament had a unique opportunity to create state institutions and build in subsequent access to state resources, in ways that bureaucrats, *ancien régime* economic or security apparatus elites, or other political actors did not. They could delay, enfeeble, or politicize formal institutions of the state, building in loopholes that favored themselves – or, if constrained by robust competition, build early and powerful formal institutions of monitoring and oversight.

Second, political parties took advantage of the shortcomings left behind by communist legacies. The communist state had no civil service: Bureaucrats were subject to the general labor code, rather than to a civil service code that could both ensure their political neutrality and offer state employees protection against political reprisal. Ministries hired their own employees (and could continue to do so after 1989 if no civil service laws were adopted). Moreover, considerable budgetary and distribution discretion existed, the result of a multiplicity of sectoral ministries and soft budget constraints necessitated by state planning and ownership of the economy. Finally, few structures of public accountability existed, such as independent courts or regulatory commissions. State structures were responsible to the

[42] Nunberg, B., ed. 1999. *The State After Communism*. Washington: World Bank; Ágh, A., ed. 1994. *The First Steps*. Budapest: Hungarian Centre of Democracy Studies.

communist party alone, through informal rules and party functionaries sec-onded to state enterprises and organs.[43] Political parties could thus maintain discretionary hiring practices and fail to regulate the various extrabudgetary funds and institutions that existed. As a result, a considerable opportunity existed to lock in the advantages of power, leaving as much discretion as possible in the access to and distribution of state resources such as jobs, contracts, or privatization deals.

Third, specific policy projects meant opportunities for exploitation. Governing parties could continue many of the discretionary practices of the communist regimes. For example, the communist regimes set up numerous quasi-independent agencies and funds to administer state property, resource redistribution, and investment. They continued to emerge after the com-munist collapse, and were often poorly managed and vulnerable to takeover by enterprising political actors. As we will see in Chapter 3, these projects were established and expanded both to gain party control over specific sec-tors – and to justify additional funding for such projects. Similarly, there was no pressure, other than from the opposition parties, to formulate civil service laws: Existing labor laws were on the books and gave political parties enormous discretion in hiring and firing.

Post-communist privatization and democratization further meant enor-mous discretion in distributing these resources, given the lack of exist-ing institutions of monitoring and oversight, the lack of fit between com-munist legal institutions and market conditions, and the weakness of the nascent contract and property rights. The privatization of state enter-prises and party holdings meant an unprecedented availability of state resources for "carrying off" by state representatives for their own use.[44] Enormous state holdings were now to be restructured, privatized, and sold off, and the profits ploughed back into the reconstruction of the state and the polity. Political actors in charge of this process were now to eradi-cate the overweening role of the state in the economy, even if this meant undermining their own economic position. Specific privatization strategies also meant distinct opportunities for political parties: The slower and less

---

[43] Hirszowicz, Maria. 1980. *The Bureaucratic Leviathan*. Oxford: Martin Robertson, pp. 22–3; Fainsod Merle. 1958. *Smolensk Under Soviet Rule*. Cambridge: Harvard University Press; Hough, Jerry. 1969. *The Soviet Prefects*. Cambridge: Harvard University Press.

[44] Similar carrying off of state resources took place as part of the rise of the state and its infrastructural power. See Mann, Michael. 1988. *States, War, and Capitalism*. Oxford: Basil Blackwell, p. 29.

well-regulated the privatization process, the greater the opportunity for state exploitation.[45]

Finally, political parties could take advantage of the shortcomings of formal institutions and instead use informal networks and alliances.[46] These provided the information and the access to obtain resources from the state, as shown by the cases of "spontaneous privatization" in 1987–90 by state enterprise managers.[47] These sources of information were often more reliable than their formal counterparts: A decade after the transition, state officials across the region admitted that no state institution had full information about state finances.[48] Not surprisingly, the lines between public property and individual profit remained blurred.

Competing Explanations

Political parties in all post-communist democracies could exploit the state in these ways – yet we see considerable variation in state exploitation. Several explanations emerged to account for this divergence. The first argues that the *functional demands* of new states and the challenges of building new markets and democracies lead to the expansion and exploitation of the state.[49] Capitalism and new market regulations require an extensive public administration in order to be properly implemented.[50] With these new responsibilities, the state expands: Following "Wagner's Law," the size of

---

[45] Thus, by mid-1996, the private sector share of GDP ranged from 45 percent in Bulgaria and Slovenia, to 60 percent in Latvia and Poland, to 70 percent in Hungary and Slovakia, to 75 percent in the Czech Republic. The rates of regulation and oversight were highest in Slovenia and in Hungary, followed by Poland, the Czech Republic, Slovakia, Latvia, and Bulgaria. By 1999, financial regulation ratings (on a 1 to 5 scale) ranged from 4 for Poland and Hungary and 3+ for Slovenia and Slovakia to 3 for the Czech Republic and 3– for Latvia and Bulgaria. See European Bank for Reconstruction (EBRD). 1996. *Transition Report*. London: EBRD.

[46] Humphrey, Caroline. 2002. *The Unmaking of Soviet Life*. Ithaca: Cornell University Press.

[47] Stark, David, and Bruszt, Laszlo. 1998. *Postsocialist Pathways*. Cambridge: Cambridge University Press, pp. 180–2. For an analysis of the informal use of state administrative resources as a way of hindering political competition, see Allina-Pisano, Jessica. 2005. "Informal Politics and Challenges to Democracy: Administrative Resource in Kuchma's Ukraine." Unpublished mss, Harvard University.

[48] Wojciech Misiąg, former Polish deputy finance minister, *Wprost*, 3 June 2001.

[49] Poggi, Gianfranco. 1990. *The State: Its Nature, Development, and Prospects*. Stanford: Stanford University Press, p. 117; Przeworski, Adam. 1990. *The State and the Economy Under Capitalism*. London: Harwood Academic Publishers, p. 58

[50] Goldsmith, Arthur. 1999. "Africa's Overgrown State Reconsidered," *World Politics*, 4: 520–46.

state grows as the economy does.[51] Growing societal demands for public goods, the complexities of public policy, and capital's need for legal regulation all expand the state and bring it under political control. In turn, as the bureaucracy expands, so do the opportunities for staffing it with party allies and for extracting resources from increasingly opaque state structures.

Yet this clear and linear relationship does not appear in the post-communist states. Instead, parties have extracted the most resources where the *fewest* regulations of the market or devolution of state powers arose. If anything, the expansion of the market and its regulation is correlated with lower state growth and exploitation rates, as in Hungary and Slovenia. Here it is important to distinguish exploitation from growth itself: As we will see, these are correlated in the post-communist cases where no prior bureaucratic autonomy or civil service laws established meritocratic, nondiscretionary hiring in the state administration. However, exploitation and state administrative growth do not logically presuppose each other in other contexts.

Another functional demand may be found in *newly forming states*. For example, Czech and Slovak state exploitation could be the result of having to build separate states after Czechoslovakia split into two constituent republics in 1993. Since many Czechoslovak institutions became de facto Czech ones, Slovakia was left with an "administrative deficit" that it sought to overcome through state expansion. In contrast, "the Czechs inherited the fully functioning state and political know-how of the former Czechoslovakia."[52] Similarly, once the Baltics and the Balkans regained their independence, we should have observed similar shortcomings, resulting in delayed or absent formal institutions and considerable growth in state administration.

However, the *rate* of state growth did not change in independent Slovakia before or after independence. By the same token, if the Czech Republic inherited the administrative structures of Czechoslovakia, its rates of expansion should have been lower than those of other new states: A republic of 10 million citizens inherited a state designed for 15 million. Instead, the rates of growth have been far closer to Slovakia's. More importantly, other newly independent states, such as Estonia and Slovenia, did not expand.

---

[51] Schavio-Campo, Salvatore, do Tommaso, G., and Mukherjee, A. 1997a. "Government Employment and Pay in Global Perspective." World Bank Policy Research Working Paper No. 1771.

[52] Szomolányi, Soňa. 1997. "Identifying Slovakia's Emerging Regime," in Szomolányi, Soňa, and Gould, John, eds. *Slovakia: Problems of Democratic Consolidation*. Bratislava: Friedrich Ebert Foundation, p. 9.

Thus, even as such demands or deficits clearly present additional challenges in post-communist state rebuilding, they are not directly responsible for state expansion or exploitation.

A second set of structural forces behind state exploitation may lie in *broad communist regime legacies*. Under communism, state employment and functions (if not effectiveness) grew.[53] Subsequently, once communism fell, "administrative agencies continue[d] to be run by the same bureaucrats and operate[d] according to the same basic procedures as before."[54] Personnel continuities would have meant additional manpower to exploit the state, especially for parties with allies in the state administration. Where asset stripping began in the late communist era, as in the "spontaneous privatizations" in Hungary and Poland, we would thus expect to see greater exploitation.[55] And since in one view "parliamentary parties lack the political power or administrative capital to enact comprehensive organizational change,"[56] the expectation is of perverse continuities with the communist system.

Yet this expectation of overwhelming and negative legacies ignores the differences among the communist regimes. For example, the Hungarian emphasis on technocratic skill rather than political affiliation in recruiting state employees made this state less structurally vulnerable than others. And, as the history of communism shows, personnel continuity does not preclude enforcing the norms and policies of a very different regime; for example, as late as 1932, half of the Soviet administrative staff had earlier been tsarist bureaucrats.[57] Finally, the rates of post-communist elite administrative turnover are similar,[58] yet there is considerable variation in subsequent state exploitation.

---

[53] Szoboszlai, György. 1985a. "Bureaucracy and Social Control," in Szoboszlai, György, ed. *Politics and Public Administration in Hungary*. Budapest: Akadémiai Kiadó, p. 167.

[54] Hojnacki, William. 1996. "Politicization as a Civil Service Dilemma," in Bekke, Hans, Perry, James, and Toonen, Theo, eds. *Civil Service Systems in Comparative Perspective*. Bloomington: Indiana University Press, pp. 137–64, p. 156.

[55] Staniszkis 1999.

[56] O'Neil, Patrick. 1998. *Revolution from Within*. Cheltenham: Edward Elgar, p. 215.

[57] Friedrich, Carl, and Brzezinski, Zbigniew. 1956. *Totalitarian Dictatorship and Autocracy*. Cambridge: Harvard University Press, p. 181.

[58] Only half of nomenklatura power position holders in 1988 were in power in 1993. The specific rates are 51.7 percent in the Czech Republic, 43.1 percent in Hungary, and 51.2 percent in Poland. Eyal, Gil, Szelényi, Ivan, and Townsley, Eleanor. 1998. *Making Capitalism Without Capitalists*. London: Verso, p. 117.

A third explanation focuses on the *sequencing and timing of state development*. If the state bureaucracy arises before mass enfranchisement, Martin Shefter argued, parties cannot encroach on the state easily.[59] If the sequence is reversed, cadre parties that arise within the legislature will have the greatest opportunity and incentive to exploit the state.[60] However, state administration arose in all post-communist cases before the mass enfranchisement of 1989 – yet the patterns of exploitation vary. Moreover, as noted earlier, parties founded outside of the parliament could easily extract state resources. Finally, the mechanisms differ: Unlike the United States or Italy in the nineteenth century, post-communist states did not face establishing state authority over an expanding or new territorial domain. Post-communist state development was not the result of a deliberate project, but of the emergence of new structures atop existing state institutions.

Finally, exploitation is not the product of widespread *elite collusion*, despite numerous suspicions. One analysis has argued that "one reason there has been no effective 'clean hands' movement in any postcommunist society may be that there are so many assets being divvied up that even the opposition gets its cut."[61] Similarly, the 1998 regional reform in Poland is said to have created a massive increase in patronage and in regional employment as a way to build up weak party organizations by colluding political parties.[62] And, as Japan shows, such cartels do not require extensive party organizations or memberships. Most post-communist parties exhibit the fluid ideology and low grassroots presence that allow party cartel strategies.[63]

Yet post-communist volatility makes such deals impermanent and unenforceable. Two fundamental conditions for both cartel-like collusion among parties and the side payments that accompany logrolling are long time

---

[59] Shefter 1994. See also Ansell, Christopher, and Burris, Arthur. 1997. "Bosses of the City Unite! Labor Politics and Political Machine Consolidation, 1870–1910," *Studies in American Political Development*, 11 (Spring): 1–43; O'Dwyer 2004 applies Shefter to the post-communist context.

[60] Shefter 1994.

[61] Holmes 1996, p. 68.

[62] O'Dwyer, Conor. 2002. "Civilizing the State Bureaucracy: The Unfulfilled Promise of Public Administration Reform in Poland, Slovakia, and the Czech Republic (1990–2000)." Berkeley Program in Soviet and Post Soviet Studies, Occasional Paper, Spring. However, government statistics posit these positions were *shifted*, not created.

[63] Della Porta 2000.

horizons and the continuity of the involved actors.[64] Without the expectation that the contract can continue indefinitely, the cartel deal falls apart. And without the expectation that the same actors will be around to reciprocate and repay a party's concession, there is little reason for the party to make the concession. Yet because of the post-communist parties' organizational weakness and the low barriers to entry, there was little expected continuity among the political actors. Offers of side payments would not have been credible, since the offering party could renege on the deal and choose another coalition partner. In the end, parties had no means of enforcing the logroll or maintaining the cartel.[65]

The one place we observe such collusive behavior is in the low-competition environment of the Czech Republic, where the ODS (Občanská demokratická strana) and the ČSSD (Česká Strana Sociálně Demokratická) created the cooperative Opposition Agreement in 1998.[66] It was then that the two parties openly agreed to change the electoral law to benefit large parties, to refuse votes of nonconfidence against each other, and to exchange parliamentary support from the ODS for several government portfolios that normally went to senior coalition partners, including the leadership of both houses of parliament. Yet even this arrangement did not last beyond the next elections, as new electoral entrants (including a splinter from the ODS) entered the new governing coalition.

In short, these compelling reasons do not adequately explain the variation we observe. Both inherited weaknesses and functional deficits provide

---

[64] Cartels further demand keeping internal factions in line, the ability to enforce and punish transgressions, and the ability to ride out demand and supply slumps. See Spar, Deborah. 1994. *The Cooperative Edge: The Internal Politics of International Cartels*. Ithaca: Cornell University Press. Side payments can be effective in buying support if preferences over policy are held with unequal intensity, there are multiple issues over which the parties can bargain, and repeated play is ensured. Buchanan, James, and Tullock, Gordon. 1963. *The Calculus of Consent: Logical Foundations of Constitutional Democracy*. Ann Arbor: University of Michigan Press. Barry Weingast and William Marshall emphasize the temporal aspects of logrolling and the nonsimultaneity of exchanges. Weingast, Barry, and Marshall, William. 1988. "The Industrial Organization of Congress; or, Why Legislatures, Like Firms, Are Not Organized as Markets," *Journal of Political Economy*, 96, 1: 132–63.

[65] Since political sovereignty rests with the voters, "no government can fully precommit all future governments." Adam Przeworski. 1997. "The State in a Market Economy," in Nelson, Joan, Tilly, Charles, and Walker, Lee, eds. *Transforming Post-Communist Political Economies*. Washington: National Academy Press, p. 418.

[66] The leaders of the two parties thus went from denouncing a grand coalition as a "deception of the voters" and "an idiocy" to announcing that it would best ensure stability and pragmatism in politics. See *Pravda*, 2 May 2002.

opportunities for exploitation but do not explain why some parties could take advantage of these so much more than others.

The Impact of Competition

If structural factors such as functional demands, inherited institutions, or developmental sequencing do not explain the variation, one alternative is to turn to the *agents* behind the post-1989 transformations. As noted earlier, the main policy actors and architects in these new parliamentary democracies were the parties in the legislatures. They were ones to reconstruct the state, and the only actors with direct access to policy making.

To be sure, a diverse set of religious, civil society, and economic actors could all influence democratic policy making.[67] The judiciary, the media, nongovernmental organizations (NGOs), and international organizations can all monitor and even sanction the exploitation of the state. Free and assertive media are especially important in disseminating and publicizing the criticisms and opinions of political parties, and serve as a key channel of reaching out to potential voters and constituencies. They can thus monitor and criticize party behavior.

However, in post-communist cases, analysts noted the weakness of civil society, the inconsistency of media influence, and the absence of international oversight.[68] The media themselves depended on leaks and reports from political parties for many of their most damning stories. Further, the role of NGOs, the judiciary, and the media may itself be endogenous to party competition and state support.[69] For example, governing parties in the Czech Republic and Slovakia tried to consolidate their hold over television broadcasts[70] as part of a broader drive to exclude civil society from policy decisions.[71] In the Czech Republic, a "deeply entrenched revolving door

---

[67] For specific examples of these pressures in post-communist countries, see Róna-Tas, Ákos. 1997. *The Great Surprise of the Small Transformation*. Ann Arbor: University of Michigan Press.

[68] Howard, Marc Morjé. 2003. *The Weakness of Civil Society in Post-Communist Europe*. Cambridge: Cambridge University Press.

[69] McMann, Kelly. 2003. "The Civic Realm in Kyrgyzstan: Soviet Economic Legacies and Activists' Expectations," in Jones Luong, Pauline, ed. *The Transformation of Central Asia: States and Societies from Soviet Rule to Independence*. Ithaca: Cornell University Press, pp. 213–45.

[70] Lewis 2000, p. 115.

[71] Terra, Jonathan. 2002. "Political Institutions and Postcommunist Transitions." Paper presented for the Fourth Annual Society for Comparative Research Graduate Student Retreat, Budapest, May.

relationship between the media and the political elites"[72] also existed. As a result, "for much of the time when [Václav] Klaus was in office, most of the Czech media followed his line slavishly. There was little unencumbered public debate."[73] Similarly, the controversies in both Hungary and Poland over the media oversight boards, in charge of granting broadcasting concessions,[74] suggest that media are often battlegrounds for party competition rather than its effective substitutes.

Similarly, several existing explanations have focused on monitoring by the electorate and its influence,[75] even if the empirical tests are less conclusive.[76] The reelection imperative can motivate opposition criticism, and higher electoral accountability can translate into a greater impetus for regulatory reforms.[77] However, in nascent multiparty systems, parties that criticize the government may not be the ones to benefit electorally from such criticism. Post-communist incumbents were punished for poor performance in office,[78] but neither the incumbent nor the opposition could predict which individual party would benefit from electoral dissatisfaction. And, unless a party could easily predict that *its* votes would increase,

---

[72] Stein, Jonathan. 1998. "Still in Bed Together," *New Presence* (January). Journalists moved from newspapers to the National Property Fund, the editor of *Respekt* magazine became a special adviser to Prime Minister Josef Tošovský, and Social Democratic deputies contributed to the editorial pages of the newspaper *Lidové Noviny* both before and after their election.

[73] Stroehlein, Andrew. 1999. "The Czech Republic 1992 to 1999," *Central Europe Review*, 13 September.

[74] Czabański, Krzysztof. 2003. "Rywin TV," *Wprost*, 26 October, pp. 30–2.

[75] Persson, Torsten, and Tabellini, Guido. 2002. *Political Economics*. Cambridge: MIT Press; Holmstrom, Bengt 1982. "Managerial Incentive Problems: a Dynamic Perspective," in *Essays in Economic and Management in Honor of Lars Wahlbeck*. Stockholm: Swedish School of Economics; Geddes, Barbara. 1994. *The Politician's Dilemma*. Berkeley: University of California Press; Ferejohn 1986; Przeworski 1995, Przeworski et al. 1997, p. 426; Vachudová, Milada Anna. 2005. *Europe Undivided: Democracy, Leverage and Integration After Communism*. Oxford and New York: Oxford University Press, ch. 1; Stepan, Alfred. 1994. "Corruption in South America," in Trang, Duc, ed. *Corruption and Democracy*. Budapest: CEU.

[76] Thus, Holmstrom 1982 and Persson and Tabellini 2002 assume, rather than demonstrate, monitoring by voters. Such assumptions may be warranted in established democracies, but not in post-communist countries.

[77] Mattli, Walter, and Plümper, Thomas. 2002. "The Demand-Side Politics of EU Enlargement: Democracy and the Application for EU Membership." *Journal of European Public Policy*, 9, 4: 550–74, p. 559. See also Montinola and Jackman 2002.

[78] Latvia is perhaps the most extreme example of intracamp fluidity: Each winning party was formed less than a year before the election. Auers, Daunis. 2002/2003. "Latvia's 2002 Elections: Dawn of a New Era?" *East European Constitutional Review*, 11/12, 4/1 (Fall/Winter): 106–10.

even popular demand for reform would have little impact. For the same reason, protest parties may be beneficiaries of other parties' criticism, but are unlikely to constrain the government effectively themselves.[79] In short, the direct influence of voters on political party behavior was limited and indirect.

Yet if political parties and their interactions are to explain the variation in exploitation, then it is necessary to specify the *kind* of competition that constrains or promotes exploitation, and *how* it does so. As it stands, several existing measures gauge the impact of party competition on policy and institutional outcomes. Among the most widely used indicators of political competition are fragmentation and the effective number of parties in parliament, turnover and party system openness, ideological polarization, and electoral volatility.[80] Research on both political party systems and on democratic governance has found these factors to affect policy making and outcomes.[81]

First, parliamentary *fragmentation* has been argued to constrain exploitation by making party collusion far more difficult and by further increasing the electoral uncertainty that leads parties to establish mutual guarantees.[82]

---

[79] Moreover, as James Fearon has noted, voters may choose on the basis of "good types" rather than expecting direct accountability of officeholders to the electorate. In effect, voters delegate power rather than monitor policy makers directly, and rely on elections as sorting mechanisms rather than as establishing accountability. Fearon, James. 1999. "Electoral Accountability and the Control of Politicians: Selecting Good Types Versus Sanctioning Poor Performance," Przeworski, Adam, Stokes, Susan, and Manin, Zernard. 1999. *Democracy, Accountability, and Representation*. New York: Cambridge University Press, 55–97.

[80] Frye, Timothy. 2002. "The Perils of Polarization," *World Politics*, 54 (April): 308–37; Orenstein, Mitchell. 2001. *Out of the Red: Building Capitalism and Democracy in Post-Communist Europe*. Ann Arbor: University of Michigan Press; Hellman 1998; Montinola and Jackman 2002, p. 151 (Montinola and Jackman hypothesize that turnover plays a critical role, but use a measure that is a composite of opposition freedom, political rights, and parliamentary effectiveness); McChesney, Fred. 1987. "Rent Extraction and Rent Creation in the Economic Theory of Regulation," *Journal of Legal Studies*, 16: 101–18.

[81] Cotta, Maurizio. 1996. "Structuring the New Party Systems after the Dictatorship," in Pridham, Geoffrey, and Lewis, Paul, eds. *Stabilising Fragile Democracies*. London: Routledge, pp. 69–99; Olson, David. 1998. "Party Formation and Party System Consolidation in the New Democracies of Central Europe," *Political Studies*, 46, 3: 432–64; Mair, Peter. 1997. *Party System Change: Approaches and Interpretations*. Oxford: Oxford University Press; Lewis, 2000, Pettai, Vello, and Kreuzer, Marcus. 2001. "Institutions and Party Development in the Baltic States," in Lewis, Paul, ed. *Party Development and Democratic Change in Post-Communist Europe*. London: Frank Cass; Kitschelt et al. 1999; Mainwaring 1993.

[82] Grzymała-Busse, Anna. 2003. "Political Competition and the Politicization of the State," *Comparative Political Studies*, 36, 10 (December): 1123–47.

Barbara Geddes, for example, has found that where several equally powerful parties exist in parliament, they alone have the incentives to reduce patronage and clientelism for fear of losing seats if they do not reform.[83] Policies take longer to be formulated, but there is less of a chance for any one set of party interests to dominate.[84] Alternatively, fragmentation may scupper state and other policy reforms because it hampers the rise of integrative forces or policy coherence.[85] Second, the entrance of new parties, whether through *electoral turnover* or *party system openness*, is said to limit the accumulation of private benefits from one electoral term to another by an individual party. Longer incumbency promotes corruption, and the entrance of new parties precludes it.[86] Alternation in power also limits the purely predatory behavior associated with the certainty of losing office permanently.[87] Third, ideological *polarization* and the rise of extremist parties may prevent construction of mutual guarantees and harm reform outcomes.[88] Another possibility is that such threats may lead voters and parties to coordinate, and thus to establish formal safeguards that would protect the state.[89] Fourth, *volatility* (the shift in voter support for given parties from election to election) may raise the stakes of the electoral game. Politicians who are certain of losing office will try to grab all they

---

[83] Geddes 1994. The exact role of popular demand in Geddes's account is unclear: If several large parties share equally in patronage, reform will occur thanks to the electoral gains possible from reform (p. 86). However, even huge popular support for reform does not translate into policy, even though the electoral payoff is said to be equal to popular demand (p. 85ff).

[84] Remmer, Karen. 1998. "The Politics of Neoliberal Economic Reform in South America," *Studies in Comparative International Development*, 2, 2: 3–30.

[85] Toonen, Theo. 1993. "Analysing Institutional Change," in Hesse, Joachim Jens, ed. *Administrative Transformation in Central and Eastern Europe*. London: Blackwell. See also Nunberg, Barbara, ed. 1999. *The State After Communism*. Washington: World Bank; Roubini, Nouriel, and Sachs, Jeffrey. 1989. "Government Spending and Budget Deficits in the Industrial Economies." NBER Working Paper No. 2919; Tsebelis, George. 1999. "Veto Players and Law Production in Parliamentary Democracies: An Empirical Analysis," *American Political Science Review*, 93, 3: 591–608.

[86] La Palombara, Joseph. 1994. "Structural and Institutional Aspects of Corruption," *Social Research*, 61, 2 (Summer): 325–50. See also Grzymała-Busse 2003.

[87] Rose-Ackerman 1978.

[88] Mainwaring 1993, p. 220; Frye 2002, pp. 308–37; Meyer-Sahling, Jan-Hinrik. 2006. "The Rise of the Partisan State? Parties, Patronage, and the Ministerial Bureaucracy in Hungary," *Journal of Communist Studies and Transitional Politics*, 22, 3 (September): 274–97.

[89] Markowski, Radosław. 2001. "Party System Institutionalization in New Democracies: Poland: A Trend Setter with No Followers," in Lewis, Paul G., ed. *Party Development and Democratic Change in Post-Communist Europe*. London: Frank Cass, pp. 74–5.

can while in office.[90] Volatility further breeds short-term voting, rather than long-term identifications, and more appeals to the broad electorate, rather than to loyal voters.[91] As a result, it may reduce accountability and make coordination between voters and parties difficult.[92] Finally, *composite measures* combine several indicators of party competition. For example, one index melds fragmentation, volatility, turnover, and openness to argue that patronage-led state building is constrained when no party is dominant and that "elections present voters with the choices among a manageable number of stable parties with familiar coalition-building preferences."[93] Table 2.2 summarizes how post-communist democracies fared on these indicators of competition.

These proxies for party competition, widely used in the literature, all point to important trends in the patterns of political competition. However, they are less reliable as predictors of state exploitation or its constraints. As Table 2.3 shows, there is no clear relationship between the existing measures of competition and the two clusters of less and more exploited states. We cannot reject the null hypothesis that the mean values of fragmentation, turnover, openness of competition, polarization, or volatility do not differ significantly from each other in the two clusters of state exploitation. In both the highly and less exploited polities, we see heterogeneous patterns of competition. Nor is it the case that these measures correlate with other indicators of the private use of state resources, such as corruption, for example: Table 2.4 shows that these same measures of competition (across the post-communist world) do not correlate with Transparency International and World Bank corruption ratings.[94]

Similarly, parliamentary institutions and structures themselves are unlikely to constrain the government. For example, formal opposition access to policy making does not explain how parties take advantage of

---

[90] Birch, Sarah. 2001. "Electoral Systems and Party System Stability in Post-Communist Europe." Paper presented at the American Political Science Association (APSA) Annual Meeting, 30 August–2 September, San Francisco.

[91] Gunnar Sjöblom's causal arrows can be reversed: Parties themselves may be responsible for the electoral volatility. Sjöblom, Gunnar. 1983. "Political Change and Political Accountability: A Propositional Inventory of Causes and Effects," in Daalder, Hans, and Mair, Peter, eds. *West European Party Systems*. London: Sage.

[92] Persson et al. 2001.

[93] O'Dwyer 2004, p. 521.

[94] The patterns hold both for democracies alone and for the entire post-communist sample. The one difference is that incumbency gains substantive and statistical significance in the broader sample, to correlate positively with corruption at .48 (.025 significance, two-tailed).

Table 2.2. *Indicators of Competition*

	Robust Competition	Fragmentation	Effective of Parliamentary Parties[a]	Incumbency	Openness[b]	Polarization[c]	Electoral Volatility[d]	Excluded Vote (avg)[e]
Hungary	3	.68	3.1	.27	<1.0	11.4	25.0	13.0
Estonia	2	.79	4.8	.36	7.2	12.0	39.5	10.1
Slovenia	3	.84	6.2	.57	7.4	19.3	21.5	10.4
Lithuania	2	.72	3.6	.36	11.0	11.9	35.0	23.4
Poland	3	.77	4.9	.27	15.8	31.8	29.0	14.0
Czech R.	1	.71	3.4	.75	2.1	12.0	17.0	12.5
Slovakia	1	.78	5.2	.50	17.1	4.9	31.5	14.6
Bulgaria	1	.71	2.7	.27	18.6	30.9	19.0	12.6
Latvia	0	.76	4.2	.71	24.7	14.6	44.5	10.3
Diff. of means[f]	P = .003 t = 9.0	P = .24 t = 1.48	P = .19 t = 1.7	P = .25 t = −1.42	P = .29 t = −1.28	P = .47 t = .82	P = .71 t = .41	P = .65 t = .51

[a] Mair 2001, 1999 data. $1/\Sigma\ S_i^2$, where S_i is seat share of ith parliamentary party.

[b] Average % of parliament seats held by new parties/parties that did not participate in previous elections. $\Sigma\ S_i/N–1$, where S_i is seat share of ith new party and N is the number of electoral terms.

[c] Frye 2001. Measured as the difference in votes between presidents and governments of opposing parties.

[d] Mair 2002.

[e] Percentage of votes for parties that failed to enter parliament.

[f] Two-tailed t-test, null hypothesis (H0): difference between means = 0. Hypothesis tested (Ha): difference between means ≠ 0. Pr (|T| > |t|) = P.

these channels.[95] As Table 2.5 shows, there is little variation among the levels of opposition influence allowed by post-communist democratic parliamentary institutions, such as how many standing committees there are, whether committee assignments are proportionally distributed among parties, or how fixed their jurisdictions are. All but Lithuania score the same four out of five possible points, yet there is considerable difference in party behavior. These parliamentary institutions do not explain the variation.[96]

[95] Strøm, Kaare. 1990. *Minority Government and Majority Rule.* Cambridge: Cambridge University Press.

[96] The one exception here is the two-thirds supermajority requirement for major legislation in Hungary, which significantly increased the opposition's access to policy making.

Table 2.3. *Bivariate Correlations Between the Corruption Index and Measures of Competition, All Post-Communist Cases*

		Robust Competition	Fragmentation	ENPP[a]	Gov't Continuity	Openness of Competition	Polarization	Volatility	Average Excluded Vote
Corruption Index	Pearson Correlation	-.854[b]	-.226	-.120	.476[c]	.443	-.091	-.077	.540[b]
	Sig. (2-tailed)	.000	.313	.596	.025	.050	.688	.740	.025
	N	22	22	22	22	20	22	21	17

Notes:
[a] Effective numbers of parliamentary parties.
[b] Correlation is significant at the .01 level (two-tailed).
[c] Correlation is significant at the .05 level (two-tailed).

Table 2.4. *Bivariate Correlations Between Corruption and Competition, Democracies Only*

		Robust Competition	Fragmentation	ENPP	Gov't Continuity	Openness of Competition	Polarization	Volatility	Average Excluded Vote
Corruption Index	Pearson Correlation	-.865[a]	-.403	-.423	.183	.358	.118	.117	.531[b]
	Sig. (2-tailed)	.000	.122	.102	.497	.173	.664	.665	.034
	N	16	16	16	16	16	16	16	16

Notes:
[a] Correlation is significant at the .01 level (two-tailed).
[b] Correlation is significant at the .05 level (two-tailed).

Table 2.5. *Formal Access to Policy Making of Parliamentary Opposition*

	Number of Standing Committees	Fixed Jurisdictions?	Correspond to Ministries?	Max Number of Committees per MP?	Proportional Distribution?	Index Score
Hungary	10–12	No	Yes	2 or more	Yes. 4–5 led by opposition, 1990–8	4
Estonia	10	No	Yes	2 or less	Yes. 2 led by opposition	4
Slovenia	14	No	Yes	2 or more	Yes	4
Lithuania	15	Yes	Yes	2 or less	Yes	5
Poland	25–8	No	Yes	2 or more	Yes. 7 led by opposition in 1993–7	4
Czech R.	11	No	No	2 or less	Yes. 3–4 led by opposition in 1996–8	4
Slovakia	16	Yes	Yes	2 regular	No. Opposition Excluded in 1994–8	4
Bulgaria	14–20	No	Not in 1990–1 Yes after 1991	1 only	Yes. 1–2 led by opposition	4
Latvia	17	No	Yes	2 or less	Yes	4

Source: Criteria and coding from Strøm 1990.

Second, these accounts provide few *mechanisms* of constraint. Fragmentation and its mathematical analogue – the effective number of parties – have an indeterminate impact by themselves. Indicators such as "effective number of parties" measure neither the viability of alternative governments nor the fragility of existing ones.[97] As Barbara Geddes shows, it is not clear whether it is electoral accountability or seat share that drive

---

[97] The effective number of electoral/parliamentary parties is a measure of seat dispersion: $1/\Sigma S_i^2$, where S_i is the seat share of the ith party. The effective number of electoral parties is calculated by substituting V_i, the vote share of the ith party, for S_i. To use these as a measure of competition would be to assume that strong competition is correlated linearly and positively with the number of rivals and their similar size. (See Stigler, George. 1972. "Economic Competition and Political Competition," *Public Choice*, 13: 91–106.)

reform.[98] Turnover mechanically limits the accumulation of resources by any one governing party but does not constrain exploitation.[99] For example, Slovenia has had the same party in power for nearly ten years, yet it has a relatively nonpoliticized state. Conversely, both Latvia and Poland see new competitors enter and win elections, but the state was more exploited in the former than in the latter. The significance of ideological polarization lies in the fact that it may eliminate certain parties from being effective critics of the government, if their extremism makes them unacceptable coalition partners or governors. By itself, however, such polarization has little direct effect. Finally, existing composite indices suffer from two problems: Their individual components do not covary with state exploitation, and they fail to specify the logic of constraint. Conor O'Dwyer, for example, predicts that parties with stable and predictable vote shares will not rely on patronage. However, he also argues that dominant parties will use patronage, even though they too have a stable and predictable share of the vote.[100] More fundamentally, if "too many parties for the voters"[101] produce patronage, it is not clear what the "right" number of parties would be, possibly as a result of particularly problematic codings.[102]

---

[98] Geddes 1994.

[99] Orenstein 2001 argues that alternation in power creates opportunities for elite learning and policy adjustment. However, the pace of the transformation was so rapid that it made disentangling causes from outcomes, or learning from each other's mistakes, difficult to sustain.

[100] O'Dwyer 2004. "Dominance" itself is unclear: Is it over time, other parties, or policy making?

[101] Ibid. p. 531.

[102] O'Dwyer's (ibid.) particular measure of fractionalization counts all members of an *electoral* coalition as individual parties. He uses this measure to argue that Poland had a far more fractionalized government and opposition than either Slovakia or the Czech Republic. Yet if we count the members of an electoral coalition as one party (which is how they are presented to voters in campaigns and on the ballot, and to potential coalition partners), the picture changes dramatically. For example, Poland in 1997 thus has a very high fractionalization rate, responsible in his argument for weak competition. Once we recode the Electoral Action Solidarity (AWS) as the single electoral choice it was, however, the fractionalization rates drop to 1.56 for the government and 1.4 for the opposition, well below the Czech 1.9 and 2.3, respectively. Yet O'Dwyer claims that Poland continues a "runaway state building" trajectory, expanding its state administration far more than the Czechs. Moreover, even if one accepts his coding, it is unclear why Slovakia, which fares far better on all measures of the party system than Poland, would have far higher rates of patronage. Similarly, the Czech ODS was a dominant party with a weak opposition from 1992–6, and Poland had an extremely united opposition and a divided government during 1997–2001: So, for much of the time period O'Dwyer examines, these patterns predict runaway Czech state building and Polish constraint, the opposite of what he argues happened.

In short, these factors capture important aspects of political competition. However, they neither correlate with, nor explain, state exploitation. They may limit the accumulation of benefits or make collusion more difficult, but are not enough to prevent parties from exploiting the state. Some may be related to robust competition – for example, low turnover can be a result of weak opposition. However, only robust competition implies a mechanism of constraint.

Robust Competition

If we are to examine which aspects of party competition are critical in constraining exploitation, we need to take a step back analytically. Political competition has become a favored explanation for variation in rent seeking,[103] and recent public choice perspectives have argued that the differences in political or economic competition are responsible for the variation in the levels of corruption and other rent seeking across countries.[104] Despite some caveats,[105] the general consensus favors competition as a well-recognized constraint.[106] The very legitimacy of competition, as Schumpeter, Downs, and others have argued, rests on the notion that it produces third-party benefits.[107] Yet if party competition can constrain corruption

---

[103] Specifically, political competition explains elite corruption: the rents sought and gained by highly placed political actors and state officials, rather than the everyday experiences of petty bureaucratic corruption. The latter has not been measured systematically.

[104] See Rose-Ackerman, Susan. 1999. *Corruption and Government: Causes, Consequences, and Reform*. Cambridge: Cambridge University Press; Tullock, Gordon. 1967. "The Welfare Costs of Tariffs, Monopolies, and Theft," *Western Economic Journal* 5: 224–32; Krueger, Anne. 1974. "The Political Economy of the Rent-Seeking Society," *American Economic Review*, 64, 3: 291–303.

[105] Scott 1972, p. 96; Dyson, Kenneth. 1977. "Party, State, and Bureaucracy in Western Germany." Sage Professional Papers in Comparative Politics, No. 01–063. Beverly Hills: Sage; Rose-Ackerman 1978.

[106] Rose-Ackerman 1978; Lancaster, Thomas D., and Montinolla, Gabriella. 2001. "Comparative Political Corruption: Issues of Operationalization and Measurement," *Studies in Comparative International Development*, 36, 3 (Fall): 3–28; Mauro, Paolo. 1995. "Corruption and Growth," *Quarterly Journal of Economics*, 110, 3: 681–712; Ades, Alberto, and Di Tella, Rafael. 1999. "Rents, Competition, and Corruption," *American Economic Review*, 89, 4 (September): 982–93.

[107] Schumpeter 1948; Downs 1957; Bartolini, Stefano. 2002. "Electoral and Party Competition: Analytical Dimensions and Empirical Problems," in Gunther, Richard, Montero, Jose Ramon, and Linz, Juan, eds., *Political Parties*. Oxford: Oxford University Press, pp. 84–110; Bartolini, Stefano. 1999. "Collusion, Competition, and Democracy," *Journal of Theoretical Politics*, 11, 4: 435–70, p. 441.

and exploitation,[108] it is also not an automatic check.[109] And, as we have seen, existing indicators of party size or seat share do not capture the capacity of competitors to constrain incumbent behavior.[110] What, then, lies at the core of competition and its beneficial aspects? What ought a new indicator capture?

As noted earlier, for competition to constrain exploitation (or other rent seeking), incumbents must worry about being replaced. Some analysts have even argued that the relevant aspect of competition, the prospect of reelection itself, is a constraint on elected officials.[111] The more threatening these potential government substitutes, "the fewer degrees of freedom the ruler possesses, and the greater the percentage of incremental income that will be retained by the constituents."[112] Thus, without democratic competition, and in the absence of existing institutions, government actors can extract freely and their rate of extraction is limited chiefly by their time horizons. Democratic competition itself changes these calculations: Even where there is no electoral accountability (winners are chosen by a lottery), competitors may still moderate their behavior and uphold the democratic system so long as their probability of future wins is high enough and the payoff is sufficiently large.[113]

A competition that is robust, in turn, further lowers the payoffs of extraction by linking extraction to sanctions and punishment. It also acts as a guarantor of democratic rules: It requires and reifies the rules of democratic competition. Opposition parties have a stake in constraining the government, to ensure that governing incumbents do not exploit the state so much that the survival of other parties is hampered by exclusion from either benefits or office. The lower their certainty of survival, the greater their incentives to do so. Robust competition also leads incumbent governments

[108] For an extensive review of the public choice literature on competition as constraint, see Rose-Ackerman 1999; Shleifer, Andrei, and Vishny, Robert N. 1993. "Corruption," *Quarterly Journal of Economics*, 108: 599–617.

[109] Rose-Ackerman 1978, p. 211; Ades, Alberto, and Di Tella, Rafael. 1995. "Competition and Corruption." Applied Economics Discussion Paper Series No. 169, Oxford University.

[110] Nonetheless, such typologies were the mainstay of earlier efforts to classify parties, driven by the analytical need to distinguish between one-party, two-party, and multiparty regimes.

[111] Rose-Ackerman 1978; Geddes and Neto 1992.

[112] North 1981, p. 27.

[113] Przeworski, Adam. 1999. "Minimalist Conception of Democracy: A Defense," in Ian Shapiro, Ian, and Hacker-Cordón, Casiano, eds. *Democracy's Value*. Cambridge: Cambridge University Press.

to establish formal state institutions that benefit both electoral losers and incumbents more equally, limiting the potential for exploitation – and in the process, leading the losers to abide further by the rules of democratic competition. Political competition thus first constrains state exploitation, rather than exploitation limiting competition. In short, robust competition lowers the incentives for rent seeking – and bolsters the competitive system itself.

As defined in the introduction, such competition requires opposition that is a distinct and plausible governing alternative, and that is an effective critic of the government. While existing analyses have emphasized some of these aspects of competition individually, this account argues that all three facets of competition are jointly responsible for curbing rent seeking. They help to provide the microlevel mechanisms and incentives of competitive constraint that lead governing parties to establish institutions inhibiting incumbents and opposition alike.

These three characteristics of the opposition also resonate with existing understandings of what we prize more broadly about competition. A clearly profiled opposition is one that voters and other parties easily recognize as a distinct target and source of mutual suspicion. Such distinct parties form mutually hostile camps, and their suspicion is fundamental to curbing rent seeking.[114] This differentiation is not limited to the ideological distance among the parties or other spatial understandings of political competition, such as those put forth by William Riker and Peter Ordeshook.[115] Parties that are quite close ideologically can be enormously hostile to each other, such as the Polish Freedom Union (Unia Wolności, UW) and the SLD (Sojusz Lewicy Demokratycznej). Alternatively, parties with considerable ideological distance can cooperate closely, such as the Czech ČSSD and ODS did.

A plausible opposition is a subset of Giovanni Sartori's *relevant* parties. Relevant parties are either necessary to form a government in the past, or if not included in government coalitions, able to affect policy.[116] Such parties, including antisystem and ostracized parties, affect the direction of competition – whether it is centrifugal or centripetal. Credibility, however,

---

[114] It further may increase accountability to voters, since it makes alternative governments more identifiable. See Powell, Bingham. 2000. *Elections as Instruments of Democracy*. New Haven: Yale University Press.

[115] Riker, William, and Ordeshook, Peter. 1968. "A Theory of the Calculus of Voting," *American Political Science Review*, 62: 25–43. Bartolini 2002 reviews these approaches.

[116] Sartori, Giovanni. 1976. *Parties and Party Systems: A Framework for Analysis*. Cambridge: Cambridge University Press, pp. 120–5.

calls for a narrower standard because it seeks to capture the pressures on incumbent behavior rather than on all competitors. For a party to affect the tactics of governing parties, it must itself be capable of governing, lest its threats are seen as empty. Therefore, plausible opposition parties must have either governed in the past or be accepted as potential coalition partners by other parliamentary actors. Parties excluded from governance do not pose such a threat and are far less likely to affect coalition behavior. And, if the main challenge posed by the opposition lies in its ability to formulate alternative governments, the more seats held by plausible opponents, the greater the number of alternative governments, as Ferejohn 1986 found.

The extent to which the opposition is a vociferous critic is a measure of the conflict of interest among competitors that is fundamental to the accounts of competition put forth by Axelrod 1970 or De Mesquita 1974.[117] The conflict here is over who should occupy office or what policies ought to be adopted, not over the rules of the game. Indeed, one of the necessary conditions for both democratic competition in general and the opposition in particular to have their effect is that all actors share the same respect for democratic rules. Moreover, these parties must have the capacity to criticize, and to publicize this criticism.

The Sources of Robust Competition

As noted in the introduction, the *sources* of robust competition are diverse. In the context examined here, however, communist parties that exited power and reinvented themselves are likely both to be robust competitors and to foster robust competition.

First, they are a clear option, given the "regime divide" that exists in most countries between the former communist parties and those whose origins were in the anticommunist opposition.[118] Their reinvention leads to the formation of two clear camps: one with roots in the former communist party, and one with roots in its former opposition. And, when communist parties transform themselves into moderate social democratic parties, they

---

[117] Axelrod, Robert. 1970. *Conflict of Interest*. Chicago: Markham; De Mesquita, Bruce Bueno. 1974. "Need for Achievement and Competitiveness as Determinants of Political Party Success in Elections and Coalitions," *American Political Science Review*, 68, 3: 1207–20. Kaare Strøm 1989 notes that whereas competition is a cause of conflict for de Mesquita, it is its consequence for Axelrod. Strøm, Kaare. 1989. "Inter-Party Competition in Advanced Democracies," *Journal of Theoretical Politics*, 1, 3: 277–300.

[118] Kitschelt et al. 1999.

not only gain considerable electoral success but become the most obvious and plausible alternative to governments with roots in the anticommunist opposition.[119]

The former communists and their former opponents have the strongest incentives to monitor and criticize each other's misdoings, due both to existing antagonisms and to the electoral threat each poses to the other. Communist successor parties are especially keen critics, since they are also defending their own existence and their historical record.[120] They also have the *capacity* to criticize: The same elite skills that allowed the communist successors to transform after the communist collapse make them able critics and highly competent governors. The reinvention of communist parties is the result of the communist willingness to engage the opposition and implement liberalizing reforms.[121] Both the communist parties and their opposition gained years, if not decades, of experience in monitoring each other and formulating both criticisms and policy alternatives. One result is that in almost all post-communist countries (except Estonia) where a critical opposition exists, communist successor parties have regenerated (the converse also holds). Another consequence was that where the communist successors were forced to exit and then reinvent themselves, reforms of the state were often political exercises in anticommunism.

In contrast, communist parties that stayed in power will have the least incentive to break with the communist system, since they stand to continue to benefit from its fusion of party and state and discretionary access to state assets. They can continue to privilege themselves and to lock out other parties. As a result, Kitschelt's logic that "success of the democratization process is often linked to the failure of the *ancien régime* forces to maintain a

---

[119] An alternative measure is the share of votes given to parties with elites blended from both the communist and the opposition camps. This measure thus captures both the prevalence and the voter acceptance of parties that tend to blunt criticism. However, blended parties may still serve as effective critics once they develop their own identities and voters differentiate them from other competitors. Values for this indicator range from 3 percent (DeSus in Slovenia), 6 percent (MiEP in Hungary), 7 percent (UP in Poland), 8 percent (Republicans in the Czech Republic), 12 percent (the Coalition Party in Estonia), 24 percent (BANU, BE, and NS in Bulgaria), 31 percent (Latvian Social Democratic Party [after 2001]), 40 percent (LC, LTF, LVP, DPS, and LDLP in Latvia), and 49 percent (HZDS, SMER, and DU in Slovakia).

[120] Staniszkis 1999 argues that post-communist and the post-opposition forces colluded and bought off each other's opposition with privatization deals. However, there is little empirical evidence of such deliberate collusion.

[121] Cf. Grzymała-Busse 2002.

strong bargaining position"[122] needs to be augmented: *Ancien régime* forces both need to exit power to enable democracy to take root *and* best serve its consolidation by returning as committed democrats.

Mechanisms of Constraint

As noted in the introduction, the fundamental mechanisms of constraint took place in parliament and relied on the parliamentary opposition's ability to influence incumbent behavior.[123] The major challenge posed by the opposition thus lay in its ability to formulate alternative governments, rather than simply in making competing offers to the voters.

First, robust competition created incentives to formulate mutual formal guarantees against exploitation. Faced with such an opposition, ruling parties fear losing office. This electoral uncertainty leads them to build in formal institutions that offer guarantees for all parties rather than benefit the incumbent alone. They do so because they fear losing everything when they are no longer the incumbent – and they know they are likely to lose the next election. In short, a critical opposition offers the incumbents incentives to limit opportunities for state exploitation and to create judicial appeal and independent oversight. The result is the creation of state institutions that limit exploitation – for example, the fusion of the oversight offices in Hungary or the stricter regulations on Polish party funding.

This pattern of self-constraint in the short term to ensure survival in the long term is a classic pattern of institutional engineering in new regimes, as the seminal work of Jon Elster, Douglass North, Adam Przeworski, Barry Weingast, and others has shown. However, it is not driven by negotiations between powerful actors wishing to extract mutual concessions.[124] Instead, it is the result of the incumbents' anticipation of exit from office and their unilateral construction of institutions that would protect themselves and their constituents when they are out of power. For example, the Hungarian MDF agreed to generous (if highly monitored) public party financing in 1990, knowing it could benefit its opponents as well. Similarly, the creation of the Polish Securities and Exchange Commission in 1991 or the Slovenian

---

[122] Enyedi, Zsolt. 2006. "Party Politics in Post-Communist Transition," in Katz, Richard, and Crotty, William, eds. *Handbook of Party Politics*. London: Sage, pp. 228–38. See Kitschelt et al. 1999.

[123] Demsetz 1982.

[124] See North and Weingast 1989; Przeworski, Adam. 1991. *Democracy and Market*. Cambridge: Cambridge University Press.

Court of Audit in 1994 limited their creators' access to state resources – but also established that their successors would be similarly constrained.

Second, the opposition moderated incumbent behavior through constant mutual monitoring. Parties questioned each other's actions via the institution of parliamentary interpellations (questions), threats of stripping immunity, and parliamentary committees. Such public investigations relied on free and critical media and their ability to disseminate and evaluate such criticisms. Thus, opposition parties easily called for investigation committees in Hungary, effectively bringing attention to suspicious dealings.[125] In Poland, both the SLD-PSL and AWS-UW governing coalitions were rife with internal, mutual accusations that their coalition partners were using state office for private gain.[126] Similarly, in Slovenia, the constant criticism of opposition parties destabilized coalitions six separate times so that the incumbents lived under a constant threat of coalition collapse.

This mutual monitoring led governments to preempt opposition criticism, as with the civil service reforms in Hungary, Lithuania, and Slovenia in the early 1990s or the introduction and strengthening of ombudsmen in Estonia and Poland. Without a critical opposition, such investigations did not take place, and opposition calls had gone unheeded. For example, the Czech opposition vainly called for investigations of government misdeeds throughout 1994–7.[127] Government representatives eventually criticized the opposition itself for wasting its interpellations on the "hoity-toity behavior of the doorman in the Ministry of Finances," rather than on cases of financial malfeasance.[128]

Third, robust competition induced the governments to build greater consensus and to share power. Several governments adopted Lyndon B. Johnson's strategy (if not his earthy formulation) and attempted to coopt the opposition.[129] Such power sharing across political parties and levels of government has preserved both markets and the integrity of the state,

---

[125] Freedom House. 2002. *Nations in Transit, 2001*. Washington: Freedom House, p. 201. The Fidesz-led government (1998–2002) suspended this practice; opposition parties called seven times for such committees but none was ever formed.

[126] Rydlewski, Grzegorz. 2000. *Rządzenie Koalicyjne w Polsce*. Warsaw: Elipsa, p. 87.

[127] Appel, Hilary. 2001. "Corruption and the Collapse of the Czech Transition Miracle," *Eastern European Politics and Societies*, 15, 3 (Fall): 528–53, p. 534.

[128] *Respekt*, 22 January 1996.

[129] Johnson rejected the suggestion to fire J. Edgar Hoover by declaring, "It's probably better to have him inside the tent pissing out than outside the tent pissing in." See Dallek, Robert. 1998. *Flawed Giant: Lyndon B. Johnson, 1960–1973*. New York: Oxford University Press.

preventing "state capture" by economic interests and enterprises.[130] More immediately, if norms of sharing power held, they inoculated fragile incumbents against marginalization in the next legislative terms. Over time, the opposition's critiques and the resulting turnover meant that the electorates increasingly perceived the entire parliament as responsible for policy making, no longer blaming the government but the entire parliament passing and regulating policy. This both increased the opposition's incentives to differentiate itself through criticism *and* the government's incentives to coopt the opposition and share power.[131]

In Estonia, Hungary, Lithuania, Poland, and Slovenia, informal rules evolved, such as sharing power within committees, handing over oversight institutions to the opposition, or ensuring that opposition parties would have equal access in questioning experts and government officials testifying in parliamentary committees. Governing parties also opened up their actions to greater monitoring, in order to reassure voters and other parties alike, as in Hungary.[132] In contrast, where the opposition was weaker, fewer incentives for power sharing existed. For example, the 1994–8 Slovak and the 1992–6 Czech governments shunted opposition representatives from influential committees into ones with trivial impact on policy.

Critical to each of these mechanisms is the actors' recognition of the incentives they face: Governing parties that are too confident or too obtuse to perceive a threat of replacement are unlikely to be constrained. Similarly, the opposition's *capacity* to act as an effective monitor and critic of government action is independent of the incentives. For example, when Fidesz (Fiatal Demokraták Szövetsége, then Fidesz-Magyar Polgári Szövetség) defeated the MSzP in the 1998 Hungarian elections, the defeated MSzP's subsequent period of intense introspection muted its criticism and dulled its attention to government behavior, allowing Fidesz to start denying the opposition access to parliamentary oversight.[133]

Finally, there is little altruism in these calculations; rather, "the government *anticipates* possible criticisms and acts so as to rob them of force. It

---

[130] Geddes 1994. Geddes and Neto 1992 argue that excessive fragmentation led to higher rates of corruption in Brazil after 1985. See also Hellman 1998.

[131] *Wprost*, 28 November 1999, "Opozycja Totalna."

[132] Ferejohn, John. 1999. "Accountability and Authority: Toward a Theory of Political Accountability," in Stokes et al.

[133] The Fidesz government in Hungary (1998–2002) decreased the frequency of parliamentary meetings from weekly to once every three weeks, changed the opposition–government balance in committees in its favor, and began to attack the Hungarian Constitutional Court.

65

empowers the opposition through anticipated reaction."[134] Where a robust competition existed, governing parties still had the *incentive* to exploit the state. They faced their own uncertainty about the future, the demands of party factions and regional leaders to whom elites owed their elected positions, or narrow constituencies to whom particularist goods were promised. However, such parties had far less *ability* to do so. Given the constant monitoring and oversight by opposition parties, no one party could get away with extensive incursions into the state. Just as importantly, the opposition often behaved tactically, not strategically: The immediate goal was to prevent the governing parties from monopolizing state resources and thus repeatedly winning elections. A state that was less exploited was a consequence, but not necessarily the goal, of robust competition.

Patterns of Competition in Post-Communist Democracies

How, then, did party competition arise in the post-communist democracies, and how clear, plausible, and critical was it? In Hungary, Poland, Slovenia and Estonia, the post-communist and the post-opposition camps were clear, plausible, and critical. In all four cases, the communist parties exited power. In Hungary, Poland, and Slovenia, they then rapidly and comprehensively transformed themselves into committed democratic competitors and the key component of a robust competition. Along with the Center Party (Eesti Keskerakond, EK) in Estonia, the communists were vociferous critics of the new democratic governments, and faced enormous criticism themselves as they tried to defend their record and survive on the political scene as alternative governing parties.

In Hungary, the rise of five clearly differentiated opposition parties in 1989[135] led both to immediate mutual monitoring and the exit of the communist party from power (and its subsequent radical transformation). When the Round Table negotiations began, each party was uncertain regarding its electoral popularity or its future. Each wanted to ensure that the others would not get an electoral advantage. Since none had the wherewithal or the desire to allow any other to benefit exclusively, all agreed to mutual constraints. Subsequently, the rapidly increasing acceptance of the transformed communist successor, the MSzP, further increased the set of

---

[134] Coppedge, Michael. 1993, April. "Parties and Society in Mexico and Venezuela: Why Competition Matters," *Comparative Political Studies* 26, 1 (April): 253–74, p. 267.

[135] These were the Fidesz, FkGP, KdP, MDF, and SzDSz.

potential coalition partners, as well as the uncertainty for the ruling parties. Nearly all parties were plausible government parties, with the exception of the extremist Justice and Life Party (Magyar Igazság és Élet Pártja, MIEP), which held 3.7 percent of the seats in 1998–2002.[136]

As a result, all Hungarian governments faced enormous criticism, "starting from [the extremist] István Csurka's choleric arguments . . . to the systematic analysis provided by the opposition."[137] Parties alternated in power, with the anticommunist parties taking the 1990 and 1998 polls and the communist successor MSzP winning the 1994 and 2002 elections. The MSzP moderated and monitored state exploitation both in and out of office. From 1990–4, the first democratic government led by the nationalist-conservative MDF was under fire both from the MSzP and Fidesz, "offering radical, intelligent, and relentless criticism . . . against the government's attempts to test the limits of the democratic institutional order, or to control the media."[138] During the 1994–8 MSzP-SzDSz coalition, the MSzP was determined that its absolute majority not create the appearance of free license for the governing party. Similarly, the SzDSz (Szabad Demokraták Szövetsége), since it was entering a coalition with a controversial communist successor party, went out of its way to ensure that it could not be accused of malfeasance or a less than a perfectly democratic record. The government shared power with the opposition, and it increased the supermajority necessary for passing major legislation "as a way of making sure the opposition have a say."[139] In short, "the political struggle between the coalition government and the opposition parties means that compromises and concessions will often be reflected in legislative amendments."[140]

With the exception of the 1998–2002 Fidesz government, governing parties tended to share power.[141] This Fidesz government, on the other hand,

---

[136] Bernhard, Michael. 2000. "Institutional Choice After Communism," *East European Politics and Societies*, 3: 316–47.

[137] Keri, Laszlo. 1994. *Balance: The Hungarian Government 1990–1994*. Budapest: Korridor, p. 85.

[138] Kiss, Csilla. 2003. "From Liberalism to Conservatism: The Federation of Young Democrats in Post-Communist Hungary," *Eastern European Politics and Society*, 16, 3, 739–63.

[139] "Country Updates," *East European Constitutional Review*, Summer 1995.

[140] Szabó, Gábor. 1993. "Administrative Transition in a Post-Communist Society: The Case of Hungary," in Hesse, Joachim Jens, ed. *Administrative Transformation in Central and Eastern Europe*. Oxford: Blackwell, p. 91.

[141] After Viktor Orbán took over power in Fidesz in 1993, many liberal members left for the SzDSz, and the party itself moved in a conservative, Christian, nationalist direction.

took advantage of the confusion following the 1998 election (the MSzP gained the most votes, but lost the election to Fidesz) to institute several changes that curtailed opposition access to information and to power, weakening the ability of the opposition to monitor and moderate government behavior. Fidesz also began a mass mobilization strategy by wooing conservative groups, the clergy, and veteran organizations into the "Civic Circles," or around eleven thousand groupings allied with (but not part of) the party. However, this tactic could not prevent the party's loss in 2002, as the MSzP and the SzDSz mounted their criticism beginning in 2000.[142]

In Poland, once the anticommunist opposition movement Solidarity won the semifree elections of 1989, governments rapidly came and fell (with five governing coalitions between 1989 and 1993), generating considerable uncertainty over any party's ability to remain in government. Once in power, "each government was under enormous policy pressure: from its own coalition or from other parties, individuals, or trade unions."[143] Opposition parties not only questioned the government constantly and publicly, but informally monitored its behavior (and gleefully informed the media at every possible turn). Coalition partners themselves monitored each other.[144] Partly as a result of this vociferous criticism, the post-Solidarity and post-communist blocks alternated in power, in 1991, 1993, 1997, and 2001. The opposition was also clear, given the communist exit and subsequent reinvention, and plausible.

The opposition was not as consistent as in Hungary, Estonia, or Slovenia, however. The appearance and disappearance of parties from the former anticommunist opposition took their toll on the opposition's ability to serve as a critical and plausible alternative. For example, opposition criticism initially waned after the electoral victory of the communist successor SLD in 1993. The former anticommunist opposition issued contradictory criticisms and lacked the parliamentary discipline that would have made it a more formidable opponent. In another episode, after the SLD's 2001 victory,

---

[142] Enyedi, Zsolt. 2003. "Cleavage Formation in Hungary: The Role of Agency." Paper presented at the 2003 Joint Sessions of the European Consortium for Political Research (ECPR), Edinburgh.

[143] *Polityka*, 2 July 1994.

[144] The SLD constantly hindered and monitored the PSL during 1993–7, while the UW was highly suspicious of AWS's reform commitments from 1997 to 2001. *Wprost*, 25 June 2000.

parties from the former democratic opposition to communist rule were not a fully plausible governing alternative: Close to a third of the opposition consisted of populist parties with limited acceptance as coalition parties.[145] As a result, the main constraints on the communist successor's behavior were its own shortcomings.[146] Finally, the disarray into which the opposition fell after the 2005 elections bode ill for the Polish state administration and its exploitation.[147]

Nonetheless, no one party could centralize power for itself, nor did it have the incentives to do so: Given the likelihood of exit from power in the next elections, it made more sense to build in formal constraints that applied to the next ruling coalition as well.[148] Further, all parties recognized the need for common initiatives and consensus behind some major reforms and were willing to make concessions to other parties to achieve these goals.[149] Investigations and criticisms were institutionalized with the 1997 introduction of formal investigative commissions in parliament. These provisions were then taken up by the opposition, and extensive investigations were launched to investigate accusations of media lobbying of the government to procure favorable media ownership laws ("Rywingate") or of inappropriate management of a state oil company ("Orlengate.)[150]

Poles recognized the advantages of such competition. As one parliamentarian argued, "we should avoid the Czech situation at all costs. These two parties, the governing and the opposition, have come to an agreement, divided their spheres of influence, and pulled out money, wherever it is possible. Another pattern, of clans and oligarchs, is in Russia and Ukraine. Is this

---

[145] These were the League of Polish Families (Liga Polskich Rodzin, LPR) (8 percent of the seats) and Samoobrona (10 percent of the seats). They were acceptable to each other as coalition partners, but to no other party.

[146] In 1999, the new leader, Leszek Miller, consolidated his authority within the party by giving enormous power to regional "barons," who then developed independent power bases, refused to countenance the leadership's demands, and fomented a crisis within the party that culminated in the 2004 departure of several members of parliament and the founding of a new party.

[147] The infamous Kaczyński brothers became president and prime minister of Poland in 2005 and 2006, respectively. Meanwhile, the SLD was riven by internal conflict and unable to offer robust criticism, and the key other opposition party, the Civic Platform (Platforma Obywatelska, PO), flirted with both the government and the opposition.

[148] See Szczerbak, Aleks. 2006. "State Party Funding and Patronage in Post-1989 Poland." *Journal of Communist Studies and Transition Politics*, 22, 3 (September): 298–319.

[149] See the summary of state reform debates in parliament, *Biuletyn 1829/ IV*, 9 May 2003.

[150] *Wprost*, 10 August 2005.

what we want?"[151] Yet, Polish competition was not as robust as in Hungary or Slovenia: The anticommunist opposition was internally riven with conflict and personal animosities, so that new parties arose only to disappear, without offering sustained criticism of the governments. Thus, while Czech parties had few alternative coalitions because the set of potential partners was constrained by ostracism, Polish parties had difficulty finding partners who would survive elections – or even a full electoral term. Nonetheless, twice as many Polish and Hungarian voters evaluated the opposition positively than did Czech respondents.[152]

In Slovenia, the rise of a democratic opposition (Demokratska Opozicija Slovenije, DemOS) and the communist party's own pro-independence stance led to pluralist competition and free elections by April 1990, before the country gained its independence from the (still socialist) Yugoslav federation. DemOS won the elections, and the communist party transformed itself into the Liberal Democrats (Liberalna demokracija Slovenije, LDS), which subsequently won the 1992 elections and thus ensured that the opposition would be clear. The LDS governed from 1992 to 2000, a lengthy incumbency by post-communist standards. However, the clear opposition created a credible threat of replacement, ably demonstrated by several major coalition crises and collapses.[153] Moreover, the opposition was entirely plausible: no party was excluded from consideration as a governing coalition partner.

Above all, the opposition was critical. Parliamentarians asked more questions in Slovenia than anywhere else, averaging over four a year per member of parliament (MP). These interpellations took on the character of formal investigations cum votes of confidence. The opposition's "relentless onslaught-by-interpellation" throughout the 1990s examined, criticized, and constrained the actions of governing parties. It took the opposition ten parliamentarians (out of a total of ninety) to launch investigations of government actions and intentions, and they became a "standard practice."[154] LDS Foreign Minister Zoran Thaler, for example, was the focus of seven such investigations, which eventually led to his resignation.

---

[151] Interview with Miroslaw Czech, Unia Wolnosci, *Nowe Panstwo*, 16 March 2001.

[152] Thirty-two percent of Hungarian and 33 percent of Polish voters thought the opposition did a good job, whereas 17 percent of Czech voters did. Among Czech voters, 56 percent thought the opposition did a poor job, compared to 39 percent of Hungarian and 33 percent Polish voters. CBOS, IVVM, and TÁRKI poll, July 1999.

[153] Coalition crises occurred in 1991–2, 1993, 1994, 1996, and 2000.

[154] "Country Updates," *East European Constitutional Review*, Summer 1999, 8, 3.

From 1990 onwards, opposition criticism directly led to the creation of new mutual guarantees and reified the central role of the parliament:

> ... coalition members [were] eager to monitor each other's moves so as to prevent any single competitor from gaining any political advantage that might later translate into a big electoral gain. ... The state, it was thought, would provide the procedural rules for allocation and flow of resources, formulation of policies, and distribution of appointments. Since all important decisions would have to be approved by the Parliament, all parties would be granted equal opportunity to register and respond to their competitors' initiatives.[155]

Formal confrontations between journalists and party representatives further publicized this party criticism.[156]

Finally, both Lithuania and Estonia developed robust competition, if anchored in different configurations. In Lithuania, the former communist party was among the first in the region to not only transform itself into a moderate social democratic party, but to return to power, winning the 1992 parliamentary elections. Subsequently, power alternated between the communist successor – the Lithuanian Democratic Labor Party (Lietuvos demokratinė darbo partija, LDDP) – and the heir to the anticommunist opposition Sajudis, the Homeland Union/Lithuanian Conservatives (Tėvynės Sajunga/Lietuvos konservatoriai, TS/LK), until 2000 and the victory of the center-left New Union party (Naujoji sajunga, NS). In contrast to either Estonia or Latvia, ethnic minority parties were not seen as a threat, and all parties were included rather than marginalized in coalition considerations.[157] Parliamentarians questioned and criticized each successive government, with an average of three questions per MP per year, a rate higher than in Hungary. Finally, until the LDDP (the communist successor) and the Social Democratic Party merged in 2001, the lines between the former communists and their former opposition remained crystalline.

Estonia is the one country where robust competition flourished, yet the communist party failed to remake itself into a moderate and successful democratic competitor. The idiosyncratic nature of Estonian party competition – centered as it was around a commitment to free-market reforms, the rule of law, and close supervision of democratic procedures and market

---

[155] Rus, Andrej. 1996. "Quasi Privatization: From Class Struggle to a Scuffle of Small Particularisms," in Benderly, Jill, and Kraft, Evan, eds. *Independent Slovenia: Origins, Movements, Prospects.* New York: St. Martin's Press, p. 241.

[156] Krašovec, Alenka. 2001. "Party and State in Democratic Slovenia," in Lewis 2001, pp. 93–106, p. 101.

[157] Lieven, Anatol. 1994. *The Baltic Revolution.* New Haven: Yale University Press.

reforms by its Finnish ally – is partly responsible. More importantly, competition was polarized by mutual suspicions and divides arising from communist era. However, the fulcrum of competition was not a communist successor, but the heirs to the anticommunist opposition: specifically, the controversial figure of Edgar Savisaar and his populist Center Party. Savisaar led the opposition Estonian Popular Front since 1988 and was the prime minister from 1990–2, when Estonia was still part of the Soviet Union. He returned to office in 1995, only to be forced to resign as a result of a scandal over the taping of private conversations with other politicians. Subsequently, he threatened to bring down both the national governing coalitions and the Talinn city government. Such episodes showed Savisaar to "be bent on political intrigue, while the coalition was forced to take desperate measures in order to stay in power."[158] In 2002, even though the Center Party won the elections, it was unable to form the government coalition, and remained in opposition until March 2005.[159] In its dual role as the most vehement critic of successive governments and the biggest magnet for controversy and criticism, the Center Party acted as an equivalent of the communist successor parties – both the source and target of the opposition.

At the same time, opposition parties were both widely plausible and highly vociferous critics. With the restrictive citizenship laws passed in 1991–2, moreover, few Russians could vote initially.[160] Ironically, this limitation on participation meant strengthened contestation; no Russian minority party arose to be ostracized in parliament.[161] All parties were thus included in coalition considerations, and the number of alternative governments posed a considerable threat of replacement to governing parties.[162]

---

[158] *East European Constitutional Review*, Winter 2001.

[159] See ibid.; *Weekly Crier*, 15–22 March 1999. Available at http://www.balticsworldwide.com/wkcrier/0301_0322_99.htm, accessed 9 February 2006, and *RFE/RL OMRI Daily Digest Report*, 29 July 1996.

[160] After the restrictive citizenship laws were passed in the early 1990s, 90 percent of the Estonian electorate was ethnically Estonian, but only 75 percent of the Latvian electorate was ethnically Latvian: 25 percent of the voters were non-Latvian, and many supported the Russian equal rights parties.

[161] In 1995, Our Home Is Estonia, a Russian bloc, entered parliament. By late 1996, however, the six-member faction fractured, and the possibility of a cohesive party did not materialize. Pettai, Vello. 1997. "Political Stability Through Disenfranchisement," *Transition*, 3, 6 (4 April).

[162] As Allan Sikk noted, "there are very far inconceivable coalition combinations in Estonia." Sikk, Allan. 2006. "From Private Organizations to Democratic Infrastructure: Political Parties and the State in Estonia." *Journal of Communist Studies & Transition Politics*, 22, 3 (September): 341–61, p. 344.

This was all the more so given the vociferous nature of Estonian party competition: Representatives averaged over 3.5 questions annually. Governments fell under opposition criticism and accusations of malfeasance,[163] and parliamentary parties continually kept watch over each other's actions.

Elsewhere, however, the communist failure to reinvent (or to exit power) augured poorly for robust competition. In both the Czech Republic and in Slovakia, the parliaments were initially dominated by the Civic Forum (Občanské fórum, OF) and Public Against Violence (Verejnos' proti násiliu, VPN) anticommunist opposition movements. These subsequently splintered, but beginning with the 1992 elections, both parliaments were dominated by the chief successors to these movements: the Civic Democratic Party (ODS), led by Václav Klaus in the Czech Republic, and the Movement for a Democratic Slovakia (Hnutie za Demokratické Slovensko, HZDS), led by Vladimír Mečiar in Slovakia. As Czechoslovakia peacefully split into the two constituent republics in 1993, these two parties continued to dominate politics; the opposition to their rule was effectively marginalized and splintered, well into the 1990s. The same set of elites governed for over eight years, and the governing ODS and HZDS won elections three times each. Repeatedly reelected into office and left to formulate the terms of the political debate,[164] they acted much like dominant parties,[165] able to delegitimize the opposition and to blur the line between state and party.[166]

In the Czech Republic, the communist party exited power, but failed to reinvent itself and thus to clarify the competition. The ruling ODS had a slim majority in parliament, never exceeding 5 seats (for 105 out of 200).[167] However, it faced almost no parliamentary opposition: The two

---

[163] For example, the post-1995 government of Tiit Vähi fell, and Vähi himself resigned, when the Isamaa's party Mart Laar revealed that Vähi privatized flats for little of their market value, and that Vähi's daughter was one of the beneficiaries. Smith, David, Pabriks, Artis, Purs, Aldis, and Lane, Thomas. 2002. *The Baltic States.* London: Routledge, p. 100.

[164] Duverger, Maurice. 1965. *Political Parties.* New York: Wiley and Sons, p. 308. See also Arian, Alan, and Barnes, Samuel. 1974. "The Dominant Party System: A Neglected Model of Democratic Stability," *Journal of Politics*, 36, 1: 592–614.

[165] See Di Palma, Giuseppe. 1990. "Establishing Party Dominance," in Pempel, T. J., ed. *Uncommon Democracies: The One-Party Regimes.* Ithaca: Cornell University Press. Unlike the parties in Italy or Japan, however, neither the ODS nor the HZDS can be characterized as moderate or delegitimizing political extremes in their countries. See also Levite, Ariel, and Tarrow, Sidney. 1983. "The Legitimation of Excluded Parties in Dominant Party Systems," *Comparative Politics*, 15, 3 (April): 295–327.

[166] Di Palma 1990.

[167] Bruszt and Stark 1998.

biggest opposition parties, the Communists (KSČM) and the Republicans (Sdruženi Pro Republiku-Republikanská Strana Česka, SPR-RSČ), were both excluded a priori from all governing coalitions, leading one analyst to conclude that "the major parties have pushed one-fifth of the parliament out of the game. In this regard not so much openness but rather overdetermination seems to characterize coalition building."[168] With 20 percent of the seats held by parties that could not enter government, the opposition was far less plausible than in the other cases.

Nor were there other plausible and critical opposition parties for several years; it took the Social Democrats (ČSSD) seven years to create an alternative that could credibly threaten the ruling ODS. Until the late 1990s, it had less than 6 percent of the vote and 8 percent of the seats and offered little threat. It could rely neither on generous parliamentary subsidies (which were given to parties in proportion to their seat share) nor on its members. Thus, throughout the 1990s, it is difficult to discern "two deeply entrenched political rivals, each of which has the organizational strength to survive without being in the government"[169] in the ČSSD and the ODS. Instead, "the parliament basically functioned as an office with rubber stamps for ODS policies."[170] Not surprisingly, only one investigation of government behavior was launched in the Czech parliament before 1996.[171]

An anti-ODS coalition was impossible until the 1996 elections (won by the ODS). Even then, the ČSSD could only have governed if it formed a coalition with the Communists and the Republicans – an alliance disavowed by all Czech parties. A prominent opponent concluded, "there is no centrist alternative in parliament to the governing parties."[172] In the intervening period, the ODS assumed a "governing strategy focused on maximizing central control over all important aspects of economic decision making, while simultaneously erecting barriers to participation for competing interests."[173] Coalition members were in charge of all eleven parliamentary committees, breaking with the practice of proportional assignments briefly implemented in 1990–2. Since "the opposition itself has long been fragmented and incoherent,"[174] the ruling ODS-led coalition could

---

[168] Enyedi 2006, p. 231.
[169] O'Dwyer 2002.
[170] *Respekt*, 1 July 1996.
[171] *Mladá Fronta Dnes*, 30 September 1996.
[172] *Lidové Noviny*, 21 March 1995.
[173] Terra 2002.
[174] Kettle, Steve. 1995, April. "Straining at the Seams," *Transition*.

confidently centralize power and refuse either to reform the state administration or to regulate the market.[175] Further, the ODS dominated the government; it pushed through its wishes even when its coalition partners united against it.[176]

Nor did opposition parties bring down the ODS – rather, defections from its own ranks were responsible. The ODS's excesses grew increasingly unacceptable to some of its elites, who broke with Klaus and founded the Freedom Union (Unie Svobody, US). As a result of this fissuring and the continued unacceptability of the extremist opposition, the ODS could not form a governing coalition once the 1998 elections resulted in a virtual deadlock. Nor could the ČSSD form a coalition, and neither party had the votes to rule by itself. Rather than either party opposing the other, the two concluded the Opposition Agreement, a political nonaggression pact that allowed the ČSSD to govern. The two parties split up parliamentary leadership positions between themselves and agreed both to abstain from undermining or criticizing each other. This government was heavily criticized for its lack of transparency and for its discretionary use of public tender decisions, where only one applicant would be allowed.[177]

Despite the protests of other parties, and the calls for President Václav Havel to ignore the agreement, the system lasted until 2002. This duopoly received so many seats in parliament (64 percent of the seats) that it no longer bothered to enforce voting discipline in many cases.[178] Of the twenty-one laws vetoed by the president, only four had any parliamentary changes made to them. The rest became law as a result of overriding the presidential veto.[179] In return for not supporting votes of nonconfidence against the ČSSD, the ODS received ministerial posts and economic acts

---

[175] But see Kitschelt et al. 1999; O'Dwyer 2002. O'Dwyer argues that the ODS and ČSSD had enormous "strength to survive without being in the government," so that they did not need to exploit the state. However, the ČSSD had a very weak organization and barely survived as a party until 1995. The ODS organizational strength, meanwhile, was a direct function of its access to state resources. Once key leaders departed in 1997–8 to form the US and DU, the ODS organization began to crumble. And, rather than being "two deeply entrenched political rivals," ODS and ČSSD cooperated under the Opposition Agreement in 1998–2002.

[176] *Transition*, 9 June 1995; *Mlada Fronta Dnes*, 3 June 1996.

[177] Linek, Lukáš. 2002. "Czech Republic," *European Journal of Political Research*, 41: 931–40, p. 938.

[178] Linek, Lukáš, and Rakušanová, Petra. 2002. "Parties in the Parliament: Why, When, and How Do Parties Act in Unity?" Institute of Sociology, Czech Republic, Sociological Paper No. 02:9.

[179] Terra 2002.

that "strengthen the positions of the existing dominant market players"[180] (often tied to the ODS).

The two parties also pushed for a majoritarian electoral law, explicitly to ensure their long-term primacy. While the Supreme Court declared this law unconstitutional in January 2001, it came close to consolidating the centralization of power and the elimination of opponents that the ODS had previously sought. Since the communists continued to be ostracized, the only critical and plausible opponents in the parliament were the Christian Democrats (Křest'anská a demokratická unie–Česká strana lidová, KDU-ČSL) and the Freedom Union (Unie Svobody, US),[181] which together held thirty-nine seats, or 17.5 percent. The coalition's domination of the political scene was so complete that critics spoke of "the stability of the graveyard" and "virtual unrecallability" when evaluating its imperious rule.[182] When the ČSSD eventually won the 2002 elections, the years of easy spoils would gainsay its claims of "clean hands" campaigns and efforts to reform the state.

In Slovakia, little clear or critical opposition existed for most of the period under consideration. *All* governments were post-communist to some degree until 1998. Rather than remaining with and reinventing the communist party, former communist elites diffused into many political parties, including the HZDS, the Slovak National Party (Slovenska národná strana, SNS), the Association of Slovak Workers (Združenie Robotnikov Slovenska, ZRS), and the Democratic Union (Demokratická Únia, DU), and the official communist successor, the SDL'. As a result, no clearly profiled or mutually critical camps arose. The communist successor SDL' remained committed to democratic norms, but its flirtations with joining the HZDS coalition dampened its role as an opposition party. The Christian Democratic KDH fought internal battles rather than government short-comings, and the Hungarian minority parties were unacceptable to all as coalition partners until 1998. These parties thus presented little threat to the HZDS. Its own coalition partners, the ZRS (in parliament 1994–8) and the SNS (1990–2002), were completely beholden to the HZDS for their position since their extremist views made them unacceptable to other parties.

---

[180] Linek 2002, p. 932.
[181] The US later joined with the Democratic Union (Demokratická Unie, DEU) to form US-DEU.
[182] *Lidové Noviny*, 11 July 2001.

The weakness of the opposition let Mečiar's HZDS exploit the state with little constraint. Two brief departures from office, in 1991 and 1994, did little to stymie the HZDS's dominance. Both times, the HZDS's exit from power was the result of Mečiar supporters defecting rather than of opposition efforts. In both cases, the opposition was subsequently further weakened and demoralized,[183] while Mečiar consolidated his power: The coalition took over all committees and leaderships, changed the parliamentary rules, changed the electoral law to discriminate against parliamentary parties, and stripped the president of all informal powers. It took the opposition several years, and the threat of legal extermination of the opposition by the HZDS,[184] to mobilize and join forces. As a result, the HZDS still won the 1998 election, but was unable to form a coalition,[185] effectively ending its power. It was only then that civil service, regional, oversight, and regulatory reforms began.

In both the Czech Republic and Slovakia, powerful and unchallenged parties were relatively certain of a return to office. They had no incentive to constrain party behavior by instituting civil service reforms, strengthening and making autonomous formal oversight institutions, or devolving power downward by decentralizing. All such moves would remove considerable decision-making and material resources from governing party hands. These parties were still constructing the state, but they did so by delaying formal institutions of oversight and regulation and instead building in greater discretion to extract state resources.

The significance of a robust competition is further illustrated by Latvia. Ostensibly, its party system is highly competitive, with high turnover and fragmentation. However, little clear, plausible, or critical opposition arose in the early years of the transition: Instead of a clear division of elites through a communist reinvention, a "merged elite" (reform communists, former

---

[183] In 1991, Mečiar founded the HZDS just as his coalition partners withdrew their support for his prime ministership. In 1994, the vote of nonconfidence was enabled by the departure of Minister of Foreign Affairs Milan Knažko and the defection of eight other deputies from the HZDS and the SNS, a silent coalition partner at the time. The replacement government, including the SDL,' SZS, SDSS, and KDH, lost votes in the 1994 elections held six months later: The first four expected to get 25 percent of the vote but received 10 percent instead, while the KDH lost a seat.

[184] In 1997–9, HZDS introduced redistricting and new thresholds for coalitions that would have given it three-fourths of the parliamentary seats.

[185] ZRS did not enter parliament. SNS's fourteen seats gave a potential HZDS coalition only 57 out of 150 seats.

communists, noncommunists, and émigré Latvians) wielded political power since 1991.[186] All the governments after the communist collapse were anti-communist, nationalist coalitions, which excluded a priori the participation of the main opposition party, the pro-Russian PCTVL (which held as many as 19 percent of the seats).[187] And there was less parliamentary criticism than in the other cases under consideration, with the lowest rates of questions asked annually by parliamentarians.

One democratic party, Latvia's Way (Latvijas Ceļš, LC), became the linchpin of all democratic coalitions – and their main beneficiary. It became one of the most powerful political actors in Latvia: In a survey of former ministers, a plurality identified the LC as "the most important political actor" in Latvia.[188] It delivered five prime ministers and controlled both the foreign ministry and the transport ministry, both highly lucrative posts given the importance of Russian oil pipelines traversing Latvian territory. Relatively certain of a return to power, the LC had no incentives to build in constraints or to demand them as part of its coalition negotiations, so that most formal state institutions were either weak or delayed until 1999–2000.[189] In the meantime, its control of the transport ministry and its refusal to countenance administrative reform meant that oil pipeline profits would be ploughed back to the party and administrative hiring could go unchecked.

Where the communists continued in power, as they did in Bulgaria (or elsewhere, in Romania and Albania), the opposition was further handicapped.[190] While no party was excluded from governance, this high rate of plausibility meant little since the opposition was neither critical nor clear. Parliamentarians asked few questions (about 1.5) a year, and there were few other conduits for the opposition to issue or to publicize its criticism of the government. And the communist successor did not exit power, much

---

[186] Plakans, Andrejs. 1998. "Democratization and Political Participation in Postcommunist Societies: The Case of Latvia," in Dawish, Karen, and Parott, Bruce, eds. *The Consolidation of Democracy in East-Central Europe*. Cambridge: Cambridge University Press, p. 273.

[187] See Lieven 1994, pp. xx, 301.

[188] Nørgaard, Ole, Ostrovska, Ilze, and Hansen, Ole Hersted. 2000. "State of the State in Post-Communist Latvia: State Capacity and Government Effectiveness in a Newly Independent Country." Paper presented at the 2000 ECPR Joint Sessions, Copenhagen.

[189] See Vanagunas, Stan. 1997. "Civil Service Reform in the Baltics." Paper presented for the conference Civil Service Systems in Comparative Perspective, Indiana University, Bloomington, 5–8 April.

[190] Karasimeonov, Georgii. 1996. "Bulgaria's New Party System," in Pridham and Lewis 1996, pp. 254–65.

less transform itself, during the critical transition period, when the major decisions regarding institutional creation and continuity with communist practices were made.

With little opposition, the communist party and its successor, the Bulgarian Socialist Party (Balgarska Socialisticheska Partija, BSP), continued to extract resources from the state and thus build in advantages for itself. The communists were democratically elected into office in June 1990 and governed until internal divisions within the BSP and social unrest brought about elections in October 1991. The new opposition government lasted only a year, and was replaced by BSP rule lasting until 1997. Subsequently, the BSP and its fractured opposition, the Union of Democratic Forces, alternated in power until the Simeon II Movement (named for the scion of the prewar monarchy of Bulgaria, now returned from exile) won the 2001 elections. Until 2001, however, Bulgaria "was governed by either former communists or coalition governments in which they retained a strong and uncontested veto power."[191]

Conclusion

Political parties in post-communist democracies chose to exploit the state because they had both the democratic commitments that made predation and fusion unacceptable, and scarce organizational resources with which to pursue classic clientelism. Instead, in reconstructing the post-communist state, they had the motives, opportunities, and specific means that allowed them to pursue exploitation – the simultaneous building of state institutions and channels of access to state resources.

These parties' fear of backsliding into an authoritarian system explains why even if little robust competition existed, governing parties were unlikely either to squelch the opposition outright or simply prey on the state. As weak and recent organizations, they feared an overthrow from power and a subsequent expropriation of the benefits gained. The parties that have come closest are the Bulgarian BSP and the Slovak HZDS, who also have the greatest number of ties to the communist system, as an unregenerated communist organization and a shelter for many of its managerial elites, respectively. Yet even they did not become simply rapacious, since they needed to build in some institutional stability in the absence of other guarantees of power.

[191] Ganev 2005, p. 43.

The patterns of reconstruction and exploitation of the post-communist state show how political parties seek benefits from the state in new democracies. In constructing a new institutional order, they both attempt to ensure their own survival and to maintain the new democratic system. As the next chapter argues, parties facing robust competition would craft formal mutual guarantees against exploitation for each other – and for the state.

3

Developing the Formal Institutions of the State

> The time [to build institutions and] fight against corruption will come after, once the swamp settles.
>
> Prague District Attorney, 1993[1]

Thanks to the collapse of communist rule, post-communist democratic parties had the opportunity to gain enormous private benefits with few constraints. Why would they fail to take full advantage of such privileged access to state resources? This is a fundamental question of post-communist state development, since building the formal institutional framework of the state was both a key challenge of state reconstruction and an enormous opportunity for governing parties to build in benefits for themselves.

This chapter argues that faced with a high probability of having to leave office, incumbents would rather constrain themselves, and all subsequent governments, than allow their successors to have access to state resources. Where a robust competition produced a credible threat of replacement to governing parties, post-communist governments deliberately chose to tie their own hands and to limit their leeway in disposing of and redistributing state resources. They built formal state institutions of monitoring and oversight, such as national accounting offices, civil service laws, auditing chambers, or ombudsmen that subjected their actions to legal review and limited their freedom to extract resources needed for their survival. They even turned over the leadership of these agencies to their political competitors: the opposition.

As a result, all the states under consideration privatized state enterprises – but only some developed independent regulation of the auctions and sales.

---

[1] Frič, Pavol, et al. 1999. *Korupce na Český způsrb*. Prague: G Plus G, p. 144.

All promoted private investment and stock markets – but only some established securities and exchange commissions. All built democracies and markets, and all demonstrated democratic commitments. But some, nonetheless, were able to build in continued benefits for themselves, while others constrained their successors, their opponents – and themselves.

This chapter examines the significance of formal institutions in limiting discretion – the unregulated and unmonitored use of state resources – and how the patterns of institutional emergence vary across the post-communist democracies. The variation defies the expectation that the pull and push of the European Union decided the development of formal state institutions. To demonstrate how robust competition produced formal restraints on exploitation, this chapter then examines in depth the mechanisms of institutional creation in two polities that diverged in startling ways: the Czech Republic and Hungary.

Why Formal Institutions of Oversight Matter

Formal institutions of monitoring and oversight provide insight and control over party behavior – and also provide a new standard by which party behavior can be judged, criticized, and brought to account. These formal institutions were not simply "cheap talk": The enormity of the battles fought over formal institutions in post-communist legislatures suggests they certainly mattered to post-communist political parties. Of course, "not all written rules constrain effectively, and not all effective constraints are written rules,"[2] and some formal institutions are easily ignored.[3] Nonetheless, any discussion about the efficacy of an institution is predicated on its existence. Moreover, in other democracies, institutions such as ombudsmen and national accounting offices effectively ensured bureaucratic accountability.[4] Even if these institutions were not perfectly enforced or autonomous of the governing parties, competitors, the media, and nongovernmental organizations had grounds on which to call attention to transgressions.

---

[2] Carey, John. 2000. "Parchment, Equilibria, and Institutions," *Comparative Political Studies*, 33, 6/7: 735–61, p. 736.

[3] Kaufmann, Daniel. 2003. "Rethinking Governance: Empirical Lessons Challenge Orthodoxy," Working Paper. Washington: World Bank.

[4] Barzelay, Michael. 1997. "Central Audit Institutions and Performance Auditing." *Governance*, 10, 3: 235–60. Bennett, Colin. 1997. "Understanding Ripple Effects: The Cross-National Adoption of Policy Instruments for Bureaucratic Accountability," *Governance*, 10, 3: 213–33.

Moreover, the temporal dynamic to institutional creation was critical. Some authors have argued that neither traditional nor legal-rational state authority "can be created, generated, or imposed rapidly."[5] Other analysts have found that policy makers themselves sometimes assume that formal state institutions simply arise endogenously in response to the market and popular demands for such institutions.[6] As we will see in this chapter, however, robust competition launches anticipatory mechanisms that lead government parties to monitor new domains of state action deliberately as they arise, and act accordingly to develop new state institutions. And, unless formal state institutions of oversight are quickly established, their regulatory authority may not develop properly.

State reforms that were adopted earlier were more likely to be full-fledged constraints on political behavior, with their own supporters and beneficiaries, rather than façades imposed for the sake of domestic or international demands. The earlier they were introduced, the harder they were to "undo" subsequently, both because potential foes of regulation and monitoring had less time to mobilize and because establishing regulation in nascent domains is more effective than imposing regulation on existing and developed domains. Therefore, a securities and exchange commission that arose concurrently with a stock market was far better positioned to regulate the standards for establishing ownership and stock trading rules than one that arose once murky banking and unclear property rights had consolidated. The importance of the simultaneous rise of a regulatory domain and the introduction of its regulating institution also explains why some state institutions are notoriously weak across the post-communist world – for example, civil service laws imposed on an existing, politicized bureaucracy tend to be ineffective.

The new potential formal legal constraints were manifold. Given the enormous amounts of state resources that were now to be privatized and transferred out of state hands, and the nascent nature of the market itself, market oversight institutions such as independent privatization boards and securities and exchange commissions were critical to ensuring that state assets were not simply appropriated by private actors. Public finance institutions, such as national auditing offices and anticorruption laws, would limit discretionary access to state resources. Institutions such as civil ombudsmen

---

[5] Jackman, Robert. 1993. *Power Without Force.* Ann Arbor: University of Michigan Press, p. 75.
[6] Herrera 2001.

increased societal oversight over government action. Finally, civil service regulations lowered discretionary hiring in state administration, as explored in the next chapter. In short, such reforms constitute self-imposed constraints on the access of political parties to state resources, helping to establish both equitable and transparent distribution of state assets.[7]

Post-communist governing parties could avoid such self-limitations in three ways. First, they could *deliberately fail to design institutions or delay their creation*, thus building in enormous license and opportunity to seek private gains. This is the "dog that did not bark" of institutional analysis: Even if the majority of existing research has focused on the characteristics of nascent institutions, and the processes by which they were constructed, political actors have the option not to create *any* formal institutions in a given domain of state authority. Thus, several post-communist democratic governments simply did not build formal state institutions, such as securities and exchange commissions, regional governments, conflict of interest laws, and so on. They could avoid doing so largely because they faced few demands to build state institutions, and in the overwhelming task of building markets and democracy, it was all too easy to overlook state institutions unless parliamentary pressures existed.

In addition to delaying or failing to implement formal institutions, political actors (political parties in the cases under consideration) can construct *politicized* institutions. These privilege a few extant actors, by making supposedly neutral formal institutions of monitoring and oversight loyal to governing parties. One way to measure politicization is to examine who is named as the chair of the oversight institution: a representative of the government, the opposition, or a widely recognized apolitical expert. Where these institutions are chaired by government representatives, they may not be as vigilant as those headed by the opposition. Likewise, to whom is the institution answerable? Where oversight institutions are under the control of a government ministry, they cannot as freely constrain the actions of the governing parties as when they are independent agencies or report to parliament as a whole and have set terms and set budgets. Nonetheless, even politicized institutions can still serve to constrain party behavior, since they

---

[7] Low levels of rent seeking can coexist with high formal discretion, and vice versa. The former demands high levels of self-restraint by the relevant actors. The latter is formalized predation: Political actors and the rents they seek are isolated from domestic and international pressures. Neither set of conditions obtained in the cases examined here.

provide a legal standard that government parties have taken on – one that a robust competition can exploit.

Third, we also see the rise of *weakened* formal institutions. Such "Potemkin" institutions cannot constrain governing party discretion effectively, because they are deliberately enfeebled and contain few provisions for enforcement. Accordingly, the *scope* of institutional action is another measure of its strength. Specifically, can the institution initiate investigations and even impose penalties, as the Estonian chancellor of the judiciary is able to? Can it directly investigate the actions of political parties? Or, as has been the case with the Czech ombudsman, for example, can it only respond to parliamentary requests and issue recommendations?

Post-Communist Variation

Post-communist democracies provide both a rich source of variation on each of these three institutional dimensions and an opportunity to examine how and why institutional choices are made. Several countries built formal state institutions that severely constrained the discretion with which political parties could extract state assets. In Hungary, Poland, Estonia, Slovenia, and Lithuania, these institutions arose early, functioned autonomously, and could extensively investigate and limit the discretion of both politicians and bureaucrats. These countries adopted formal constraints on government discretion and state vulnerability, and did so "spontaneously," with minimal external pressure. Formal institutions did not favor the governing parties; in fact, informal norms quickly placed opposition representatives in control of these state structures.

In contrast, in the "latecomer" group of institution builders, which included the Czech Republic, Slovakia, Latvia, and Bulgaria, formal oversight institutions were absent for most of the crucial decade after communism's collapse – the period when state assets were privatized, new legal frameworks were set up, and actors learned how to compete and succeed in the new market and regulatory environments. Governing parties had considerably more discretion to obtain state assets for themselves. Reforms that would remove state assets from the grasp of the governing parties – civil service laws, central oversight institutions, or regulatory agencies – were significantly delayed. Some were passed in 2001–2, more than a decade after the first economic or political reforms, and only under pressure from the European Union.

The timing, control, and scope of formal state institutional development and reform vary considerably among the post-communist democracies.[8] Figure 3.1 shows these patterns of institutional emergence, using a newly constructed database of over sixty-five formal institutions of oversight and monitoring. These include national accounting offices, securities and exchange commissions, government procurement regulations, civil rights ombudsmen, and transparency laws. Each cell represents a different institution and the year in which it arose. Parentheses indicate either limited scope or politicized control; for example, the 1996 Slovak local government reform increased the discretionary power of the central government to withhold funds from politically opposed regions. This database also indicates how formal institutions were adopted: The critical threshold here is the year 1997. Prior to this year, there were few external demands for building formal state institutions, and such institutions arose as a result of domestic politics, not international imposition.

Here again, two clusters emerge: one of early and avid adopters of formal institutions of oversight and monitoring, and another where parties delayed formal institutions, politicized their authority, and limited their scope. Discretion-limiting reforms of the state took different trajectories: incomplete and delayed in the Czech Republic, Slovakia, Bulgaria, and Latvia, and were pursued far more avidly and earlier in Hungary, Poland, Slovenia, Estonia, and Lithuania.

Explaining Discretion in Resource Extraction

How can we explain these patterns? Several analyses have noted a prominent external force behind the reform of formal state institutions: the European Union.[9] As part of its accession talks, the EU devoted considerable energy to the question of administrative capacity in implementing and enforcing EU laws in the new member countries. It repeatedly demanded that that state capacity in the candidate countries needs to be developed and enforced, with greater transparency, monitoring, and oversight capacities. To that end,

---

[8] Since the institutions are endogenous to the parliaments, it is extremely difficult to accurately assess enforcement. The focus on control and scope is in keeping with Huber and Shipan 2002, who also focus on policy instructions, rather than outcomes. Huber, John, and Shipan, Charles. 2002. *Deliberate Discretion?* Cambridge: Cambridge University Press.

[9] For an excellent summary, see Lippert, Barbara, Umbach, Gaby, and Wessels, Wolfgang. 2001. "Europeanization of CEE Executives: EU Membership Negotiations as a Shaping Power," *Journal of European Public Policy*, 8 (6 December): 980–1012.

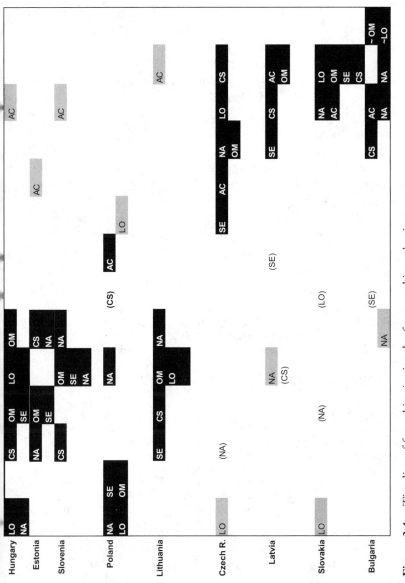

Figure 3.1. Timeline of formal institutional reforms and introductions

Notes: CS = Civil Service, OM = Ombudsman, AC = Anticorruption Laws, LO = Local Government, NA = National Audit Office, SE = Securities and Exchange Commission. Black: early timing predicted by robust opposition, late timing predicted by less robust opposition. Gray: not predicted by robust opposition or its absence. Parentheses: politicized and limited institutions.

the 1997 Luxembourg Council made administrative capacity a key condition of membership. This attention to the state was unprecedented, since "the EU has not devoted significant attention to administrative capacities as a membership criterion in earlier enlargements."[10]

These conditions applied forcefully to all the candidate countries (and all the countries considered here except Bulgaria joined the EU in May 2004). The EU backed up these commitments with assistance programs to remedy the perceived administrative shortcomings of the candidate countries.[11] Technical assistance consisted of providing strategic blueprints and information dissemination, as well as training specific bureaucrats. Twinning programs seconded "pre-accession advisers" from EU countries to the candidate country institutions, in order to provide technical assistance and "best practices" advice to a variety of bureaucrats and government officials.[12] Finally, the EU issued the Progress Reports, starting in 1997, which examined candidate country performance in areas ranging from taxation to audiovisual policy.[13] The EU formalized many of these demands with the

[10] Verheijen, Tony. 2002. "The European Union and Public Administration Development in Central and Eastern Europe," in Baker, Randall, ed. *Transitions from Authoritarianism: The Role of the Bureaucracy.* London: Praeger, p. 247. Bugaric 2005 argues that not only were the EU demands unprecedented, but they were erected chiefly to delay the post-communist round of accession. Bugaric, Bojan. 2005. "The Europeanization of National Administrations in Central and Eastern Europe: Creating Formal Structures Without Substance?" Paper prepared for the *Apres Enlargement* Workshop, EUI, Florence, 29–30 April.

[11] Grabbe, Heather. 2001. "How Does Europeanization Affect CEE Governance? Conditionality, Diffusion, and Diversity," *Journal of European Public Policy*, 8 (6 December): 1013–31. Thus, PHARE (Poland Hungary Assistance for the Restructuring of the Economy) expanded to "channel technical, economic, and infrastructural expertise and assistance to recipient states." European Parliament. 1998. "The PHARE Programme and the Enlargement of the European Union," Briefing No. 33 (December). Available at http://www.europarl.eu.int/enlargement/briefings/pdf/33a1_en.pdf. SIGMA (Support for Improvement in Governance and Management in Central and Eastern European Countries) was established in 1992 as a unit of the Organization for Economic Cooperation and Development's (OECD) Public Management Service (PUMA) to promote good governance, build institutional capacity, and support public administration reforms.

[12] SIGMA. 1998. Paper No. 26 (December), p. 16. During 1998–2001, the first four years of the program, over five hundred twinning projects took place in candidate countries. European Commission Enlargement Directorate General. 2001. "Twinning in Action." Occasional paper, March.

[13] Other areas of examination included internal markets, consumer protection, agriculture, transport, social policy and employment, science and research, education and training, telecoms and information technology, cultural policy, the environment, justice and home affairs, unions, financial control, sectoral policies, economic and social cohesion, minority rights, fisheries, maritime safety, and statistics.

Accession Partnerships in 1998. Their implementation was the key bench-mark for accession progress and the main source of conditionality for aid and other benefits.[14]

All these instruments of evaluation, conditionality, and assistance re-flected the apparent consensus in the EU: that the new members had to introduce a slew of formal reforms to ensure proper implementation and enforcement of the body of EU laws.[15] In a subsequent scholarly evalu-ation, the direct result of EU conditionality was that the EU "promoted valuable reforms: creating an independent civil service, overhauling the judiciary, improving oversight of financial markets, and blocking bailouts of uncompetitive but influential sectors."[16] Given the candidates' (often unreciprocated) desire to join the EU, these powerful policy tools could be responsible for the imposition of formal institutions of oversight and control, and for the variation we observe.

Yet while the EU demands were extensive and nonnegotiable, they do not account for the patterns of institutional adoption. The pressures exerted by the European Union came too late, and too inconsistently, to explain the observed variation. The EU did little to influence developments directly in state administration prior to 1997 and the Luxembourg meeting, when the European Union's explicit emphasis on state structures and their reform began in earnest. It was this council that issued new priorities, including twinning projects, technical assistance programs, and the progress reports on the candidates. The EU's insistence that "administrative capacity is a crucial ingredient of the readiness to assume the obligations of both *becoming* and *being* a European Union Member State"[17] thus emerged long after many post-communist countries had finished erecting the basic insti-tutional framework.[18]

---

[14] Grabbe 2001, p. 1022.

[15] Vachudová, Milada Anna. 2005. *Europe Undivided: Democracy Leverage and Integration After Communism*. Oxford: Oxford University Press; Jacoby, Wade. 2004. *The Enlargement of the EU and NATO: Ordering from the Menu in Central Europe*. New York: Cambridge University Press; Ekiert, Grzegorz, and Zielonka, Jan. 2003. "Introduction: Academic Boundaries and Path Dependencies Facing the EU's Eastward Enlargement," *Eastern European Politics and Society*, 17, 1(Winter): 7–23.

[16] Moravcsik, Andrew, and Vachudová, Milada Anna. 2003. "National Interests, State Power and EU Enlargement," *Eastern European Politics and Societies* 4, 17, 1 (Winter): 42–57.

[17] SIGMA. 1998. Paper No. 23.

[18] European Parliament. 1998. "The Phare Programme and the Enlargement of the European Union." Briefing No. 33 (4 December).

Prior to 1997, "neither the commission nor the various Councils progressed beyond a banal impression that 'administration mattered.'"[19] Initial accession criteria consisted of the Copenhagen 1993 obligations of democracy and the free market, and had little to say on the topic of public administration.[20] As late as its 1995 Madrid meeting, the EC concluded only broadly that membership candidates have to ensure their administrative and judicial capacity to enforce the *acquis communautaire*, the body of EU laws and regulations. No specific reforms were mentioned, however, until 1997.

Even after 1997, much of the EU's influence was indirect and passive, demanding reforms but not necessarily specifying their content.[21] The late hour at which the EU decided to emphasize state administration also meant haphazard directives and off-the-shelf solutions that did little to address the underlying problems. The EU provided little targeted oversight or resources, so that many of the formal reforms fulfilled EU expectations in form but not function.[22] As a result, "the candidate countries have been adopting EU legislation hastily and half-heartedly, and it may therefore take many years before this legislation is actually implemented in both letter and spirit."[23] Many EU projects were criticized for paying little attention to what would best serve the candidate countries, or improve administration. Rather, "institution building through twinning" often meant the duplication of EU structures by individual bureaucrats.[24]

In short, the EU had a direct effect only in a subset of cases. While the EU influenced the adoption of various formal state institutions after 1997 in some of the "laggard" countries, its demands do not explain the variation in state exploitation prior to 1997. Further, EU conditionality neither explains the early adoption of formal state institutions in many of

---

[19] Scherpereel, John. 2003. "Appreciating the Third Player: The European Union and the Politics of Civil Service Reform in East Central Europe." Paper prepared for presentation at the Annual Meeting of American Political Science Association, Philadelphia, 28–31 August.

[20] In 1993, the Copenhagen meeting set out broad political criteria for potential members: democracy, rule of law, human rights, and the presence of a functioning market economy. Copenhagen European Council. 1993. 21–22 June. Available at http://www.europarl.eu.int/enlargement/ec/cop-en.htm.

[21] Scherpereel 2003.

[22] Jacoby 2004.

[23] Ekiert and Zielonka 2003, p. 16.

[24] One reason was that EU shifted in 1997 from "demand-driven" programs – wherein recipient countries asked for specific forms of assistance – to "accession-driven:" programs – conceived and implemented by the EU alone. Verheijen 2002, p. 256.

the countries under consideration, nor does it account for the variation in the timing and substance of institutional emergence. Nor was it the case that accession frontrunners simply chose to preempt future EU demands: both because it was not clear what these would be, and because several slow institutional adopters are found in the ranks of accession frontrunners.[25]

If the European Union were responsible for institutional adaptation, we should see a pattern of institutional development in direct response to EU demands. Yet several countries were able to adopt institutions *before* the EU itself decided what kind of institutions it would and should specify, suggesting that other forces were at work. This is not to say that the EU was not an influential force in the region or its democratic development.[26] In some areas, such as minority rights, it exerted a direct and powerful authority, leading government parties to change laws and adopt EU standards.[27] However, it did not have a systematic or extensive impact on the building of state administration.

Nor did other international institutions exert pressure for the building of formal state institutions. The Council of Europe, EU, Organization for Security and Cooperation in Europe (OSCE), and North Atlantic Treaty Organization (NATO) made numerous agreements and benefits contingent on democratic and economic transformations, but without an accompanying focus on state institutions.[28] The EBRD, for example, made many of its loans conditional on meeting democratic conditions, such as free elections, rather than on oversight institutions or administrative capacity. IMF conditionality, meanwhile, focused on meeting economic targets, such as price and trade liberalization, restrictive monetary policies, fiscal discipline, and privatization, rather than institutional or even political demands.[29] Other international financial institutions shared this focus on economic targets but not their institutional underpinnings.[30]

---

[25] Kopstein, Jeff, and Reilly, David. 2000. "Geographic Diffusion and the Transformation of the Postcommunist World," *World Politics*, 53, 1: 1–37.

[26] Vachudová 2005.

[27] Johns, Michael. 2003. "Do as I Say and Not as I Do: The European Union, Eastern Europe, and Minority Rights," *East European Politics and Societies*, 17, 4 (November): 682–99.

[28] Smith, Karen. 2001. "The Promotion of Democracy," in Zielonka, Jan, and Pravda, Alex, eds. *Democratic Consolidation in Eastern Europe. Vol. 2: International and Transnational Factors*. Oxford: Oxford University Press.

[29] Vreeland, James Raymond. 2003. *The IMF and Economic Development*. Cambridge: Cambridge University Press.

[30] Nello, Susan Senior. 2001. "The Role of the IMF," in Zielonka and Pravda 2001.

Domestic Determinants

If international imposition does not account for the variation, two alternative accounts analyze interactions between domestic political actors. First, the balance of power among bargaining actors can determine whom the institutional framework will benefit.[31] In accounting for the broad patterns of institutional choices in post-communist countries, scholars have examined the grand bargains struck between opposing forces during the communist collapse. The outcomes of these negotiations included the major institutional decisions necessary for the dismantling of the communist monopoly and building a new democratic system, such as electoral laws and representative systems, constitutions, and the judiciary.[32]

If this account is correct, the resulting configuration of institutions would reflect the political balance of power. The greater the bargaining power of the particular actors, the more likely they were to impose their preferred institutional outcome,[33] such as changes in the electoral law that would benefit the parliamentary standing of their proponents.[34] One implication

[31] Knight, Jack. 1992. *Institutions and Social Conflict*. Cambridge: Cambridge University Press; Firmin-Sellers, Kathryn. 1995. "The Politics of Property Rights," *American Political Science Review*, 89, 4: 867–81; North and Weingast 1989, Weingast, Barry. 1997. "The Political Foundations of Democracy and the Rule of Law," *American Political Science Review*, 91 (June): 245–63. For an excellent overview, see Jones Luong, Pauline, and Weinthal, Erika. 2004. "Contra Coercion: Russian Tax Reform, Exogenous Shocks and Negotiated Institutional Change," *American Political Science Review*, 98: 139–52.

[32] Ishiyama, John. 1997. "Transitional Electoral Systems in Post-Communist Eastern Europe," *Political Science Quarterly*, 112, 1: 95–115; Remington, Thomas, and Smith, Steven. 1996. "Institutional Design, Uncertainty, and Path Dependency During Transition," *American Journal of Political Science*, 40, 4: 1253–79; Stepan and Skach 1993; Lijphart, Arend, ed. 1992. *Parliamentary Versus Presidential Government*. Oxford: Oxford University Press; Linz, Juan. 1994. "Introduction: Some Thoughts on Presidentialism in Postcommunist Europe," in Taras, Ray, ed. *Postcommunist Presidents*. Cambridge: Oxford University Press: 1–14; O'Neil, Patrick. 1993. "Presidential Power in Post-Communist Europe: The Hungarian Case in Comparative Perspective," *Journal of Communist Studies*, 9, 3: 177–201; Hendley, Katherine. 1996. *Trying to Make Law Matter*. Ann Arbor: University of Michigan Press; Frye 1997; Sadurski, Wojciech, ed. 2002. *Constitutional Justice, East and West: Democratic Legitimacy and Constitutional Courts in Post-Communist Europe*. The Hague: Kluwer Law International; Smithey, Shannon Ishiyama, and Ishiyama, John. 2000. "Judicious Choices: Designing Courts in Post-Communist Politics," *Communist and Post-Communist Studies*, 33: 163–82.

[33] Colomer, Josep. 1995. "Strategies and Outcomes in Eastern Europe," *Journal of Democracy* 6, 2: 74–85; Frye 1997. For a critique of this approach, see Bernhard, Michael. 2000. "Institutional Choice After Communism," *Eastern European Politics and Societies*, 3: 316–47.

[34] See also Benoit, Kenneth. 2004. "Models of Electoral System Change," *Electoral Studies*, 23: 363–89. Jones Luong 2002 provides a bargaining model that incorporates both the

of these analyses is that when multiple and evenly matched actors bargain, discretion for rent seeking will be reduced[35]; no actor can single-handedly impose institutions that allow her to run away with the spoils of the state. Multiple and equally powerful political actors promote the provision of public goods, cutting down on transaction costs and constraining the pursuit of private interests via public office.[36] One observable implication is that parliamentary fragmentation promotes power-sharing institutions and limits on discretion.

A second perspective focuses on the incentives and means of insulating policies and state agencies from politics. Electoral and legislative design itself creates several incentives to formalize constraints as a way of protecting policies from reversal by opponents. Terry Moe and Michael Caldwell, for example, contrast the American congressional system of divided government and checks and balances with the Westminster system of majority party rule and the fusion of executive and legislative.[37] In the former, divided government leads to compromise solutions and to extensive (and inefficient) formalization. In the Westminster system, undivided authority produces no such compromises, and no incentives to formalize any institutions (since a subsequent government, with its total control of policy making, could simply undo any formalizations).[38] Instead, informal norms and reputations constrain the domain of government action. In this account, the predictions for parliamentary proportional representation systems are weaker, but parties in these systems will formalize constraints on discretion when power is divided among coalition members, party responsibility for policy is weak, turnover is limited, and changes in the status quo are made difficult.[39] Changes in the status quo were made relatively easy after

perceived gains from electoral institutions and the changes in perceived power that occur during the bargaining. Emphasizing the bargaining process, Smithey and Ishiyama found that the greater the number of competing actors, the less independent the judiciary that arose. Smithey and Ishiyama 2000, p. 177.

[35] Geddes 1994; Rose-Ackerman 1999; Shleifer and Vishny 1993.

[36] Kang, David. 2002. *Crony Capitalism: Corruption and Development in South Korea and the Philippines.* Cambridge: Cambridge University Press; Geddes 1994.

[37] Moe, Terry M., and Caldwell, Michael. 1994. "The Institutional Foundations of Democratic Government: A Comparison of Presidential and Parliamentary Systems," *Journal of Institutional and Theoretical Economics,* 150/1: 171–95.

[38] Moe and Caldwell 1994 argue that political uncertainty and the fear of the state are enormous in both systems.

[39] Without a division of powers, Kaare Strøm argues, the main tool of institutional checks in parliamentary systems will be the ex ante screening of prospective parliamentarians and ministers by political parties. Other potential tools of containing agency losses include

the communist collapse. Therefore, we would expect the introduction of formal constraints where governments are fragmented (which both divides power and lessens policy responsibility of any individual party) and turnover is low.

In a related perspective, numerous analyses have focused on the relations of accountability and delegation between principals and the agents they select to act on the principals' behalf.[40] The focus has been on the difficulty of ensuring that agents fulfill rather than shirk their obligations to principals: How, for example, do politicians make sure bureaucrats implement policies? Discretion here is the leeway of the bureaucratic agents in fulfilling the political parties' directives. To simplify these complex and systematic analyses, one general implication is that the more certain a government is that the future favors its program, the more discretion it will grant to state agents.[41] More specifically, political parties build in the greatest discretion for bureaucratic actors, and thus delay or avoid formal institution building, under conditions that include the absence of conflict over policy, low levels of fragmentation, the existence of nonstatutory regulators such as civil law courts, and an undivided government.[42] All of these strengthen the government's conviction that its policies will be implemented – and that it will be around to propose further policies to implement. Of these, civil law systems and parliamentary (and thus undivided) governments are found in all the cases under examination. We thus expect formal institutions of

contract design, monitoring and reporting requirements, and third-party vetoes. Strøm, Kaare. 2000. "Delegation and Accountability in Parliamentary Democracies," *European Journal of Political Research*, 37: 261–89.

[40] See, for example, Huber and Shipan 2002; Kiewet, D. Roderick, and McCubbins, Matthew D. 1991. *The Logic of Delegation: Congressional Parties and the Appropriations Process*. Chicago: University of Chicago Press; Lupia, Arthur, and McCubbins, Matthew. 2000. "The Institutional Foundations of Political Competence," in Lupia, Arthur, McCubbins, Matthew D., and Popkin, Samuel L., eds. *Elements of Reason: Cognition, Choice, and the Bounds of Rationality*. New York: Cambridge University Press, pp. 47–66; Strøm 2000; McCubbins, Matthew, Noll, Roger, and Weingast, Barry. 1987. "Administrative Procedures as Instruments of Political Control," *Economics and Organization*, 72 (March): 243–72. For an extensive review of this literature, see Bendor, Jonathan, Glazer, A., and Hammond, T. 2001. "Theories of Delegation," *Annual Review of Political Science*, 4: 235–69. See Strøm 2000 for a delineation of the chain of accountability and delegation that spans from voters to representatives to cabinet ministers to bureaucrats.

[41] Moe, Terry M. 1990. "Political Institutions: The Neglected Side of the Story," *Journal of Law, Economics and Organization*, 7: 213–53; Moe and Caldwell 1994.

[42] Epstein, David, and O'Halloryn, Sharyn. 1994. "Administrative Procedures, Information, and Agency Discretion," *American Journal of Political Science*, 38/3: 697–722; Huber and Shipan 2002.

Table 3.1. *Party Competition, 1990–2003*

	# of Govts[a]	Mean Government Duration (Days)[b]	Fragmentation	Polarization[c]
Hungary	4	1096	.68	11.4
Estonia	8	477	.79	12.0
Slovenia	6	604	.84	19.3
Poland	9	449	.77	31.8
Lithuania	7	447	.72	11.9
Czech R.	4	869	.71	12.0
Slovakia	6	593	.78	4.9
Bulgaria	6	590	.71	30.9
Latvia	10	340	.76	14.6
Diff of means	P = .82	P = .52	P = .24	P = .47
test*	t = .24	t = .73	t = 1.48	t = .82

* *Note:* Two-tailed T-test.

Source:

[a] Müller-Rommel, Ferdinand, Fettelschoss, Katja, and Harst, Philipp. 2004. "Party Government in Central East European Democracies: A Data Collection (1990–2003)," *European Journal of Political Research*, 43: 869–93.

[b] Müller-Rommel et al. 2004.

[c] Frye 2002.

oversight and monitoring to arise in party systems that are more driven by competition and conflict – that is, once again, those that are more fragmented and polarized.[43]

In sum, the explanations focusing on the conditions for bargaining and insulation predict that turnover, fragmentation, and polarization should covary with the timing and scope of formal institutions that constrain discretion. Yet as Table 3.1 shows, there are no clear correlations between these measures and the two clusters of early and late adopters of formal institutions. Countries with considerable turnover can be found in both clusters: Both Poland and Estonia have greater than average turnover, but so does Latvia. The countries with the highest and lowest observed parliamentary fragmentation, Slovenia and Hungary, are both the earliest adopters of formal institutions of monitoring and oversight.[44] Finally, countries whose

---

[43] Divided government is not an issue in parliamentary democracies, and all the countries under consideration have civil law systems. Only policy conflict and party fragmentation vary.

[44] Parliamentary fragmentation is an indicator of the concentration of seats in parliament, consisting of $1-1/\Sigma\ S_i^2$, where S_i is the seat share of the ith party.

institutional outcomes place them both in the "late adopter" category can take very high (Bulgaria) or very low (Slovakia) values on polarization.[45]

Nor are the predicted mechanisms observed. The bargaining model predicts that we should see bargaining among the key political actors, with the balance of power deciding the outcome. Rather than bilateral bargaining, however, we observe unilateral moderation, anticipation, and cooptation in the face of a credible threat of replacement. Once parliaments and the concomitant representative institutions were established, governments conceded to and tried to coopt the opposition, but rarely bargained outright.

Post-communist institution builders, moreover, were concerned not with protecting the state or policies, but with insulating themselves against their competitors and preventing them from gaining access to state resources. The desire to prevent bureaucratic shirking was not the main motivation for building formal institutions of monitoring and oversight (as we will see in the next chapter, such considerations did prompt some attempts to purge communist officials from the post-communist administrations).[46] Instead, political parties concentrated chiefly on who would gain access to state resources, which were about to become available to multiple actors with the privatization or redistribution of state holdings.

Both models of bargaining and insulation predict the *kind* of institutions that arise, but not when or whether they do. Their mechanisms presuppose either the absence of parliamentary arenas for party interactions (the "foundational bargaining" approach) or well-established parliamentary competitors who need to protect their policy investments from their opponents (the "policy insulation" approach). Neither focuses on institution building as a survival strategy for new governments, attempting to make themselves less vulnerable to political competition. Yet that was the main mechanism behind the variation we observe.

Robust Competition and Formal Institutions

As noted earlier, no matter what their ideological orientation, political heritage, or organizational goals, fragile new democratic political parties

---

[45] The polarization measure captures the extent to which legislators and the executive come from different parties.

[46] More generally, political parties are both agents (of voters) and principals (of the bureaucracy).

needed considerable resources to survive. Since political party elites decided how state assets would be distributed and which state institutions would be constructed, they could retain and further build discretionary access to state resources, such as jobs, contracts, or privatization tenders. These resources would provide a stable material base for the impoverished political parties. Oversight institutions would thwart such opportunities. Nor were there functional reasons to build new institutions, since the communist state structures existed as a default, however flawed.[47] Thus, as these governing parties ostensibly built the institutions of market and democracy, they could also build in conduits to state assets and profit from them.

Robust competition changed this calculus by generating a credible threat of replacement to the governing parties. Since parties ran a high risk of losing the next elections, they would want to constrain the opposition by creating new institutions of monitoring and oversight as they opened up new domains of state action, such as privatization or property rights enforcement. They could thus ensure that no successor would benefit from the state to the detriment of the others, even if this meant constraining themselves. One implication is that parties that felt less vulnerable – either because of misperception or because they had alternative means of survival (such as strong grassroots organizations) – would feel these pressures less keenly and thus be more "immune" to robust competition.

How did the three mechanisms produced by robust competition – anticipation, moderation, and cooptation – constrain discretion in formal institutions? First, robust competition led to the preemptive adoption of formal institutions of monitoring and oversight by parties that expected to be out of office in the next electoral term – a way of constraining one's political opponents from exploiting their access to state resources for their own gain. This anticipatory mechanism generated formal institutions of oversight as their bailiwicks arose; securities commissions were established simultaneously with stock exchanges, national auditing offices arose before privatization got underway, civil ombudsmen were strengthened as new civic rights were established. The opposition, in turn, when it assumed office, tended to adopt and strengthen these institutions further, in an attempt to constrain *its* successors.[48]

---

[47] Bruszt and Stark 1998; Grzymała-Busse and Luong 2002.

[48] This correlation also explains why incumbency as an indicator of competition (the inverse of turnover) is the only one to take on a relatively high P value in Table 3.2, making it more difficult to reject the null hypothesis.

Second, opposition parties questioned and criticized government actions in parliament, and government parties responded by limiting their extraction and justifying their actions for fear of electoral retribution. Where the opposition constantly monitors and publicizes government actions, government parties are more likely to limit their discretion to extract state resources if they fear the adverse publicity would lead them to lose votes. Robust competition thus both changes the calculation of governing parties regarding the desirability of formal constraints on discretion and itself offers informal constraints on discretion. This second set of constraints is less powerful in creating institutions, but it can strengthen (or weaken) existing institutions.

Third, the threat of replacement also leads governing parties to try to coopt the opposition or to share power and responsibility with opposition parties. By doing so, governing parties attempt both to dilute the strength of the opposition attacks, by making the opposition at least partly responsible for the policy outcomes, *and* to prove their probity by including their most vociferous critics in oversight and regulatory positions. This mechanism figured less prominently in establishing formal institutions than in determining the *informal* norms of staffing, regulation, and power concentration.

If robust competition is responsible for generating institutions of monitoring and oversight, we should observe parties facing robust competition rapidly adopting formal institutions of monitoring and oversight. Regulatory institutions should arise with the new domains of state action they are to monitor. Successive governments, no matter what their ideological stripe, should strengthen formal institutions, so long as the competition remains robust. Further, anticipation, moderation, and cooptation are independent of the numerical supremacy of the government. Rather, they are a function of the robustness of the competition and the opposition parties' ability and willingness to investigate and publicize government actions. Whether or not parties respond to these stimuli depends on their perceptions of their electoral vulnerability – and as we will see, governing parties can miscalculate their reelection chances. They may also perceive the threat correctly but try to insulate themselves by building networks of loyal electoral supporters.[49]

---

[49] Formal investigations and policy demands are more likely a function of political strength – that is, whether the governing coalition needs the opposition's vote, whether the rules for parliamentary investigations allow the opposition to launch formal inquiries, and so on. A

Where competition is less robust, we should see delayed regulation, few anticipatory moves, and either the failure to build formal institutions of monitoring and oversight or the building of highly discretionary ones. Little power sharing or cooptation would be observed. These forces should operate independently of fragmentation, polarization, or the demands of the EU. In short, a clear, plausible, and critical parliamentary opposition produces incentives for the government to anticipate the opposition's coming to power, to moderate parliamentary behavior, and to attempt to include the opposition in these new institutions.

How did robust competition produce early and avid institutional adoption? To answer this question, the remainder of this chapter will first examine the broad variation across the cases. It will then focus on an in-depth comparison of two countries that ought to have produced similar institutional configurations if the other existing explanations determined institutional design outcomes: Hungary and the Czech Republic. The key institutions of monitoring and oversight, the dates of their founding, and their powers are all summarized in Table 3.2.

Patterns of Institution Building

A strong correlation between a robust competition and the early adoption of formal state institutions holds across the cases. In countries with more robust competition – Hungary, Slovenia, Estonia, Poland, and Lithuania, 85 percent of the formal institutions of oversight and monitoring (twenty-nine out of thirty-four from Figure 3.1) adopted in these countries were established by 1997.

Thus, within three years of Slovenian independence, the Ombudsman for Human Rights, Civil Service Law, National Accounting Office, and Securities and Exchange Commission were all in place. Despite low turnover (the same party was in power since 1991), competition was robust; its intensity "made coalition members eager to monitor each other's moves so as to prevent any single competitor from gaining any political advantage that might later translate into a big electoral gain. The parties searched for monitoring mechanisms that would enable all the parties to learn

government with enough votes to command the supermajorities required for constitutional amendments or major institutional changes could be immune to even the most vociferous opposition critique.

Table 3.2. *Key Institutions of Monitoring and Oversight*

	Civil Service	Ombudsman	National Accounting Office	Securities and Exchange Commission
Hungary	1992 Apolitical Extensive scope	1993 Parliamentary Commissioner for Human Rights (Országgyűlési Biztosok Hivatala) (two other ombudsmen for minority rights and data protection) Apolitical Extensive scope	1990 State Audit Office (Állami Számvevőszék) Apolitical Powers greatly strengthened in 1990	1993 Financial Supervisory Authority (Pénzügyi Szervezetek Állami Felügyelete) Apolitical Extensive scope
Estonia	1995 Apolitical Extensive	1993 Chancellor of Judiciary (Vabariigi Õiguskantsler) Extensive scope	1995 State Audit Office (Riigikontroll) Apolitical Extensive scope	1993/1997 Securities Inspectorate (Finantsinspekt-sioon) Controlled by Ministry of Finance until 1997
Slovenia	1992 Apolitical Extensive scope	1994 Defender of Human Rights (Varuh Človekovih Pravic) Apolitical Extensive scope	1994 The Court of Audit (Računsko Sodišče) Apolitical Extensive scope	1992 Securities and Market Agency (Agencija za Trg Vrednostnih Papirjev) Apolitical Strict reporting requirements
Lithuania	1995/1999 Vague specifications corrected in 1999	1994 Seimas Ombudsman (Seimo Kontrolierių Staig) Apolitical Controls political parties	1995 State Control Board (Valstybės Kontrolė) Apolitical: recalled by parliament Extensive scope: can launch investigations	1996 Securities Commission (Vertybinių popierių komisija) Apolitical: accountable to parliament Extensive scope

Developing the Formal Institutions of the State

	Civil Service	Ombudsman	National Accounting Office	Securities and Exchange Commission
Poland	1996/1999 1996 law politicized: rewarded SLD allies Law corrected in 1999	1990 Civic Rights Ombudsman (Rzecznik Praw Obywatelskich) Apolitical Strengthened greatly in 1990	1994 Supreme Control Chamber (Najwyższa Izba Kontroli) Opposition Extensive scope: controls parties	1991 Securities and Markets Commission (Komisja Papierów Wartościowych i Giełd) Apolitical Strict reporting requirements: monthly
Czech R.	2002 Introduced in response to EU demands	2000 Public Defender of Rights (Veřejný Ochránce Práv) Apolitical Limited powers	1992/2000 Supreme Audit Office (Nejvyšší Kontrolní Úřad) Gov't controlled until 2000: no independent investigative powers	1998 Securities Commission (Komise pro Cenné Papíry) Ministry of Finance until 1998 Limited scope: no binding regulations for capital markets
Slovakia	2002	2002 Public Defender of Rights (Verejný ochranca práv) Apolitical	1993 Supreme Audit Office (Najvyšší Kontrolný Úrad) Gov't control No independent investigative powers	2002 Financial Market Authority (Úrad pre Finančný Trh) No prior control of stock market until 1998
Latvia	1994 Political: excluded Russian minority 1999 new law	2002 National Human Rights Offfice (Valsts Cilvēktiesību Birojs)	1994 State Audit Office (Valsts kontrole)	2000 Securities Markets Commission (Finanšu un Kapitāla Tirgus Komisija)
Bulgaria	2000 Direct response to EU demands	Not adopted	1995/2001/2002 National Audit Office (Smetna Palata) Under Ministry of Finances control Limited scope: could not originate audits	1995 Securities and Stock Exchanges Commission (Komisija po tsennite kniha) Limited scope: no binding market regulations

through them and react on time. . . . "[50] The robust competition led to extensive regulation and constraint: The 1991 Slovenian privatization law was even said to "overregulate" privatization, since parties "defend themselves against each others' potential abuse by taking all possible contingencies into account."[51]

The capacity and incentives of the opposition to change government behavior are demonstrated by Slovenian market regulations and the sequence of privatization oversight decisions. In 1991, a proposed privatization law would have given firms, managers, and employees full discretion in ownership restructuring. The Christian Democrats argued that this would only perpetuate the economic power of the former Communists and their elite networks. (Not coincidentally, the law would also interfere with the party's own plans to gain influence over the economy.) But by the time the draft law reached the parliament, the argument that the law would end communist influence no longer worked: "[B]ickering for their share of the pie, the other parties were uneasy with the idea of letting the Christian Democrats have it all."[52] As a result, the bill underwent massive rewriting, to ensure that no party would benefit unduly. Similar worries about potential discretion for the government also led to the consolidation of public finances. Prior to 1991, less than a fifth of total public budget expenditure was in the budget, but the 1991 fiscal reform consolidated all earmarked funds except for the pension fund.[53]

Other countries with robust competition moved quickly to establish formal institutions of monitoring and oversight. Within two years of the collapse of the communist regime, Poland had strengthened or established a National Auditing Office, the Ombudsman, and conflict-of-interest laws. A Securities and Exchange Commission arose in 1991, with strict reporting requirements: Companies had to report their earnings every month rather than every quarter. Similarly, both Estonia and Lithuania also established ombudsmen, civil service laws, independent national accounting chambers, and securities and exchange commissions within four years of the collapse of the Soviet Union, by 1995. These institutions were given extensive scope,

---

[50] Rus, Andrej. 1996. "Quasi Privatization: From Class Struggle to a Scuffle of Small Particularisms," in Benderly, Jill, and Kraft, Evan, eds. *Independent Slovenia: Origins, Movements, Prospects*. New York: St. Martin's Press, pp. 225–50.

[51] Ibid., p. 234.

[52] Ibid., pp. 233–4.

[53] Žižmond, Egon. 1993. "Slovenia – One Year of Independence," *Europe-Asia Studies*, 45, 5: 887–905, pp. 893–4.

and in most cases were independent of political control (the exception here is the Estonian Securities Inspectorate, which fell under the Ministry of Finance until 1997).

In each of these cases, the establishment of formal institutions of monitoring and oversight was both a form of insurance against the communist resurgence (even reinvented communist successors were initially feared) and against eventual exit from office. More generally, these institutions help to ensure that incumbents do not endanger the survival of other parties. And even powerful governments could be constrained; for example, the opposition Freedom Union (UW) party used subterfuge in the committees, exploited internal conflict within the coalition, and mobilized public opinion to ensure that educational reform, local government financing, and banking reform would continue even when the 1993–97 governing coalition held an absolute majority.[54]

Among these countries, Hungary and Poland had an unusual advantage: existing communist institutions of monitoring and oversight that could now be given a new life. During the last years of communism, the Polish ruling party constructed several institutions of oversight and control that had "the explicit aim of monitoring and enforcing the legality of the state and its representatives."[55] The National Control Chamber (NIK) functioned by 1977 (and was placed under parliamentary supervision in 1980), an Ombudsman by 1987, and a Constitutional Tribunal in 1986. A Superior Administrative Court was established in 1980 gave citizens a venue to complain about administrative decisions they believed violated the law, while a Tribunal of the State, established in 1982, adjudicated cases involving the highest state dignitaries.

This leads to the possibility that the causality could be reversed – that is, that robust competition flourished where formal institutions of oversight and monitoring had already limited discretion. However, communist-era formal institutions were only the skeletons of their democratic successors: They only gained real muscle once communism fell. First, they were given new, enormous scope; for example, the Ombudsman's office, which initially met with considerable skepticism, could now directly refer a case to the Constitutional Court, request extraordinary revision by the Supreme

[54] *Gazeta Wyborcza*, 29 July 1994, and 16 April 1996.
[55] Łoś, Maria, and Zybertowicz, Andrzej. 1999. "Is Revolution a Solution?" in Krygier, Martin, and Czarnota, Adam, eds. *The Rule of Law After Communism*. Aldershot: Ashgate, p. 280.

103

Court, make legislative recommendations to the government, and make those recommendations available to the public. In only 3 percent of the cases were the Ombudsman's requests not respected by the administration.[56] Above all, the Ombudsman could now investigate the actions of all political actors rather than merely investigating the conditions of prisons, health care, or the environment, as it did under communism.[57] Similarly, the NIK and the strengthened Constitutional Court were now no longer appointed by and for only the communist party. Instead, an informal rule rapidly developed that the NIK would be led by a member of the opposition, a practice followed from its founding. The reasoning was that "the opposition has the greatest incentive to investigate the government, so if it gives the governing parties a clean bill of health, we could all rest more easily."[58] This is not to say that the Polish state had the reputation for integrity that the Estonian, Hungarian, or Slovenian states did; yet even critics acknowledged that discretion was highly limited "due to internal disagreements within the ruling coalition, criticism by the opposition parties and independent experts and the Constitutional Tribunal's rulings."[59]

Where the competition was weaker, in the Czech Republic, Slovakia, Latvia and Bulgaria, only 31 percent (ten out of thirty-two) of formal institutions were adopted prior to the EU beginning the push for administrative reform. Of these, as we will see, several were either explicitly politicized or deliberately enfeebled. Most reforms were not passed until 2001–2, and only under considerable EU pressure. Even then, governments often vehemently opposed formal state institutions as "expensive and unnecessary."[60] These parties, relatively certain of a return to office, could disregard the creation of formal institutions, or create weakened versions to reinforce their hold on power.[61]

---

[56] Kurczewski, Jacek. 1999. "The Rule of Law in Poland," in Přibán, Jiří, and Young, James, eds. *The Rule of Law in Central Europe*. Aldershot: Ashgate, pp. 188–9.

[57] See *Sprawozdanie Rzecznika Praw Obywatelskich za okres od 1 stycznia 1988 r. do 30 listopada 1988*. 1989. Warsaw: Government Printing Office. This last report issued by the office of the Ombudsman prior to the collapse of communism. By 1993, the Ombudsman was investigating political discrimination, party behavior, electoral law, political associations, local government, and so on.

[58] Interview with Marek Zieliński, 7 May 2002, UW headquarters, Poznan.

[59] Łoś, Maria, and Zybertowicz, Andrzej. 2000. *Privatizing the Police State*. New York: St. Martin's Press, p. 143.

[60] Both the ODS and the HZDS announced they would scrap the passed laws if elected into office in the 2002 elections in the Czech Republic and Hungary, respectively.

[61] Issacharoff, Samuel, and Pildes, Richard. 1998. "Politics as Markets: Partisan Lockups of the Democratic Process," *Stanford Law Review* (February): 642–717, p. 643.

Without a robust competition, formal state institutions were absent, politicized, or effectively stripped of independent regulatory powers. In Slovakia, the Supreme Control Office (NKÚ) and the Special Control Body (OKO), which monitored the security services, were the two institutions of monitoring and oversight established in 1993 to continue the role of federal Czechoslovak institutions. Just as quickly, however, they were brought under the complete control of the ruling HZDS party. During an all-night session of parliament that decimated non-Mečiarites from state administration in 1994, the HZDS recalled the heads of the NKÚ, OKO, and the general attorney and his office. All were replaced with HZDS loyalists. The HZDS completely excluded the representatives of opposition parties from these bodies, and continued to do so for the duration of its stay in office.[62] Simultaneously, it removed the opposition from parliamentary committees and leadership, packing the opposition into the toothless Environmental Committee.

Existing institutions were weakened: The Supreme Control Office had the power only to supervise the use of state budget funds, but could not audit any organizations in which the National Property Fund held shares or any funds from foreign sources.[63] The National Property Fund (FNM), founded in 1991 in the old Czechoslovak federation, became a source of enormous private benefits to the HZDS government. The FNM was a quasiprivate joint stock company created to administer privatization. Once the HZDS replaced the Fund's executives with its loyal appointees, it turned over all privatization decisions to the FNM. As a result, parliament had no oversight over the lucrative privatization process,[64] and HZDS leaders were direct members of supervisory boards of profitable enterprises.[65]

These moves gave the Mečiar administration enormous leeway in disposing of state assets. The HZDS, which nurtured the links between privatizing investors and top politicians, made privatization bids contingent

[62] Szomolányi, Soňa. 1997. "Identifying Slovakia's Emerging Regime," in Szomolányi, Soňa, and Gould, John, eds. *Slovakia: Problems of Democratic Consolidation*. Bratislava: Friedrich Ebert Foundation, 1997, p. 10.

[63] Zemanovičová, Daniela, and Sičáková, Emília. 2001. "Transparency and Corruption," in Mesežnikov, Grigorij, Kollár, Miroslav, and Nicholson, Tom, eds. *Slovakia 2001*. Bratislava: Institute for Public Affairs, pp. 537–52, p. 545.

[64] Szomolányi 1997, p. 17.

[65] Mesežnikov, Grigorij. 1997. "The Open-Ended Formation of Slovakia's Political Party System," in Szomolányi, Soňa, and Gould, John, eds. *Slovakia: Problems of Democratic Consolidation*. Bratislava: Friedrich Ebert Foundation, p. 45.

on party contributions, and the contracts themselves went to party allies.[66] The FNM turned privatization into a means of rewarding and enriching government allies. The circle was completed with "political control over [banking] institutions and the clientelist nature of the business environment, [which] meant that state-controlled banks continued to provide politically motivated loans and did not demand repayment from inefficient companies."[67] Finally, the regional reform of 1996 only insulated the HZDS from potential electoral discontent, by making the regions financially and politically dependent on the HZDS (and by gerrymandering the new regions to reflect HZDS political strength). The opposition remained largely powerless – both because one significant set of players was ostracized (the Hungarian minority parties) and because no regenerated communist successor acted as the linchpin of the opposition (instead, the flirtation of the communist successor SDL' with the HZDS only blunted its critique and blurred the alternatives for voters).

In Latvia, the coalition linchpin, Latvia's Way (Latvijas Ceļš, LC), was able to maintain control of particular sectors of the state – the lucrative Ministry of Transportation, for example. LC could torpedo inconvenient reforms, especially those that would impose oversight on "its" sectors. Without a plausible threat of replacement and held hostage by a key coalition party, governing parties did not build formal institutions of monitoring and oversight; all but one were implemented after 1997. Since Latvian "cabinets often tend[ed] to be formed by the same parties, they also tend[ed] to feel limited responsibility for promises and decisions made by previous governments."[68] Until the EU began to exert pressure for formal institutional reform, "political parties were not really interested in the success" of formal state institutions of oversight and monitoring.[69] A Constitutional Court law was not passed until 1995; prior to then, there was no judicial review of the constitutionality of parliamentary laws. A civil service law was established in 1994, but it was chiefly designed to verify the Latvian citizenship and language abilities of the civil servants and their possible connections to the

---

[66] Freedom House 2000.

[67] Slovak Government Information Service. 1999. *Analysis of the Inherited State of the Economy and Society*.

[68] Tisenkopfs, Tālis, and Kalniņš, Valts. 2002. "Public Accountability Procedures in Politics in Latvia." Report, Baltic Studies Center, Riga, Latvia, February.

[69] Kalniņš, Valts, and Čigāne, Lolita. 2003. "On the Road Toward a More Honest Society." Policy report, January. Available at http://www.politika.lv.

KGB. It was overhauled under EU pressure in 2000, since it also excluded several important public sectors (such as the Ministry of Interior) and failed to provide for merit qualifications.

In Bulgaria, the communist party did not exit from office during the regime collapse, and the opposition was often more focused on internal squabbles than on government actions. As a result, in the eyes of several commentators, the 1990–97 period was lost to reform: The communist successor BSP continued to exploit the state and enrich itself at its expense. Facing a weak opposition, the BSP governments used its absolute majority to delay several reforms of the state, including civil service, national accounting, and anticorruption offices. It sought to maximize discretion, as "de-facto control over publicly owned assets shifted from state to party officials."[70] Judicial reform was deliberately delayed: The three-tier judicial system called for by the 1991 constitution went unfulfilled, despite repeated opposition efforts to put the issue on the parliamentary agenda.[71] Instead, when the Constitutional Court ruled the BSP's moves unconstitutional, the BSP simply cut its judicial funding. The National Audit Office (NAO) was introduced in 1995. However, the NAO was weak: As one critic charged, "there is little or no emphasis on measuring results achieved against objectives."[72] It was only given real teeth, and the capacity to easily start investigations, in 2001, and under EU pressure.

In all three of these countries, the impetus for introducing institutions of monitoring and regulation was the European Union. Serious state reform in Slovakia began only in 1999, when a new, non-HZDS government coalition began to reform state institutions. (The HZDS won the plurality of the votes in 1998 elections but was unable to form a coalition after it became clear that the EU would not let in an HZDS-led Slovakia.) Civil service, regional, oversight, and depoliticization reforms then began in earnest. In July 2001, the National Control Chamber could finally audit and control all economic subjects with state funds.[73] It was also then that the Ombudsmen's office was established, with the civil service law following in 2002.

---

[70] Ganev 2005.

[71] *East European Constitutional Review*, Fall 1996.

[72] International Monetary Fund. 1999, August/2000, March. Report on Observance of Standards and Codes.

[73] "Správa o boji proti korupcii na Slovensku." 2001. Report of the Slovak government, October. Available at http://www.government.gov.sk.

In Latvia, similarly, "the focus on administrative reforms came back only as recently as 1999 largely due to criticism from the European Union."[74] Several laws were revamped in 2000. Market oversight institutions, civil service laws, anticorruption offices, and an ombudsman were all established only in 2000–2. Thanks to EU pressures, further reforms followed: The administrative center reform was adopted in 2001, to be implemented in 2003, establishing new citizen rights and independent judicial review. A securities and exchange commission (FKTK) was founded in 2000. Conflict-of-interest laws were passed in 2002, when the anticorruption agency (KNAB) was founded.

Finally, once Bulgaria was officially invited to begin negotiations for EU membership in 1999, the prime minister himself, Ivan Kostov, took over the Ministry of State Administration and began to implement an ambitious plan of formal institutional reform. The government promised to reform laws further, including the reorganization of the administration and public procurement. Civil service laws were passed in 1999. A national Anticorruption Strategy was adopted in 2001, as was a new law on the National Audit Office. However, no ombudsman or regional reform was introduced. Given "the doubtful commitment of the ruling elite to implement these changes,"[75] the EU was perceived as the key force behind the belated formal institutional reform in Bulgaria.[76]

In these cases, weaker competition created few incentives for closing loopholes in formal institutions. Where governing parties faced little opposition, they had no incentive to constrain themselves by establishing formal oversight institutions. The access of other parties to policy making and administrative decisions was limited. This was especially the case for opposition parties whom the governing parties denounced as "illegitimate," such as the Communists or the Republicans in the Czech Republic, the Russian minority parties in Latvia, and the Hungarian minority parties in Slovakia. The opposition had little capacity to monitor or investigate government actions. Nor was there much of an incentive for the governing parties to moderate their behavior and try to share responsibility for governance, given their relative certainty of a return to office. And, given

---

[74] The commercial banking crisis in 1995 depressed the GDP and occupied most of the policy debates that followed in 1995–7. Tisenkopfs and Kalniņš 2002.

[75] Todorova, Rossitsa. 2001. *EU Integration as an Agent of Public Administration Reform*. Unpublished manuscript, American University in Bulgaria.

[76] Verheijen, Tony. 1999. "The Civil Service of Bulgaria: Hope on the Horizon," in idem, *Civil Service Systems in Central and Eastern Europe*, Cheltenham: Edward Elgar, pp. 92–130.

the electoral dominance of the Czech ODS and Slovak HZDS, and the centrality of the LC to Latvian government coalitions, there were fewer marginal voters to capture via such public reports of these parties' misdoings. Governing parties were certain enough of future victories to continue to build in advantages for themselves.

Comparing the Czech Republic and Hungary

A comparison of institutional development in the Czech Republic and Hungary shows how the mechanisms of robust competition promoted the limiting of discretion and the building of formal constraints on the extraction of state resources for private gain. The two countries diverged considerably in their institutional outcomes: While Hungarian institution building was largely completed by 1995, the Czech Republic did not begin to consider a securities and exchange commission, independent national auditing office, regional government reform, an ombudsman, or civil service reform until the government crises of 1996–7. At the same time, we observe variation over time: The Hungarian Fidesz government of 1998–2002 attempted to undermine the monitoring and regulatory capabilities of several formal institutions (and the parliament itself) and to insulate itself from competition.

This divergence is all the more surprising given the many similarities between the two. After the collapse of communism, both countries underwent extensive economic and democratic reforms, becoming the favorites of foreign investors and financial institutions alike. Despite multiple differences in their communist regimes,[77] they shared many democratic traits: The communist party exited in both cases, with an anticommunist opposition that was initially uncertain of its popular support.[78] However, the regeneration of the Hungarian communists into a moderate social democratic party made them a credible threat and a catalyst for reform that was absent in the Czech Republic.

Both were the undisputed frontrunners of EU accession: Hungary applied in April 1994, the Czech Republic a year and a half later in 1996. Along with Poland, these countries were widely perceived to be a sure bet as the

[77] The Hungarian regime was widely considered to be far more liberal than the Czechoslovak orthodox conservatives.

[78] See Bernhard 2000; Bruszt, Laszlo, and Stark, David. 1991. "Remaking the Political Field in Hungary: From the Politics of Confrontation to the Politics of Competition," *Journal of International Affairs*, 45, 1 (Summer): 201–45.

first group of countries to enter the EU together. Both had the longest-lived governments in the region, with mean government duration of 1,096 days in Hungary and 869 in the Czech Republic (the longest-lived cabinet in the Czech Republic lasted 1,455 days, and 1,451 in Hungary).[79] During the critical period of 1990–4, when so many Hungarian institutions arose, the rates of parliamentary fragmentation were nearly identical: .67 and .68, respectively (their 1990–2003 averages were .68 and .71). Not surprisingly, analysts have categorized both as having the most institutionalized and consolidated party systems in the region.[80]

Accordingly, models of external imposition, foundational bargaining, and policy insulation all predict that the two countries would follow similar paths of institutional development. If the EU were the dominant force in institutional development, we would expect the countries to develop formal institutions at the same time. Once the Czech Civic Forum splintered into multiple parties over the course of 1990, both countries had similar balances of power among the political forces, so both should have developed power-sharing institutions that constrained all competitors' discretion. In contrast, their relatively low rates of turnover, fragmentation, and cabinet duration predict few constraints on discretion, if the institutional explanations of discretion are correct. Since the government was undivided and constitutional courts functioned in both countries, there is further expectation that neither would limit discretion. Instead, the two countries diverged in their institutional development.

Nor did the institutional legacies of the communist state and new independence make the Czech challenges of institution building so enormous as to account for the lag in building formal institutions. First, as noted earlier, even in Hungary or Poland the communist-era institutions of monitoring and oversight had to be strengthened and empowered after the collapse of their communist patrons, and the advantages they provided were often offset by the need to renovate them thoroughly. Second, in one account of communist legacies, the bureaucratic-authoritarian Czech state ought to have limited discretion far more after its collapse than the Hungarian national-accommodative state, which attempted to buy off popular support

---

[79] Müller-Rommel, Ferdinand, Fettelschoss, Katja, and Harst, Philipp. 2004. "Party Government in Central East European Democracies: A Data Collection (1990–2003)," *European Journal of Political Research*, 43: 869–93.

[80] O'Dwyer 2004; Mair 1997.

by relaxing strictures on state jobs and finances.[81] Finally, communist legacy-centered accounts would have a difficult time accounting for changes over time: why Czech governments eventually built institutions after 1998, and why the Hungarian government attempted to expand discretion in 1998–2002. Instead, the configurations of party competition explain both the variation between the two countries and across time.

Hungary

Hungary illustrates both the importance of robust competition and the ways in which governing parties attempt to insulate themselves from the threat it presents. It was the first post-communist country to institute a raft of formal state institutions of oversight, monitoring, and exploitation control. Governments throughout 1990–8 further strengthened them. Several administrative decisions were taken out of the hands of national political parties, as the administration decentralized extensively in 1990, and a strong Constitutional Court reviewed policies, acting as a powerful check and oversight institution. While Hungary's politicians were hardly blameless,[82] their actions were rapidly exposed, and the forced resignations, public scandals, and parliamentary sanctions served to moderate governing parties.

Members of government investigative committees made clear that robust competition was crucial to moderating rent seeking. Corruption and malfeasance were exposed in three ways: by democratic government institutions, political party criticism, and leaks to the press.[83] Above all, competitors had enormous incentives to build institutions "aimed at preventing each other from exploiting state resources for political purposes."[84] Accordingly, Hungary was the first post-communist country to institute a civil service law and regional decentralization. The 1990 and 1992 Civil Service Acts made whole sets of state positions incompatible with party membership,

---

[81] Kitschelt et al. 1999.

[82] In the Postabank scandal, the bank made numerous loans to political and society figures, costing the Hungarian taxpayers some 150 billion forints, and the 1998–2002 Fidesz-MPP government also attempted to meld the financial and political worlds. Ilonszki, Gabriella. 2000. "The Second Generation Political Elite in Hungary: Partial Consolidation," in Frentzel-Zagórska, Janina, and Wasilewski, Jacek, eds. *The Second Generation of Democratic Elites in East and Central Europe*. Warsaw: PAN ISP.

[83] Federal Broadcast Information Service (FBIS), 21 July 1994.

[84] Bartlett, David. 1997. *The Political Economy of Dual Transformations*. Ann Arbor: University of Michigan Press, p. 156.

including most of the civil servants. The 1990 Act on Local Government devolved power away from the center. It was the earliest and most comprehensive local government reform in the region.[85]

Opposition criticism led to the protection of state assets. The State Property Agency was established in March 1990 to regulate privatization and oversee its implementation. In the 1988–90 period, the number of economic units expanded from ten thousand to thirty thousand, largely driven by the expansion of limited liability companies, which grew from four hundred to eighteen thousand.[86] Once these excesses of late-communist "spontaneous privatization" emerged, the first democratic Hungarian governments established a stringent regulatory regimen that monitored privatization decisions and prevented banks and enterprise managers from striking special deals or stripping the state of its assets, in sharp contrast to Czech and Slovak practice.[87] By January 1990, a powerful State Audit Office began to investigate, unannounced, any entity with even partial state funding.[88]

Public finances were further brought under parliamentary oversight with the 1992 Law on Public Finances, the 1994 merging of the State Privatization Agency and the State Asset Holding Company, the 1995 Act on Public Procurement, and the 1995 creation of the Treasury, the first among the post-communist countries. These laws centralized decision making and provided for considerable oversight. Ironically, the 1992 law, passed by the anticommunist parties, ratified a number of legal arrangements left behind by the communist party: a large number of extra-budgetary funds, wide autonomy for the Central Budget institutions (spending agencies), and local governments.[89] In contrast, the 1995 laws, passed by the post-communist coalition, did away with these arrangements. The new laws eliminated hybrid forms of ownership, created real owners, and specified property rights more strictly.[90] The post-communist

---

[85] The side benefit of devolution was that opposition parties won 35 percent of local mandates, the largest share in the region.

[86] Schamis, Hector E. 2002. *Re-Forming the State: The Politics of Privatization in Latin America and Europe.* Ann Arbor: University of Michigan Press, p. 152.

[87] Barnes, Andrew. 2003. "Comparative Theft: Context and Choice in the Hungarian, Czech, and Russian Transformations 1989–2000," *Eastern European Politics and Societies,* 17, 3: 533–65, p. 548.

[88] Hesse, Joachim Jens. 1993. "From Transformation to Modernization: Administrative Change in Central and Eastern Europe," in Hesse, Joachim Jens, ed. *Administrative Transformation in Central and Eastern Europe.* Oxford: Blackwell, p. 241.

[89] Schamis 2002, p. 160.

[90] Ibid., p. 163.

MSzP government was eliminating discretionary access to state resources for its competitors – and for itself.

Oversight institutions exercised direct, apolitical, and powerful control. The Government Control Office was established in 1994 as a "central state organization with nationwide competency, to exercise budgetary control over executive bodies and assess the implementation and enforcement of decisions taken by the government."[91] The Ombudsman, introduced in 1994, was a further formal oversight innovation, and two other ombudsmen, in charge of minority rights and data protection, respectively, were further introduced. All three ombudsmen could bring cases to the Constitutional Court, lodge cases with the prosecutor's office, and demand that the head of an offending institution remedy abuses by the institution.

Similarly, governments increased power-sharing provisions, limiting their capacity to control the state administration and devolving power downward. Hungary was also the first post-communist country to institute a civil service law and regional decentralization. The 1992 Civil Service Act made whole sets of state positions incompatible with party membership, including most of the civil servants. A distinctive system of state secretaries clarified differences and coordinated reconciling them prior to cabinet meetings, serving as an additional check on policy formulation. Political state secretaries served as deputy ministers, substituting for ministers in parliamentary meetings. Administrative state secretaries were apolitical appointments with indefinite terms and represented the administration of a given ministry rather than the interests of a particular government. The 1990 Act on Local Government devolved power away from the center. It was the earliest and most comprehensive local government reform in the region.[92]

---

[91] OECD. 2001b. *Issues and Developments in Public Management: Hungary 2000.* OECD, p. 3.

[92] It also introduced democratically elected municipal councils, giving the parties another round of political competition and access to power. Hegedüs, József. 1999. "Hungarian Local Government," in Kirchner, Emil, ed. *Decentralization and Transition in the Visegrad.* Basingstoke: Macmillan. The side benefit of devolution was that opposition parties won 35 percent of local mandates, the largest share in the region. Baldersheim, Harald, et al. 1996. "New Institutions of Local Government: A Comparison," in Baldersheim, Harald, Illner, Michal, Offerdal, Audan, Rose, Lawrence, and Swaniewicz, Paweł, eds. *Local Democracy and the Processes of Transformation in East-Central Europe.* Boulder: Westview Press. New parties won 7 percent of the mandates in Poland, 26 percent in the Czech Republic, and 34 percent in Slovakia. The bloc civic opposition movement (Solidarity, Civic Forum, and Public Against Violence) won 32 percent, 47 percent, and 47 percent, respectively.

Institutions that had existed prior to 1989, such as the Constitutional Court and the National Audit Office, were now given new capacities and regularly monitored and investigated government actions. The Hungarian Constitutional Court was highly active, and acted as a very strong safeguard against potential abuses.[93] The Court was one of the few institutions left over from the communist era that acted as an effective constraint; robust competition established the rest. In the last days of the communist regime, the Court struck down the death penalty, abolished the use of a universal personal identification number, changed the abortion law, and did away with a tax on mortgage payments that the party-state attempted to impose to cover budget deficits five months before the first free elections in 1990.[94] In each case, the ruling communist party obeyed the court. Subsequently, in the first five years of its work, the court nullified about one-third of all laws brought before it.[95] The court's most public moment came in 1995, with its rulings on the constitutionality of the austerity package brought forth by the MSzP government and its striking down of the social spending cuts promulgated in the package. As a result, "rulings by the constitutional court have repeatedly necessitated substantial modifications to existing legislative acts in order to bring them into line with constitutional law."[96]

When Hungarian governing parties transgressed, their actions were rapidly exposed, and any one party's gains limited. Critics noted that "throughout its four years in power, the [1990–3 MDF Jozsef] Antall government came under fire for purging state officials associated with the communist regime, loading the bureaucracy with political sycophants, appropriating privatization revenues for patronage and meddling with the judiciary."[97] Yet when the MDF tried to politicize the National Bank's independence in October 1991,[98] the opposition mobilized in parliament. It

[93] Örkény, Antal, and Scheppele, Kim Lane. 1999. "Rules of Law: The Complexity of Legality in Hungary," in Krygier, Martin, and Czarnota, Adam, eds. *The Rule of Law After Communism*. Aldershot: Ashgate, p. 59.

[94] Ibid., p. 59.

[95] Scheppele, Kim Lane. 2002. "Democracy by Judiciary." Paper presented at the conference "Rethinking the Rule of Law in Post-Communist Europa: Past Legacies, Institutional Innovations, and Constitutional Discourses," EUI, Florence, 22–3 February, p. 22.

[96] Szabó. 1993, p. 91.

[97] Bartlett, David. 1996. "Democracy, Institutional Change, and Stabilisation Policy in Hungary," *Europe-Asia Studies*, 48, 1: 47–83, p. 64.

[98] Prime Minister Antall fired the head of the Bank, György Suranyi, for signing the Democratic Charter, a protest against the MDF's centralization of power. Suranyi was brought back in 1995.

immediately turned to press criticism, calls for formal investigations, and threats to hold up other legislation requiring a supermajority (and thus opposition support). As a result, the Central Bank was given considerable autonomy, and made answerable to the parliament as a whole, rather than to the prime minister alone. Similarly, when the MDF attempted to pack the media oversight boards in 1990–1, the opposition killed the government media law.[99] The liberal criticism of the MDF led its members to "publicly indict the leadership."[100] In other words, "the advent of genuine electoral competition and development of credible oversight capabilities in the Hungarian Parliament permitted opposition parties to hold the government's conduct up for public scrutiny – factors that contributed to the Forum's crushing defeat in the second post-communist election."[101]

Both formal and informal power-sharing prevailed. Diverse actors, ranging from foreign investors to the bar and the chamber of notaries to the churches and local governments, scrambled for resources and "used Parliament to push through their parochial interests."[102] The result was that no single powerful beneficiary emerged. Informal constraints also developed: As early as 1990, parties agreed that parliamentary committees would be filled and led by opposition parties in proportion to their votes. After 1994, a special investigative committee category arose, which could be set up at the written request of a fifth of parliament.

A pattern of anticipatory institutional creation and power-sharing evolved, irrespective of the ideology or regime roots of successive governments. The 1994–8 coalition government of the MSzP and SZDSz signed a post-election pact under which the liberal parties controlled the budget committees of the parliament. And these committees expanded their oversight activities, "subjecting the Finance Ministry's reports to line-by-line scrutiny."[103] Since committees were headed by opposition members throughout the post-1990 period, it is not surprising they were used "to

---

[99] Vass, László. 1994. "Changes in Hungary's Governmental System," in Ágh, Attila, ed. *The Emergence of East Central European Parliaments: The First Steps.* Budapest: Hungarian Centre for Democracy Studies, pp. 186–97, p. 193.

[100] Bartlett 1997. p. 155.

[101] Bartlett 1996, p. 64.

[102] Sajo, Andras. 1998a. "Corruption, Clientelism, and the Future of the Constitutional State in Eastern Europe," *East European Constitutional Review*, 7, 2 (Spring): 37–46, p. 41.

[103] Bartlett 1996, p. 65.

scrutinize the government more extensively."[104] The anticipation of such scrutiny was so strong that it was one reason why the 1994–8 MSZP-SzDSz coalition increased the supermajority requirements for constitutional changes from two-thirds to four-fifths of the parliament, even as the coalition held two-thirds of the seats.

In short, for most of the 1990s and the critical period of institution building, a robust competition led governments both to introduce formal institutions and to alter their behavior. Yet Hungary also shows the limits of the formal channels for robust competition, and how, paradoxically, informal pressures exerted by the opposition could be more powerful than that of their formalized counterparts. This paradoxical situation arises because formal channels of parliamentary sanction and action come up against the hard rule of parliamentary life: The government's majority allows it to ignore the opposition, if only temporarily. In contrast, informal criticism and investigations do not rely on numerical supremacy.

The 1998–2002 Fidesz – Magyar Polgári Párt (MPP) government recognized the constraints placed on earlier governments by a robust competition, and attempted to insulate itself from this forceful criticism by restricting the power of the opposition. Fidesz first changed the frequency of parliamentary plenary sessions from weekly to every three weeks. It then obstructed the opposition's efforts to launch special investigative committees, which would have investigated government actions such as the consolidation of the controversial Postabank and state television finances.[105] The coalition also established the National Image Center, founded shortly after the 1998 elections to promote Hungary's image abroad, which rapidly became a sinecure for party loyalists and a profitable source of funding (via contract tenders) for firms allied to the governing parties, such as the aptly named Happy End, Ltd.[106] The National Image Center itself was a subdepartment of the prime minister's office, and answerable only to the prime minister himself.

---

[104] Ilonszki, Gabriella. 2002. "A Functional Clarification of Parliamentary Committees in Hungary, 1990–1998," in Olson, David, and Crowther, William, eds. *Committees in Post-Communist Democratic Parliaments: Comparative Institutionalization.* Columbus: Ohio State University Press, pp. 21–43, p. 24.

[105] Act 46, adopted in 1994, specified that if 20 percent of MPs so desire, parliament is to establish such committees for any field of government activity, and twenty such attempts were made in 1998–2002.

[106] Happy End was headed by the 1998 Fidesz election campaign manager, for example.

However, the opposition continued to criticize the government and moderated some of the Fidesz governments' subsequent plans to funnel funds to party-allied businesses.[107] Despite the fewer sessions of parliament, the high number of interpellations remained largely unchanged, as the opposition increased the intensity of questioning of the governing parties and their policies.[108] And, the opposition continued to hold press conferences, investigate government behavior, and publish incriminating documents. As one newspaper editorial commented, "the opposition is there day in and day out, with access to much the same information as the Government, and ready to pounce on any wrongdoing – slight or major, actual or perceived – that can be used to political advantage."[109]

By 2000, the resurgent opposition renewed its impact on policy and appointments. When the time came to reappoint the three ombudsmen (civil rights, minority rights, and data protection) in spring 2001,[110] Fidesz first proposed abolishing the data protection ombudsman, and the Independent Smallholders' Party (FKGP) argued that the ombudsman could be replaced by a parliamentary commission. When that proposal failed in light of the parliamentary opposition's criticism, Fidesz turned to personnel decisions. In filling the three positions, and the deputy general ombudsman's, the coalition proposed that two of the ombudsmen (civil rights and data protection) be named by the government and two by the opposition. The opposition, however, rejected this proposal, and demanded the departing ombudsmen be reappointed. To resolve the stalemate, President Ferenc Mádl made his own proposals (which included the reappointment of the minority rights ombudsman), which passed in three out of the four cases.[111] In short, while the Fidesz government was able to limit formal investigations and opposition access by using its majority to change the rules, it was unable to prevent the opposition from informally investigating, criticizing, and publicizing its actions.

The power of robust competition can be seen in two responses of the Fidesz government. First, it was forced to abandon both discredited policies

---

[107] Interview, anonymous MSzP official, July 2002.

[108] In 1994–8, the opposition issued 804 interpellations, and in 1998–2002, 696. Freedom House 2002, p. 203.

[109] *Budapest Sun*, 10 June 1999, "Bank fracas shows gains and defects," editorial.

[110] The ombudsmen had six-year terms.

[111] The candidate for the data protection ombudsman, Mihály Maczonkai, received 198 votes, but since a two-thirds majority was required, the seat remained vacant until it was filled in late 2001 by Attila Peterfalvi.

and politicians. Its September 1998 proposal to lower the number of MPs from 386 to 220 required the support of the opposition. Despite courting the MSzP as the other largest party in parliament that stood to benefit, Fidesz was unable to receive the two-thirds of the votes necessary to pass the measure. The head of the Tax Authority (APEH) police unit, established in January 1999, faced huge criticism from the opposition for his close ties to both Fidesz and shady businesspeople. His superior, President of the Tax Authority Lajos Simicska, had to resign himself in September 1999, a year after his appointment, in the face of heavy criticism from the SzDSz. The SzDSz held a series of press conferences and published several documents that showed personal ties between various companies led or managed by Simicska and Fidesz.[112]

Opposition criticism hit hardest the junior coalition partner, the FKGP. József Torgyán, the minister of agriculture and FKGP leader, faced allegations of nepotism when his daughter-in-law and her mother were named to the boards of the national airline and a major firm with state interest. Both resigned by December 2000 under opposition party pressure. Béla Szabadi, formerly the state secretary of the Ministry of Agriculture and Rural Development (FVM), was forced to resign from parliament in 2001 and was arrested on nineteen counts of embezzlement, fraud, and mismanagement. Zoltán Székely, the FKGP chair of the Parliamentary Procurement Committee, was caught taking a Ft 20 million bribe ($65,000) and forced to resign in the fall of 2000. Torgyán himself resigned in February 2001, after months of opposition investigation and charges of improperly reporting his income and accepting bribes. In the early fall of 2000, the opposition launched a formal conflict-of-interest procedure to investigate Torgyán's misdoings. When the parliamentary Committee on Immunity and Conflict of Interests, headed by the governing coalition, refused to initiate an investigation against Torgyán, the opposition pressed for the publication of his financial statements. It led by example, with opposition MPs and the mayor of Budapest publishing their statements. Government officials, including Prime Minister Viktor Orban, followed.[113] When Torgyán continued to refuse to publicize his financial documents, the government coalition put forth a set of amendments to the law on the status of

---

[112] Gábor Kuncze, the head of the SzDSz parliamentary faction, charged that Fidesz politicians benefited from Postabank investments. Specifically, Simicska, the former financial director of Fidesz then appointed to run the Hungarian Tax Office, led the Mahir media chain, which had several contracts with Postabank.

[113] *East European Constitutional Review*, Fall 2000, 9, 4.

parliamentarians to include the release of annual financial reports. The opposition held these hostage: Until Torgyán divulged his financial dealings, they refused to support the measures (and without the opposition's support, the amendments could not get the required two-thirds supermajority). The political pressure, and the negative publicity surrounding his financial irregularities, led to his resignation and bitter complaints of a "hounding" by the press.[114]

The onslaught of opposition criticism and publicity had its effects on government parliamentarians, who wanted to cut themselves off from the excesses committed in their name. Eventually, corruption allegations during 1998–2002 led to the defection of half the FKGP parliamentary representatives and to the complete collapse of the party's parliamentary role. Similarly, when the Fidesz government established the Tax Authority police force in January 1999, its parliamentary faction soon requested that the head of the Tax Authority reconsider his appointment of the police force head, László Pelikán, who had been tied to criminal businesspeople and accused of purchasing smuggled jewelry. Their stated motive in seeking the dismissal was that both opposition politicians and the press would generate enormous negative publicity for the government.[115]

Fidesz also attempted to insulate itself against the electoral threat from the MSzP-SzDSz opposition by building loose grassroots organizations that would give it a stable and loyal electoral constituency without having to expend many resources. Initially founded after the 1998 elections, the circles grouped together Fidesz sympathizers on a local basis, but were neither formally affiliated with nor led by the national party itself. Their total membership by 2002 was estimated at 150,000. The number, as Orban's spokesperson explained, was "higher than the membership of all parliamentary parties together," offering a security net for Fidesz and a source of electoral mobilization.[116] (These same civic circles would then lash out in protest after Fidesz lost the 2002 elections, demanding recounts and investigations in Fidesz's name.)

As part of the strategy of electoral insulation, Fidesz began to fund local governments with the Fidesz-FKGP leadership much more generously than those local governments controlled by the opposition. Twenty-nine local governments controlled by the ruling party received a combined

[114] Fraser, Allan. 2001. "Torgyán Bows to Pressure to Quit." *Budapest Sun*, 15 February.
[115] Balazs, Ester. 1999. "Tax Police Chief Under Attack." *Budapest Sun*, 4 February.
[116] *Budapest Sun*, 23 January 2003.

Ft 8.53 billion (over \$30 million), with towns and cities earning Ft 294.1 million (over \$1 million) per tender. In contrast, the twenty opposition-run local governments received less than a fourth of the funds: Ft 1.17 billion (over \$4 million), averaging Ft 28.91 million (over \$100,000) per tender.[117] Another strategy to insulate the party electorally was to propose and adopt a two-year budget in 2000, which meant that Fidesz could rule in a minority coalition if necessary until the next parliamentary elections in 2002. In short, Fidesz tried its hardest to insulate itself from an opposition it knew would curtail its current and planned resource extraction.

Yet formal institutions themselves controlled and regulated government actions if headed by independent leadership and answerable to the parliament as a whole. The State Audit Office (ÁSZ) audited the state budgets and sharply criticized the Fidesz government for its inability to account for state-owned assets and missing records. Such criticism was then taken up by opposition parliamentarians, who added that balance sheets were falsified and nearly Ft 94.5 billion (\$350 million) was spent without parliamentary approval in 2000 alone.[118] Similarly, some of these institutions expanded their domain: Over the course of the 1990s, the State Audit Office began to audit budget chapters and ministry expenditures, even though the law did not require it to do so.[119] Most importantly, the office investigated the controversial National Image Center (NIC), which the opposition accused of awarding contracts worth billions of forints without any competitive tenders, and the financial malfeasance of the corporations that received noncompetitive tenders from the NIC: Happy End, Ltd., and Silver Ship, Ltd.[120]

In contrast, formal institutions run by Fidesz allies and answerable to the government alone, such as the Tax Office, were often used to further the government's informal agenda and insulate it further from opposition threats by cowing potential critics. As one opposition parliamentarian charged, the Tax Authority became "a modern house of terror. If anyone says anything against the Government that they don't like then immediately APEH is there. . . . And it's not even denied because they want people to feel that this is the consequence."[121] Similarly, the government politicized the

---

[117] *Budapest Nepszabadsag*, 4 July 2001.
[118] "Auditors Criticize Government," *Budapest Sun*, 4 October 2001.
[119] *Magyar Hirlap*, 25 April 2003.
[120] *Magyar Hirlap*, 29 July 2002.
[121] *Budapest Sun*, 7 March 2002.

Hungarian state television, making it into what one critic called "a virtual open propaganda instrument of the outgoing [Fidesz] Government."[122]

Even here, there were limits. To set up or change a formal state institution, the government needed the opposition's approval, thanks to the two-thirds supermajority requirements. As a result, the "glass pocket" anticorruption law of 2000 and the Hungarian Financial Supervisory Authority (PSZÁF, founded in 2000, which consolidated the Hungarian Banking and Capital Market Supervision, the State Insurance Supervision, and the State Pension Fund Supervision) were both passed only with the opposition's approval and after considerable concessions to the opposition's demands.[123] The anticorruption measure, for example, included numerous opposition proposals and amendments.

The excesses of the Fidesz coalition became campaign fodder during the elections of 2002. The two main opposition parties, the SzDSz and the MSzP, charged that the government was corrupt, in areas ranging from highway construction to the privatization of state farms. Both parties repeatedly cited the FKGP malfeasances, the National Image Center fiasco, and the politicization of the tax office as further evidence of the coalition's corruption and degeneration. Their election campaign chiefly focused on criticism of the administration.[124] Meanwhile, Fidesz and the MDF grew increasingly confident that their insulation efforts ensured a stable constituency and attempted to move even further to the nationalist right to capture the extremist MIEP voters – thus making it easier for the opposition to charge that Fidesz was irresponsible and arrogant.

Once the Fidesz coalition was out of power in 2002, several of its excesses were curbed. The National Image Center was abolished. Supervision of both the State Privatization Corporation (ÁPV Rt) and the Hungarian Development Bank (MFB) returned to parliament: These were no longer under the purview of the Chancery (the Office of the Prime Minister). The "reference desks," established by Fidesz to curtail ministerial autonomy and ensure greater prime ministerial control, were now also abolished.

---

[122] *Budapest Sun*, 2 May 2002.
[123] In a bizarre twist, the PSZÁF head, Károly Szász, was found severely beaten in 2003, as a supposed result of his investigations into an equities holding company, K and H Bank. The subsequent scandal would be among Hungary's biggest, since Fidesz had a field day with the discovery that a former head of the bank was Laszlo Csaba, the finance minister in the new MSZP government of 2002. In 2005, Szász himself was investigated for giving unwarranted bonuses to his employees.
[124] *Budapest Sun*, 2 May 2002.

In all these areas, domestic competition, rather than the pressures of the EU or other external agents, was the key determinant of the institutions, programs, and policies that arose. The institutional reforms were completed by the time the EU turned its attention to the state, and accordingly, progress reports found far less to criticize in Hungary. As a final note, in Hungary, as elsewhere in the region, the EU, the World Bank, and other international financial organizations emphasized anticorruption efforts. Thus, in early 2000, the Hungarian Ministry of Justice announced that fighting corruption was the highest priority for Hungary in preparation for joining the EU.[125] Much of the groundwork for these efforts had already been laid down, however, as a direct result of earlier party competition.

The Czech Republic

In contrast, the ODS government in the Czech Republic saw no reason to constrain itself throughout 1990–8. The weak parliamentary opposition could not set into motion the moderating, anticipatory, or cooptive mechanisms. Accordingly, few formal institutional reforms occurred under the ODS's watch: Václav Klaus criticized state oversight institutions as only "adding another layer of bureaucracy."[126] Formal institutions that would have constrained discretion were either very weak or missing altogether. Czech regulation of the market was minimal: Bank reform was both delayed and minimal, regulatory mechanisms were disassembled, judicial review of privatization ceased, and privatization decisions were not justified.[127] Faced with a weak opposition, "with virtual impunity, the Klaus administration continued on its path, nodding at instances of corruption within its own electoral alliance. It ignored efforts to establish a national securities council and other measures that would have enhanced the transparency of Czech capital markets."[128]

Numerous reform attempts were scuppered by the government: The "ODS maintained a strong enough political position to dodge attacks waged

---

[125] Jednotka boji proti korupci [Anticorruption Unit], Ministry of Interior, *Zpráva o korupci v ČR a o plnění harmonogramu opatření vládního programu boje proti korupci v ČR*. [Report about corruption in the Czech Republic and about the fulfilling of the government plan for the fight against corruption in the Czech Republic], 2001.

[126] *Mladá Fronta Dnes*, 9 April 1996.

[127] Frič et al. 1999, p. 178. To be fair, the February 1991 privatization law did not allow for oversight in the first place.

[128] Orenstein 2001.

by less powerful political actors and deftly delayed legislative progress on administrative reform bills."[129] The ODS also used its domination of the parliamentary committees (none were under opposition leadership during its tenure in office) to preclude opposition bills from ever reaching the parliamentary floor. As a result, government executive bodies "operated with virtually no transparency."[130]

The main reason was the absence until 1996 of an opposition that could create the incentives for building formal institutional constraints on discretion. The deep division between the former communist rulers and their opposition meant the opposition was clear – but it was neither plausible nor critical. The two biggest opposition parties, the Communist Party of Bohemia and Moravia and the Republicans, held over 20 percent of the seats in the parliament, but were both excluded a priori from all governing coalitions. As a result, even if the ODS coalition partners left the ODS and tried to form an alternative government with the opposition, they could only get 75 seats, far short of the 101 required to govern.[131] The other potential opponent (the Social Democratic ČSSD) gained popularity only in 1995–6, and had 7 percent of the seats until the 1996 election, allowing the ODS-led coalition to set the terms of policy making and state politicization largely on its own. Few questions were asked of the government, and the ODS pushed through its wishes even if all its coalition partners united against it. Instead of strong criticism, the opposition only joined a coalition member (ODA) in "requesting in the press an explanation" of a privatization scandal.[132] Once the ODS government collapsed, moreover, the former opponents – the ČSSD and the ODS – joined to govern together, which blurred the lines between government and opposition.

Czech delays in state reform sharply contrast with the country's earlier image as the leader of post-communist economic and political transformations.[133] For the ODS governments led by Václav Klaus, liberalization of the economy was the priority, and its key component was deregulation.[134] Formal state institutions of monitoring and oversight would only wind up

---

[129] Scherpereel 2003.

[130] Freedom House 2000.

[131] The Czech ODS coalition had 105 out of 200 seats, but of the remaining 95 seats, 49 were held by parties that could not enter an alternative governing coalition. The KDU-ČSL's 15 seats, the ODA's 14, and the remaining opposition's 46 added up to 75.

[132] *Respekt*, 28 September 1992.

[133] Appel 2001.

[134] Interview with Václav Klaus, *Profit*, 29 April 2002.

"hampering the market."[135] When the ODS government first emerged in 1991, one existing aim of privatization established by the Civic Forum government was to limit corruption by subjecting the process to several administrative organs and laws.[136] However, Klaus quickly reneged on this commitment, and a new government proposal was not legally binding: Privatization institutions could now privatize what and how they wanted.

Instead of exercising cooptation or power sharing, one coalition partner, the ODA, single-handedly controlled the state institutions in charge of distributing and overseeing state property, such as the National Property Fund (Fond Narodního Majetků, FNM). The ruling coalition further tightened its grip in 1992–3 in the name of speeding up privatization.[137] With Klaus in power in 1992, the function of the original law on privatization was hugely weakened. Regulatory mechanisms were systematically taken apart. Judicial review of privatization decisions ceased, and the decisions were no longer made public or justified. As a result, those who made privatization decisions automatically decided about their appropriateness and legality. New laws passed in 1993 by the ODS coalition ensured that no judicial review of the already-secret privatization decisions existed and that the government received discretion in changing both future conditions and terms of already-approved projects.[138]

Klaus delayed the emergence of other oversight institutions, in keeping with a governing strategy described as "focused on maximizing central control over all important aspects of economic decisions making, while simultaneously erecting barriers to participation for competing interests."[139] A Securities and Exchange Commission was not established until 1998, long after the Czech stock market acquired a reputation for opacity and unclear property rights. The Commission was dismissed as an irrelevant and harmful bureaucratic intervention, leading to opaque ownership structures and

---

135 *Mladá Fronta Dnes*, 9 April 1996.

136 Frič et al. 1999, p. 177.

137 In 1992, the so-called honor system in the Ministry of Privatization began. As Jonathan Terra points out, it effectively institutionalized secrecy in the decision-making process; ministry officials could make ad hoc discretionary adjustments of submitted proposals, state regulatory power was decreased, and legal accountability was eliminated (laws c. 544/ 1992 SB and 210/ 1993 Sb.). See Terra 2002, pp. 137–8.

138 Reed, Quentin. 2002. "Corruption in Czech Privatization: The Dangers of 'Neo-Liberal' Privatization." in Kotkin, Stephen, and Sajos, Andras, eds. *Political Corruption: A Sceptic's Handbook*. Budapest: CEU Press, p. 273.

139 Terra 2002. "Corruption in Czech Privatization: The Dangers of 'Neo-Liberal' Privatization."

making property or shareholder rights difficult to enforce. Initially, the Ministry of Finances was in charge of stock market oversight, through its subordinate agency, the Center for Securities. However, in keeping with a strategy of "building an administration that is as effective and as small as possible,"[140] the Center was limited in its oversight powers and had no regulatory capacity. As a result, "tunneling" (asset stripping of privatized enterprises by their new owners) went undetected until the late 1990s.

The opposition put up little fight; for example, the parliamentary Banking Commission called for the government to put forth reforms that would insulate the Czech National Bank from political influence (as its president complained, "there is huge political pressure on banks, while at the same time, we function in a legislative and institutional vacuum").[141] However, the proposed reform bill was quickly squelched "with the political agreement of the ODS, KDU-ČSL and ČSSD."[142] By 1996, financial experts were criticizing the Czech stock market for a "certain lack of transparency."[143] Reports began to appear that foreign investors were staying away from Czech investments, given the lack of transparency and the unclear pricing mechanisms.[144] A fund manager complained that he "felt no political will that would bring about change and defend against deceptions."[145] As the pressure grew, so did the eagerness of the stock exchange for a Securities and Exchange Commission–style body with extensive regulatory and sanctioning powers.[146] The Ministry of Finance and the ODS government, meanwhile, resisted the pressure, both because it would remove stock market oversight, however weak, from the Ministry of Finances and because it was not "the job of the government to establish a capital market."[147] It was only in December 1996, five years after privatization began, that the government agreed to set up an independent securities exchange commission. The move came largely as the result of the threat of foreign investor departures, but no relevant laws were put into effect until 1998.

---

[140] *Mladá Fronta Dnes*, 26 April 1997.
[141] Former central banker Michal Tošovský, meeting of the Permanent Commission for Banking, first meeting, 13 September 1996.
[142] Meeting of the Permanent Commission for Banking, fifteenth meeting, 5 May 1998.
[143] *Mladá Fronta Dnes*, 21 December 1996.
[144] See the reports in *Mladá Fronta Dnes* and *Lidové Noviny* from late 1996 to early 1997.
[145] *Mladá Fronta Dnes*, 25 October 1996.
[146] See interviews with former Minister of Privatization and ODA MP Tomáš Ježek, *Mladá Fronta Dnes*, 11 July 1996 and 7 November 1996.
[147] *Mladá Fronta Dnes*, 10 December 1996.

Where the governments in Hungary had considerable incentives to depoliticize and regulate privatization assets, their Czech counterparts had equally powerful incentives and capacity to avoid formal oversight of the privatization processes. The biggest malfeasance was widely suspected in the privatization funds, many of which began to transform themselves into holding companies in late 1996 in an attempt to avoid regulation on their investments once the government declared its intention to build the Commission for Securities (Komise pro Cenné Papíry, KCP). As one critic declared, "besides the strengthening of oversight, it is necessary still to atone for old sins, which were brought about by a market without regulation."[148] Yet despite the urgency, two developments rendered the institution impotent. First, the existing Center for Securities, a parliamentary commission, and the Ministry of Finances began to jockey for the right to design the new institution. This meant further delay in its introduction, as the governing coalition members debated who can nominate the chair of the KCP, how it would be funded, and what its powers would be. In the end, the government would nominate the Commission, leading to charges it could not be impartial, and its powers were not as extensive as its Hungarian or Polish counterparts. It could not, for example, issue new regulations itself. Second, the delay until 1998 in introducing the institution meant that it would now attempt to reimpose control over a swamp of unclear property relations and murky contracts. During the years of weak regulation, "in the face of simple anarchy, a huge financial lobby arose,"[149] further hampering the new agency's job. A year after the founding of the KCP, Klaus acidly commented that the commission "precisely fulfilled my expectations. These were zero, and the result is a zero."[150]

Just as the ODS never seriously considered stock market oversight, it weakened the regulation and auditing of public finances. The NKÚ, or the Supreme Audit Office, was established at the federal Czechoslovak government in January 1992. Once Czechoslovakia dissolved into the two constituent republics in January 1993, however, the governing coalition immediately dissolved the NKÚ and refounded it as an institution under government (that is, ODS) control. Unlike its Hungarian or Polish counterparts, it did not report to the parliament as a whole and it had no capacity

---

[148] Interview with Miroslav Zámečník, assistant to the executive director of the World Bank, *Mladá Fronta Dnes*, 12 April 1997.

[149] Ivan Pilip, the former minister of finances, in *Mladá Fronta Dnes*, 3 November 1997.

[150] *Mladá Fronta Dnes*, 1 April 1999.

to choose where and whom it could audit.[151] The NKÚ lost the right to initiate investigations or to follow up on citizen initiatives.[152] Investigators could not pursue those accused of malfeasance unless the government filed a specific accusation, and they had to prove criminal intent. Not surprisingly, later investigations found that only 22 percent of public tenders were competitive. The rest were handed over chiefly to entrepreneurs allied with the governing party.[153] A lengthy catalog of privatization scandals began with the arrest of the head of the Center for Coupon Privatization, Jan Lizner, for taking a $350,000 bribe in late 1994.[154]

The Supreme Audit Office was more politicized than its Hungarian counterpart: After 1993, the office was headed by Lubomír Voleník of the governing ODS. Opposition candidates were not considered. Even though Voleník was widely regarded as a competent and able administrator, a deputy in the NKÚ began to circulate a petition in 1997 calling for reforms in the NKÚ, arguing that the institution was not conducting investigations in an impartial and nonpartisan manner because both the chair and his deputy were ODS members.[155] Moreover, his appointment set a precedent for political appointments. According to the 1998 Opposition Agreement, Voleník was reappointed in 2002 for another nine-year term. The Social Democrats were supposed to name the deputy chair. President Havel, however, rejected the ČSSD candidate František Brožík for not declaring his assets properly as a parliamentarian. Subsequently, when Voleník died in June 2003, both the ODS and the Social Democrats attempted to push through explicitly partisan candidates, but the post remained unfilled as of July 2005.[156] Repeatedly the parties argued that since the first NKÚ chair was a politician, subsequent chairs and deputies ought to be, too.[157] By 2004, the post became so politicized that Prime Minister Stanislav Gross was offering the post to the ODS in exchange for supporting the

---

[151] Frič et al. 1999, p. 180.

[152] Appel 2001, p. 534.

[153] *Mladá Fronta Dnes*, 2 May 2002. Of the 6,853 tenders for ministerial offers, only 1,483 were competitive.

[154] For an accounting of the various scandals, see Appel 2001 and *LIdové Noviny*, 17 January 1998.

[155] *Mladá Fronta Dnes*, 4 September 1997.

[156] The government candidate for the NKÚ chair, František Brožik, refused to make an asset declaration, despite membership on lucrative enterprise boards. He was also a former representative of the German firm Bauer Bau International, for whom he bought real estate and then resold it to the Brožik family for very low prices. See *Mladá Fronta Dnes*, 26 April 2002, 20 May 2002.

[157] *Mladá Fronta Dnes*, 18 August 2003.

government.[158] In contrast to both Hungary and Poland, no informal norm of opposition control of the office was established.

Power sharing, whether with other parties or with autonomous state institutions, was widely viewed with suspicion by the ODS leadership. The ODS was opposed to setting up the institution of an ombudsman on the grounds that it was unnecessary in a state governed by the rule of law, and too expensive. Repeated proposals for the institution, both by the president and opposition members, were ignored and kept off the legislative agenda.[159] The ODS government argued that citizens can achieve their rights in the courts, with "the president, the prime minister, each minister, parliamentarians and maybe television" serving as ombudsmen.[160] Klaus declared that "we feel there are enough institutions in our state."[161] Another, perhaps more sincere, criticism was that the ombudsman would constitute "a revision of electoral results, an attempt to dominate the political scene by means that do not reflect the balance of political power."[162]

Once the financial scandals of 1997 broke out, however, the ODS coalition partners were willing to countenance an ombudsman, chiefly because they wanted to disassociate themselves from the ODS abuses of power. In 1997, the Social Democrats submitted a proposal that some KDU-ČSL members supported. Once the ODS reasserted coalition discipline, the proposal failed on the third reading, with the KDU-ČSL parliamentarians surprising their brethren and suddenly opposing the ombudsman's office. As Klaus declared after the office was finally established in 2000, "I have always fought against the Ombudsman's Office and I am fighting against it to this very day."[163]

After the 1996 elections, also won by the ODS, the Office for Legislation and Public Administration, "the only agency dealing with public administrative reform," was abolished.[164] The ODS promised further formal state reform, including decentralization and a civil service law, but did not fulfill either.[165] Meanwhile, the parliamentary opposition had too few votes to

---

[158] *Mladá Fronta Dnes*, 7 July 2004.

[159] As KDU-ČSL Deputy Chair Jan Kasal noted, the ODS was "convinced to the marrow of the irrelevance of this institution." *Právo*, 14 May 1996.

[160] *Mladá Fronta Dnes*, 9 April 1996.

[161] *Mladá Fronta Dnes*, 1 April 1996.

[162] Senator, former Minister of Interior, and ODS MP Jan Ruml, quoted in *Mladá Fronta Dnes*, 1 April 1996.

[163] *Lidové Noviny*, 10 October 2003.

[164] OECD. 2000a. *Issues and Developments in Public Management: Czech Republic–2000*, p. 2.

[165] Ibid., p. 2.

challenge these measures, and there were few calls in the media to do so. The criticism of the communist party, the KSČM, was dismissed as the sour grapes of orthodox communists. As one critic concluded, "with virtual impunity, the Klaus administration continued on its path, nodding at instances of corruption within its own electoral alliance."[166] Not surprisingly, "the coalition of June 1992 carried with it – at least in retrospect – all the signs of a division of spoils. ODA got the privatization institutions, KDU-ČSL the ministry of defence, agriculture, and the antimonopoly office, and ODS left itself the key ministries of finance, justice and interior, and BIS [the security services]. The natural basis of this unspoken mutual agreement was to leave the other parties alone, so that they could make milk cows out of their offices."[167]

ODS thus successfully blocked institutions of monitoring and oversight. The opposition had little access to policy making, since it was excluded from the parliamentary leadership and unable to conduct investigations into government behavior. There was no counterweight to the government; the ČSSD held too few seats and could not enter into a coalition with either the ostracized former communists or the extremist Republicans. As a result, the opposition neither presented a credible alternative to the voters, nor could it constrain the government effectively. It took the party financing scandals of late 1996–7 and the subsequent defection of numerous ODS deputies to undermine the ODS's hold on power and to allow other parties to govern.

In short, government executive bodies "operated with virtually no transparency"[168] for much of the first post-communist decade and the critical years of privatizing state assets. Yet this lack of regulation backfired: The result was a spate of banking, privatization, and party donations-for-state-assets scandals that surfaced in the late 1990s, leading finally to the collapse of the ODS government in the winter of 1997. It was only once the ODS left office in disgrace in 1998 that state reforms began in earnest. Not surprisingly, Klaus likened the new government's attempts to the stifling bureaucracy communist rule, and argued that market reform "has stopped, instead of going ahead, and began to once again turn in the direction of regulation, orders, prohibitions."[169]

---

[166] Orenstein 2001, p. 110.
[167] Frič et al. 1999, p. 177.
[168] Freedom House 2000, p. 229.
[169] Interview with Vaclav Klaus, *Profit*, 29 April 2002.

With the fall of the ODS coalition after the repeated party financing and privatization scandals in the fall of 1997, the interim "government of experts," led by former central banker Michal Tošovský, attempted to begin to repair the damage. As one of its first acts in 1998, it finally set up the Czech Securities and Exchange Commission.[170] Even so, the Commission had little independent authority: It was subject to the Ministry of Finances and could not issue binding regulations for markets.[171]

The new government elected in 1998 and led by the ČSSD (with ODS support) adopted a concept for civil service and public administration reform in 1999. A Clean Hands program began after the election of 1998, in fulfillment of ČSSD electoral promises to "do away with all tunnellers."[172] The results, however, were less than spectacular, with the first chair of the investigative body set up, Jan Sula, resigning due to violent threats against him and family.[173] Anticorruption efforts began again with government resolution 125 in 1999, "The Government Program for Combating Corruption in the Czech Republic," which redoubled the scant efforts to investigate and punish incidents of corruption. By 2000, the government dissolved the Coordination and Analytic Group (KAS), which was responsible for the Clean Hands campaign but failed to meet regularly and uncover or bring to court cases of malfeasance and privatization errors.

Many of these belated reforms were a direct result of EU pressures: Not only did the EU repeatedly criticize the Czech Republic after 1997, but it began several projects under the auspices of SIGMA and PHARE to remedy administrative shortcomings. As a result, official proposals and reports regarding the reform of the state administration after 1998 explicitly referred to the demands of the EU and the specific projects that guided the belated reforms.[174] Thus, the new government began work on public administration reform, regional decentralization, and public finances, areas that had been left untouched throughout the first post-communist decade.

---

[170] Orenstein 2001, p. 93.

[171] Subcommittee for Capital and Financial Markets, first meeting, 23 September and 5 November 1998, "Report of the Functioning and Management of the KCP for April–September 1998."

[172] CTK, "Czech Government Unwilling to Face Anti-Corruption Failure," 1 June 2000.

[173] Stroehlein, Andrew. 1999. "The Czech Republic 1992 to 1999," *Central Europe Review* (13 September).

[174] Úsek pro reformu veřejné správy. 2001. "Vybrané výstupy z projekty PHARE CZ 9808.01 Posílení institutcionálních a administrativních kapacit pro implementaci *acquis communautaire*." Prague: Government of the Czech Republic.

After enormous delay and obfuscation, a Civil Service Act passed in April 2002, a decade after it a similar reform was enacted in Hungary (1990–2) and six years after it was in Poland (1996). Immediately, the ODS announced its opposition to the law. Regional government was also passed in 2000, after years of delays by the ODS (whose leadership worried that creating another level of elected governments would only allow other parties to survive and to gain strength).[175]

In late 1999, the proposal to establish an ombudsman finally passed, supported by the ČSSD, the communists, and the KDU-ČSL, with the ODS and most Freedom Union parliamentarians opposing. The ombudsman's office began functioning in 2000. However, its powers were considerably constrained: The ombudsman would only be able to point out violations to a superior body, the public, or the parliament. In contrast, the Polish and Hungarian ombudsmen could both force state bodies to change their policy implementation and bring cases to the state attorney offices and constitutional courts. Klaus continued to declare that an ombudsman's office was unnecessary, since various ministries and government offices already functioned as ombudsmen dealing with citizen requests and complaints.[176]

Delays meant inherent weaknesses. Precisely because they were now regulating existing (and consolidated) relationships, these institutions would face a far bigger challenge than similar reforms agencies (the Securities and Exchange Commission, National Accounting Offices) that were introduced simultaneously with the property rights and ownership structures they were to regulate. The ombudsman's office, for example, faced repeated questions regarding its "real chances in a situation where the Czech public administration reform is only being prepared and where neither justice nor the state administration is functioning properly."[177]

In short, the governments of Hungary and the Czech Republic, as the frontrunners of economic and democratic reforms, had the capacity and the favorable preconditions to implement state reforms and to hinder state exploitation by erecting a framework of formal state institutions of monitoring and oversight. Their paths nonetheless departed, rapidly and profoundly – and the criticism, incentives, and threat of replacement offered by the opposition parties were a key determinant of this divergence.

---

[175] *Respekt*, 18 September 1995.
[176] *Právo*, 21 October 2003.
[177] ČTK, "Czech Senate Passes Ombudsman Law," 8 December 1999.

Conclusion

Three conclusions emerge from the post-communist adoption of formal institutions of monitoring and oversight. First, parties were less interested in protecting state agencies from policy reversals and opposition influence than they were in insulating themselves from their electoral competitors. As a result, where competition was weak, so were the incentives to build new formal state institutions. Where they were built, they were often discretionary and politicized. Where competition was more robust, governments responded by building more autonomous and powerful institutions to constrain the opposition when it came into power.

Second, formal institutions of state monitoring and oversight were not simply an automatic accompaniment of market and democratic reforms. Some scholars had argued that state withdrawal from the polity and the economy itself fosters the institutions of formal state monitoring and oversight. As one analyst commented after reviewing the Hungarian case, "one of the puzzling discoveries of the East European transformation is precisely that the socialist state was a very weak one. Marketization has strengthened it, largely by triggering state formation processes."[178] But market reforms could have this beneficial effect only if party competition led to the emergence of formal state institutions that could extract taxes, enforce contracts and property rights, and adjudicate competing claims. Nor is external imposition responsible: In several cases, government coalitions preempted many of the demands of the EU by founding formal state institutions long before the EU called for them.

Finally, the early timing of formal institutional adoption is critical. Early institutions enhance the opposition's ability to constrain government action, by providing a clear standard of behavior and by serving as another check on potential state exploitation. Moreover, when institutions are established concurrently with their regulatory domains, they can function far more effectively. Formal institutions can then limit discretion before it blooms – otherwise, as the case of state administration in the next chapter shows, once unregulated and unmonitored use of state resources takes root, it becomes extremely difficult to extirpate.

[178] Schamis 2002, p. 169.

4

The Expansion of State Administration

PATRONAGE OR EXPLOITATION?

> Bureaucracy is not an obstacle to democracy but an inevitable complement to it.
>
> Joseph Schumpeter, *Capitalism, Socialism, and Democracy*

A striking aspect of post-communist state exploitation is the discretionary expansion of state administration: the unregulated and unmonitored growth in the number of those employed in the central state ministries, regulatory and tax agencies, social security administration, and their territorial offices. At the same time, we also see considerable variation among the post-communist democracies in the fifteen years after the collapse of communism, as Table 4.1 shows. The average annual growth rates ranged from .49 percent (Hungary) to 7.5 percent (Latvia). State administration as a share of total employment in 2004 represented anywhere from roughly one and a half of 1989 levels (Estonia and Hungary) to more than doubling (Lithuania, Poland, Slovenia) and even quadrupling (Bulgaria, the Czech Republic, Latvia.)[1] Both the absolute numbers of state administration employees, and their share of total employment grew considerably after the communist collapse.

Yet the mechanisms of this expansion, and the forces that drive it, defy the prevailing expectations that either classic patronage or the functional deficits of the state were behind post-communist state growth. Political

---

[1] For comparison, during its sustained expansion under American occupation from 1945–52, the Japanese state administration expanded by 84 percent. Pempel, T. J. 2000. *Regime Shift: Comparative Dynamics of the Japanese Political Economy.* Ithaca: Cornell University Press. During a comparable seven-year period after 1989, the Czech state administration expanded 120 percent, the Slovak 149 percent, and the Latvian 200 percent.

Table 4.1. *Annual Growth Rate in State Administration Employment, 1990–2004*

Country	1990 State Administration Employees	2004 State Administration Employees	% Change, Absolute Numbers	% Change, Share of Employed	Average Annual Growth Rate
Hungary	297,900	318,200	107	167	.49
	5.8% of total employed	9.7%			
Estonia	32,000	37,100	116	149	1.14
	3.9% of total employed	5.8%			
Slovenia	26,776	49,932	186	210	5.07
	2.9% of total employed	6.1%			
Lithuania	49,900 (1992)	82,400	165	211	4.55
	2.7% of total employed	5.7%			
Poland	260,700	535,100	205	244	5.02
	1.6% of total employed	3.9%			
Czech R.	91,729	205,800	225	400	5.70
	1.7% of total employed	6.8%			
Slovakia	32,833	83,500	263	300	7.57
	1.4% of total employed	4.2%			
Bulgaria	49,364	118,186	239	431	5.95
	1.3% of total employed	5.6%			
Latvia	21,000	69,000	329	467	7.54
	1.5% of total employed	7.0%			

parties expanded the state administration by hiring their allies, founding new quasistate institutions, and increasing the budgets of these agencies. Their aim, however, was increasing access to state resources rather than building electoral support. Accordingly, they attempted to expand the regulatory domains under their control and the discretionary budgets available instead of rewarding loyal supporters with jobs in the state sector. Parties both farmed out administrative hiring to allied elites and set up a slew of quasistate agencies that allowed them to govern and to seek state resources while bypassing formal legislative and executive channels. The growth in state administration employment thus indicates pervasive discretionary hiring.[2]

After examining the variation in discretionary (unmonitored and unregulated) state expansion, this chapter examines its mechanisms. Classic patronage mechanisms are not the main drivers of either the state expansion or

[2] As Meyer-Sahling 2006 argues, the growth of state administration itself is not a direct measure of patronage or other practices, unless we take into account the *mechanism* of this expansion.

the observed variation, and functional shortcomings or societal demands do not explain the differences. Instead, the two main mechanisms of exploitation here are hiring by proxy and creating new quasistate entities. As an in-depth analysis of the Polish and Czech cases shows, robust competition could curtail these expansionary strategies – and limit party discretion.

The Expansion of Post-Communist State Administration

In examining post-communist state growth, the first distinction to make is between the factors responsible for the shared "baseline" growth we observe across *all* countries and those that explain the *variation* in the expansion of state administrative employment.

The communist era left behind state administrations that were vulnerable to discretionary hiring. No neat frontier existed between the nominally parallel structures of the communist party and the state.[3] The communist party filled many of the functions executed by bureaucrats and state institutions in industrialized democracies. These included regulatory oversight, economic management and control of state-owned enterprises, and resolution of policy alternatives. As all too many of its unfortunate clients would attest, this was among the least efficient of communist state domains. Moreover, while the fused party-state was a bloated and inefficient administrative structure, the core administrative corps was small by OECD standards. State administration itself comprised only 1.5 percent of total employment by 1990, compared to nearly 5 percent found in advanced industrial democracies.[4]

The baseline expansion in state administration employment was thus partly a way of overcoming these deficits. As a result, while employment in state administration contracted worldwide in the 1980s and 1990s,[5] it has expanded both in absolute size and in its share of employment in East

---

[3] Fainsod, Merle. 1963. *Bureaucracy and Modernization*. Stanford: Stanford University Press; idem. 1953. *How Russia Is Ruled*. Cambridge: Harvard University Press; Hough, Jerry, and Fainsod, Merle. 1979. *How the Soviet Union Is Governed*. Cambridge: Harvard University Press; Friedrich, Carl, and Brzezinski, Zbigniew. 1956. *Totalitarian Dictatorship and Autocracy*. Cambridge: Harvard University Press; Bielasiak, Jack. 1983. "The Party: Permanent Crisis," in Brumberg, Abraham, ed. *Poland: Genesis of a Revolution*. New York: Vintage Books, p. 20.

[4] In another example, Russian state administration employment comprised 1.2 percent of total employment. See Brym, Robert, and Gimpelson, Vladimir. 2004. "The Size, Composition, and Dynamics of the Russian State Bureaucracy in the 1990s," *Slavic Review*, 63, 1: 90–112.

[5] Schavio-Campo, Salvatore, do Tommaso, G., and Mukherjee, A. 1997b. "An International Statistical Survey of Government Employment and Wages." World Bank Policy Research Working Paper No. 1806.

Central Europe. As noted earlier, state administration consists of central and territorial offices of the national state: the employees of the ministries, regulatory and fiscal agencies, social security and labor office administration, and their territorial branches. The category of state administration employment *excludes* employees in state health care, education, and armed forces. These are summarized in the next section in Table 4.2, but are not included here since many of these jobs were moved into the private sector.[6]

However, there are also considerable differences in both the *rates of growth* in state administration employment and the *increase* in state administration employment. Both are indicators of the expansionary forces at work, since they take into account different (employed) population sizes. As Table 4.1 shows, the variation ranges from the Hungarian state administration, which barely expanded at an average annual growth rate of .5 percent, to the burgeoning Latvian and Slovak states, which grew over fifteen times as quickly, with annual growth rates over 7.5 percent. By 2004, within fifteen years of the collapse of communism, we once again see two clear and distinct clusters, with Hungary, Estonia, Slovenia, Lithuania and Poland experiencing lower rates of growth than the Czech Republic, Slovakia, Bulgaria, and Latvia. Similarly, as Figure 4.1 shows, the increase in state administration employment as a share of total employment after 1989 ranged from 167 percent in Estonia to 467 percent in Latvia.

Competing Explanations

Three main explanations for the variation in state expansion have emerged: the formation and maintenance of patronage and clientelism, the functional needs created by the shortcomings in the communist state, and societal demands for state employment. All are plausible, yet, as we will see, none adequately explains the variation.

Patronage and clientelism have been held responsible for much of the bloat in state employment in other democracies.[7] Not surprisingly, then, the

---

[6] This coding avoids either excluding areas of party hiring within the state or including such a broad set of institutions that "state administration" is no longer a useful category. Appendix B discusses the technical issues involved in collecting the data on state administration employment, its comparability, and its accuracy. See O'Dwyer, Conor. 2003. "Expanding the Post-Communist State? A Theory and Some Empirical Evidence." Paper presented at the Annual Convention of the American Association for the Advancement of Slavic Studies (AAASS), Toronto, Canada.

[7] O'Dwyer 2004; Piattoni 2001, p. 6; Chandra 2004.

136

Table 4.2. *Changes in State Employment, in Thousands of Employees and Percentages, 1990–2004*

Country	Health Care (N)	Educational System (M)	Other Public and Social Welfare (O)	State Administration (L)	Non-L Change in Employment	1990–2004 Change in Overall State Employment
Hungary	236 → 241 102%	312 → 318 102%	194 → 162 84%	298 → 318 107%	97%	99%
Estonia	50 → 35 70%	49 → 55 112%	30 → 27 90%	32 → 37 116%	91%	96%
Slovenia 1992–2004	56 → 47 84%	52 → 55 106%	n/a → 26.2	27 → 50 186%	94%	113%
Lithuania 1992–2004	103→ 90 87%	138 → 132 96%	117 → 47 40%	50 → 82 165%	75%	69%
Poland	901→ 703 78%	1,100 → 975 89%	427 → 366 86%	261 → 535 205%	84%	96%
Czech R.	280 → 282 101%	317 → 309 97%	204 →185 91%	92 → 206 225%	97%	110%
Slovakia 1991–2003	123 → 155 126%	183 → 160 87%	62 → 78 126%	33 → 84 263%	107%	120%
Bulgaria	221→ 132 60%	272 → 198 73%	16 → 68 425%	49 → 118 239%	79%	93%
Latvia	68 → 60 88%	101 → 88 87%	83 → 53 64%	21 → 69 329%	51%	99%

Note: Unless otherwise noted, 1990 figures → 2004 figures.
Source: Statistical offices and yearbooks.

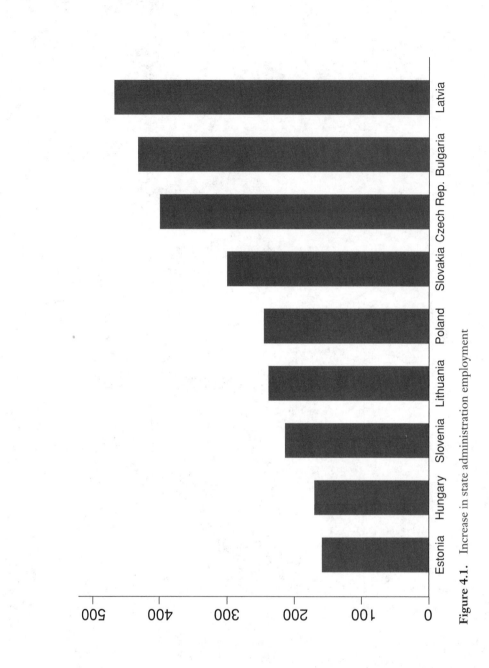

Figure 4.1. Increase in state administration employment

vulnerabilities of the post-communist state led several analyses to conclude that the "opportunities for patronage were bountiful"[8] in post-communist East Central Europe. After all, surveys of state officials in the region show that political influence in the administration is pervasive: An astonishing 100 percent of respondents in the Czech Republic, Estonia, Lithuania, and Poland consider their administration politicized.[9] Moreover, given the porousness of the post-communist state, and the timing of suffrage before civil service reforms, existing accounts predict widespread patronage.[10]

If the patronage account is correct, we should see governing parties attempt to buy votes by targeting narrow constituencies for the particularistic provision of goods such as jobs, infrastructure projects, or general government expenditures. The mechanism of state expansion would then consist of political parties meeting the increasing demand for government jobs and goods in exchange for continued support of the incumbents. The result has typically been growth over time both in the share of government expenditures in the GDP, and in the overall public employment – most particularly, in the welfare state sectors of health, education, and so on, since the government largely controls their expenditures and hiring.[11]

Yet in the post-communist democracies, neither the outcomes nor the mechanisms associated with clientelism are visible. We do not observe systematic growth in either the welfare state employment or in government expenditures as a share of GDP. As Table 4.2 shows, in all the cases under consideration, government employment in the welfare state did not expand nearly as much as in state administration. Health care, educational systems, and other state services have been the traditional target of patronage hiring; in post-communist states, however, they have *shrunk*, thanks to employee departures and the increasing privatization of these sectors.

---

[8] O'Dwyer 2002; Goetz, Klaus H. 2001. "Making Sense of Post-Communist Central Administration: Modernization, Europeanization or Latinization?" *Journal of European Public Policy*, 8, 6 (December): 1032–51, p. 1043. See also Piattoni 2001; Chandra 2004; O'Dwyer, Conor. 2004. "Runaway State Building: How Political Parties Shape States in Postcommunist Eastern Europe," *World Politics*: 520–53.

[9] King, Roswitha. 2003. "Conversations with Civil Servants: Interview Results from Estonia, Lithuania, Czech Republic and Poland." Manuscript, University of Latvia, Riga.

[10] Shefter 1994; Perkins 1996.

[11] Calvo, Ernesto, and Murillo, Maria Victoria. 2004. "Who Delivers? Partisan Clients in the Argentine Electoral Market," *American Journal of Political Science*, 48 (4 October): Gimpelson, Vladimir, and Treisman, Daniel. 2002. "Fiscal Games and Public Employment," *World Politics*, 54: 145–83; 742–57. Robinson, James, and Verdier, Therry. 2002. "The Political Economy of Clientelism." Centre for Economic Policy Discussion Paper Series No. 3205.

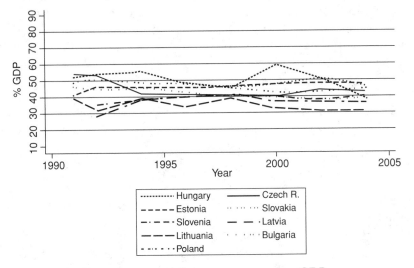

Figure 4.2. Government expenditures as percentages or GDP
Note: OECD average, 1996: 48.0 percent.
Sources: 1991–8 data: EBRD. 1999. *10 Years of Transition. Transition Report 1999.*
London: EBRD; 2000–4 data: EBRD 2005. *EBRD Transition Report Update, May
2005.* London: EBRD; OECD average: OECD. 1997. *OECD Economic Outlook,
1997.*

Moreover, if clientelism took off in these polities, we would expect
greater state spending. Yet there was no systematic increase in government expenditures after 1989, as Figure 4.2 shows. Instead, all these polities
hover around the OECD average of 48 percent of GDP spent on government expenditures. This is not to say that parties did not *attempt* to target
provision: Populist parties such as the Slovak HZDS, the Polish PSL, and
the Hungarian Fidesz each tried to reward loyal local governments with
additional (and significant) spending. But these efforts were too short-lived
and localized to account for the growth of national state administrations.
They also ran into an organizational difficulty: The distribution of benefits
took place in national parliaments, but the voters whose support might have
been bought and monitored were on the local level, isolated from national
party politics by lack of party candidates and organizations.

Parties had neither the incentive nor the capacity to engage in individual
patronage or clientelism on a grand scale. For parties to exchange individual
benefits for public support effectively, it is not enough to have control over
state resources and their distribution. Three conditions have been found to

make patronage possible. First, voters rely on the state for jobs.[12] Second, voters can make credible promises to support the party, and the party has to offer an equally credible promise to hire supporters.[13] Third, parties have the organizations to deliver the goods, so they can target individuals and individual constituencies, and the capacity to monitor the voters, so that they can identify potential defectors and target patronage benefits.

Yet few of these conditions held in the post-communist context. First, economies were increasingly privatized. Even where there was high unemployment, the opportunities within the state sector were diminishing. In fact, two of the countries where we see higher growth rates in administration employment, Latvia and the Czech Republic, were widely seen as leaders of privatization efforts, having privatized about 67 percent and 80 percent of their economies by 1997, respectively.[14] The median share of state employment in total employment was 42 percent in the region by the mid-1990s, with Slovakia and Bulgaria as two notable exceptions at 68 percent and 65 percent respectively.[15] State employment decreased subsequently.

Second, party instability across the region made it difficult for voters and parties to engage in particularistic contracts. Offering jobs to supporters, rather than extracting resources directly, was both inefficient and implausible. For one thing, high volatility and fragmentation made party disappearance all too likely a prospect.[16] If it was doubtful that a given party would be around to receive the electoral support or continue to distribute the goods, the incentives for patronage were considerably dampened for both voters and political elites. It was also unclear that passing particularist measures for the benefit of narrow constituencies would be an effective strategy of obtaining lasting electoral support. Parties had few guarantees that the beneficiaries of such measures, such as farm price supports or industrial tariffs, would respond with sustained support.

Nascent post-communist political parties needed funding more than they needed loyal party workers. Electoral campaigns were expensive,

---

[12] Chandra 2004.
[13] Robinson and Verdier 2002.
[14] Freedom House. 1998. *Nations in Transit*, Washington Freedom House.
[15] Frydman et al. 1998, p. 2.
[16] Of course, this coordination problem could be solved: If enough voters are bound to a party, its electoral fortunes will be more predictable. However, there were few factors that could resolve the coordination problem: Time horizons were short, no salient points existed, and side payments were either unavailable or contingent on resolving the coordination problem.

farmed out to international media advisers, and reliant on TV advertising, huge billboards, and radio commercials. The daily work of the party was concentrated in the parliamentary offices of the MPs. National party candidates traveled to local voter meetings, but there was little individual mobilization or canvassing.

Finally, the organizational prerequisites were missing.[17] Few post-communist parties had the organizational capacity to deliver and monitor clientelistic contracts. As already noted, outside of central parliamentary offices, where both activists and offices were maintained through parliamentary stipends, most political parties had few well-developed organizations or activist networks. Nor is there evidence of patronage at the local level: In most post-communist democracies, less than half the local government seats were captured by party-affiliated candidates, as Figure 4.3 shows.[18] If party clientelist networks were developing, we should see a rise in the number of local candidates affiliated with parties – but there was no increase over time in any of the countries.

Party loyalists were too scarce. For example, even as Polish media reports claimed that over 200,000 jobs in state administration could be filled by political parties in early 2001,[19] the total membership of Polish parliamentary parties at the time was about 195,000.[20] Even if the patronage jobs would not be delivered to members alone but more broadly to supporters, parties had limited ability to do so. Few positions in the national administration were actually nominated directly by political parties. For example, even critics estimate that the upper boundary of administrative positions named by Polish parties reached 1.8 –2.4 percent, while in Slovakia, the estimates range from 3.6–5 percent.[21] No more than 10 percent of respondents across

[17] Perkins 1996; Piattoni 2000.

[18] The high initial rates of party affiliation are the result of mass opposition movements, such as the Czech Civic Forum, the Slovak Public Against Violence, or the Polish Solidarity, running en masse against the communist incumbents.

[19] *Wprost*, 5 August 2001. See also Szczerbak, Aleks. 2006. "State Party Funding and Patronage in Post 1989 Poland," *Journal or Communist Studies and Transition Political*, 22, 3 (September): 298–319.

[20] SDL had about 75,000 members at the time, UW 16,000, and PSL 100,000. PO was not yet founded and Samoobrona was not in parliament. The membership of the LPR was negligible, and the governing AWS had no formal party membership, but did claim 2 million unionists as automatic members.

[21] These figures assume 3,200 Polish state officials and 4,000 Slovak ones as subject to party nominations and subsequent purges. See Project Syndicate. 1995. "Marching Backwards: Slovakia's Counterrevolution" (October). Available at http://project-syndicate.org/surveys/marching_bac.php4, accessed 10 September, 2004. Kevin Krause estimates that as many as

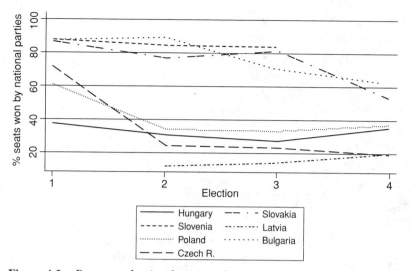

Figure 4.3. Presence of national parties in local elections: mandates won by political party candidates (not independent and not local committees)
Source: Electoral commissions; Ágh, Attila, and Kurán, Sándor. 1996. "'Parliaments' and 'Organized Interests' in Civil Society: Local Government Legislation and Elections in Hungary (1990–1995)," in Ágh, Attila, and Ilonszki, Gabriella, eds. *Parliaments and Organized Interests: The Second Steps.* Budapest: Hungarian Centre for Democracy Studies; Baldersheim et al. 1996; Horváth, Tamás, ed. 2000. *Decentralization: Experiments and Reforms.* Budapest: Open Society Institute; Swaniewicz, Pawel, ed. 2004. *Consolidation or Fragmentation? The Size of Local Governments in Central and Eastern Europe.* Budapest: Open Society Institute.

the region experienced political party affiliation as essential for obtaining a job in the state sector, even in the more exploited states of Bulgaria or Latvia (see Table 4.3 and Appendix C for full methodology). If anything, as we will see, parties relied on expanding quasistate institutions rather than hiring within existing administration standards.[22] Finally, state administration growth and patronage are not logically linked: Politicians can selectively deliver benefits outside of the state administration (via political party organizations, for example[23]) without the disbursement of patronage jobs.

---

eight hundred officials out of 22,000 were affected in late 1994 and 1995, during the height of the Mečiar purges. Krause, Kevin Deegan. 2006. *Elected Affinities.* Stanford: Stanford University Press.

[22] See Kopecký 2006, p. 268.

[23] For example, the Italian state grew from 1946 to 1958 by one hundred thousand people. In a country of 25 million, "adding 100,000 to the state bureaucracy would hardly be enough for a party to gain more seats at an election. However, since the bureaucracy distributed

Table 4.3. *Usefulness of Party Affiliation in Obtaining State Jobs: Survey Results*

	Party Affiliation Is *Useless* for Obtaining State Job – %	Party Affiliation Is *Essential* for Obtaining State Job – %
Poland	29.0	5.0
Czech R.	20.1	1.6
Slovakia	9.8	3.7
Bulgaria	19.5	2.3
Latvia	18.5	9.7

Source: Surveys conducted by TNS-OBOP, IVVM, FOCUS, GALLUP-Bulgaria, and TNS-Latvia, summers of 2003 and 2004, commissioned by the author. For anchoring vignettes that were used to provide interpersonal comparability, see Appendix B. Data were subjected to Chopit analysis, controlling for age, gender, urbanity, and education level.

Since no *new* party had the requisite organizational reach, the one group of actors who could use patronage strategies were communist-era parties that had retained their organizational networks.[24] These included the Bulgarian BSP, the Romanian PDSR, and the Polish PSL. Some were able to deliver localized benefits, thanks to their surviving organizational networks and virtual monopolies on certain budget sectors. Yet even here the links were fragile; for example, the Polish Peasants' Party (Polskie Stronnictwo Ludowe, PSL), an unreconstructed communist satellite party, lost many local affiliates after its coalition partner curtailed its access to state resources. As a result, even established parties with extensive organizations did not sustain classic patronage.[25]

Strong party organizations, on the other hand, were not needed for discretionary elite hirings and firings, or for the founding of new state institutions. If anything, the familiar causal arrows of organizational strength promoting electoral success are reversed: Electoral success let post-communist

allegedly universal resources, such as social security benefits, only at its discretion, politicians had ample opportunity to take the middleman's role, brokering the exchange of state resources for party favors." Warner, Carolyn. 2001. "Mass Parties and Clientelism: France and Italy," in Piattoni 2001, p. 130.

[24] Note that this is an argument about communist successor organization, not about its ideology; the latter does not predict organizational investments. Kitschelt, Herbert. 2001. "Divergent Paths of Postcommunist Democracies," in Diamond, Larry, and Gunther, Richard. *Political Parties and Democracy*. Baltimore: Johns Hopkins Press, p. 304.

[25] O'Dwyer 2004 argues that the Slovak HZDS was a patronage party by dint of its dominance and the weakness of the opposition. The ODS, however, also won elections twice, had a stable governing coalition (for lack of alternatives) in parliament, and also faced a weak opposition, yet by O'Dwyer's account, the party did not build patronage structures. The connection between dominance and patronage strategies is thus unclear.

democratic parties strengthen their organizations, since it increased party access to state resources, and delivered state funding based on their seat share. For example, the membership of the Czech ODS peaked during its stay in office, at over 22,000 in 1995, only to drop by nearly a third to 16,000 once the party was forced out of government in 1998.

Functional Explanations

If patronage does not explain state expansion, more functional explanations focus on administrative shortcomings and the exigencies of nation building. Post-communist growth thus might result from the enormous personnel and institutional deficits of the communist state. However, there is little evidence that the *variation* in expansion was motivated by these shortcomings, or conversely, accompanied by increased effectiveness or regulation. Post-communist states that expanded their state administration employment have not collected taxes more effectively or provided better services.[26] In fact, state administration employment grew the least in Hungary, where the state was widely seen as effective and autonomous even under communism.[27] The equally efficient Slovenian and Estonian states remained even smaller.

Nor is the variation explained by the needs of nation building.[28] Both newly independent and "old" states expanded. Some new states (Latvia and Slovakia) grew far more than others (Slovenia and Estonia). Among the newly independent states in the sample, Czechoslovakia peacefully split into its constituent republics in January 1993, while Estonia, Latvia, Lithuania, and Slovenia gained independence from the Soviet Union and Yugoslavia, respectively, in 1991. Yet Estonia and Slovenia's rates of growth are considerably lower than the other newly independent countries', suggesting that independence is not a sufficient condition for higher rates of growth, as Table 4.1 shows. Just as importantly, if new independence itself gives rise to state administration growth, we would expect the *rate* of state employment growth to rise after independence. Yet the split of Czechoslovakia in 1993 did not change the rates of expansion, either before or after independence.

---

[26] Grzymała-Busse 2003.

[27] Szoboszlai 1985a; Kaminski. 1992. For example, in 1981, 44 percent of the party and 78 percent of the state cadres had a college education. In 1989, 78 percent of the party and 93 percent of the state cadres had a college education. See Gazsó, Ferenc. 1992. "Cadre Bureaucracy and the Intelligentsia," *Journal of Communist Studies* (September): 76–90.

[28] Scott, James. 1972. *Comparative Political Corruption*. Englewood Cliffs, Prentice Hall.

Similarly, Estonian state administration actually slowed down its growth immediately after independence, growing by only .65 percent from 1990 to 1992, against an average yearly growth in Estonian state administration of 1.14 percent. Slovenia is the only case where the greatest growth came in 1991–3, shortly after the republic gained independence and the communist regime collapsed.

Societal Demands

If neither patronage nor functional needs explain administrative expansion, government growth may also be a function of demand from specific sectors of society, such as socioeconomic classes, specific voter constituencies, bureaucrats eager to expand their ranks, or administrative regions. In Allan Meltzer and Scott Richard's median-voter model, decisive voters are the force that translates voter preferences into bigger government.[29] In turn, the growth of a middle class broadens the political base that stands to benefit from redistribution and expanded government programs, leading both to growth in government expenditures and associated growth in state administration.[30] The propensity of specific constituencies to demand particularistic benefits varies with their socioeconomic characteristics: Impoverished voters are more likely to take lower-paying state jobs, and parties can gain more voters from disbursing many low-paid jobs rather than a few high-paying ones.[31] Thus, the state will expand as the middle class does, and parties targeting poorer voters stand to benefit especially from patronage tactics.

Yet there is little evidence that such demands led to expanded post-communist state administration employment. Redistributive issues certainly assumed enormous importance across the region.[32] However, parties

---

[29] Meltzer, Allan H., and Richard, Scott F. 1981. "Rational Theory of the Size of Government," *Journal of Political Economy*, 89, 5: 914–27.

[30] Peltzman, Sam. 1998. *Political Participation and Government Regulation*. Chicago: University of Chicago Press.

[31] Robinson and Verdier 2002; Calvo and Murillo 2004; Kitschelt 2000. Torbin Iversen and Anne Wren argue that party ideology may account for different preferences regarding public employment; however, given the overwhelming elite consensus on the need for reform and the constraints of international financial institutions, we see no change in 1998 growth rates across government coalitions of different ideological stripes. Irersen, Torbin, and Wren, Anne. 1998. "Equality, Employment, and Budgetary Restraint. *World Politics*, 50, 4: 507–46.

[32] Kitschelt et al. 1999.

rarely promised to expand state spending, and few would have been able to do so given the enormous pressure for liberal market reform emanating from international financial institutions in the early 1990s. Some parties did attempt to target their constituencies with particularistic benefits, most notably the PSL in Poland, the HZDS in Slovakia, and the Smallholders' Party in Hungary. However, these parties focused on targeting financial transfers and subsidies to their supporters rather than government jobs.

Alternatively, a predatory bureaucracy itself may cause state administration employment to expand.[33] In one post-communist example, regional governors in the Russian federation were said to use public employment to build local support, and to extract resources from the center. In this view, the regional governments eventually accumulated considerable wage arrears, but avoided punishment by shifting the blame onto the central government and blackmailing it into providing more resources for fear for public unrest and strikes.[34] Yet no matter how predatory, the bureaucracy needs legislative cooperation (or budgetary discretion) to expand. We do not see any evidence of successful regional demands in the cases under consideration, not least because they were all unitary governments. Nor is the mechanism of state expansion via blackmail clear: Why would the central government bail out regional politicians? If the electoral futures of the center are linked to the regions, presumably the center would exercise greater control over expenditures in the first place. If center–region ties are so loose as to allow such regional discretion, then it is unclear how regional governors can shift the blame to the center.[35]

State Expansion: Discretion and Privatization

Instead, the state grew as governing parties created new state institutions and new outposts of party discretion within existing institutions. Exploitation here took the form both of discretionary hiring (via the placement of elites allied to parties in positions where they could hire and expand a given

---

[33] Terry Moe and Gerry Miller augmented this model by including government legislators as joint decision makers with the bureaucracy, answering Peltzman's (1998) criticism that in the Niskanen model, politician have incentives to restrain the bureaucracy since they do not gain from its expansion. See Moe, Terry, and Miller, Gary. 1983. "Bureaucrats, Legislators, and the Size of Government," *American Political Science Review*, 77: 297–323.

[34] Gimpelson and Treisman 2002.

[35] Another potential problem with the analysis is that the figures for employment in health, education, and similar fields do not distinguish between public and private employees.

government agency or ministry) and of founding new state institutions that maximized discretion, such as funds administered outside of the budget and agencies functioning outside of parliamentary purview. The goal was expanding control over state resources rather than buying electoral support, and the beneficiaries were party elites rather than party supporters.[36]

The expansion of state administration was thus an aspect of state exploitation rather than a fulfillment of functional needs or popular demands for clientelism. State administration expanded in the process of gaining control over state resources, not as a result of patronage: "[W]here there are lots of state assets to be distributed ... access to government jobs – the traditional form of patronage – was secondary to such opportunities."[37] State assets – and especially the proceeds of their privatization – were a tempting and lucrative proposition. Parties tried to ensure their survival by capturing the centers of economic power, gaining access to the enormous holdings of the state now under the purview of the ministries of finance, privatization, and transport and the various privatization agencies.

Robust competition braked these mechanisms of state administration growth. As one domestic critic argued, "leading politicians have no interest in following or limiting the growth of bureaucracy, because this would decrease their field of action ... so long as any coalition decides about the filling of places in state administrations on the basis of political criteria, excessive exploitation is mitigated only by the mutual competition of coalition (or opposition) parties."[38]

First, as we saw in the last chapter, robust competition led to the earlier imposition of formal institutions of monitoring and oversight, including civil service laws, fiscal reforms, and transparency laws that dismantled quasistate agencies and funds. Second, robust competition precluded any one party's monopoly on state resources. Criticism led parties to moderate their actions, for fear of electoral backlash (and post-communist parties tended to be especially vulnerable, since they lacked alternative sources of voter support, such as extensive organizations). Opposition also tended to

---

[36] Of course, once control is gained over state resources, it then can be used to develop patronage – but given the other difficulties in developing the requisite party organizations, we see few such attempts in post-communist East Central Europe. See Müller, Wolfgang. 2006. "Party Patronage and Party Colonization of the State," *Handbook of Party Politics*. Katz, Richard, and Crotty, William, eds. London: Sage, pp. 189–95.

[37] Sajo 1998a.

[38] Novotný, Vít. 1999. "Deset lat po listopadu: Omezme moc české politické oligarchie," *Britské Listy*, 29 November.

constrain the accumulation of posts by any one party, exchanging rather than increasing the number of employees. It did so by increasing the likelihood of turnover in office, which prompted cycles of hiring and purging that lowered the overall expansion over time. Finally, informal power-sharing norms developed, so that no one party could monopolize seats on supervisory boards or access to privatization resources.

If parties engaged in opportunistic reconstruction of the state that resulted in exploitation rather than patronage, we should see the expansion of the state occur even when the incumbents were unable to deliver patronage, under governments led by parties with weak organizations and a small corps of activists. Growth should occur in these areas where political parties move the protest access and face the feeblest constraints. If robust competition limits exploitation, then we should see not only lower overall rates of state expansion but the earlier implementation of civil service laws – and a drop in growth rates once these laws are in place. Robust competition should also lead parties to decrease, rather than to build, the number and scope of quasistate institutions and extrabudgetary funds.

How, then, did parties expand the state administration to their own benefit? The next two subsections examine the two main strategies: discretionary hiring and the founding of quasistate institutions and extrabudgetary funds and agencies. These served twin purposes: They carried out market and democratic reforms, and they expanded party access to the state.

Discretionary Hiring

Post-communist political parties relied on discretionary hiring, unmonitored and unregulated by formal institutions. In the absence of civil service regulations, government ministries (headed by political party representatives) hired at will. Since "each ministry wants its own network of offices and institutions," agencies and employment positions proliferated.[39] Immediately after the communist collapse, governments avoided layoffs in the state sector.[40] Subsequently, industrial branch ministries (industries and industrial sectors had corresponding government ministries) were consolidated

---

[39] PHARE and NVF. 1998. "An Analysis of Public Administration of the Czech Republic." Summary report. (September). Prague.

[40] Amsden, Alice, Jacek Kochanowicz, and Lance Taylor. *The Market Meets Its Match*. Cambridge, Harvard University Press, 1994, p. 192; Rice 1992, p. 119.

and reduced in number, but their employees were simply shifted to new jobs in the enterprises of their corresponding sector. This was a defensive reaction by ministries fighting for survival during a time of flux and consolidation of government cabinets.

Parties attempted to staff the *managerial* positions in the ministries – and then gave their affiliated elites discretion to hire ever-increasing numbers. Expansion of these institutions would justify greater state financing, offer insurance against the weakening of a ministry's cabinet role, and make it harder to audit and observe the actions of the state agencies involved. Given the difficulties in ensuring that bureaucratic agents left over from the communist era were fulfilling their duties, party-nominated managers then hired whom they wished to ensure a loyal staff.[41]

Across the cases discussed, no civil service laws or other legislation initially existed to limit these practices, or to provide a pool of qualified civil servants, whose expertise and training were the basis for their hiring. In a few cases, as in Hungary in 1992 or Slovenia in 1993, these laws were established very quickly. Subsequently, even if "no government has an interest in the creation of a civil service, because the natural desire of the governing is to preserve the status quo, which allows them to pick friendly officials, since each team seeks political loyalty first and foremost,"[42] fear of replacement led some parties to promote civil service laws in an attempt to prevent other parties from packing the administration.

Where they faced a weak opposition, governing parties found it to their advantage to leave state hiring unregulated, allowing ministries and state offices to hire freely. As a critic of the Czech state argued, "leading politicians have no interest in following or limiting the growth of bureaucracy, because this would decrease their field of action."[43] Further opportunity came in the initial chaos of the transition, and the neglect of the state. Immediately after the collapse of communist regimes in 1989, "the new political elites were, at least initially, unable to introduce reforms in the civil service. Given their concentration on political problems and the everyday details of government, they were probably not even conscious of the scope of the necessary changes."[44] Consequently, civil service laws were often delayed, staffing ceilings did not exist within the ministries and state

---

[41] *Respekt*, "Nenápadný půvab byrokracie," 10 May 1993.
[42] Paradowska, Janina. 1998. "Kierowca z nomenklatury," *Polityka*, 31 October, p. 27.
[43] Novotný 1999.
[44] Amsden et al. 1994, p. 192.

offices, and there were no meritocratic competitions for most jobs in state sectors.[45]

Political parties obtained several benefits from discretionary hiring and expansion in the state administration. First, these gave the parties direct access to state resources that could be used for a variety of ends, including national media campaigns and individual elite enrichment. The more highly placed allies they had in the ministries and in the agencies, the more access they had to privatization contracts and decisions. Such parties were then more attractive as targets of bribes (the Czech ODS) and more powerful as rent seekers (the Latvian LC).

Control meant both resources and decision-making power. The bigger a given ministry or agency, the greater its budget – and presumably, the discretionary funds available to the party that controlled it. Not surprisingly, parties attempted to control specific domains. For example, in both Poland and in Hungary, peasants' parties obtained the ministry of agriculture when in a coalition government, and used these as launching pads to create agricultural funds, banks, and quasipublic agencies. Other cases included the Czech ODA and the Finance Ministry, or the Latvian LC and the Ministry of Transport. Here, the state administration expanded to increase party control over a ministry and to increase its budget.

Second, political parties also wanted a "loyal" administration, one that would fulfill their directives. This consideration was especially important if parties perceived that the bureaucracy would resist or oppose policies favoring the party. All the new democratic parties in power feared a communist fifth column in the bureaucracy, slowly subverting and undermining the implementation of the new reform projects. In other cases, parties simply feared a skeptical bureaucracy, as the HZDS did in Slovakia. This was all the more so since higher-level civil servants "very often had a high degree of freedom to decide on the allocation of public funding."[46]

Finally, these strategies of awarding allied elites with discretion over hiring and control over new agencies were simply more efficient than attempting to establish vertical patron–client linkages as a way of ensuring party

---

[45] See SIGMA. 2002a. "Bulgaria: Public Service and the Administrative Framework: Assessment 2002"; idem. 2002b. "Czech Republic: Public Service and the Administrative Framework: Assessment 2002"; idem. 2002c. "Latvia: Public Service and the Administrative Framework: Assessment 2002"; idem. 2002d. "Slovakia: Public Service and the Administrative Framework: Assessment 2002."

[46] Bercík, Peter, and Nemec, Juraj. 1999. "The Civil Service System of the Slovak Republic," in Verheijen, 1999: 184–210, p. 193.

survival. They relied on existing elite networks to colonize the state administration rather than on laboriously establishing party organizations that would channel the exchange of votes for jobs. All these reasons made discretionary hiring so profitable that even when the government formally decided, as it did in the Czech Republic in 1995, to reduce staffing in state administration, there were few ways of implementing such measures.[47] Each ministry wanted its own network of offices and institutions, and simply circumvented formal government statements.[48]

Potential hires found state administrative jobs attractive for their numerous perks: access to foreign travel, illicit consulting fees, and additional salary bonuses (as high as 300 percent in Latvia.[49]) Not surprisingly, one study found that 87 percent bureaucrats listed "long-term career opportunities and job security as a principal motivator to stay in the civil service," even if "94 percent of respondents reported to be aware of replacements in civil service positions after new formation of government"[50] on the elite level.

Civil service laws at best gradually made inroads into discretionary state hiring: The existing state administration offered resistance to new regulations. Since civil service laws would be imposed on an existing and well-entrenched domain – state administrations had existed in the communist era, after all – they faced a far greater challenge than institutions that were established concurrently with the domains they were to regulate.[51] Many of the new civil service bureaus were understaffed and unable to revise the status of employees hired prior to their implementation. Such problems are not unique to the post-communist cases: the Pendleton Act in the United States was enacted in 1883, but was only enforced a quarter-century later – and organized interests still heavily influenced the state agencies. Given both the enormity of the task, and historical precedent from other countries, "civil service professionalization does not suffice to render the state autonomous of parties, legislative coalitions, and interest formations."[52]

---

[47] OECD 2001a, p. 11.

[48] PHARE and NVF 1998.

[49] Karklins, Rasma. 2002. "Typology of Post-Communist Corruption," *Problems of Post-Communism*, 49 (July/August): 22–32, p. 26.

[50] King 2003.

[51] The communist state featured few of the institutional gatekeepers that could limit state administration employment: formalized hiring procedures, civil service exams, educational or professional experience requirements, or hiring caps.

[52] Carpenter, Daniel. 2001. *The Forging of Bureaucratic Autonomy*. Princeton: Princeton University Press, p. 10. See also Zuckerman, Alan. 1979. *The Politics of Faction: Christian Democratic Rule in Italy*. New Haven: Yale University Press.

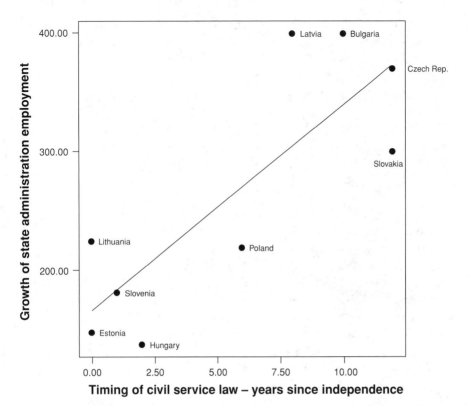

Figure 4.4. Correlation between civil service law adoption and growth of state administration (.68)

Nonetheless, where political competition created the incentives, "the idea of creating a civil service based on political impartiality and stability became increasingly attractive."[53] Where political competition was robust, the efforts to institute civil service reform were sustained as part of the larger push for formal state institutions of oversight. Parties also struck power-sharing compromises to prevent any one party from monopolizing the administration, limiting the overall accumulation of offices. Thus, as Figure 4.4 shows, civil service laws were implemented earlier where there was robust competition: in the smaller and slower-growing states of Estonia, Hungary, Lithuania, Poland, and Slovenia. And, these laws correlate

---

[53] György, Istvan. 1999. "The Civil Service System of Hungary," in Verheijen, 1999, pp. 131–58, p. 148.

negatively with the growth of the state: The average annual growth rate of expansion across the post-communist democracies was 5.92 percent prior to the introduction of civil service laws. It nearly halved once civil service laws were adopted, to 2.99 percent. Where the opposition was weaker, civil service laws were adopted later, and growth rates did not drop as precipitously.

Two caveats apply in interpreting these changes. First, these laws did more to limit hiring than to promote a meritocratic bureaucracy, given the numerous exemptions in qualification criteria.[54] Second, most civil service laws were adopted either very early on in the transition, or late in the 1990–2004 time period under consideration.[55] Comparing average growth rates before and after civil service laws is thus susceptible to an annual fluctuation throwing off the average or to other outlier effects. Nonetheless, these trends are evidence of competitive pressures to limit the discretionary expansion of the state.

The Hungarian case is an example of the import of civil service laws. The impetus for Hungarian civil service reforms emerged prior to the communist collapse, but took off only with the advent of democracy. Twenty-two different acts were passed between 1989 and 1992, and parliament enacted the first comprehensive civil service law in the region in 1992.[56] This law effectively established the independence of the state administration system from political parties. From the start, civil servants could not be party activists. More importantly, apolitical higher civil servants, such as the permanent state secretaries or municipality notaries, nominated, hired, and promoted state officials. Administrative state secretaries were hired on the basis of their technical qualifications and expertise, while political state secretaries were formal party appointments. Ministers had little leeway in hiring, except for the top political positions. As a result of these laws, the World Bank concluded, discretionary hiring was largely eliminated.[57]

---

[54] See, for example, Meyer-Sahling 2006.

[55] The early adopters were Hungary and Slovenia in 1992 and Lithuania and Estonia in 1993, and the late ones were Bulgaria in 2000, Latvia in 2001, and Czech Republic and Slovakia in 2002.

[56] György 1999, p. 132. A 2001 bill introduced competitive salaries and new ethical requirements for civil servants. For officials in sensitive positions, the refusal to file a wealth statement resulted in termination.

[57] Nunberg, Barbara. 2000. "Ready for Europe: Public Administration Reform and European Union Accession in Central and Eastern Europe." World Bank Technical Paper No. 466. Washington: World Bank, p. 274.

Political parties could nonetheless decide the top posts in the administration. Yet the 1990–4 and 1994–8 Hungarian governments did not purge the state administration: The MDF was prevented from doing so by opposition protests in 1990–1, and the MSzP by self-imposed power sharing. However, the 1998–2002 Fidesz-MPP government perceived little threat from the opposition and acted accordingly. Immediately after the 1998 election, as its key opponent, the MSzP, was busy holding a special congress and numerous meetings to analyze the reasons for its electoral defeat,[58] the new Fidesz government dismissed not only the political state secretaries but also 25 percent of the supposedly apolitical administrative state secretaries and deputy state secretaries.[59] The leaders of all 20 territorial units of the central administration had to undergo an open competition for their jobs, and coalition leaders openly declared that "certain political expectations and demands were also formulated."[60] In the end, Fidesz replaced up to 80 percent of high-ranking officials in individual ministries after 1998.[61] However, opposition leaders were able repeatedly to launch investigations into the hiring practices of the government, constraining their ability to exchange or hire new employees freely.[62] As a result, the personnel exchanges were largely limited to the ranks of political appointees rather than the administration as a whole.[63]

Where party competition was weaker, governments could more readily resist the pressures from the opposition for civil service laws or for other limits on discretionary hiring. Accordingly, in the Slovakia, the Czech Republic, Latvia, and Bulgaria, no functioning civil service laws were passed until 2001–2.

In Slovakia, discretionary hiring under Mečiar began to resemble full-fledged patronage. The HZDS government used the simple expedient of loyalty tests to retain or fire state officials. In 1995, the HZDS sent out "action fives," HZDS commissions that oversaw the purge of *okres*-level administration and its staffing with "proper people." Higher-level employees within both the state administration and the state-owned economic

---

[58] The MSzP gained absolute numbers of votes from 1994 to 1998, but lost the election.
[59] Ilonszki 2000, p. 170.
[60] Ibid., p. 170.
[61] *Budapest Sun*, 13 June 2002.
[62] Interview with Chancery Minister Elemér Kiss, *Népszabadság*, 4 June 2002.
[63] Meyer-Sahling 2006 focused on the dismissal of state secretaries as evidence or the Hungarian state's politicization – but these amounted to eighty positions within the administration.

sector had to join HZDS on pain of termination. Yet even here patronage opportunities were limited: Not only were party memberships low, but no party had more than 165 employees, making the creation and oversight of clientelistic exchanges with voters extremely difficult.[64]

Average annual growth rates approached 8 percent, and the greatest period of growth came during 1993–5, when Mečiar was consolidating his power and attempting to create an elite economic class of clients. In 1995–6, the HZDS government added administrative units at all levels in the guise of local government reform. These were stopped by the HZDS.[65] After the infamous purge of November 1994, when all heads of oversight, monitoring, and administrative bodies were summarily exchanged for HZDS loyalists, "a dominant criterion for placement in a high level job within the state administration [was] loyalty to the governing political party."[66] Under Mečiar, "management posts were, generally speaking, filled by political appointees and the freedom to recruit was at the discretion of ministers and heads of offices."[67] With no opposition to restrain it, and with a considerable degree of certainty in its own electoral prowess, the HZDS could expand the state freely in the name of "building the new Slovak nation."

Even with the arrival of the reformist of the Democratic Coalition (Slovenska Demokraticka Koalície, SDK) government in Slovakia in 1998, the distribution of posts continued, but now with parity for all the parties involved. The SDK first replaced all seventy-nine local (*okresní*) leaders and all eight regional (*krajské*) leaders loyal to the HZDS coalitions. It then distributed positions in state enterprises, banks, the oil sector, and insurance.[68] However, even if there were no formal constraints on expansionary dynamics (the ministries could still hire at will), the end of unopposed HZDS dominance after 1998 led to power sharing and a diffusion of such appointments. No party could monopolize the staffing of the state administration, and extensive intracoalition negotiations preceded each new nomination.

---

[64] The numbers ranged from 136 to 166 for HZDS, with 72,000 members, to 3 for SDK, with 114 members. See Malcická, Lenka. 2001. "Vybrané aspekty financovania politických strán a hnutí v SR." Manuscript, Bratislava, Slovakia, available at http://politika.host.sk/prispevky/prispevok_malcicka_financovaniestran.htm, accessed 21 June.

[65] Rybář, Marek. 2006. "Powered by the State: The Role of Public Resources in Party-Building in Slovakia." *Journal of Communist Studies and Transition Politics*, 22, 3: 320–40.

[66] Bercík and Nemec. 1999, p. 193; Mesežnikov 1997, p. 45.

[67] SIGMA 2002d, p. 1.

[68] "Kto jest bez viny, nech hodí kamenom [Let him who is without fault cast the stone]," *Dilema*, January 2000.

Accordingly, the rate of expansion dropped, and hiring became less discretionary.[69]

Moreover, the HZDS after 1998 ironically proved a vociferous and vigilant opposition party – one that aimed to point out the "sins of the priests" – and was all too credible a threat to the new government. Its constant criticism of what it saw as the hypocrisy of its old opponents limited the government's discretion. Accordingly, the new government passed a civil service law in 2001.[70] However, the law was criticized as designed chiefly for the satisfaction of the EU and once again allowed ministries to hire lower-level staff at will.[71] Further, it still allowed discretionary "salary bonuses," a key source of kickbacks in the previous administration.

In Latvia, a civil service law was passed in 1994, by the Latvia Way–led government, and more than fourteen thousand candidates passed the qualification exam for civil service candidate status.[72] However, the law was chiefly a way of purging ethnic Russians from the administration, and the civil service exam primarily a Latvian language test. More importantly, no secondary legislation (which would address remuneration, classification of jobs, contract guarantees) was passed. Not until 2001 was a meritocratic civil service law passed. Quasistate institutions and extrabudgetary organizations became so important that nearly two-thirds of ministers declared that the most important fora for decision making lay outside of the state.[73]

The biggest average growth occurred when Latvia's Way was the senior governing party (1993–5 and 1999). Latvia's Way served in every cabinet and led five since 1993. It had little interest in diminishing its discretion, especially since its position in government was virtually certain. In its coalition negotiations, the party also proposed other policy priorities – and as a result, the momentum for reform never took off. Parliament was largely uninterested in civil service reform, abolishing the Ministry of State Reforms in 1995. Nor were there other mechanisms to limit growth. It was not until 2000, and under EU pressure, that a new civil service law was

---

[69] Rybář 2006.

[70] *Sme*, 3 May 2002.

[71] SIGMA 2002d, p. 3.

[72] Lucking, Richard. 2003. *Civil Service Training in the Context of Public Administration Reform*. New York: United Nations Development Program.

[73] Responses of ministers serving after 1995 in the Latvian governments. The 67 percent figure represents an increase from levels prior to 1995, when 57 percent of ministers agreed that the most important decisions were made outside of the state. Nørgaard, Ostrovska, and Hansen 2000.

adopted, which went into force in 2001. As one official summarized the situation, "nothing would have happened here without the EU pressure on politicians."[74]

Similarly, it took until 2000 to pass a civil service law in Bulgaria, under heavy EU pressure. Even so, few competitions for jobs took place (once, in fact, to recruit a director general), the requirement for college education was dropped, and the subsequent governments "enlarged the notion of political appointees in order to remove certain layers of managerial civil servants."[75] Most importantly (and for the parties, profitably), fiscal discretion was still preserved, so that salary bonuses continued, while job descriptions and evaluations were "almost non-existent."[76] As a result, the rate of state expansion actually *increased* after the civil service law, chiefly because the processes of expansion now took the form of accumulation rather than exchange.

Until then, both the weakly institutionalized UDF and the extensively organized BSP dismissed and rehired personnel, as did the short-lived non-partisan caretaker governments. There is little evidence such hirings took place to build party support, all the more so since the caretaker governments had little party backing. Thus, UDF government inserted an article in 1991 into the labor law that allowed for dismissal "in the interest of the job," aimed at communist-era officials. In return, the BSP rehired thousands of communist officials who were fired by the previous administration after it won the elections in 1994.[77] Subsequently, the 1994–5 government of Renata Indzhova fired over three thousand top- and middle-level state officials, as did the interim government of Stefan Sofianski in early 1997, which expanded the firings to include the directors of state-owned enterprises.[78] Since governments were in place for too short a time to replace all of those whom they fired, we see exploitation with lower growth.[79]

In short, discretionary hiring was prevalent. Even when civil service laws were in place, we still see evidence of discretionary hiring, firing, and

---

[74] Dimitrova, Antoaneta. Forthcoming. "Europeanisation and Civil Service Reform in Central and Eastern Europe," in Schimmelfennig, Frank, and Sedelmeier, Ulrich, eds. *The Europeanization of Central and Eastern Europe*, p. 33.

[75] SIGMA. 2002a, p. 8.

[76] Ibid., p. 14.

[77] Kochanowicz, Jacek. 1994. "Reforming Weak States and Deficient Bureaucracies," in Nelson, Joan M., Kochanowicz, Jacek, Mizsei, Kalman, and Munoz, Oscar, eds. *Intricate Links: Democratization and Market Reforms in Latin America and Eastern Europe*. Washington: Overseas Development Council, p. 216.

[78] Verheijen 1999, p. 97.

[79] Ibid., p. 106.

remuneration, given the poor specification and enforcement of the laws. Nonetheless, civil service laws went hand in hand with other institutional attempts by parties to constrain each other. When imposed early, civil service laws are thus a symptom of heightened vigilance as much as an attempt to impose a direct constraint. As a result, where we see robust competition, we see *both* lower expansion rates and the earlier introduction of civil service laws.

Privatizing the State: Parastatal and Extrabudgetary Organizations

As parties sought to govern and to gain state resources, they created quasipublic agencies and funds that were funded by the state outside of the formal budget, and were often outside the purview of parliament. As a result, for example, the average number of formal cabinet ministries in these countries dropped in each country, but the number of administration employees did not.[80] These parastatal organizations and extrabudgetary entities included funds, agencies, and intermediary bodies, such as health insurance boards, privatization agencies, regulatory commissions, and state-owned bank boards.

These parastatal organizations were founded to channel funds and bolster state capacity, by granting concessions, licenses, and exemptions. Their stated aims was to administer privatization, public funds distribution, and welfare provisions. While their employees were part of the state administration, these structures themselves were often outside of the state budget and parliamentary purview, which further allowed hiring to proceed unchecked. They greatly expanded party discretion, since the privatization of state services permitted "radical increases in the salaries of managers and middle-level employees."[81] Contracts could be more easily awarded to party allies, regulatory influence for the parties could be broadened, and control over the institutions' budgets expanded. Moreover, expanded parastatal employment justified a greater flow of funds to these agencies and funds, since agencies and government ministries could simply set their own budgets. This both expanded party control over increasing sums and profited parties directly, through the "tithing" of official salaries to the parties. The result was governance by proxy – and profit by expansion.

---

[80] Protsyk, Oleh. 2003. "Reforming Cabinets in Post-Communist Countries; Political Determinants of Cabinet Organization and Size." Manuscript, University of Ottawa, Canada.

[81] Sajo 1998b.

Table 4.4. *Estimates of Extrabudgetary Funds and Quasipublic Agencies, 1990–2003*[a]

	# Set Up	2003 Status	2002 # as % of 1990
Hungary	35 funds	2 funds (by 1995)	6
Estonia	9 funds	4 funds	45
Slovenia	47 funds[b]	2 funds	4
Lithuania	20 funds 20 agencies	8 funds 10 agencies	45
Poland	30 funds 40 agencies	7 funds 22 agencies	41
Czech R.	14 funds 8 agencies (1993–7)	13 funds 12 agencies (2000)	113
Slovakia	12 funds 18 agencies: 1994–8	11 funds (2004) 13 agencies	80
Latvia	2 funds 10 agencies	2 funds 18 agencies	167
Bulgaria	100 funds and agencies	12 funds (2001) 27 agencies (2000)	39

[a] Mean change in robust competition cases: 28.2. Mean change in cases without robust competition: 100. Difference of means test: $P = .028$, $t = -2.77$.
[b] Parliamentary Institute estimate; precise numbers are unknown.

Sources: IMF Reports on the Observance of Standards and Codes, *Raport Otwarcia*, Polish Ministry of Treasury, May 2002. Goetz, Klaus, and Wollman, Hellmut. 2001. "Governmentalizing Central Executives in Post-Communist Europe," *Journal of European Public Policy*, 8, 6 (December): 864–87.

Many of these extrabudgetary funds dated to the pre-1989 era, as communist party-states attempted to circumvent hard-currency restrictions and to gain fiscal flexibility. (As a result, we see the greatest initial numbers where the communist parties had earlier set up these entities, in Hungary, Poland, and Slovenia; see Table 4.4.) After 1989, such funds were set up to channel funds for specific goals, rather than having ministries constantly argue over competencies and budget funding. The goal was greater efficiency, via the quasiprivate delivery of funds and expertise to specific policy areas. The biggest funds included housing funds, social security and pension funds, and health care funds. Smaller ones ranged from the Nuclear Fund (a Slovak entity set up to replace old nuclear plants) to the Czech Cinema Fund (set up to support the film industry). Many of these were initially benign entities, but since they were funded from general state expenditures, not the formal state budget, they could go unaudited.

Once such agencies, funds, and offices were established, they tended to proliferate. As one critic noted, "the creation of new administrative units often happens without much thought: someone decides that a new office is needed, so it is created. Then it turns out that something similar already exists."[82] Critically, these agencies were not part of the regular budgetary and oversight structures, so they held the attraction of access to state resources but with far greater discretion than was available in the budget sector. Since they were funded outside of the budget, the new agencies were not directly competing for resources with existing ministries and state structures, which further allowed them to grow unhampered. As Table 4.4 shows, they survived where competition was weak; on average, there is no change in the number of these agencies and funds in these cases. Where the competition was more robust, the number of these funds and agencies fell considerably, with 2002 levels representing less than 29 percent of the numbers in 1990.

In addition to establishing extrabudgetary funds, government ministries also created quasistate institutions. Many of these quasipublic agencies arose prior to 1989 as an attempt to increase state capacity to implement social policies. Others were brand-new creations of political parties after 1989. They ranged from the agricultural development agencies, to privatization agencies, to road and infrastructure investment. With few budgetary constraints and little parliamentary oversight, these agencies then split up and spawned further entities, creating the demand for more legislation and more staffing, while expanding the discretion of party ministers over both state monies and hiring.[83] At the same time, the ministries who created and ran the agencies pressured the central government to increase the funding for these structures and to create more.

Privatization itself contributed to state expansion via both new agencies devoted to administering and overseeing privatization, and structures of privatization oversight, such as the supervisory boards that regulated state enterprises. The state (usually the treasury) set up these boards to represent state interests before the state firms were privatized. Positions on the boards were filled both by the privatization authority and the governing coalition.[84] Governing parties appointed their elite allies: members of parliament,[85] informal allies, and regional activists. The boards thus served

---

[82] Antoni Kamiński, quoted in *Wprost*, 31 January 1999.

[83] Interview with Zyta Gilowska, by Elżbieta Misiąg, 3 September 2001, available at http://www.platforma.org/new/wywiady/10.shtml.

[84] *Wprost*, 5 March 2000.

[85] In Hungary, as of 1995, MPs could no longer serve on boards of companies with more than a 10 percent state interest, and could no longer serve on the boards of some private sector companies, such as insurance agencies, credit institutions, and public or private procurement agencies.

both as an additional source of party income and an incentive to slow down privatization and expand party control over state holdings.

These strategies are not without precedent: Privatization policies in Great Britain under Margaret Thatcher created similar quasipublic agencies. Privatization and agency creation was accompanied by a drop in the levels of civil service employment from 762,000 in 1976 to 481,000 in 1998.[86] In post-communist East Central Europe, however, the creation of such agencies had exactly the opposite result: the expansion of state employment through the withdrawal of the state from the market. Rather than shifting personnel out of the state, as British agency creation had done, East Central European agency creation led to new hiring, since the state structures were too small and too unqualified as a source of staff. The ironic result was that the privatization of state assets expanded state employment, by creating new employment both within formal state structures and within quasistate institutions.

The profitability of staffing agencies and boards to political parties was clear. Where party leaders were direct members of supervisory boards of profitable enterprises, they could draw considerable salaries.[87] To benefit further party-allied interests, "state agencies retained the ability to control the field by providing subsidies from state funds to select groups."[88] Finally, hiring in the extrabudgetary funds or quasistate agencies was not necessarily a political award to the employees, but a way to justify increasing the fund's assets, and the parties' potential financial benefit from those assets.[89] Given the considerable discretion both in the financing of these agencies and in distributing their money, political parties could skim from these funds. Moreover, not only were these agencies funded outside of the budget, but

---

[86] Suleiman 2003, p. 253. As Paul Heywood notes, however:

> Rather than create a clear distinction between public and private sectors, privatization programmes have often been characterized by the emergence of a series of quasi-governmental regulatory agencies . . . This process of "agencification" linked to the doctrine of "new public management" has created significant opportunity structures for influence-peddling, as well as removing many regulatory agencies from direct public accountability (Heywood, Paul. 1997. "Political Corruption: Problems and Perspectives," *Political Studies*, 45, 3: 417–35, p. 429).

[87] Mesežnikov 1997, p. 45.

[88] Malová, Darina. 1997. "The Development of Interest Representation in Slovakia After 1989," in Szomolányi, Soňa, and Gould, John, eds. *Slovakia: Problems of Democratic Consolidation*. Bratislava: Friedrich Ebert Foundation, p. 100.

[89] *Polityka*, 17 February 1996.

in some cases (as in the Czech Republic) they did not have to return unspent money. The surplus could be used at the discretion of the agency heads. The result was that "2–3 people would be hired to do the job of the original one. Functions were duplicated across the board, resulting in state 'self-multiplication.'"[90]

Not surprisingly, these agencies and funds were a far more attractive prize than hiring within the general state administration.[91] In Poland, for example, the majority of the hundreds of state officials replaced by each new administration worked for extrabudgetary funds and agencies.[92] Even when these entities were eventually abolished, under IMF and EU pressure (as in Bulgaria in 2000) or by new administrations determined to clean house (as in the Czech Republic and in Slovakia), employees were not fired but reshuffled into the administration. State employment did not decrease.

The creation of these funds was a reflection of competitive dynamics. Where party governments ruled without serious opposition, as in communist Poland, Bulgaria, Latvia, or 1992–8 Slovakia, funds multiplied and gained both assets and employees. Where a robust competition created incentives for mutual constraint, as in Poland after 1989, Hungary, or Slovenia, the number and size of these funds decreased considerably. Party competition limited state hiring expansion in the quasistate sector both by abolishing these agencies and by building in formal constraints on their actions, such as launching parliamentary investigations or referring the cases to the National Audit Chambers.

Examples of these dynamics abound. The first democratic government of the Hungarian Democratic Forum (MDF) initially came under fire for appropriating funds and privatization resources through the State Privatization Agency.[93] Once the Hungarian Socialist Party came to power in 1994, facing intensive monitoring and criticism of its actions, and especially those that appeared to continue communist practices, it radically reduced the number of funds, from thirty-five to two. The decision came as part of the

---

[90] Interview with Vlastimil Aubrecht, Public Administration Parliamentary Committee (CSSD), 25 April 2002.

[91] See Kopecký, Petr. 2006. "Political Parties and the State in Post-Communist Europe: The Nature of the Symbiosis," *Journal of Communist Studies and Transitional Politics*, 22, 3: 251–73.

[92] Interview with Michał Kulesza (secretary of state and government plenipotentiary for state structural reforms, 1940–3, 1997–9), 23 April 2002.

[93] Bartlett, 1996.

1995 austerity reforms, and was designed both to reduce government spending and to bring it under parliamentary control.[94] A conflict-of-interest law in 1996 further forbade national government representatives from serving on the boards of directors and supervisory councils of companies within which the state had more than a 10 percent share.[95]

In contrast, in Slovakia under Mečiar, over eighteen agencies and twelve funds arose from 1994 to 1997 alone, the peak of Mečiar's power. According to one state official, these were largely plums handed out to HZDS allies, who would then exercise power over hires – and in expanding staffing, justify increasing funding to the funds.[96] Numerous ministerial functions were handed over to these agencies, with the HZDS exercising a "preference for direct control."[97] The HZDS also created two additional central state bodies: the Ministry of Construction and Public Works and the Office for Strategy for Development of Society. Both bodies were in charge of awarding highly lucrative infrastructure contracts. Second, the government oversaw the founding of "innumerable" funds and agencies on the regional and local level, all reporting to the central government.[98] Some of these were established as part of the 1996 regional reforms; others arose in a more ad hoc fashion. Minimal oversight of these funds existed: After 1994, the HZDS either transferred authority over these agencies to its own ministries or abandoned it altogether.

Privatization was hugely profitable for the governing Slovak parties. In administering the privatization processes, the HZDS and its allies nominated members of boards of directors, supervisory boards, and CEOs of state enterprises. As with the quasipublic agencies, there was little oversight of their activity: "According to the law, even if they or their close families control stocks in other companies, they are not obliged to disclose these facts either to their respective ministries or to the FNM."[99] Not only did the HZDS establish a monopoly over FNM positions and its oversight, but

---

[94] Čekota, Jaromír, Gonenç, Rauf, and Yoo, Kwang-Yeol. 2002. OECD Economics Department Working Paper No. 336, 30 July.

[95] Freedom House 2002, p. 204.

[96] Interview with Roman Vavrik (SDK), member of the Council on Public Administration and deputy major of Bratislava, 30 April 2002.

[97] INEKO for the Slovak Government. 2000. "Zaverečná správa o výsledkoch a odporučaniach audity súladu činnosti a financovania úsredných orgánov štátnej správy." Unpublished report (August), p. 6.

[98] Interview with an anonymous Ministry of Finances official, May 2002.

[99] Zemanovičová and Sičáková 2001, p. 447.

it also increased its role vis-à-vis parliament.[100] Given the limited capabilities of the opposition parties, it was only after 1998 that the full extent of these activities became known, and the "Black Book" of HZDS excesses was published by the new government.

Once a new government entered power in Slovakia in 1998, this time subject to considerable opposition oversight, the quasiprivatization of state functions slowed down enormously. A government audit emphasized the need to eliminate many medium-level organizations, sections, committees, and divisions.[101] The former anti-HZDS opposition now eliminated several hundreds of institutions still under control of central state institutions, broadened state management instead of using independent agencies, and ended the funneling of ministerial functions to the myriad budgetary and extrabudgetary organizations.[102] The 1998–2002 government initially wanted to continue political appointments of top managers of strategic companies. But "the partisan nomination system proved too dangerous to coalition stability, as management shuffles at strategic firms created hard feelings."[103] The previous practices of governing parties nominating the members of boards of directors and supervisory boards and CEOs of state enterprises also ended.[104]

Bulgarian state administration employment also expanded via the privatization of state functions and considerable discretion. The first government, led by the unreconstructed former communist BSP, rapidly began to create new agencies and funds, numbering over one hundred by 1997. These new agencies were directly subordinate to the BSP-run Council of Ministers, but not under any parliamentary supervision.[105] These were kept in place or expanded by the successive governments that followed, which either did not pay attention to the state (the nonparty Popov government of December 1990–December 1991) or attempted to place their loyalists in

---

[100] Krause 2006. The FNM now had the right to approve privatization sales, which was previously held by the parliament, and eliminated the oversight of the Supreme Audit Office.

[101] Slovak Government Information Service. 2000. "Audit súladu činností a financovania ústredných orgnov šttnej sprvy" (August). Also available at http://www.vlada.gov.sk/INFOSERVIs/DOKUment UOSS 2000/audit UOSS 2000 august.shtml.

[102] INEKO 2000, p. 6.

[103] Mesežnikov, Grigorij. 2001. "Domestic Politics," in Mesežnikov et al., p. 33.

[104] Zemanovičová and Sičáková 2001, p. 447.

[105] Goetz, Klaus, and Margetts, Helen. 1999. "The Solitary Center: The Core Executive in Central and Eastern Europe," *Governance*, 12, 4 (October): 425–53, p. 429.

government administration (the UDF governments tried to place political affiliates in top civil service positions in order to ensure the political loyalty of the administration).[106] No oversight was exercised over these agencies and funds, and the degree of discretion in their funding meant that sources ranging from privatization revenues to selling information to donations all filled their coffers.[107] It was only in 2001, and only under heavy EU pressure, that these agencies were drastically consolidated into twelve funds.

Thus, where a robust competition existed, the number of funds and agencies steadily declined. Parties fought to reestablish parliamentary control over these state satellites. Where competition was less robust, it took external actors such as the EU to impose order and control over these highly discretionary aspects of state administration.

The Impact of Robust Competition: Comparing the Czech Republic and Poland

To examine in greater depth the mechanisms of discretion building and the impact of competition on the expansion of state administration, we turn to two "unlikely cases": Poland and the Czech Republic. Poland was notorious for its ineffective pre-communist bureaucracy and highly troubled democracy during the interwar period (which ended with Marshall Piłsudski's coup in 1926). As the Polish communist regime slid into a quagmire of debt and fiscal problems, it established a series of quasistate institutions and extrabudgetary funds that functioned outside of the official oversight and budget structures. By 1989, there were over thirty such funds and forty such agencies, and reducing their number proved difficult. Its national-accommodative communist rule and the immense growth of discretion and lax regulation in the late-communist era should have made discretionary state expansion eminently feasible in Poland.

In contrast, the Czech Republic was noted for its pre-communist legacy of professional state bureaucracy and stable democracy, bureaucratic-authoritarian communist rule, and lack of late-communist laxity or discretion.[108] The Czech Republic did not inherit a slew of informal quasistate institutions and concomitant practices. The funds and agencies that were established only arose after the collapse of communism. All of these factors

---

[106] Verheijen 1999, p. 96.
[107] Ganev 2005, pp. 105–6.
[108] Kitschelt et al. 1999.

Table 4.5. *State Administrations in Poland and the Czech Republic*

	Poland	Czech Republic
Increase as % state employment, 1990–2004	244%	400%
Absolute increase, 1990–2004	205%	225%
Change, as reported by state administration office	80%	211%
Annual growth rate, central ministries	1.9%	7.5%
Change in quasistate agencies and funds	41%	113%

should have meant considerably lower growth and exploitation of the state administration in the Czech Republic.

Yet post-communist state growth, in both its extent and its mechanisms, shows an opposite pattern, as Table 4.5 shows. State administration as a share of total employment grew 244 percent in Poland and 400 percent in the Czech Republic, despite a far higher unemployment rate in Poland.[109] State administration was less likely to be a sponge for absorbing unemployed workers in Poland than in the Czech Republic: As a World Bank study concluded, "government employment was apparently (and fortunately) not used as an employment-fighting (or hiding) device"[110] in Poland. In absolute terms, the state administration grew 205 percent in Poland and 225 percent in the Czech Republic. Using data from state administration self-reporting, however, the growth rates show even greater disparity: 80 percent in Poland and 211 percent in the Czech Republic (see Appendix B).

The key differences between Poland and the Czech Republic lay in the dynamics of state expansion. In the Polish case, the incentives to go after state offices were far bigger than in the Czech Republic, considering the inherited discretion from the communist funds and agencies, and the share of the economy was in state hands. Yet the rates of expansion were lower, since the opposition constrained growth, constantly raising an alarm.[111] In the Czech Republic, in contrast, privatization was far faster, and the country inherited fewer communist-era agencies and funds. However, the ODS and other governments had far more capacity to expand and exploit the state.

[109] Until 1997, Polish unemployment rates exceeded 11 percent, while Czech ones remained well below 5 percent. In 1998, the Czech unemployment rate began to climb, topping out at 10 percent in 2004. (The Polish unemployment rate in 2004 was 19 percent.)
[110] Crombrugghe, Alain de. 1997. "Wage and Pension Pressure on the Polish Budget." Report for World Bank Project RPO 678–96, Policy Research Working Paper No. 1793, p. 25.
[111] Polish state expansion was thus far more publicized than that of the Czech Republic, both because of a more robust opposition and fewer ties between parties and the media.

The two countries also show different mechanisms of state growth. In the Czech Republic, the state was centralized (regional reform was not implemented until 2002) and the parties of the ODS coalition monopolized the control of specific ministries for years. As a result, growth in state administration employment occurred in the central state administration (ministries and central offices) at far higher rates than elsewhere. These ministries then went on to found new institutions and hire at will. In Poland, in contrast, the state administration was less centralized, in that an extensive system of territorial governance existed, augmented by the further deconcentration of power as a result of the 1997 regional reform. No party held a ministry or other central state sector in a hegemonic grip, given the fragility of Polish governing coalitions. As a result, growth occurred in territorial administration and in the quasistate sector rather than in the central administration itself. As the extrabudgetary funds and quasistate institutions were cut back thanks to opposition criticism, the rates of growth slowed down, despite the fact that in Poland opportunities for discretionary hiring were considerably greater than in the Czech Republic.

Without formal barriers on discretionary hiring, but under the eyes of a formidable political opposition, Polish state administration doubled from 1990–2002, with an average annual growth rate of 5.02 percent. Given the robust competition, strong incentives existed to eliminate discretion, and every single government attempted to put forth a version of a civil service law by 1991,[112] with a government plenipotentiary established in 1992.[113] It "was born in political conflicts,"[114] since each party wanted to ensure that no others could nominate too many officials. However, political instability delayed the law: The fall of three different governments prevented its passing. The process was speeded up by the reform of the administrative center in 1996 and the perception that it was opening up new positions to be named by government parties. As a result, no party wanted the others to benefit, and a civil service law passed in 1996 with only one opposing vote, "a success of all political groupings, government and opposition."[115]

---

[112] Torres-Bartyzel, Claudia, and Kacprowicz, Grażyna. 1999. "The National Civil Service System in Poland," in Verheijen 1999: 159–83, p. 168.

[113] The 1982 Law on State Officials had already created an employment system substantially different from the labor code and gave tenure to some categories of civil servants. It regulated job classifications for the first time, encoded employment and dismissal procedures, and guaranteed job security. Torres-Bartyzel and Kacprowicz 1999, p. 159.

[114] *Polityka*, 10 August 1996.

[115] Ibid.

The opposition immediately began to criticize the law as inadequate. For one thing, the law favored old communist state administration employees.[116] The opposition repeatedly criticized the civil service law. Once the opposition returned to power in 1997, the new AWS-UW government launched an investigation of the flaws in the 1996 civil service law and its implementation, calling forth an independent investigatory commission. The conclusions criticized the SLD-PSL government for delaying the reforms, and the first director of the civil service for allowing easy exams and fudging language requirements.[117]

The law's critics, now in government, then revamped and expanded the law in 1999, making the exams considerably more difficult, creating a class of public servants as a separate legal category, and making merit the determinant of both pay and position.[118] The communist successor SLD announced it would carefully monitor new civil service legislation, repeatedly criticizing the novelization but keeping its meritocratic proposals when it reentered office in 2001. It also heavily criticized renewed attempts by the AWS to staff the state with its allies, attempts made when AWS began to fall apart in 1999.[119] Once a new SLD-led government entered office in 2001, it amended the law with meritocratic procedures.

At the same time, *informal* constraints of competition effectively limited the size of the Polish state administration. Exploitation by individual parties was short-lived and subject to continual contestation. Any one coalition's attempts could be quickly reversed by its successor. As a result, exchanges of personnel, rather than simple accumulation, were the dominant dynamic. For example, when it came to power in 1993, the coalition of the Democratic Left Alliance (SLD) and Peasants' Party (PSL) replaced numerous officials and regional governors associated with the previous Solidarity governments. An even more explicitly political move came when immediately before the 1997 elections, SLD Prime Minister Włodzimierz Cimoszewicz nominated eighteen directors of general departments (out of seventy-two) in several ministries, all of whom passed the easy civil service

---

[116] The law specified that civil servants with more than seven years of service were exempt from passing tests and were to be favored in advancements. Needless to say, the only civil servants with this tenure were from the communist era.

[117] *Gazeta Wyborcza*, 6 March 1998.

[118] Jabłoński, A. 1998. "Europeanization of Public Administration in Central Europe: Poland in Comparative Perspective." NATO Individual Democratic Institution Research Fellowships, Final Report 1995–7.

[119] *Rzeczpospolita*, 3 April 2002.

exam, and thirty-five directors of departments at the voivodeship (regional) level. However, when the SLD and PSL were replaced with the AWS-UW coalition in 1997, many of these decisions were reversed. Seventeen central and fifteen voivodeship directors were again replaced.

Each successive administration exchanged about two thousand to three thousand high-ranking officials[120] with little difficulty. In doing so, governing parties relied on their own elites, who would be named to ministries and agencies and then hire their own, replacing and adding to the pool of existing officials. Since the opposition was the biggest constraint, it is not surprising that greatest state expansion occurred in 1993–5, when the SLD-PSL coalition governed with a relatively weaker opposition (post-Solidarity forces were in disarray after the unexpected victory of the former communists).[121] Some critics saw a new "party nomenklatura,"[122] especially when after the 1997 elections, the post-Solidarity AWS openly spoke of exchanging four thousand positions.[123] In contrast to the earlier episode, however, the opposition, especially the communist successor SLD, monitored individual institutions, and the AWS was unable to achieve its goal. The result was that, as a government critic pointed out, "for political parties, the real action could not be in the state administration [hiring]. They had to go seeking resources elsewhere."[124]

The constant monitoring and squabbling also created incentives to share power. For example, the AWS-UW government went as far as to put parity of party representation on enterprise boards in their coalition agreement; if the chair came from one party, his or her deputy had to be from the other. Opposition parties agreed to this standard, and declared they would hold it up when they got to power.[125] Thus, while domestic critics charged that the boards of state enterprises, government agencies, and local corporations were all politicized, the dispersion of power also limited the concentration of resources. Two additional informal rules developed by 1996: regional leaders (*voivodes*), appointed by the prime minister, automatically resigned with each election. And, ministers acquired "political cabinets": groups of

---

[120] *Polityka*, 11 October 1997.
[121] The annual growth rates were 10.7 percent from 1993–4 and 16.5 percent from 1994–5, compared to the 5.6 percent average.
[122] *Polityka*, 22 January 2000.
[123] *Polityka*, 18 December 1999.
[124] Interview with Michal Kułesza (secretary of state and government plenipotentiary for state structural reforms, 1990–3, 1997–9), 23 April 2002.
[125] Marek Borowski, quoted in *Gazeta Wyborcza*, 12 February 2000.

explicitly political advisers, named by the minister for his or her own needs. The latter lowered the pressures to exchange state officials, and further limited the accumulation of offices, since the cabinets resigned when the minister did.[126] No party had the capacity or the freedom to monopolize the state.

Where the opposition could reach, investigate, and criticize, governments were more likely to moderate their behavior. Where they had less organizational reach, as in the territorial branches of the central administration, they had far less ability to constrain administrative growth. One indicator of the ability of opposition parties to keep in check the accumulation of offices is that while annual growth rates for the entire administration were around 5 percent, they were under 2 percent for the central ministries and government agencies. And these relationships held not just thanks to turnover, but throughout the incumbency of a given government. For example, from 1994–6, ministerial and central agency employment increased by only 2.8 percent, at a time of massive opposition criticism that the SLD had politicized the administration.[127]

In contrast, on the *local* level, there were incidents of explicitly politicized hiring. For example, a health insurance branch asked for a "recommendation from the AWS" as part of the qualifications for building maintenance positions.[128] The regional reform of 1997 created new tiers of local government and health funds.[129] Yet there was little evidence of systematic patronage. The expansion of state administration employment or the founding of agencies and extrabudgetary organizations was not connected to the electoral cycle, nor was there any increase in their growth rate either before or after elections.[130] In sum, given slower privatization and greater state oversight of state enterprises, huge *incentives* existed to expand the state, but the parties' *capacity* to do so was constrained.

Dozens of extrabudgetary funds and quasistate agencies were set up during the period of late communism and immediately after its collapse (see Table 4.4). These were modeled after the agencies founded in Britain and in France in the 1970s.[131] Founded in the period of late communism and in

---

[126] Jacek Raciborski, sociologist at UW, quoted in *Rzeczpospolita*, 3 April 2002.

[127] *Wprost*, 25 January 1998.

[128] *Polityka*, 31 October 1998.

[129] Szczerbak 2006, pp. 310–11.

[130] Interview with Jan Pastwa, head of Civil Service, *Nowe Państwo*, 7, 2001.

[131] Majone, Giandomenico. 1994. "The Rise of the Regulatory State in Europe," *West European Politics* 17, 3 (June): 77–101.

1990, they included the Social Security Agency, the Agency for Industrial Development, the Agricultural Market Agency, and some more esoteric entities, such as the Fund for the Promotion of Creativity.[132] They were quickly criticized for administering enormous funds (hundreds of millions of U.S. dollars) with minimal control.[133] They answered only to ministers, and to the director of the agency nominated by the ministers.[134] They were also heavily criticized for blurring the boundaries between "public, party, and individual interests."[135]

Nonetheless, the mutual criticism of the opposition and the government pruned the number of quasistate institutions. The road was bumpier than in the Hungarian case, given the enormity of the mining and agricultural sectors, which claimed most of these agencies. Many of the communist-era agencies were summarily eliminated by Leszek Balcerowicz, the architect of polish privatization, as part of the radical economic reforms after 1989. Yet, given the lack of new administrative templates, administrations returned to them as a way of resolving the "spectacular problems," such as agriculture and mining.[136] Ministries responsible for these sectors pressured the center to create more extrabudgetary institutions.[137] Several were established by the governing coalition of the communist successor SLD and the peasant party PSL in 1994–5, when the opposition was busy with infighting.[138] Most were the result of the SLD trying to keep the PSL happy as a coalition partner; as thus, the Agency of Economic Development (1994) and the Agency for the Restructuring and Modernization of Agriculture (1994) arose. The AWS administration of 1997–2001 expanded the agencies further as a way to reward its fractious factions. Some funds were both warranted and competent, such as the Fund for Environmental Protection.

[132] *Polityka*, 11 February 1995. See also *Wprost*, 3 June 2001 and 31 January 1999.
[133] Regulski, Jerzy. 1999. "Building Democracy in Poland: The State Reform of 1998," Discussion Paper 9, Local Government and Public Service Reform Initiative. Budapest: Open Society Institute, p. 20.
[134] *Polityka*, 11 February 1995.
[135] Jarosz, Maria. 2001 *Manowce Polskiej Prywatyzacji*. Warszawa: PWN SA, p. 24.
[136] Interview with Marek Zieliński (member of the UW Public Administration Reform Committee, Fundusz ds Inwestycyjnych, 1993–2001), 7 May 2002, UW headquarters, Poznan.
[137] Interview with Zyta Gilowska by Elżbieta Misiąg, 3 September 2001. Available at http://www.platforma.org/new/wywiady/10.shtml.
[138] The opposition at the time was trying to unite in various formations, such as Konwent Św. Katarzyny. Interview with Gilowska by Misiąg, 3 September 2001. Available at http://www.platforma.org/new/wywiady/10.shtml.

Others became far more problematic; for example, the Fund for the Protection of the Handicapped awarded lucrative tax breaks to "workshops of protected labor," ostensibly a way of hiring the disabled. The opposition rapidly accused the fund of corruption and preferential awarding of such status, and its discretion was summarily eliminated.[139]

As soon as many of these funds and agencies arose, however, opposition parties immediately accused the agencies of wanton spending, especially in the agriculture-related agencies (not surprisingly, the traditional bailiwick of the populist PSL). Several changes limited the discretionary access to state resources by 1996. Agency projects were now evaluated by numerous outside experts at all levels and were subject to control by the National Accounting Office. More importantly, many of these agencies were eliminated in 2002 by the SLD government (now freed of its obligations to the peasant PSL) to create an administration that would be "more effective, smaller, and cheaper for the tax payer."[140] Their number decreased from thirty to seven, and all came under the purview of increasing media criticism, fueled by the rise of two new political parties that made transparency and accountability their mantra.[141] Moreover, actual employment in these organizations was tiny; most agencies had no more than 250 employees total.[142]

As noted earlier, privatization strategies (themselves endogenous to political parties) offered distinct opportunities. In Poland, after enormous debate and delays (produced by parliamentary conflict), a 1995 "commercialization" law established supervisory boards, made up of government and private representatives in enterprises with shares owned by the state. These were to be a midway step to privatization. With time, however, these supervisory boards became an end unto themselves. Board positions were both a reward to party elites and a source of income to the party.[143] The enterprise boards numbered a total of around 15,000 members, for 1,750 enterprises with partial state ownership. According to the plenipotentiary

---

[139] Interview with Zieliński, 7 May 2002.

[140] Chancellern of the Prime Minister press release, 20 March 2002.

[141] These were the Civic Platform (Platforma Obywatelska, PO), and Law and Justice (Prawo i Sprawiedliwosc, PiS).

[142] *Wprost*, 31 January 1999.

[143] Parties could use these positions in two ways: to spend the money directly for various sponsoring and advertising, and to get foreign investors and others to contribute to the party in exchange for a permit to buy company shares.

for administrative reform, this is "where the real action was" for political parties.[144] About 4,000 board memberships were decided by ministry officials, and successive governments exchanged about 70–80 percent of the members.[145] As many as 20 percent of parliamentarians were directly connected with these boards by 1993.[146]

Yet competition created a tension between these short-term benefits and longer-term electoral potential. In 1994, the Clean Hands action limited the number of board memberships held to two per individual, curtailing the profitability of membership for party representatives.[147] By 1998–2000, the Parliamentary Committee for Member Ethics in Poland reported that fewer than 5 percent of parliamentarians (twenty-one, of whom six were not paid) sat on the boards.[148] There was also considerable power sharing: Emil Wąsacz, the minister of treasury in the AWS-UW government, appointed numerous opposition figures to the councils, and many officeholders remained in their council positions despite the change in governments in 1997 and 2001.[149] Similarly, the 2001 SLD government reached across party lines to name ministers and oversight officials.[150] In short, opposition investigations, policy pressure, and parliamentary criticism brought under control the initial burgeoning of discretion in 1989 and its reassertion after the 1993 elections. The number and scope of quasi-state institutions and extrabudgetary funds decreased significantly over time, dropping to less than half their original number.

In contrast, in the Czech Republic, the opportunities appeared smaller, yet the expansion was greater. In the absence of an opposition threat, there were no formal institutional controls over discretionary hiring. As in Poland, there was little evidence of direct patronage; as one official commented, "there was some political influence in direct hiring, but political parties simply were not able to hire that many people – they were too small, and too focused on what was going on in Prague."[151] Instead, party

---

[144] Interview with Kulesza, 23 April 2002.

[145] *Polityka*, 27 February 1999.

[146] Wasilewski, Jacek. 2000. "Polish Post-Transitional Elite," in Frentzel-Zagórska, Janina, and Wasilewski, Jacek, eds. *The Second Generation of Democratic Elites in East and Central Europe*. Warsaw: PAN ISP, p. 213.

[147] Previous "recordholders" had had as many as eight memberships simultaneously.

[148] Komisja Etyki Poselskiej, 03-07-2001, Biuletyn 4398/III.

[149] *Wprost*, 5 March 2000.

[150] *Polityka*, 25 October 2001.

[151] Interviews with Jan Ruml (former minister of interior, 1992–6, senator for US), 14 July 2003, Prague.

elites took over existing and new state institutions and hired at will. Many of these plum jobs went to party leaders who failed to enter parliament, since "no party should get rid of people who have behind them lots of work."[152]

Predictably, given the centralization of the governing parties and their weak organizational reach, the biggest growth occurred in the central state administration: the ministries. The opposition parties were too weak to stop this expansion. In contrast to Poland, where the growth rates in the ministries were about half the average growth rate for the rest of the state administration, Czech ministry employment grew by about 7–8 percent a year, or roughly one-and-a-half times as fast as in the rest of the administration.[153] In short, precisely because political parties had their greatest reach in the central administration, this is where we observe both the constraining effects of competition – and the discretionary hiring in its absence.

Such jobs ranged from highly lucrative enterprise boards to ministry consultancies and high official positions. Bonuses and premiums were awarded to supplement official salaries at the discretion of the management. Funds left over from unfilled vacancies were made available for salary bonuses,[154] and "controls over the real numbers of staff are not carried out."[155] Not surprisingly, charges of thousands of "dead souls" – empty positions for whom government agencies and ministries collected salaries – were the predictable result.[156] And, without turnover or an electoral threat presented by the opposition, there were no other mechanisms that could have curbed continued discretionary hiring.

Neither formal strictures nor opposition criticism moderated government behavior. Under the guise of "neoliberal" abandonment of the state, formal institutions that could have limited discretionary hiring were simply ignored and delayed. After the elimination of regional governments in 1990, the central Czech state government was in charge of staffing all levels of the polity and used its centralized power accordingly. The ODS government approved a basic outline of the state administration code and then

---

[152] Petra Buzková, CSSD minister of education, quoted in *Mladá Fronta Dnes*, 9 September 2003.

[153] For the rates of central ministry employment for 2000–4, see, *Hospodarské Noviny*, 8 August 2005. According to Ruml, the rates grew even faster under the ODS government, from 1991–8.

[154] SIGMA 2002b, p. 8.

[155] Ibid., p. 11.

[156] *Mladá Fronta Dnes*, 30 June 2005.

shelved it.[157] A law that would have regularized the tenure of civil servants, to affect sixty-thousand employees, was briefly brought up in January 1993, but dropped without reading in the parliament.[158] Repeatedly, the ODS government criticized such plans as unnecessary, expensive, and entrenching a bureaucracy without reason. Instead, it launched an antibureaucratic commission in 1996 (which fizzled away for lack of advisory power and political support from the government within half a year).

The rule until 1996 was "that the winner takes all," according to later Social Democratic criticisms.[159] Not surprisingly, the biggest growth spurt for the state administration came under the heyday of ODS rule, from 1991 to 1995.[160] The government then announced a plan for a 5 percent decrease in the state administration, but it did not come to fruition. With no effective opposition to constrain the ODS, the governing coalition continued to create and to accumulate positions in the central state administration.

Moreover, as Hilary Appel points out, the ODS focused on staffing and controlling relevant ministries and judicial bodies that both had enormous access to state holdings and were to act as their watchdogs, including the Ministry of Privatization, FNM, the Finance Ministry, and their supervisory bodies. This further explains the unusually high growth in central ministries.[161] Other leaders in state growth were the Ministry of Labor and Social Affairs (which had at its disposal lucrative public works contracts) and the quasistate institutions and funds.[162] Since each ministry and agency set up its own budget, there was no central oversight of how state funds were spent on these employees. Nor could ministries or state organs declare how many employees were working for them: Even as public employment (which included state administration) grew by fourteen thousand in 1998, no ministry could identify where precisely the hires took place, or why.[163] Finally, the least understood, or officially justified, growth occurred in the territorial offices of the central state administration.[164] Within seven years

---

[157] OECD 2000a, p. 10.

[158] *Lidové Noviny*, 12 January 1993.

[159] Interview with Vaclav Grulich. CSSD, 25 April 2002 (Committee per Public Administration, 1992–, former minister of interior 1998–2000, CSSD).

[160] Annual growth rates averaged 13.2 percent a year during this period, against an overall average yearly growth of 5.8 percent.

[161] Appel 2001, p. 535.

[162] *Mladá Fronta Dnes*, 1 October 1997.

[163] *Mladá Fronta Dnes*, 13 August 1999. See also *Mladá Fronta Dnes*, 19 June 2000 and 5 November 2003.

[164] *Mladá Fronta Dnes*, 1 October 1997.

of the communist collapse, this sector grew by seventy thousand employees.[165]

The opposition was largely powerless to stop the ODS. By 1996, both the Social Democrats (in the opposition) and the ODA and KDU-ČSL (in the government coalition) began to criticize ODS's "arrogant centralism"[166] and hoped to brake the ODS's growing power in the state administration by introducing regional reform: "[T]he smaller governing parties do not hide that their support for regions is an attempt to constrain the power of the electoral victor."[167] Nonetheless, the ODS refused to consider regional reform for its entire duration in power.

As late as 2000, the Czech Republic came under fire from the EU for making no distinction between political appointees and career officials, and for not defining the category of civil servant.[168] The EU mournfully noted that "the occupying of positions in the state machinery according to party membership or on the basis of personal acquaintances is in contradiction with the requirements of the rule of law and with the interests of the public."[169] In fact, it was only the European Union, and its clear demand for civil service laws, that eventually led to the passing of a Czech civil service law in late April 2002, to take effect in 2004. Through a series of legislative delays, its implementation was then postponed until mid-2007. It would affect about eighty thousand government employees and restrict line ministries from continuing to hire at will. However, no legislation on job security for civil servants passed. Predictably, Václav Klaus and the ODS voted against the law as expensive and unnecessary – but the ČSSD government emphasized that the EU had been asking for such a law for years, and the coalition had to pass it as part of the preparations for accession.[170]

Yet even after the EU pressures and the departure of the ODS from power, many of these practices continued. Party representatives acknowledged that state staffing was at the discretion of political party allies, who filled various state offices down to the regional branches of the state

---

[165] *Respekt*, "V obklíčení byrokratů," 4 August 1997.

[166] Jan Kalvoda, ODA chair, *Mladá Fronta Dnes*, 30 March 1996.

[167] *Mladá Fronta Dnes*, 4 May 1996.

[168] European Union Commission. 2000. *Regular Report on the Czech Republic's Progress Towards Accession*. Brussels: EU.

[169] PHARE and NVF 1998.

[170] *Mladá Fronta Dnes*, 27 April 2002. The law stipulated that a general manager of the civil service bureau would hire state secretaries, who would then be in charge of hiring state officials.

government.[171] The Social Democratic government elected in 1998 had as its goal the "leveling of the heavy advantage, which the parties of the former governing coalition gained in the territorial offices of the central administration. An applicant for the chair of přednosta [territorial administration head] had no chance without party elite sponsorship. The situation was similar in the ministries, both at the central level and in the branches."[172]

The introduction of regional governments and decentralization in both countries curbed the rate of growth of overall state administration, but also presented considerable opportunities for discretionary hiring at the local level, prompted by personal connections and lack of central oversight.[173] The Czech Ministry of Interior guaranteed that central state employees would not lose their jobs even as their functions were transferred to the new regions in 2002.[174] At the same time, since so many functions were being transferred downward, local offices began to hire in considerable numbers.[175] There is less evidence, however, that these hirings benefited political parties directly; where they occurred on discretionary grounds, they were far more likely to benefit individual local politicians and their allies, most of whom were independent of national political parties.

Finally, and most ironically (given the nearly blank slate with which the communist regime left its successors in this department), the number of funds and agencies in the Czech Republic increased significantly after the collapse of communism. Fourteen funds were all founded after 1989, ranging from the enormous Territorial (1991) and Agricultural Support Funds (1994) and to the tiny Fund for Promotion and Development of Czech Cinematography (1992). Similarly, eight quasistate agencies also arose, such as the Czech Consolidation Agency (1991). Their overall budgets were within the same order of magnitude as their Polish counterparts, with tens of billions of Kč (hundreds of millions of U.S. dollars) under their control.[176]

---

[171] Interview with Vlastimil Aubrecht, Public Administration Parliamentary Committee (CSSD), 25 April 2002.

[172] Novotný, Vít. 1999. "Deset let po listopadu: Omézme moc České politické oligarchie," Britské Listy, 29 November.

[173] Thus the rate of growth prior to the 1998 reforms was 5.84 in Poland, dropping to 3.79 after. In the Czech Republic, it dropped from 6.86 percent to 2.10 percent after the 2000 regional reforms.

[174] Mladá Fronta Dnes, 1 August 2001.

[175] Mladá Fronta Dnes, 29 June 2004.

[176] Hospodářské Noviny, 27 August 2004. The difference, of course, is that the GDP of Poland in 2000 was $463 billion, whereas it was $172.2 billion in the Czech Republic.

The biggest extrabudgetary funds consisted of the Housing Assistance Fund (2000) and the Transport Infrastructure Fund (2000), along with the Environmental Protection Fund (founded 1991). They were not dependent on the yearly budget, nor, as importantly, did they have to return any unspent moneys. Above all, the parliament was to oversee these funds via their "shareholder boards" – but in a situation where the governing coalition faced no opposition, this control was easily subverted to party goals.[177] Throughout the heyday of privatization (until mid-1996), the Czech ODS staffed most administrative bodies with supervisory functions through politically based appointments, reserving its tightest control over ministries and judicial bodies with oversight over privatization: the Ministry of Privatization, the National Property Fund, the Ministry of Finance, and their interior supervisory bodies.[178] The long delay in privatizing and restructuring the banking sector[179] also becomes more intelligible with the realization that the ODS governments "were able to place their own appointees in the top management positions at the big state-owned banks. . . . Before long, Klaus had packed the big banks' board of directors and upper managements."[180] Until 1996, the ODS took what office it could, while its coalition partners were often limited both by their lesser clout and by their scarcer ranks of elites.[181]

The governing coalition had the only oversight over the funds, which did not have to return any unspent moneys.[182] There was no oversight over the funds' structure, scope, or effectiveness.[183] As a result, the ODS government officials "throughout most of the 1990s hired their party colleagues to direct many state and semistate enterprises and institutions, including banks and health insurance boards."[184] Czech officials agreed that the growth in state administration was driven not by direct patronage, but rather by

---

[177] Interview with Tom Zajíček, ODS, chair, Parliamentary Committee for Public Administration, Regional Development, and the Environment, 25 April 2002, Prague.

[178] Appel 2001, p. 535.

[179] See Appel, Hilary. 2004. *A New Copitalist Order*. Pittsburgh: University of Pittsburgh Press.

[180] Horowitz, Shale, and Petráš, Martin. 2003. "Pride and Prejudice in Prague: Understanding Early Policy Error and Belated Reform in the Czech Economic Transition." *East European Politics and Societies*, 17, 2: 231–65.

[181] Interview with Vlastimil Aubrecht, Public Administration Parliamentary Committee (CSSD), 25 April 2002.

[182] Interview with Oldřich Kužílek, former chair of ODA parliamentary club, FS and PSP representative for ODA, etc., 11 July 2003, Prague.

[183] *Hospodárské Noviny*, 27 August 2004.

[184] Novotný 1999.

the expansion of central state administration and the rise of central new organizations that did not exist prior to 1989 – various quasipublic agencies, financial offices, consolidation agencies, and nonprivatized state enterprises.[185] These indirect efforts intensified during the 1998–2002 Opposition Agreement, described by some of the officials as a "political-economic cartel."[186]

In short, Poland and the Czech Republic illustrate that opportunistic reconstruction was the main mechanism of post-communist party survival and state growth. Political parties focused on areas and sectors where they could gain the most direct material benefits, and this meant farming out actual hiring to party allies, as well as founding new state institutions. By the same token, precisely because so much was at stake, where political parties could constrain each other through competition, we see lower growth rates, as in the Polish central state hiring. Where they could not do so, growth proceeded with far less restraint, as in the Czech ministries and funds.

Conclusion

Exploitation in state administration consisted of discretionary hiring that expanded party bailiwicks and extended control over key fiscal, budgetary, and extrabudgetary sectors. Just as importantly, it meant founding new, quasistate agencies, enterprise boards, and extrabudgetary funds that both administered the new market structures and expanded the access and influence of political parties over state holdings.

Political competition constrained both the discretionary growth of state administration and the resources it provided for parties. Nonetheless, robust competition was not a failsafe guarantee; even in Hungary, political parties who ignored the opposition threat (such as Fidesz) could ride roughshod over newly established civil service norms and regulations. Nor does competition force bureaucracies to be an optimal size.[187] Independent civil service systems take decades, if not centuries, to consolidate, and the process is neither straightforward nor easily managed. And for every Great

---

[185] Interviews with Ruml, 14 July 2003; Oldřich Kužílek, former chair of ODA parliamentary club, FS and PSP representative for ODA, etc., 11 July 2003, Prague; Tom Zajíček, ODS, chair of Committee for Public Administration Reform, 25 April 2002, Prague.

[186] Interview with Ruml, 14 July 2003.

[187] Wittman 1995, p. 95. Wittman argues that competition for funding within bureaucracies would reduce their size; however, such competition was missing, circumvented through extrabudgetary funds and quasipublic agencies.

Britain, there is an Italy, where clientelist factions continued to expand the bureaucracy and the resources controlled by government.[188]

Expanding the state administration by maintaining discretionary hiring and creating new agencies and funds was a strategy of increasing the authority of political parties, who could now control ever-larger agency budgets and discretionary funds. State exploitation was thus an indirect source of power, prestige – and the survival of fragile new democratic parties. As the next chapter shows, political parties also used these same state institutions to skim and funnel money directly into party coffers.

[188] Zuckerman 1979, p. 37.

5

Privatizing the State

PARTY FUNDING STRATEGIES

> Party finances are one of the most important, and, for obvious reasons, the
> least transparent chapters of the history of political parties.
>
> Max Weber, Economy and Society

For observers of the post-communist transformation, the financing of political parties comprised one of the murkiest and most suspect aspects of
democratic party politics. Scandals involving mysterious party donors, film
producers, oil pipelines, fire-sale privatizations, and suitcases full of cash
emerged in the 1990s, wrecking popular trust in political parties. However
desperate or tragicomic, these forays show that securing funding was as
controversial as it was pressing for the political parties involved. Nascent
democratic political parties quickly had to find sources of material support, at a time when electorates were impoverished and fickle, fledgling
private firms had little spare capital and were initially uninterested in supporting political parties, and party members were neither numerous nor
generous.[1]

For parties in search of capital, the state was a far more attractive and
potentially stable source of funding. In addition to yielding formal subsidies, the impending privatization of state enterprises and holdings meant
enormous informal opportunities. This is not to say that state funding or
privatization by themselves indicate exploitation; however, leaving formal
state funding unregulated and concentrated, pocketing resources from the
processes of privatization, allowing discretionary access to state resources,

---

[1] Membership itself was a double-edged sword. Had they become a major source of funding,
members would limit the party's strategic flexibility. Similarly, private enterprises and nongovernmental organizations can be generous and steady in their support – but even so, they
exact their price in subsequent policy concessions.

and concentrating the benefits among the ruling parties are all symptoms of exploitation.

Political parties thus benefited both from their direct access to the state and its resources and from the indirect transfers they engineered. To be sure, the real extent of party funding is in many ways unknowable: The channels that pour funding into party coffers are often twisted, change their names and provenance, and disperse funding through multiple, diverse, and fictitiously named sources. What we *can* observe more systematically and readily, however, is the *regulation* of party funding whether constraints arise, how they are enforced, and how transparent the sources of party funding are. We can also examine the *access* of parties to state resources, and whether it was formalized or discretionary – and especially how and where parties abused the processes of privatization, which held the greatest potential material benefit for political parties. Finally, we can also measure the *concentration* of benefits: whether the beneficiaries are one or two incumbent parties, or whether all parties can benefit.

The more robust the competition, the more stringently regulated, transparent, and formalized the access to state resources. All parliamentary parties (and many nonparliamentary parties) benefited. Conversely, less robust competition was associated with unregulated, opaque, and discretionary access, where the parties extracted resources wherever they could from the state. Such "covert" access tended to favor incumbent parties, who could freely extract informal state resources while limiting their competitors' access; opposition or extraparliamentary parties were largely excluded from such funding. Lax regulations of party financing allowed *state* agents, such as state-owned firms and banks, to contribute to the parties and establish few reporting requirements, while offering few sanctions for the violation of laws.

The broad variation ranges from the relatively transparent Hungarian and Slovenian party funding regimes to the covert Latvian and Slovak counterparts. Estonian, Hungarian, Slovenian, and (to a lesser extent) Lithuanian and Polish laws on party financing quickly eliminated several potentially worrisome sources of party funding: business and other economic activity by political parties, foreign and anonymous donors (which were not only hard to trace but often concealed illegitimate gains from other sources), and both state enterprises and local governments. As Tables 5.1 and 5.2 show, all these loopholes had been closed off in polities with robust competition. Both legal sources of party funding and party funding regulations were far more strictly monitored and regulated where robust competition existed.

Table 5.1. *Legal Sources of Party Funding as of 2002*

	NGOs	Economic Activity[a]	Foreign Donors	Local Gov'ts	State Firms	Anonym Donors	State Subventions
Hungary	No	No	No	No	No	No	1% threshold, all parties and candidates
Estonia	No	No	No	No	No	No	5% threshold, parliamentary parties
Slovenia	No	Ltd	No	No	No	No	1% threshold, all parties and candidates
Lithuania	No	Ltd	No	No	No	No	3–5% threshold, all parties and candidates
Poland	No	No	No	No	No	No	3% threshold, all parties
Czech R.	Yes	No[b]	Yes	Yes	Yes	Yes	3% threshold, parliamentary parties
Slovakia	Yes	Ltd	Yes	Yes	Yes	Yes	3% threshold, parliamentary parties
Bulgaria	Yes	No	Yes	Yes	No	Yes	1% threshold, all parties, amount variable
Latvia	Yes	Yes	No	Yes	Yes	Yes	None

Notes:
[a] Defined as ownership or management of profit-making enterprises, services, or real-estate holdings.
[b] From 1992–6 and 1997–2001, economic activity was allowed.

In contrast, where robust competition was weaker, both the official legal framework and informal monitoring by the opposition left considerable loopholes. As a result, state firms and enterprises often funded national party activity, as did local government coffers. Similarly, the benefits were concentrated among a few parties in Bulgaria, the Czech Republic, Slovakia, and Latvia: critically among the BSP, the ODS, the HZDS, Latvia's Way, and the People's Party, respectively. Not surprisingly, public opinion regarding parliamentary corruption varied similarly; it was seen as corrupt

Table 5.2. *Party Funding Regulations as of 2002*

	First Law	Donation Caps	Expenditure Caps	Financial Declarations	Election Accounts	Sanctions
Hungary	1990	Yes	Yes	Yes	No	NAO audits all parties funded by budget, fines
Estonia	1994	Yes	Yes	Yes	Yes	NAO audits all parties
Slovenia	1990	Yes	Yes	Yes	Yes	NAO audits all parties, fines (80K–5M tolars)
Lithuania	1990	Yes	No	Yes	Yes	NAO audits all parties
Poland	1990	Yes	Yes	Yes	Yes	NAO audits all parties funded by budget, fines
Czech R.	1990	No	No	Yes	No	No NAO audits
Slovakia	1994	Yes	Yes	Yes	No	Fines for failure to report finances, no audit
Bulgaria	2001	Fluctuate	Fluctuate	No	No	None
Latvia	1995	No	No	Yes	No	Weak, primarily administrative

Sources: Government laws; Ministries of Finance; Walecki, Marcin, Smilov, Daniel, and Ikstens, Jānis. 2001. *Party and Campaign Funding in Eastern Europe.* Washington: IFES.

by 58 percent of the respondents in Slovakia, 49 percent in Bulgaria and the Czech Republic, and 40 percent in Poland.[2]

This chapter first examines two existing explanations for the patterns in party extraction of state resources: collusion and predation. It then examines both the formal and informal forms of state funding for political parties. Robust competition constrained the exploitative financing of parties through three different mechanisms. Two paired comparisons conclude the chapter: Poland and the Czech Republic show how robust competition limited the parties' ability to extract resources from the most lucrative indirect and informal state sources. Latvia and Slovakia show that formal state

[2] USAID public opinion poll, Radio Free Europe/Radio Liberty broadcast, 10 November 1999, Slovakia.

funding alone does not indicate or influence rent seeking, but that the regulation, access, and concentration of funding do.

Cartels or Predators?

Existing explanations posit that parties can either collude together or prey individually to obtain state resources. First, political parties could form a cartel to split the spoils of the state, making side payments to prevent defection.[3] Such cartels ensure long-term access to state resources for the colluding parties. In many ways, the post-communist political context resembles the one faced by West European "cartel parties" analyzed by Richard Katz and Peter Mair, with expensive competition, dependence on state subsidies in lieu of member dues or close voter relationships, and, above all, parties as "part and agent of the state."[4] Parties in these circumstances, they argue, have a mutual interest in organizational survival and will cement their joint access to state resources without allowing new challengers. Such close cooperation then results in a spiral where parliamentary parties gain office, increase their state funding, and swell the ranks of parliamentary personnel. Isolated further from the voters, these parties then need even more state resources to survive.[5]

Alternatively, governing parties could engage in outright predation (the direct and unrestrained extraction of resources).[6] Uncertain of their future access to office but fully aware of the enormity of state holdings, parties can strip assets from the state. Unlike clientelism, predation does not presuppose any exchanges of support for resources – and it also requires no extensive organizational presence. Such predation implies that parties have short time horizons and face few constraints. Frequent turnover would promote extensive extraction of state resources: In the Philippines, for example, "each group in turn would busily set about lining its own pockets, aware that in the next round its fortunes might well be reversed."[7] Alternatively, political actors certain of a long-term stay in office also adopt predatory strategies.

---

[3] Bartolini 1999–2000.

[4] Katz, Richard, and Mair, Peter. 1995. "Changing Models of Party Organization and Party Democracy," *Party Politics*, 1: 5–28, p. 15.

[5] Mair 1995.

[6] See Goldsmith, Arthur. 1999. "Africas Overgrown State Reconsidered," *World Politics*, 4: 520–46. Rose-Ackerman 1999; Bates, Robert. 1981. *Markets and States in Tropical Africa*. Berkeley: UC Press.

[7] Kang 2002, p. 150.

Yet neither strategy was viable for post-communist political parties. Collusion demands both extensive cooperation and a high certainty that the same players will be around to enforce and benefit from the contract in the future.[8] It requires a stable set of actors and the long-term time horizons – themselves the result of already consolidated competition. As noted earlier, however, post-communist fluidity (high rates of entry and exit, turnover, electoral volatility) meant that political parties could not be certain that their potential partners in collusion would be around in the next electoral term, or even that they themselves would survive the next elections. The party systems remained "too unstable to conclude that a party 'cartel' of privileged insiders is emerging."[9] Moreover, as Ruud Koole points out, party cooperation itself has not been successful in keeping out new entrants.[10] And, if contracts between donors and politicians are not enforceable,[11] neither are contracts among parties, even in the short term. As a result, some evidence of collusion is apparent only where competition is severely dampened, as in the Czech Republic during the Opposition Agreement of 1998–2002.

Similarly, both domestic commitments and external constraints prevented predation. First, as noted earlier, the perceived costs of predation included the high risk of a reversion back to authoritarian rule and the abolishment of competing parties (with the expropriation of their assets) that would follow. And, even if the European Union did not promote state reform until the late 1990s, it consistently made clear that a commitment to democracy by all major political actors was a basic precondition of potential membership. Such commitments precluded purely predatory strategies by political parties. As a result, where we see asset stripping during privatization, individual owners and investors, rather than political parties, were typically responsible. Such entrepreneurs (some of whom gained their ownership through favorable privatization deals and close party alliances) exploited the lax shareholder rights and murky property laws to "tunnel out" the companies they bought from the state.[12] Post-communist democratic

---

[8] Spar 1994; Weingast and Marshall 1988.

[9] Szczerbak 2006.

[10] Koole, Ruud. 1996. "Cadre, Catch-All or Cartel? A Comment," *Party Politics*, 4: 507–23. Koole further points out that the systemic notion of cartel cannot be used to characterize individual parties.

[11] Samuels, David. 2001. "Does Money Matter? Credible Commitments and Campaign Finance in New Democracies," *Comparative Politics* 34, 1 (October): 23–42, p. 29.

[12] Fidrmuc, Jan, Fidrmuc, Jarko, and Horvath, Julius. 2002. "Visegrad Economies: Growth Experience and Prospects." GDN Global Research Project: Determinants of Economic Growth.

parties themselves, however, had both the long-term commitments and the immediate fears that precluded simple predation.[13]

Formal and Informal Extraction

Yet if these strategies were either unavailable or unattractive, post-communist parties could rely on the discretionary strategies delineated earlier: the lax regulation of party finances, building in access to informal gains from privatization and its lucrative profits, and the concentration of formal benefits among the governing parties.

Political parties seeking resources from the state could rely both on formal institutions and informal practices as well as on direct extraction and indirect transfers. The resulting four configurations of party funding are summarized in Table 5.3. Political parties used both formal and direct party funding through the state or the more indirect benefits conferred by electoral laws. They also directly but informally gained state assets by forcing state institutions and state-owned sectors to contribute to political parties; along with privatization profits, parties considered these to be the most lucrative sources of party funding. Finally, informal and indirect sources included bribes and interest-free loans with infinite repayment deadlines contributed to party coffers. These were indirect because they largely came from private investors hoping to curry favor with the parties in obtaining privatization deals and state contracts.[14] These four configurations are examined in turn in the following subsections.

Formal Party Financing

Formal aspects of party financing comprised direct state subsidies for political parties and, far more indirectly, electoral laws. Electoral laws provide

---

[13] If the authoritarian party remained in office, it had neither the democratic commitment nor the fear of authoritarian reversion. Such parties were far more likely to begin to prey on the state, as can be seen in several post-Soviet republics.

[14] Parties also receive *private* donations for numerous reasons: ideological convictions, hope of social access and appointments, promises of specific favors and contracts, the specter of policy change and favorable legislation, or the general benefit of a friendly government in office. This chapter examines these donations insofar as they were made in exchange for awarding state assets or access to policy making, but the analytical focus is on the extraction of state assets in various forms. See Pinto-Duschinsky, Michael. 1985. "How Can Money in Politics Be Assessed?" Paper presented at the International Political Science Conference, Paris, p. 23.

Table 5.3. *Party Strategies of Resource Extraction from the State*

	Formal Institutional Sources	Informal Practices
Direct extraction	Party funding laws	State firm and local government support, legal loopholes
Indirect transfers	Electoral laws	Privatization deals, loans, bogus companies, party taxes

one weak form of *indirect* formal party financing. They regulate free media access and electoral thresholds, both of which could make campaigns more expensive for the parties. However, the variation in these laws has been found to have a tenuous impact on political exclusion or representation, and at most they marginally affected the potential for exploitation.[15] Thus formal and indirect state support in the form of electoral laws was not a significant source of party resource extraction.

Direct and *formal* party financing consisted of parliamentary subventions, electoral campaign funding, and funding for the maintenance of party offices and staff. All these ensured the survival of parties that cleared the thresholds for state financing. Parties received support both for campaign expenditures and for the maintenance of parliamentary offices. Nearly all post-communist democracies developed state subventions for political parties (the exceptions are Latvia, and, until 1996, Estonia). This was the most direct way for parties to benefit from their role as state builders – but not necessarily the most lucrative.

The endogeneity of state funding to its beneficiaries has led some to suspect that it indicates a party takeover of the state – a substitute for membership support.[16] The state is increasingly important in financing parties across Western Europe, with anywhere from 25 percent (Austria) to 84 percent (Finland) of party funds coming from the state.[17] Such funding is said to result in dwindling party membership and central party hierarchies growing in power.[18] The situation would be exacerbated in post-communist

---

[15] Birch, Sarah. 2002. *Electoral Systems and Political Transformation in Post-Communist Europe.* London: Palgrave MacMillan.

[16] O'Dwyer 2003.

[17] Mair, Peter. 1994. "Party Organizations," in Katz, Richard, and Mair, Peter, eds. *How Parties Organize.* New York: Sage, p. 9.

[18] Mendilow, Jonathan. 1992. "Public Party Funding and Party Transformation in Multiparty Systems," *Comparative Political Studies,* 25, 1 (April): 90–117.

Europe, where parties subordinate the search for members to the search for votes and look for secure funding from all possible sources.[19] Others rejoin that state subventions were introduced with very different aims: to "contribute to less corruption, more control of lobbying, more equal opportunities in party competition and some control of the cost explosion,"[20] and have no bearing on party system configurations or membership levels.[21]

In resolving this debate, a key starting point is that political parties themselves decide who can benefit and how much from formal party financing.[22] Depending on the configurations of competition, then, state funding could amplify the incumbents' advantage (if they were awarded on the basis of parliamentary seats) or it could allow multiple extraparliamentary parties to survive (if, for example, they were awarded on the basis of thresholds lower than those for entry into parliament).[23] The more that parties anticipated losing votes, the more generous they tended to be to small parties and nonparliamentary actors. Thresholds for state funding would then fall well below parliamentary entrance thresholds, for example.

Yet if formal state funding is a function of competition, why would governing parties with a weak opposition bother with sharing state funding at all? The devil lay in the details of regulation, access, and concentration of benefits. Much as with formal institutions of monitoring and oversight, ruling parties could build in advantages for themselves at the expense of their competitors – by awarding funding on the basis of seats, for example. As a result, governing parties could formally play by the democratic rules of the game (thus avoiding criticism from international organizations, who were concerned with the observance of democratic norms far more than with state institutions), yet continue to benefit unduly.

Thus, formal funding itself is not necessarily evidence of party exploitation of the state.[24] If anything, as Table 5.4 suggests, the more exploited the state, the lower the share of the public subsidy in financing political parties. Rather, state financing of parties more plausibly indicates exploitation if it

[19] Heywood 1997, p. 431.
[20] Nassmacher, Karl-Heinz. 1989. "Structure and Impact of Public Subsidies to Political Parties in Europe," in Alexander, Herbert, ed. *Comparative Political Finance in the 1980s.* Cambridge: Cambridge University Press, pp. 236–67, p. 238.
[21] Pierre, Jon, Svasand, Lars, and Widfeldt, Anders. 2000. "State Subsidies to Political Parties: Confronting Rhetoric with Reality," *West European Politics*, 23, 2 (July): 1–24. See also Sartori 1976, p. 95.
[22] Mair 1997, p. 106.
[23] This was the case in Hungary, Poland, and Slovenia.
[24] Mair 1997, p. 106. See also Katz and Mair 1995.

190

Table 5.4. *Estimated Sources of Party Income by 2004, in Percentages*

	Public Subsidy	Membership Dues	Private Donations
Hungary	69	<3	25
Estonia	85	<1	10–15
Slovenia	70–5	<1	25
Poland	50	<1	50
Czech R.	35	5	55
Slovakia	30	4	60
Bulgaria	<20	<7	76
Latvia	N/a	>2	85
W. Europe	52	10–15	20–40

Sources:
Author's calculations, obtained by $\Sigma\ S_i/\Sigma\ T_i$, where S = state contribution to ith party, and T = total funds received by ith party. Ágh, A. 1995. "Partial Consolidation of the East-Central European Parties," *Party Politics*, 4: 491–514; Walecki, M. 1999. *Wybrane aspekty finansowania partii politycznych w Polsce* [Selected aspects of party financing in Poland]. Warsaw: ISP; Czech and Slovak ministries of interior; Pierre et al. 2000; *Lidové Noviny*, 2 September 1996; Dmitrova 2002; Sikk 2006.

is unregulated, allows discretionary access, and is concentrated among the most powerful parties. State subventions by themselves can be the result of party collusion, existing norms about state provisions, or simply functional demands. But they indicate exploitation only when they are poorly regulated and clearly and unduly benefit incumbent parties. Where funding was informal and discretionary, the state was much more likely to be exploited. As a result, as we will see in this chapter, both Latvia (with no state funding) and Slovakia (with extensive state funding of parties) saw considerable resource extraction from the state by political parties.

Conversely, where funding was regulated, transparent, and dispersed among parties, we see far less exploitation, no matter what the level of direct formal party financing by the state. The generous state party funding in Hungary was highly regulated and informal funding constrained. The extensive compromises made between the communist party and the opposition, and within the opposition camp, in 1989–90[25] resulted in the distribution of former communist party property to all the political parties after the first elections. This both kept the parties afloat financially and led to

[25] Bernhard 2000; Körösényi, Andras. 1999. *Government and Politics in Hungary*. Budapest: CEU Press.

continued public state funding for parties since then.[26] Nearly two-thirds of the new law on parties was concerned with the methods of funding distribution, use, accounting, and limits on potential donations. Party funding reports were made public, and an independent monitoring agency, the Government Control Commission, was set up. Subsequently, in May 1991, professional accounting standards for parties were introduced, which were repeatedly upheld.[27] As a result, despite the rise of foundations closely allied with the parties and the ties of business with parties (especially the communist successor MSzP, with its links to "spontaneous privatizers"), party finances were more public, more stringently controlled, and allowed less rent seeking than in the other cases considered here.[28]

Conversely, Estonia introduced state funding of political parties only in 1996. Yet, because of the increasingly strict regulations imposed on parties before and after, they could not exploit the state. Financing itself was introduced "with the aim of limiting the undue influence of other sources of financing, including both corrupt corporate donations and foreign donations."[29] Formal state financing of parties was then greatly increased in 2004, partly to compensate parties for a major new constraint: the banning of all corporate donations. Despite some shortcomings in the regulation of party financing (for example, a parliament committee took over the auditing of party financial reports from the National Election Commission), the 2004 law further strengthened the strictures, and the monitoring, of party finances.

The Slovenian state funded political parties from the start, and increased the regulation and strictures on party financer over time. At the start of the democratic period, liberal funding laws did not expressly forbid foreign funding and allowed for public subsidies, membership fees, and donations from individuals and enterprises. Reporting requirements were in place, but only a few parties reported their income. However, as a result of the LDS–Christian Democratic rivalry and a raft of mutual accusations, major

---

[26] According to the October 1989 law, parties receiving more than 1 percent of the vote were eligible for state funding. Each party received additional state funds in proportion to the number of candidates it presented. A quarter of state funding was distributed among all parties in parliament, and 75 percent on the basis of votes received. Van Biezen, Ingrid. 2004. "Political Parties as Public Utilities," *Party Politics*, 10, 6: 701–22.

[27] Petroff, Włodzimierz. 1996. *Finansowanie partii politycznych w postkomunistycznej Europie.* [The financing of political parties in Europe]. Warsaw: Polish Parliamentary Bureau of Analyses and Expertises.

[28] Körösényi 1999, p. 168.

[29] Sikk 2006.

changes were introduced with the 1994 Law on Political Parties: The Court of Auditors took over the oversight power and would now institute heavy fines for parties that did not meet the reporting requirements. Sources of funding were curtailed; no anonymous donors were allowed, all donations over $2,000 had to be reported, all parties had to declare their assets to parliament and to the Supreme Audit Office, and subsidies were stopped if the parties failed to report their earnings properly. As a result, by 1996, Slovenian parties were funded mostly by public subsidies.[30]

Informal Party Financing

Informal extraction from the state took both direct and indirect forms. One *direct* source of informal state funding comprised state firms and local governments, which incumbents sometimes forced to contribute to national party coffers, lest their budgetary appropriations suffer. Lax laws also promoted informal state funding. In some cases, laws that allowed anonymous donors and foreign sources or failed to establish caps on donations and expenditures made extraction easier. In other polities, these legal gaps were quickly and effectively filled, to the point that some Polish businesspeople complained that "no firm trading on the Warsaw Stock Exchange can possibly contribute to political parties,"[31] since the law forbade firms with even 1 percent state ownership or foreign ownership to fund parties.

In using *informal* and *indirect* sources of state funding, political parties took advantage of conduits they built in to the market and democratic institutions. The most desirable and lucrative sources of funding were to be found in the redistribution of communist state assets, which were difficult to monitor and supervise given the extent of these processes. The extent of the communist state holdings – which included industrial enterprises, real estate, and natural resources – meant that these sales were potentially a very lucrative source of assets. The tenders, bids, contracts, and direct profits from the sales were especially attractive in the first few years of privatization, when the biggest plums were available. Governing coalitions awarded contracts and sales to party allies and assumed control over the privatization process and its regulation. They obtained kickbacks from both domestic and foreign investors in exchange for favorable investment and procurement decisions. These decisions could both benefit existing party

[30] Krašovec 2001.
[31] Paradowska, Janina. 2000. "Lewa kasa, Prawa kasa," *Polityka*, 22 January 2000.

allies and create new ones. These allies were the source of another indirect source of state funds: loans made to parties, often by banks that were partly state-owned, with little promise of repayment.

The specific strategies of gaining rents from privatization varied from state to state. Where privatization was gradual but with considerable oversight, as in Poland and in Slovenia, parties colonized the supervisory councils of partially state-owned enterprises, staffing them with their own members. The party representatives on the supervisory boards then funneled back a portion of their salary to the party. In the Czech Republic and Latvia, where privatization was relatively fast and the oversight less extensive, private investors tended to bribe parties directly. In Slovakia, rapid direct sales resulted in favoring party allies, who would then funnel money back to the party. Not surprisingly, 83 percent of Slovak property that was privatized was sold via noncompetitive sales to a predetermined buyer.[32] Finally, in Bulgaria, stalled privatization with minimal oversight led to the direct takeover of state assets by party allies.[33] By late 1992, 100 percent of the privatization revenues in Bulgaria were funneled into the discretionary extrabudgetary funds controlled by parties directly.[34] As a result, while privatization scandals related to political parties occurred in each of the cases under consideration, the specifics of party involvement varied considerably.

Other, if less lucrative, sources of informal and indirect party funding included salary paybacks and entrepreneurial activity. Parliamentarians and state officials paid anywhere from 5 to 10 percent of their salaries back to the party that appointed them to these positions.[35] These party "taxes" were levied on those who obtained political positions: parliamentarians, councilors, and members of enterprise boards. Such tithing meant that state resources would flow back to the political parties. Political party allies also created private firms, who would then provide consulting and other services to state-owned enterprises. The profits from these services would then be funneled back to political party coffers.[36]

---

[32] Fidrmuc et al. 2002, p. 86.

[33] Frydman et al. 1998; Ganev 2005.

[34] Ibid., pp. 105–6.

[35] Wealthy but unknown political hopefuls paid up to $10,000 to gain entry onto some of the political party candidate lists. *Gazeta Wyborcza*, 28 November 1997. Otherwise, parties first picked central and local party leaders, then prominent personalities, and subsequently mayors and other local officials, as well as members of sympathetic societal organizations. *Polityka*, "Klucze i Wytrychy," 17 July 1993; Walecki, Marcin, ed. 2002. *Finansowanie Polityki*. Warsaw: Wydawnictwo Sejmowe, p. 93. See aslo *Dziennik Polski*, 15 December 1999.

[36] Paradowska 2000.

Impact of Robust Competition

Political party competition constrained the exploitative aspects of both formal and informal funding through several mechanisms. First, a robust competition led governments to establish quickly formal funding institutions, which also limited the rents parties could gain from privatization. The shared worry that governing parties would entrench themselves as a result of their privileged access to state resources led to a consensus on the need to close loopholes, monitor and regulate financing effectively, and eliminate as much of the informal and covert funding as possible.[37] As a result, party funding was more stringently regulated, formalized, and transparent, and increasingly so over time. Not only did the formal regulation arise earlier, but it tended to disperse funding rather than concentrating it among the electoral winners. Such support is more of a "public good," since it is nonexclusive and its use by one party does not diminish the others' benefits.

Second, competition also directly constrained informal funding from the state by monitoring the government and publicizing transgressions. Robust competition constrained rent seeking from privatization and government contracts, both because diverse parties were in charge and because of informal monitoring. For example, a key form of informal state funding for Hungarian political parties consisted of informal commissions from state contracts received by party allies. Thus, in 1996, the APV (State Privatization and Holding Company) hired a lawyer, Marta Tocsik, to negotiate with local governments regarding compensation for local real estate holdings that were privatized. For negotiating a better deal for the APV, Tocsik received $3.2 million, or 10 percent of what she had saved the APV. She then transferred half of this money to firms closely allied to the MSzP. However, once the deal was exposed by the opposition Fidesz party and the media, Tocsik was subsequently indicted and found guilty of malfeasance, as were the managers of the firms to whom half her commission had gone.

Similarly, robust competition in Slovenia meant that financing scandals resulted in immediate sanctions. Thus, Marjan Podobnik, head of the Slovenian People's Party (Slovenska Ljudska Stranka, SLS), was accused of developing fictitious bank accounts and of blackmailing large enterprises slated for potential privatization.[38] Podobnik was also involved in accepting

---

[37] Ibid.

[38] For example, the construction company SCT was offered approval of its privatization if it gave the party 200,000 German marks ($100,000).

funds from a state-owned company (Lek), which was legal at the time, in 1992. However, since the funds were channeled through another corporation (to get around Lek's supervisory board, which did not want to make the donation), Podobnik and his associates were charged with accepting illegal financing. The opposition Social Democrats brought these stories to light, a media scandal ensued, and the Podobnik group was ousted from the party.[39]

Third, the opposition monitored how and where parties extracted resources from privatization processes. Where privatization did not take place, political parties were able to hold onto and take over state assets directly. With minimal oversight, the links between parties, state assets, and potential third-party beneficiaries could grow unimpeded. For example, because of the lack of consistent provisions on party property in Bulgaria, some parties turned into commercial entities, "dealing primarily with property management instead of political issues"[40] Parties sublet their offices (subsidized by the state); awarded contracts to renovate party offices to allied firms, who would then overcharge the state treasury; and extracted assets from state firms sold to party allies at favorable prices. Most notoriously, the BSP government of 1995–6 forced the National Bank of Bulgaria to prop up failing enterprises and other banks allied to the governing party.[41]

Where no robust competition exposed the practice, parliamentarians were also put on the direct payroll of firms and companies. While their Polish counterparts, for example, served on the supervisory councils of state-owned enterprises, Bulgarian MPs received salaries and commissions from entrepreneurs directly in exchange for favorable contract awards and privatization deals. Informal rules developed: "[I]f the MP acted on behalf of his party, the commission was supposed to go into the party treasury."[42] If the MP acted alone, only a portion would go to the party coffers. Some went a step further: Euroleft leader Alexander Tonov, for example, established a firm fee schedule for his party's parliamentary services, along with

---

[39] Another major scandal of post-communist Slovenian politics was the arms smuggling affair: Minister of Defense Janez Jansa was dismissed in April 1994 after allegations of high-level Slovene officials' involvement in smuggling arms to Bosnian Muslims came to light. The United List of Social Democrats also accepted illegal indirect funding from the British Labour Party in 2000, to the tune of $20,000 U.S.

[40] Center for Study of Democracy Brief, Bulgaria, Sofia, July 2004. Available at http://www.csd.bg, accessed 19 November 2004.

[41] *East European Constitutional Review*, Spring/Summer 1996.

[42] *Novinar*, 16 March 1999.

strict conditions regarding secrecy, deposits, and so on.[43] Given the lack of effective opposition, either against the BSP in 1994–7 or against the UDF in 1997–2001, there were few forces to curtail these activities. Not surprisingly, over 42 percent of Bulgarian companies, the highest such percentage in the region, paid money to political parties in return for favors, and 28 percent paid bribes at least once.[44]

Fourth, in countries with a robust competition, the concentration of benefits was far lower; no one party monopolized informal sources of funding. Further, as in Poland and in Slovenia, businesses refrained from making large donations to any one party that would call attention to their political activity, which in turn minimized the ability to bribe parties to get favorable treatment in privatization deals or other contracts. However, where robust competition was weak, such concentration went unimpeded; for example, when the Bulgarian UDF government was accused in November 1999 of financing improprieties over the past ten years, it refused to answer the press allegations. President Petar Stoyan eventually interfered, asking for a response to the accusations, to no avail, and the two main opposition parties at the time, the BSP and Euroleft, were too weak to capitalize on these problems.[45]

Because it comprises both formal and informal sources and sanctioning mechanisms, party financing is thus highly vulnerable to changes in the robustness of competition – and immediately so. The processes of institutional creation that characterized the building of formal state oversight and the expansion of the state administration are slower moving, and as a result, they take longer to respond to the changes in the robustness of party competition. Several aspects of exploitative party financing, however, such as selling state assets, direct party skimming of privatization profits, or bribe taking, do not rely on the construction of new laws or agencies, but on immediate opportunities and lack of monitoring.

---

[43] *168 Chassa*, 26 March 1999. In addition, elites who financed political parties obtained lucrative contracts – most notably, Maxim Dimov, who financed the Nacionalno Dvizhenie Simeon Vtori (NDSV, National Movement Simeon II) electoral campaign in 2001, became the deputy chair of Roseximbank. The state channeled all Tax Office and Customs payments through Roseximbank, as well as the operations of the biggest taxpayers, such, Lukoil and Mobiltel. Lukoil and Naftex, two oil companies, both financed NDSV Campaigning, including handing over their billboards and issuing credit cards to party officials. Dimitrova, Zoya. 2002. "Financing Election Campaigns." Unpublished Ms. Ljubljena: Peace Institute, p. 18.

[44] Business Environment and Enterprise Performance Survey, World Bank, 1999.

[45] *East European Constitutional Review*, Winter/Spring 2000.

This sensitivity of financing to competition began with the communist exit, and whether it forced a dispersal of communist assets across all parties. A negative example serves as an illustration: The communist successor Bulgarian Socialist Party was never forced to divest itself of either its organizational holdings or its bank accounts. The opposition's weakness until the late 1990s meant that it "did not press for Communist Party funds to be dispersed or examined."[46] The BSP thus had the formal advantage of its resources, while retaining the profitable informal connections it held. Since party financing regulations allowed parties to conduct business activities, the BSP could benefit especially from laws that allowed all parties to buy, manage, and sell property, real estate holdings, and enterprises.

Another manifestation of the sensitivity of party funding strategies to robust competition is that even whereas robust competition has constrained parties in the past, its weakening immediately allows governing parties to begin to plunder the state. When the Hungarian Fidesz coalition government gained office in 1998, for example, several competitive constraints were loosened. The opposition MSzP spent most of 1998–9 recovering from the shock of losing elections and focused on internal party reform, holding congresses, changing officials, and launching committees to address its electoral shortcomings. In the process, Fidesz quickly moved to eliminate several of the vantage points from which the opposition had earlier constrained the government: The parliamentary immunity/conflict-of-interest committee, headed by the opposition throughout the post-communist era, now became a coalition bailiwick, and the public prosecutor, a Fidesz appointee, did not take action in the fifty-odd complaints of criminal behavior against Fidesz appointees. Perceiving little threat of replacement, Fidesz felt free to act as it wished, even though it ended many of its excesses once MSzP regained its strength in 2000–1.

Under Fidesz, informal party funding grew increasingly intense, and its beneficiary was chiefly Fidesz and its coalition partner, the Smallholders' Party. Bribery was the preferred channel, as private and state firms vied for the favor of the coalition. Thus, in 2000, the chair of the Procurement Committee in parliament was caught accepting a bribe of Ft 20 million ($80,000 U.S.). In 2000, the controversial leader of the Smallholders and the minister of agriculture, József Torgyán, was accused of accepting bribes in a series of scandals. The coalition-led Immunity Committee refused to censure him or to initiate proceedings against him. However, by this

---

[46] *RFE/RL Report on Eastern Europe*, 9 March 1990.

point, the opposition had reawakened and began to exert enormous informal pressure, with politician after politician publishing his or her financial statements when Torgyán refused to do so (see Chapter 3). Even Fidesz began to consider openly a new conflict-of-interest law, and Torgyán was compelled to resign in February 2001.

In extreme cases, the endogeneity of party funding to competition meant that governing parties themselves determined the amount of funding available during each electoral term. Not surprisingly, where there was little robust competition, governing parties "gradually scaled down public funding, because they realized that by being in power they were in a much more favorable position in terms of fundraising than the opposition."[47] Rather than tying their hands with direct, regulated, formal state funding, such parties had the opportunity to avail themselves of indirect funding, both formal and informal. Such discretion allowed governing parties to try and build in advantages for themselves. For example, in Bulgaria, both electoral laws and party funding regulations changed from electoral term to electoral term, as the government tried to "calculate how to write the rules for its own benefit"[48] (a possibility made all the more feasible by the absolute majority held by the BSP in the 1994–7 parliament). This discretion was so profitable that not even EU pressure prompted immediate change. In 2001, annual government subsidies were made proportionate to the number of votes gained, for parties with 1 percent or more of the vote.[49] The amount of the subsidy, however, was not specified and clearly favored the incumbent party. It was not until 2004, moreover, that anonymous donors had to be made public, and even then parties could continue their business activities.

This is not to say that political parties Hungary, Slovenia, or Poland were somehow more virtuous – where they could, they too extracted state resources. The slower pace of privatization and restructuring of state enterprises offered considerable opportunities. For example, in Poland, charges surfaced of malpractice in public procurement, favorable awarding of concessions, and unregulated lobbying.[50] New rules in 1997 prevented Polish parties from having economic interests in even partly state-owned

---

[47] Ikstens, Jānis, Smilov, Daniel, and Walecki, Marcin. 2002. "Campaign Finance in Central and Eastern Europe," *IFES Reports* (April). Washington: IFES.

[48] *East European Constitutional Review*. Winter 2001, 10, 1.

[49] Ibid.

[50] World Bank. 1999. *Corruption in Poland: Review of Priority Areas and Proposals for Action*. Warsaw: World Bank.

firms,[51] but party members were still assigned to the supervisory boards (*rady nadzorcze*) of state corporations, and a portion of their salary flowed back to benefit their party finances.

However, while there were several privatization scandals, most centering on the links between late-communist elites and their economic holdings, governing parties were rarely implicated (with the notable exceptions of the Rywin and Orlen scandals, discussed later in this chapter). Moreover, the vigilance of the opposition parties meant that such scandals would be publicized immediately; allegations that privatization processes skimmed funds for the MSzP came to light in 1995, a year after the MSzP began to govern. Similarly, the Postabank scandal immediately revealed that the state-owned bank sponsored various firms and politicians, giving them preferential interest rates.[52] In contrast, the many excesses of the Czech ODS in the early 1990s only became known years later.

Rethinking Party Finances

Three implications follow. First, state funding alone does not correlate with or indicate exploitation; its regulation and oversight, both formal and informal, are more relevant. Second, fluctuations in the levels of opposition criticism and access can have immediate repercussions on party financing, more so than either the building of formal institutions or the expansion of the state administration. Third, party competition is more likely to affect the availability and regulation of state funding than vice versa.[53] Political parties determined the levels and regulation of party financing from the very start. Therefore, it is unlikely that state funding itself determined political party competition. Similarly, it is not clear that state funding had a direct influence on volatility, party entrance, or membership rates, as recent studies have suggested.[54] As a result, it is not necessarily the case that state funding is responsible for preventing parties from building roots in civil society.[55] Rather, parties with weak roots and low organizational presence

---

[51] *Polityka*, 19 April 1997.

[52] Lewis 2000, p. 111; Ilonszki 2000. The bank's eventual collapse cost the taxpayers some 120–180 billion forints ($500–700 million U.S.).

[53] Jóhanna Birnir argues that state funding lowers volatility and the entry of new parties in post-communist states. Birnir, Jóhanna Kristín. 2005. "Public Venture Capital and Party Institutionalization," *Comparative Political Studies*, 38, 8 (October): 915–38.

[54] Ibid., Katz and Mair 1995.

[55] Van Biezen, Ingrid. 2000. "Party Financing in New Democracies," *Party Politics*, 6, 3: 329–42.

turned to the state as the main source of resources necessary for their survival. The causal arrows run from configurations of party competition and organizations to state-funding regimes, not vice versa, as the next section demonstrates.

Comparing Party Financing Regimes

The next section relies on two paired comparisons. First, the cases of Poland and the Czech Republic show the impact of informal and indirect forms of state funding. The more robust competition in Poland both constrained informal party funding and influenced where and how parties could indirectly extract privatization rents. Second, the cases of Slovakia and Latvia show how state exploitation was not a function of party funding but of the extent and strength of its regulation. Slovakia had high levels of state funding, and Latvia none – yet in both countries, political parties heavily exploited the state.

If robust competition constrains state exploitation in the realm of party financing, we ought to observe lower rates and greater sanctioning of informal funding where more robust competition exists. We ought also to observe greater regulation (reporting requirements and transparency enforcement) and greater dispersion of benefits among parties. The mechanisms ought to be both responsive and anticipatory – that is, parties react both to scandals and evidence of malfeasance, in anticipation of losing office. State financing for parties, if this explanation is correct, should not reflect robust competition, but the *regulation* of privatization, spending, and sanctions should.

Privatization and Informal Funding

Polish and Czech party funding differed along the three dimensions of exploitation in party funding: the extent of regulation, the access to state resources via privatization, and the concentration of benefits. Czech party funding was less regulated and the benefits concentrated in the hands of the incumbents far more than in Poland. The extent of informal funding – the resources gained from the processes of privatization – differed considerably, with Czech parties benefiting far more directly and extensively. This is all the more surprising given that Poland implemented slower privatization, with an intermediate stage of "commercialization" for state enterprises slated for privatization, which engendered extensive party involvement in enterprise oversight. In contrast, Czech privatization was more rapid and did not involve political parties to the same extent in supervisory or regulatory roles.

In Poland, due to constant monitoring by the opposition and the media, regulation of and constraints on party funding increased steeply in the first decade of democratic competition. This is not to say that all regulations were enforced effectively or that the state institutions were impervious. Nonetheless, the concentration of resources remained low; no party had high and consistent access to the state, and the one party that consistently tried to privilege itself, the PSL, was punished both by its parliamentary opposition and, subsequently, the electorate.

Formal party funding legislation grew out of the initial conflict between the communist PZPR and the anticommunist opposition Solidarity forces. The communist proposal for state funding came as part of a package that would have disadvantaged Solidarity. Political parties could not expect money from either state enterprise or foreign sources, ten thousand signatures would be necessary to register a party, and workplace organizations would be allowed.[56] Solidarity opposed each of these measures, since it had several foreign allies, worried about its organizational ability, and knew that the communists already had access both to state funding and workplace party organizations. The compromise constrained both actors: Neither foreign nor state funding for election campaigns was allowed, but workplace organizations were abolished. For fear of communist domination, no state funding arose initially, but each senator and member of parliament received state funds to keep up local offices (about $125 a month, at a time when the average salary was about $90 a month). Many parliamentarians opened up their local offices at the seats of the local party organizations, thus indirectly supporting the political parties.[57]

Subsequent compromises further increased regulations. The largest two parties in the 1991–3 parliament, the Democratic Union (Unia Demokratyczna, UD) and the Party of the Democratic Left (SLD), allied to change the electoral law to favor bigger parties. However, because even these two parties each commanded fewer than 14 percent of the seats and thus needed to get the other parties' support, they provided state funding for other parliamentary parties as a "carrot." Uncertain of their future prospects, the

[56] *Rzeczpospolita*, 7 November 1989.
[57] *Rzeczpospolita*, 21 October 1992.

other parties (with one libertarian exception) supported the proposed state financing.

The 1993 electoral law introduced subventions for party parliamentary activity and gave more free media time to all parties with national lists. It also continued the cap on the amount of private campaign spending[58] and broadened the definition of "state involvement" in firms and enterprises that could not contribute to parties, further limiting informal access to state resources. After seventy-seven of forty-three parties failed to declare assets properly after the 1991 elections,[59] financial declarations were now enforced more rigorously: After Solidarity lost its right to budget subventions in 1993 when it was late by one day with its declaration, all those committees with the right to state subvention submitted their declarations on time.[60] Additional funds were awarded by parliamentary seat rather than only by votes gained, thus rewarding the incumbents – who then changed the rules in the light of the rise of the AWS as a potent political force.[61] In 1997, state funding was broadened to include all parties with 3 percent of the *vote* (rather than seats). The threshold rewarded parties with more votes, as well as those that conducted cheap campaigns, since parties could keep the surplus. The 1997 law further strengthened reporting requirements and their enforcement, but did not propose full state funding, for fear of taxpayer revolt.[62]

After several years of funding parliamentary representations and partially refunding campaign costs for all parties, Poland continued to move to greater public state funding. A new law in 2001 mandated full reporting and more effective sanctions.[63] As one author commented, "all agree that to limit corruption it is necessary to publicize the sources of

---

[58] Vinton, Lucy. 1993, "Poland's New Election Law: Fewer Parties, Same Impasse?" *RFE/RL Report*, 7–17 (8 July); International Foundation for Electoral Systems. 1996. *Electoral Laws.* Washington: IFES. Spending was capped at the equivalent of sixty average monthly wages.

[59] *Wprost*, 15 May 1993.

[60] Walecki, Marcin, ed. 2002. *Finansowanie Polityki.* Warsaw: Wydawnictwo Sejmowe, p. 143.

[61] This also meant that some parties actually made a profit on the elections, such as PSL and SdRP in 1993. Lewis and Gortat 1995, p. 607. In both Poland and Hungary, parties were dependent on state funding, receiving anywhere from 24 percent to 95 percent of their funding from the state. Agh, Attila. 1995. "Partial Consolidation of the East-Central European Parties: The Case of the Hungarian Socialist Party," *Party Politics*, 4: 491–514, fn7. The FKGP received 93 percent, the Christian Democrats 88 percent, Fidesz 84 percent, SzDsz 58 percent, MDF 45 percent, and the MSzP 24 percent.

[62] *Polityka*, 16 April 1997.

[63] Parties not submitting a report, or those that did not pass the forensic accountants' scrutiny, would not receive state funds for that electoral period.

party financing."[64] As a result, the new law eliminated public fundraising campaigns and further capped contributions. More importantly, it stipulated that all campaign spending had to come from a public electoral fund set up by each party and monitored by an independent commission. The new law further ended all entrepreneurial activity by parties and issued generous state subventions for parties – provided that they could account for how they spent their money, and that these public reports pass audits by independent public accountants.[65] (In 2003, three parties lost their right to state subventions for three years when their annual reports were rejected as inadequate.[66]) Any nonstate gifts had to go through an official bank account, set up exclusively to cover campaign funds. As a result, the 2001 law made formal state the main form of financing for political parties.[67]

No party could concentrate funding, whether private or state, in its hands. Polish businesspeople were not particularly eager to support individual parties financially.[68] Only 4 percent of Polish private managers polled complained about corruption, but more than half were convinced that a third of the politicians were dishonest.[69] Among those surveyed, the majority declared that "they should not tie themselves to any existing party" and that "they should temporarily support certain tried-and-true persons, not parties at the peaks of the political ladder."[70] Instead, most firms either financed several political parties at once, or none.[71] As a result, most parties received roughly half of their funding from the larger-scale donations from various businesses and individuals.[72] In comparison to the Czech Republic, the donations were tiny. As a result, despite constant opposition monitoring, bribery scandals were rare until 2002 and the spectacular trial of Lew Rywin. Rywin was a film producer accused of attempting to mediate

---

[64] *Rzeczpospolita*, 19 May 2000.

[65] Interview with Kazimierz Czaplicki, head of the Polish Electoral Comission personal communication, June 1, 2001.

[66] Szczerbak 2006, p. 305.

[67] Ibid.

[68] *Polityka*, "Koszt Fotela," 19 June 1993.

[69] *Wprost*, 15 May 1993.

[70] Filas, Agnieszka, and Knap, Jarosław. "Wybór Biznesu," *Wprost*, 20 April 1997.

[71] Walecki 2002, p. 82. Iain McMenamin and Roger Schoenman find that "chaste" relationships, where firms do not develop relationships with any party, dominate in Poland. McMenamin, Iain, and Schoenman, Roger. 2004. "Political Competition, The Rule of Law and Corruption in Successful Post-Communist Countries." *Working Papers in International Studies*, No. 7, Dublin City University.

[72] Centrum Bandanie Opinii Publicznej (CBOS, Center of Public Opinion Research). 2001. "Finansowanie partii politycznych," Komunikat z badań, Fall.

a deal between the Agora publishing company and the SLD government that would exchange $150,000 for a media law that favored future Agora acquisitions. The deal never went through, but the opposition had a field day with the subsequent investigation, which subpoenaed the luminaries of the SLD government.

What makes this relatively equitable distribution of resources all the more surprising is that the communist successor party continued to hold a financial advantage over the others. As in Hungary and Slovenia, the communist party was forced to divest itself of its considerable holdings. In all three cases, the party nonetheless held onto significant funds; in fact, the first party funding–related scandal in Poland came with the founding of the communist successor SdRP in 1990, which was rumored to be financed with suitcases of cash smuggled in from Moscow by party elites. Much as in Hungary, the communist party attempted to preempt the dispersal of its assets to other parties. As communism was falling, regional committees of PZPR went to work, investing party assets into new firms and corporations in late 1988 and 1989. Of the fifty-one firms associated with PZPR prior to 1991, thirty-seven declared bankruptcy before the declaration regarding the nationalization of PZPR assets. Subsequently, the post-communist governing coalition founded in 1993 the Agency for Economic Development (Agencja Rozwoju Gospodarczego) to give out credit on favorable terms. Among the beneficiaries were businesspeople associated with politicians from PSL, the coalition's junior partner.[73] Nonetheless, there was little evidence that party-affiliated businesspeople could systematically profit from the ties to the state and the ruling party.[74] Bank privatization further weakened the ties of parties to banks, such as BGH's ties to the Center Alliance (Porzumienie Centrum, PC) or Pekao's to UW, including the infamous ties or PSL to its "vassal," the BGZ.[75]

A key difference between Polish and Czech state exploitation lies in the processes of privatization. In Poland, by the late 1980s, the Polish communist party had already liberalized the economy and began to set up commercial banks with private components (such as the Bank Inicjatyw Gospodarczych, or BIG) and special accounts to deal with debt servicing. As communism fell, the party founded its own firms and lent money to allies, who then repaid the party in material support. Many of these practices

[73] "Kapitał Rodzinny," *Wprost*, 19 November 1995.
[74] "Apetyt na pieniądze," *Polityka*, 10 April 1993.
[75] *Polityka*, 12 February 2000.

rapidly ended, however, with the ascent to office of the opposition Solidarity after the semifree elections of 1989. While Poland pursued a rapid liberalization policy during the "extraordinary time" of 1989–90, successive governments delayed privatization and reduce its scope, as they faced opposition both in parliament and in their own coalitions.[76] Given the organizational and symbolic clout of the trade union Solidarity, employee councils could veto privatization proposals at each state-owned enterprise. It took until 1995–6 for privatization to begin in earnest, with the "commercialization" law that transformed state enterprises into joint-stock companies owned by the Treasury. These companies had boards made up of state and political representatives, and it is here that political parties began to draw direct benefits from privatization, by placing allies on the boards and tithing their salaries.

Czech privatization took the form of mass voucher privatization, in two waves: 1991–2 and 1994–5. The rapid pace of privatization (as much as 80 percent of state holdings were privatized by 1995) was accompanied by minimal regulation of property rights or ownership structures. As Hilary Appel demonstrates, two consequences followed. First, the state continued to own large blocks of shares following voucher privatization, and "maintained an ownership position indirectly . . . as a consequence of the success of investment privatization funds founded by the main national banks."[77] Banks were still majority-owned by the state, and thus became both creditors and owners of nominally privatized enterprises. Since 71 percent of vouchers in the first wave and 64 percent in the second went to the funds, the state continued its involvement in the economy.[78] Second, legislation for secondary market in privatized shares was not developed, so "investment groups could acquire shares without disclosing the emergence of a new block of ownership and without compensating small stakeholders."[79] The result was "tunneling" of privatized enterprises. Third, without a regulatory infrastructure and oversight bodies (other than a government-controlled National Accounting Office), there were few ways of monitoring privatization tenders or subsequent ownership. The result of this rapid but unregulated privatization was a spate of party-financing scandals that traded donations to parties for favorable access to shares and ownership

---

[76] Orenstein 2001, p. 98.
[77] Appel, Hilary. 2004. *A New Capitalist Order: Privatization and Ideology in Russia and Eastern Europe.* Pittsburgh: University of Pittsburgh Press, p. 61.
[78] Ibid., p. 61.
[79] Ibid., p. 65.

of enterprises – which could then easily be gutted of their assets. Since such entrepreneurs tended to buy their way into favorable privatization deals, their contributions had to be considerably larger than in the Polish case, where privatization decisions fell under the joint purview of employee councils, independent state officials, and political party representatives.

Privatization deals, and the bribes paid to gain them, became a key source of Czech party funding.[80] As a result of the loose regulations, parties freely reached out to banks and firms, with relative impunity. In several cases, investors funded parties in exchange for favorable privatization deals. In 1994, investor Kamil Kolek gave the ODA 1.5 million Kč to buy a department store successfully, despite coming third in the bidding process.[81] (He later demanded back his gift, claiming he was blackmailed into giving a total of 2 million Kč to the party lest he lose his holdings.[82]) The ODA denied that a similar donation affected the ODA-held Ministry of Trade and Industry's decision to sell the donor an enterprise for 35 million Kč less than the agreed-upon price.[83] The ODS and KDU-ČSL stood accused of accepting bribes from the U.S. computer company EDS in exchange for canceling a public tender for the staff information system for ministries run by KDU-ČSL and ODS.[84] All three governing parties in 1996 were found to have false names of donors on lists, and all three received huge anonymous gifts while claiming ignorance of the donors' real identities.[85]

Such informal state funding was made possible by a lax regulatory framework that promoted not only the extraction of state assets, but concentration of the benefits in the hands of the governing parties. From the start, given the antiparty rhetoric of the opposition Civic Forum in 1989, the interim "government of national reconciliation" formulated a rather vague law on parties in January 1990. It did little to address finances other than to stipulate that the Civic Forum, the Communist Party and its four satellites, and the Slovak Public Against Violence could make use of their own funds. Since the communists had enormous resources that led the other parties to

---

[80] Frič argues that there were three separate sites for influencing political parties: the decision over which privatization projects to pursue (parliament), the choice of who would privatize them (the FNM), and voucher privatization (the Ministry of Finances). Frič 1999, p. 155.

[81] Ibid., p. 199.

[82] *Lidové Noviny*, 12 February 1998.

[83] *Rudé Právo*, 10 January 1996.

[84] Government of the Czech Republic. 1999. 125/1999. Resolution: "Government Program for Combating Corruption in the Czech Republic (17 February)." Prague: Ministry of Interior.

[85] Frič 1999, p. 153.

fear for their survival, the new democratic legislature abolished this disparity after the June 1990 elections by forcing the communist party to give up 95 percent of its assets.[86]

As Václav Klaus's ODS arose from the Civic Forum, it "reluctantly allowed" state funding but refused to expand the regulatory framework, creating a persistent pattern. According to a 1991 law, the state funded parties that received 2 percent or more of the vote. These funds were to be used for daily activities of the parties. Parties could not establish their own businesses, but could share in owning and running enterprises. Financial reports were to be made annually and loans were to be stated. However, there were no stipulations regarding the conditions of the loans or strictures on the banks that made them.

Nor did the degree of regulation increase over time. By the 1992 elections, as the ODS became more certain of its support, state funding levels increased while regulations actually decreased. The law now made it possible for state funds to be used for electoral campaigns as well as daily activity. In 1994–5, the coalition moved to financing from the state for vote totals exceeding 3 percent of the electorate and an additional 500,000 Kč ($15,000 U.S.) subventions per MP, in effect limiting which parties could obtain state funding but making it more profitable for the ones who did. Donations over 100,000 Kč ($3,000 U.S.) were to be named, but since the Supreme Audit Chamber could not audit parties as of 1995, there was no effective monitoring of these donations.[87] Business activities were curtailed. In early 1997, however, these constraints were eliminated again and parties could engage in business activities more freely. In contrast to the Polish opposition, which vehemently protested when it perceived unfavorable changes in party funding[88] the Social Democrats, the one plausible opposition party at the time, neither tried to stop the legislation nor criticized it.

Attempts to concentrate benefits continued. When the opposition Social Democrats began to govern in 1998, the new government declared the reform of the party financing system as one of its priorities.[89] Both the ODS and the ČSSD now moved to reform party funding – and in the process, to increase the entrance thresholds for potential competitors. The new

---

[86] Petroff 1996, p. 8.

[87] Reed 2002, p. 280. Not surprisingly, the party registers revealed dozens of faked names.

[88] Szczerbak 2006, p. 305.

[89] "Programové prohlašení Vlády České Republik," [Programmatic Declaration of the Government of the Czech Republic], 27.1.1998. Available at http://www.vlada.cz/ASC/urad/historie/vlada98/dokumenty/progrprohl.il2.htm.

July 2000 law stipulated that all donors must be declared yearly, placed a limit on donations to political party, and limited foreign donations (to foreign parties, foundations, and foreigners residing in the Czech Republic). The subvention for individual MPs was doubled to 1 million Kč ($300,000 U.S.) but gifts could remain anonymous until the 100,000 Kč ($3,000 U.S.) threshold.[90] In many 2000, parliament even voted to abolish the taxation of party donations. Gifts were limited, but loans were not, and parties did not need to provide information regarding the loans or their payment.[91]

The new law also effectively shut down investigations into secret party bank accounts and loans.[92] Not surprisingly, then, loans became a key instrument of party funding. Both the ODA and the ODS received loans of 25 and 50 million Kč, respectively, from Antonín Moravec, head of the Credit and Industry Bank, which they then repaid via favorable privatization deals.[93] Moravec and other party donors, such as Jiří Čadek, Viktor Kožený, and Alexander Komanický, became known as the most prominent of the "tunnelers" – entrepreneurs who bought state firms and rapidly stripped them of all assets via complicated systems of daughter companies and liability transfers. The lack of transparency made these bank "loans" to parties especially attractive, and the parties did not have to state the conditions or guarantors of their loans. These loans were issued by banks owned partially by the state and then paid off by third actors, including state enterprises.[94] Parties could even break up large gifts into smaller ones, thus getting a tax break, and could retain anonymous bank accounts, allowed even under the 1996 law on money laundering.[95]

Access to privatization resources, and to the state more broadly, went unregulated. The lax Czech funding laws also created enormous incentives

---

[90] *Parlamentní Zpravodaj.* 1999. "Jaké jsou klady a zapory aktualního navrhu novely zakona o politických stranach" [What are the bases for the current proposal for the novelization of the law on political parties]. See also Vládní program boje proti korupci v Česke Republice 1998. "Zpráva o korupci v České republice a možnostech účinného postupu proti tomut negativnímu společenskému jevu." 17 February.

[91] *Parlamentní Zpravodaj.* 2000. "Rozhovor s Vojtěchem Šimíčkem o financování politických Stran" [Interview with Vojtěch Šimíček About Party Financing], 5.

[92] Terra, Jonathan. "Political Institutions and Postcommunist Transitions." Paper prepared for the Fourth Annual Society for Comparative Research Graduate Student Retreat, Budapest, May.

[93] *Respekt,* 16 February 1997.

[94] Reed, Quentin. 1996. *Political Corruption, Privatisation and Control in the Czech Republic.* Ph.D. Dissertation, Oxford University.

[95] *Lidové Noviny,* "Bezzubý zakon na špinave penize" [A Toothless Law on Dirty Money], 17 February 1996.

for extracting resources from the state covertly. First, despite formal requirements for reporting party finances, no sanctions were applied to parties that failed to report or falsified their reports. Moreover, under the 1995 ruling of the Supreme Court, the National Control Commission could no longer monitor or sanction party financing. The NKÚ now had no oversight or access to party financial activities, at the request of members of parliament, who also ensured that the law precluding parties from business activity would be abolished.[96] Technically, the Ministry of Finances would cease paying parties its state contributions for failure to declare its finances properly. But in 1996, the ministry (headed by ODS member Ivan Kočarník) refused to do this in the case of ODS.[97]

Unlike Polish or Hungarian regulations, Czech and Slovak laws allowed *state* firms and enterprises to contribute to parties. State-owned firms – including those owned entirely by the state, such as the Petrof piano manufacturer – regularly contributed to governing coalitions.[98] In a notable incident, the ODS held a fund-raising dinner in November 1994, attended by over two hundred businesspeople, most of whom ran state enterprises. State firm donations were limited in 1999, but state foundations could continue to contribute. The loophole enabled state firms to continue to finance parties by setting up foundations.

Local governments were also allowed to donate, and the ODS refused to consider proposals to limit these donations. In September 1998, the press revealed that the ODS was subsidized by numerous corporations that won public orders from the ODS-controlled Prague City Council. Several firms and public utilities run by the local governments contributed to the party coffers.[99] Finally, Czech parties themselves were allowed to undertake business activities until 1994. Then, in a reversal of the regulations engineered by the parliamentary committees, parties were again allowed to conduct business activities in 1997.

In addition to lax regulation, the legislative framework and the weak opposition also facilitated the concentration of resources. Not surprisingly, given its dominant legislative role, the ODS was the biggest beneficiary of all these maneuvers. Over time, all these changes "dramatically increase[d] the gap between the 'haves' and 'have nots' on the party political scene.

---

[96] *Český Tydenník*, 7–9 May 1996.
[97] Reed 1996.
[98] Ibid.
[99] Frič 1999, p. 155.

Moreover, the numerous modifications to constitutional, electoral and parliamentary rules in the Czech Republic since 1993 show a rather consistent trend to establish and reinforce institutional rules where both party strength and the rule of majority play a crucial role."[100] At each point, the governing parties benefited more than their counterparts. For example, although all parties had to put up deposits for their candidate lists in Czech elections, the funds for the parliamentary parties came from state sources, whereas parties outside of parliament had to raise the money themselves.

The most notable scandal occurred with the discovery that the two main donors to the ODS in 1995–6, Lajos Bacs and Rajiv Sinha, were a dead Hungarian and a Mauritian, respectively. Accusations surfaced that Milan Šrejber, an entrepreneur and potential beneficiary of a steelworks privatization deal, was behind the gifts of nearly half a million dollars.[101] The ODS further concealed over 170 million Kč in Switzerland[102] and the reason it received 7.5 million Kč ($240,000) from Moravia Steel after the latter was allowed to lower its bid for Trinecke Žéelezarne by 300 million Kč.[103] In addition, the Investiční a Poštovní bank's funds were used, via the Czech Cultural Trust (a quasi-NGO founded by ODS supporters), to lend 50 million Kč ($2.5 million U.S.) to the ODS in the 1992 campaign, with no repayment deadline. Despite considerable irregularities in its dealings, the bank was subsequently left alone by regulators and continued a revolving door between party leaders and bank directors.[104] One of the bank's daughter companies was headed by ODS affiliate Libor Prochazka, who also owned the newspaper *Denní Telegraf* and held shares in the television stations TV Nova and Prima.[105] Neither the ODS nor the ČSSD returned the funds, nor did it suffer any legal consequences.

[100] Van Biezen, Ingrid, and Kopecký, Petr. 2001. "On the Predominance of State Money: Reassessing Party Financing in the New Democracies of Southern and Eastern Europe," *Perspectives on European Politics and Society*, 2, 3: 401–29, p. 422.

[101] Czech Radio News, 22 November 1997. Available at http://search.radio.cz/news/CZ.

[102] *Respekt*, 1 December 1997.

[103] The ODS also claimed it had received over 2 million Kč from the American Committee for the Support of ODS, despite the latter's denial it had ever paid the money.

[104] The vice chair of ODS, Libuše Benešová, was on the board of the bank from 1996–8. Klaus adviser Jiří Weigel is still one of the managers of the Prague IPB. The ČSSD also developed a relationship with the bank: Jan Klacek was both a high-ranking official within the ČSSD (its shadow vice prime minister) and the head of the bank. Jiří Tesař, former head of bank, wrote the ČSSD program in 1990, and a controversial ČSSD figure, Miroslav Šlouf, emerged as the key defender of IPB interests.

[105] *Mladá Fronta Dnes*, 20 June 2000.

If the ODS dominated rent seeking, other parties valiantly tried. The KDU-ČSL signed a murky agreement with the Italian entrepreneur Leone Mosca, who then sent 3 million Kč ($115,000 U.S.) to its coffers. KDU-ČSL also saw a surprising jump in membership dues (from 7.4 million to 17.7 million Kč) over the course of 1996.[106] Another coalition partner, ODA, received over 6 million Kč ($200,000 U.S.), ostensibly from the TMC Company in the Virgin Islands, which turned out to be Philip Morris, the First Privatization Fund, and the Vitkovice steel mill.[107] ODA incurred debts of over 60 million Kč ($3 million U.S.) in 1992, which the bank owner then offered to erase. A new loan of 58 million Kč ($2.9 million U.S.) was then paid up by a private firm.

In the "Bamberg affair," Social Democrats were accused of promising key government posts in exchange for favorable loans to a group of Czech-German businesspeople in 1996. In 1998, the ČSSD revealed that its hidden sponsors included the British Westminster Foundation for Democracy, the Swedish Olof Palme Foundation, and the Dutch Alfred Mozer Foundation.[108] But the Swedish foundation did not exist, the Dutch denied ever giving money to the party, and the British supporters announced that they gave well over a million dollars, while ČSSD claimed far less. It subsequently transpired that one of the Social Democrats' biggest donors in 1998 was associated with the largest investment fraud in Czech history.[109]

Czech parties received three to ten times as much corporate funding as their Polish counterparts did, largely the result both of lower regulations – and the greater temptations of the privatization processes in the Czech Republic. In Poland, the biggest donors were Arthur Andersen, which gave 50–80,000 PLN ($15,000–20,000 U.S.) to the SLD, UW, and AWS, and the Agora publishing company, which gave 300,000 PLN ($85,000 U.S.) to UW over the course of 1997–2000. Finally, the wealthy businessperson Aleksander Gudzowaty paid for 80 percent of Lech Walesa's 1995 presidential campaign in Poland.[110] All these figures paled in comparison to the largesse of firms supporting the Czech parties.

No party benefited as much as the ODS, whose electoral victories in 1992 and in 1996 made it seem invincible – and for entrepreneurs eager to benefit from the party's lax corporate regulation, irresistible. These repeated

---

[106] As early as 1993, Mosca gave 3 million Kč to KDU-CSL.
[107] *Lidové Noviny*, 14 February 1998.
[108] *Lidové Noviny*, 17 February 1998.
[109] Reed 2002, p. 283.
[110] *Polityka*, 22 January 2000.

scandals eventually brought down the ODS government in the winter of 1997. (Specifically, news of a secret Swiss bank account led several MPs to abandon the coalition.) After several notables left the party to form the Freedom Union (Unie Svobody), the ODS subsequently adopted several steps to clear its reputation, including hiring an outside auditor and donating 7 million Kč of its false donations to the victims of the floods that took place in the late summer of 1997.[111] As the scandals piled up, parties were now to name all donors, employees, wages paid, and so on, but no enforcement mechanisms were put in place to control this informal party financing, despite the Clean Hands campaign.[112] In short, the largely unchallenged concentration of power meant that the governing parties could enrich themselves considerably, if indirectly, from the state and privatization processes.

In short, more robust competition in Poland meant greater regulation and deconcentration of assets held by political parties – and a far more limited ability to benefit from the processes of privatization. In contrast, the weaker opposition in the Czech Republic allowed incumbent parties to benefit unduly for years, and to create a system of privatization that created incentives for direct and unregulated contributions to political parties in the hopes of preferential treatment.

Formal State Funding as Exploitation?

If party competition affected how (and how much) political parties gained informal funding, this section argues that formal funding itself was neither a boon nor a bane to state exploitation. Parties could exploit the state independently of the existence of state funding, with or without formal state funding provisions, as in Slovakia and Latvia, respectively.

Slovakia shows the opportunities for state exploitation with considerable state funding provisions. Initially, the Slovak party funding scheme was identical to the Czech, since the two were in the Czechoslovak federation. In 1992, the law was revised to stipulate that parties without mandates would lose their funds. This benefited the newly ascendant Movement for a Democratic Slovakia (HZDS), led by Vladimír Mečiar, both by eliminating funds for potential new challengers and by permitting a flexible

---

[111] Appel 2001, p. 537.

[112] Jednotka boji proti korupci, Ministry of Interior. 2001. *Zpráva o korupci v ČR a o plnění harmonogramu opatření vládního programu boje proti korupci v ČR* [Report about corruption in the Czech Republic and the fulfillment of the schedule for the government program of the fight against corruption in the Czech Republic].

interpretation of what it meant for a party to gain mandates. Given the constant splitting and fusing of parties in parliament, the latter benefit proved an especially important loophole, one that Mečiar fully exploited once he began to appoint the judiciary in charge of interpreting the law. The 1992 law further abolished provisions for state funding to new political parties, stipulated by the 1990 law. A 1994 revision stipulated that donors making gifts over 50,000 Ks ($1,425 U.S.) could not remain anonymous. Foreign contributions remained legal, which led to Slovak companies funneling large amounts of money to political parties from fake businesses or individuals outside the country.[113]

Little regulation of party finances existed until 2000. Under the 1991–8 HZDS governments, the state financed parties with 3 percent of the vote, but did not regulate this funding. Moreover, there were no stipulations limiting the amount of contributions from private firms or state-owned enterprises, nor were there any contribution limits. A 1994 law formally allowed political formations to promote their business activity only in clearly defined areas. But in 1996, Slovak media revealed that HZDS members had founded businesses that participated in privatization projects in spheres of business activity not covered by the Law on Political Parties and Movements. Moreover, HZDS often informed would-be participants in the privatization process that partnership with HZDS-tied companies was a "necessary precondition of the successful realization of their privatization projects."[114]

The law on party financing was largely left unchanged until 2000, when new subventions for mandates (500,000 Sk per MP per year or $1,500 U.S.) and parliamentary activities were introduced. Under the previous law, each party that received at least 3 percent of the vote received 60 Sk ($1.8 U.S.) per vote. The new system increased substantially the amount of state support: Parties now received an additional 75 million Sk ($2.2 million U.S.) from the state budget. The 2000 law further obolished anonymous donations and stipulated that parties publish financial declarations for the first time, but without introducing any monitoring or sanctioning of reports moreover, loans and other indirect sources would remain anonymous. The law's revision in 2004 made sponsorship a matter of written agreements if the donation exceeded 5,000 Sk ($150 U.S.). It also limited membership fees, a move that would hit the opposition ANO, the New Citizens' Alliance, the hardest, since its founder single-handedly funded most of the

---

[113] *East European Constitutional Review*, 9, 4, Fall 2000.
[114] Mesežnikov 1997, p. 38.

party's budget. The law also more than doubled the subsidy per vote to over 140 Sk and made state subventions a function of the average wage, thus ensuring a long-term increase in state funding.[115]

Informal exploitation also grew to epic proportions under the Mečiar government. Stunningly, bribery was no longer illegal. As a result, the HZDS became the wealthiest party in Slovakia – and because its finances were dominated by covert deals and extensive personal ties, its brief exits from power in 1991 and in 1994 did not change its dominant position. Instead, the party continued to receive "astronomically high" amounts from anonymous donors,[116] such as the 40 million Ks ($12 million U.S.) it received in 1998, in addition to gifts from named donors, state funding, and unreported contributions.

Benefits were concentrated and the HZDS was the key beneficiary. The 1994 law on parties prohibited the *founding* of enterprises, but allowed parties to enter *existing* enterprises and corporations. As a result, party fundraising was dominated by favorable privatization deals, as the Mečiar administration distributed both posts and contracts. With minimal oversight or regulation, the HZDS benefited from such deals disproportionately – far more than its coalition partners, the ZSL and the SNS.[117] The HZDS, which nurtured the "links between privatizing investors and top politicians in the civil service,"[118] made privatization bids contingent on party contributions, and the contracts themselves went to party allies.

The real money, as usual, was in privatization deals. When the second wave of voucher privatization was canceled in favor of direct sales in 1994, coalition parties deliberately privatized enterprises so as to maximize the benefits for themselves.[119] It became "obvious to all that governing parties do not live on the state subvention alone."[120] During the first three years of the privatization program, the National Property Fund received 35 billion Sk ($1 billion U.S.) for firms sold. In the first six months after Meciar fully consolidated his rule in 1994, the NPF

[115] Rybař 2006, p. 328.

[116] Malčická, Lenka. 2000. "Vybrané aspekty financovania politických strán a hnutí v SR" [Selected aspects of party and movement financing in Slovakia], *Politika*.

[117] *Dilema*, "Kto jest bez viny, nech hodí kamenom." [Let him without fault cast the stone], January 2000.

[118] Freedom House 2000, p. 582.

[119] Slovakia had undergone the first wave of voucher privatization in the united Czechoslovakia in 1991–2. The second wave, scheduled for 1993–4, never took place and direct sales began in 1994.

[120] Dilema, "Kto jest bez viny, nech hodi kamenom," January 2000.

received 3 billion Sk ($86 million U.S.) for property valued at 20 billion Sk ($550 million U.S.).[121] Slavomír Hatina, a supporter of HZDS from its inception and a key financial backer of HZDS, controlled Slovnaft, through the 39 percent shares he bought at fire sale prices from HZDS. The former transportation minister now controlled the steelmill VSZ Košice, driving it into bankruptcy (but not before getting a hefty payout when the firm was sold to US Steel). Julius Tóth, the former finance minister, controlled Slovakia's sole private bank.[122] Other beneficiaries included coalition deputies and close associates of the HZDS outside of parliament.

As in the Czech Republic, state enterprises and local governments financed national political parties. Real estate deals on the local level were used to launder funds for political parties. Even after 1998, the governing Christian Democrats (KDH) placed all of its regional and local secretaries in the employ of the media ownings of a businessperson and a KDH leader.[123]

However, changes in the structures of competition could bring about changes in the system of party financing. When the HZDS was finally voted out of power in 1998, the regulatory framework began to change. Bills introduced by the new SDK government in late 1999 would cap the funds the parties could use, increase the amount of state funding, and mandate greater transparency in party accounts (although the lists of donors still remained secret).[124] So long as the ODS and the HZDS ruled in the Czech Republic and Slovakia, however, they could freely extract resources for their survival from the state with little constraint on the nature or amount of this funding. The weakness of the opposition also meant that the full extent of governing party rent seeking was not made public until the late 1990s. Because of the lack of regulation and legal accountability, covert party funding held sway.

A similar pattern of relatively rapid privatization with less oversight made it possible for Latvian parties to survive through rent seeking. However, and in contrast to Slovakia, no formal state funding provisions arose in Latvia. Attempts by various parties to institute such funding were largely stymied by Latvia's Way, the kingmaker party in all governing coalitions. Latvia's Way argued that taxpayers would rebel. At the same time, however,

---

[121] See "Marching Backwards: Slovakia's Counterrevolution." October 1995. Available at http://project-syndicate.org/surveys/marching˙bac.php4, accessed 10 September 2004.
[122] Ibid.
[123] Peter Gabura was a member of the broader leadership circle. *Pravda*, 2 November 1999.
[124] RFE/RL broadcast, 10 November 1999, Slovakia; *Gazeta Wyborcza* 14 June 2000.

both Latvia's Way and the People's Party were the greatest beneficiaries of informal ties to businesspeople who depended on state contracts. The advantages of incumbency favored Latvia's Way, much as they had helped the ODS and the HZDS in the former Czechoslovakia: Latvia's Way, "the dominant force in the government since 1993, was also the best financed party."[125]

Few incentives for increasing regulation of party finances existed. Not surprisingly, the first law on party financing put forth in 1995 was both general and very lax. It formally prohibited national or local government funding, as well as either foreign or anonymous donors. However, the Latvian National Independence Movement faction, supported by several other parties, ensured that donors would not be made public, and could contribute via shell companies and foundations. The party financing law was followed by the more strict Corruption Prevention Law, passed in 1996, which for the first time prohibited parliamentarians from holding private sector jobs. The Corruption Prevention Law also instituted question time in parliament for the first time, in order to introduce greater transparency to the political process.

The first major change to this lax and exploited regime was the 2002 law on party financing. For the first time, limits on donation were lowered, so that the base of donors could widen, diminishing the familiar specter of parties being "owned" by entrepreneurs. The National Anti-Corruption Board (KNAB) now assumed control of party finances; parties would now submit declarations to KNAB, which had the power to regulate and sanction parties, imposing fines for noncompliance with declaration requirements and donation limits. When KNAB asked the Supreme Court to stop the activities of eleven political parties for not submitting annual declarations, the Court agreed in five cases.[126]

However, throughout the post-1991 period as an independent democracy, no state financing was available for parties and no limits were placed on party spending. Nor did the 2002 law change the situation. Income

[125] Plakans, Andrejs. 1998. "Democratization and Political Participation in Postcommunist Societies: The Case of Latvia," in Dawish, Karen, and Parott, Bruce, eds. *The Consolidation of Democracy in East-Central Europe.* Cambridge: Cambridge University Press, pp. 245–89.

[126] KNAB. 2003. "Progress and Results in the Field of Corruption Prevention and Combat." Periodic update, 24 November. Available at http://www.knab.gov.lv/ru/actual/article.php?id=18863, accessed 12 February 2004.

received from donations was exempted from income tax, and donors partly freed from taxes on donations.[127] As a result, "the concentration of funds enables the ruling-coalition partners to use these funds to increase their chances to express their political views and opinions, compared to opposition parties not represented in the Saeima."[128] Not surprisingly, Latvia's Way and the People's Party were also the biggest spenders, responsible for well over half of campaign expenditures.[129]

Privatization benefited the parties directly, and by the same token, politics and business mixed indiscriminately. Since campaign costs doubled from year to year, political parties needed to build, rather than simply maintain, such ties.[130] Several parties "reported substantial donors of the "corporate" variety, Harmony [party] benefiting from a large contribution by a well-known Russian businessmen in Latvia."[131] Repeatedly, high-ranking officials stood accused of violating corruption and conflict-of-interest norms, yet retained their positions and their access. Thus, in 1997, the heads of critical ministries – economy, transport, agriculture, and health and culture – all held private positions in various companies at the time of their government service. Similarly, a third of parliamentarians, as well as President Guntis Ulmanis (1993–9), all held private positions along with their official posts. Some of these were in direct conflict with each other: Vilis Kristopanis of Latvia's Way was on the board of LatRosTrans, a joint oil pipeline venture, over which he held direct jurisdiction as the minister of transport.[132] Not only did most of these officials retain their positions, but they did so in spite of a coalition collapse and re-formation.

Many of the biggest excesses came to light years after they took place. For example, Prime Minister Andris Šķēle (nonparty prime minister 1995–7, People's Party prime minister 1999–2000) received enormous amounts of funds from privatization and a promissory note for $29 million from the trust company he entrusted to manage Ave Lat, his food processing company.[133] A new scandal erupted in 2001 when Šķēle was accused of promising

---

[127] Snipe, Arta. 2003. *Financing of Political Parites: Effectiveness of Regulation. The Latvian Example.* Master's Thesis, Riga Graduate School of Law, Riga, Latvia.

[128] Čigāne, Lolita. 2002. "A Reflection of the Shortcomings in Legislation on Party Financing in the 2001 Finance Declarations," Soros Foundation Latvia and Transparency International "delna," Riga, Latvia, April. Available at http://www.politika.lv.

[129] Ibid.

[130] Snipe 2003.

[131] Plakans 1998, p. 269.

[132] *East European Constitutional Review*, 6, 23 (Spring/Summer 1997).

[133] *East European Constitutional Review*, Summer 2000.

a $1 million U.S. bribe to the parliamentary speaker to ensure that the privatization of the Latvian Shipping Company would benefit the People's Party and its associated businesses.[134] The New Era (Jaunais Laiks, JL) party managed to run afoul of the 1996 anticorruption law even before it was established in February 2002, by accepting large corporate donations and offering the central bank president a huge fee to become the party's chair in late 2001. In short, the lack of formal regulation or informal oversight made possible a direct and unconstrained extraction of state resources.

As a final additional note, the Estonian case shows that robust competition could constrain the exploitation of the state, even in the absence of formal party financing. As noted earlier, parties did not receive state funding until 1996. (After 1996, the threshold for financing remained the highest in the region: Only parties with over 5 percent of the vote could receive funding.) Laws on party funding forbade state agencies and local governments, as well as foreign governments and public institutions, from supporting political parties financially. Parties received a subvention for parliamentary authority but no other state funding. Strict reporting requirements meant parties had a week after a donation to submit a report to the Register of Nonprofit Associations and Foundations. Similarly, parties had to report all campaign expenditures within a month of the election to both the Riigikogu and the Local Government Council.[135] Since a 1,000 kroon limit existed on private contributions, businesses and individuals who contributed had to make multiple small contributions – and as in Poland, many hedged their bets by spreading their donations among parties. While some critics have charged that the private financing was relatively permissive,[136] the constant monitoring of opposition parties led to a party financing regime with the reputation for being the cleanest in the region.

These cases show that formal state funding itself is not an influence on or an indicator of state exploitation. More broadly, the more robust the competition, the more it would constrain governing parties from either writing the laws to benefit themselves or simply failing to specify laws in the first place. The less robust the opposition, the greater the governing parties' discretion in extracting resources – both from the formal legal framework

---

[134] *East European Constitutional Review*, Winter 2001.

[135] SIGMA. 1999. "Public Management Profiles of Central and East European Countries: Estonia." October.

[136] Sikk, Allan. 2003. "A Cartel Party System in a Post-Communist Country? The Case of Estonia." Paper prepared for the European Consortium for Political Research ECPR General Conference, 18–21 September, Marbury, Germany.

and from informal sources. Where competition was less robust, bribery was more straightforward, and both state and private economic actors attempted to buy favorable government policies by contributing to party coffers either directly or by loaning enormous sums. By the same token, party officials could more readily extract funds by openly obtaining and awarding state contracts. Such efforts were far more constrained where the opposition launched continual investigations of government action. As a result, we see more far less concentration of benefits to one party, and considerably less volume flowing through any one channel.

Conclusion

This chapter suggests that we carefully specify rent seeking in party funding. State financing of political parties by itself is not necessarily an indicator of exploitation or elite collusion, as some analyses have argued. Instead, such financing can be evidence of party efforts to rein in state exploitation, if it is transparent, regulated, and well enforced.

As this chapter shows, we need to examine both formal and informal forms of state financing, in both their direct and indirect guises. Some analyses have argued that post-communist party funding patterns are simply the result of moneyed interests such as oligarchs or newly powerful businesspeople wishing to consolidate their gains via elections.[137] Yet this chapter suggests that the extent of such informal and indirect state funding not only varies with the extent of competition but is only one form of party financing in the post-communist democracies.

The countries examined in this book sequenced reforms so that democratic political actors were established before the economy was opened to market forces. As a result, the process was less state "capture," where political parties were hostage to outside economic interests, than opportunistic state reconstruction, where political parties built in advantages for

---

[137] Treisman, Daniel. 1998. "Dollars and Democratization: The Role and Power of Money in Russia's Transitional Elections," *Comparative Politics*, 31, 1 (October): 1–21. Treisman argues that private funding had little impact on electoral outcomes, unlike changes in regional budget funding, which produced more votes for incumbent and pro-reform parties. Given the difficulties in enforcing contracts between spenders and politicians, private funding was not effective. It is unclear what the mechanism by which such increases should target specific parties. More importantly, as David Samuels points out, the problem of donor-party contracting is endemic to all democracies, not just Russia. Samuels, David. 2001. "Does Money Matter? Credible Commitments and Campaign Finance in New Democracies," *Comparative Politics*, 34, 1 (October): 23–42.

themselves as much as they could. Political parties took advantage of the opportunities inherent in privatization, and the less-regulated the privatization, the greater the opportunity for state exploitation. The more robust the competition, the more state funding was regulated, access to privatization resources limited, and the benefits dispersed across several parties. While it is not possible to measure all the benefits that parties extracted from the state, this chapter shows that parties extracted private benefits from the state through both formal and regulated institutional channels and via informal and indirect practices. These might escape legal enforcement – but not the notice of a robust opposition.

Conclusion

> There is as much difference between us and ourselves as there is between us and others.
>
> Michel de Montaigne, *Essais*

Post-communist state exploitation leads us to reconsider political parties as competitors and as state builders – and to rethink states as the set of institutions that can emerge willy-nilly from political party competition. Thrust into the constantly shifting landscape of an authoritarian regime collapse and rising democratic and market competition, post-communist political parties faced unprecedented challenges. They began to rebuild state structures while learning to compete for electoral support and access to governance. These anxious and fragile parties opportunistically reconstructed the state both to ensure their own immediate survival and that of a democratic system that would prize political parties and could withstand a backslide into authoritarianism.

The swift pace and intensity of post-communist transformations placed political parties in a central policy role, giving them a *means* to exploit the state. The *motives* were straightforward: party survival and a commitment to democracy. The *opportunities* lay in the vulnerabilities of the extant communist state structures and the absence of existing institutional constraints. The same parties both designed reforms and directly stood to benefit from them. Rapid state reconstruction also meant little consultation with society or nongovernmental actors; the actions of governing parties directly influenced both who had access to power and how it was exercised.

Yet the very democracy that gave rise to these political parties could also constrain their exploitation of the state through robust competition. Such competition led to the earlier creation of formal institutions of monitoring and oversight, with broader regulatory scope and a greater role for the opposition. It placed informal constraints on the discretionary expansion of the state administration, holding in check quasistate agencies and extrabudgetary funds. And it curtailed access to the profits of privatization, leading to more formalized, transparent, and deconcentrated party financing. The resulting variation in state exploitation has three broad implications for the study of the state, of political competition, and of post-communist development.

Political Parties and the State

As post-communist democracies show, political parties are not confined to representation and contestation, fielding teams of candidates for office. Their role in reconstructing state institutions, the diversity of their strategies of survival through the state, and the importance of domestic competition even in the face of international pressure all suggest that political parties play a fundamental role in shaping the state.

First, the immediate competitive considerations of political parties heavily influence the kind of state institutions they establish, the pace and sequencing of this construction, and whose interests the new state institutions will serve. Robust competition led to the creation of formal state institutions that had broader scope to constrain party discretion, arose earlier, and acted more neutrally rather than favoring the incumbents. In turn, the timing of institutional creation had considerable ramifications for institutional efficacy; monitoring and oversight were more effective when they arose simultaneously with the domains they were to regulate. Where new regulatory institutions were imposed on existing and entrenched domains (such as civil service laws or delayed market regulatory institutions), they were far less capable of staunching the discretionary flow of resources out of state coffers and into party hands. Conversely, party competition also influenced the building of discretionary quasistate institutions – the various agencies and extrabudgetary funds that existed largely outside of parliamentary purview. These were a huge unregulated and unmonitored supply of resources. Robust competition constrained their growth and, in many cases, led to their elimination.

Party leeway to build and to shape state institutions is greatest in new parliamentary democracies where existing state institutions, civil society, and the media do not influence policy making. However, the incentives created by robust competition for governing parties to protect the state are not limited to new democracies. Where levels of competition increase in established democracies, so do the incentives to prevent rent-seeking practices. For example, in both Italy and in Austria, a more robust party competition in the last quarter of the twentieth century exposed many rent-seeking practices and began to curb them. In Austria, as parliament grew in influence, consensus lessened and policy debates began in earnest. Parliamentary investigative committees were launched,[1] and merit, rather than party membership, was emphasized.[2] A civil service training academy was established in 1975, as was an ombudsman's office and new channels of public scrutiny. In Italy, the post-1989 transformation of the communist party ended its ostracism in parliament (the party participated in informal power sharing, but had been formally excluded from all governing coalitions).[3] While this transformation was not as dramatic as in the post-communist cases (partly because the reforms addressed long-standing practices and established state domains), it meant both new governing alternatives and new criticism of the Christian Democrats.[4]

Second, opportunistic state reconstruction and the exploitation that followed comprise only one of the potential strategies of extraction from the state. Others include clientelism, predation, and the fusion of party and state. These are fundamentally constrained by party organizations, democratic commitments, and the resources that they place at the disposal of party leaders. While much of the scholarship has focused on the long-term impact of electoral institutions, socioeconomic development, or ideological traditions, these immediate constraints can also profoundly affect party strategies of survival through the state. Patronage, for example, can succeed only for parties with the organizational wherewithal to exchange state jobs

---

[1] Müller, Wolfgang. 1992. "Austrian Governmental Institutions: Do They Matter?" in Luther, Kurt Richard, and Müller, Wolfgang, eds. *Politics in Austria: Still a Case of Consociationalism?* London: Frank Cass, pp. 99–131, p. 105.

[2] Luther, Kurt Richard. 1992. "Consociationalism, Parties, and the Party System," in Luther and Müller, pp. 45–98, p. 90.

[3] The PC was part of the parliamentary majority in 1976–9, but it was never "viewed as acceptable coalition partners." Colazingari, Silvia, and Rose-Ackerman, Susan. 1998. "Corruption in a Paternalistic Democracy: Lessons from Italy for Latin America," *Political Science Quarterly*, 113, 3: 447–70, p. 449.

[4] Pujas, Véronique, and Rhodes, Martin. 1999. "Party Finance and Political Scandal in Italy, Spain, and France," *West European Politics*, 22, 3: 41–63.

for electoral support, as in the case of Italian case expansion through explicit Christian Democratic clientelism.[5]

If organization influences strategies of survival irrespective of the parties' origin, then it calls into question widely accepted views regarding the determinants of rent seeking. For example, Martin Shefter's powerful account argues that mass parties mobilizing outside of existing legislatures did not pursue patronage strategies, and internally mobilized parties did so only if no state bureaucracy or coalition for bureaucratic autonomy existed.[6] Yet this book suggests that patronage requires localized organizational resources that provide channels of goods distribution and voter monitoring. Mass party organizations, whether internally or externally mobilized, are thus very well-suited to the pursuit of clientelism.[7] More broadly, the needs and capacities of political parties are a fundamental factor in determining how the state is built – and how rents are sought.

Finally, in weighing domestic constraints against the international determinants of state reconstruction, one lesson from the rise of formal state institutions in post-communist democracies is that we should approach international imposition of formal state institutions with caution. Domestic competitive pressures can and do trump international pressures. The EU coaxed laggards into passing formal institutions – but the implementation of these institutions was often inadequate or delayed further (as in the case of the Czech civil service law). Without domestic support, such efforts can result in "Potemkin institutions." Moreover, the imposition of a policy consensus can dampen domestic political debates – and the very weapons of criticism and contentiousness used by the opposition to protect the state from exploitation.[8] In the name of improving state administration, then, international efforts may undermine it.

---

[5] One study found that up to half a million employees were hired through patronage from 1946 to 1958. Lewanski, Rudolf. 1997. "Italian Civil Service: A Pre-Modern Bureaucracy in Transition?" Paper prepared for the Conference on "Civil Service Systems in Comparative Perspective," University of Indiana, 5–8 April. In contrast, Carolyn Warner argues that only one hundred thousand jobs were created. Warner 2001, p. 130.

[6] Shefter 1994.

[7] In turn, the decision to invest in mass organization weighs the costs in both time and money of establishing a local organizational presence against the benefits of available campaign techniques (individual mobilization versus national media campaigns), the availability of local allies, the pace of democratization, and so on.

[8] See Innes, Abby. 2002. "Party Competition in Post-Communist Europe: The Great Electoral Lottery," *Comparative Politics*, 35, 1: 85–105; Grzymała-Busse, Anna, and Innes, Abby. 2003. "Great Expectations: The EU and Domestic Political Competition in East Central Europe," *East European Politics and Societies*, 17, 1: 64–73.

Studying Party Competition

The importance of robust competition to post-communist state exploitation suggests a reconceptualization of the existing indicators of competition. As the post-communist experience shows, not only are elections alone a poor indicator of functioning democracies, but many existing indicators of competition tell us little about what we prize about democratic competition: its potential for representation, contestation, and constraint. Such widely used but potentially misleading gauges include general proxies for political competition, such as experience with democracy or as overall measures of political rights and democracy, and more specific indicators such as turnover, polarization, fragmentation, openness, and volatility.

These indicators neither make meaningful distinctions between authoritarian and democratic regimes, nor do they explain the differences among democracies. For example, authoritarian Kazakhstan and democratic Poland share the same rate of openness to new parliamentary parties. Belarus and Slovenia are equally polarized. Azerbaijan and Latvia have similar government incumbency rates. At the same time, democracies with very distinct exploitation patterns and corruption scores, such as Estonia and Latvia, share similar competitive profiles. Relying on fragmentation or turnover as predictors of rent seeking leads to the surprising conclusion that Italy and Sweden, both with one governing party ruling without interruption for nearly five decades, ought to exhibit similar patterns of corruption and governance. The prevalence of such patterns suggests a rethinking of competition and its impact.

Specifically, for analyses focusing on competition as constraint, a crucial consideration is the credible threat of replacement provided by a clear, plausible, and critical opposition. Parliamentary action, rather than the distribution of seats or years in governance, determines the potential for rentseeking. Therefore, we need to examine party *behavior* in parliamentary committees, coalitions, media pronouncements, interpellations, and so on. Just as importantly, we need to focus on the mechanisms of constraint: here, in the post-communist cases, these comprised anticipatory institutional creation, moderation of extraction, and power sharing.

Competition is so important when political parties are the key actors to monitor and constrain governing party behavior – that is, in new parliamentary democracies. In established democracies, consequently, we see other sources of constraint. Specifically, where democratic parties and state structures arose over centuries rather than years, a variety of factors could constrain state exploitation and other forms of resource extraction from the state. Such gradual cases of state development include much of North-western Europe. In the Nordic states (Denmark, Finland, Norway, Sweden, Iceland), single parties have dominated politics over decades. The Swedish Social Democratic Party (SAP) for example, governed from 1932 to 1976 and again from 1982 to 1991, with over 40 percent of the vote. Yet these countries are held up as paragons of state transparency and political party restraint; there is no evidence of clientelism or exploitation, much less pre-dation or party-state fusion. In these cases, however, both parliamentary and extraparliamentary forces constrain governments.[9] Fierce partisanship in parliament meant both regular possibility of shifts in coalitions and minor-ity governments, and continual adverse publicity.[10] Corporatist channels of consultation and instruments of direct democracy (referenda in Denmark, Finland, and Sweden), along with ombudsmen and strong oversight insti-tutions, all further constrained governments.[11] Finally, a powerful and par-tisan press monitored and publicized government action.[12] In these cases, political parties had both the local organizational presence and the demo-cratic commitments to pursue clientelist policies, but they were powerfully constrained by the opposition and the multiple channels of monitoring and oversight it had helped to create.

Post-Communist Political and Economic Development

This account of robust competition as a constraint on state exploita-tion implies new perspectives on post-communist political development. The debates surrounding post-communist transformations have tended to assume that "all good things go together" – and as several authors have shown, democratic performance and market reforms go hand in hand. Yet this overwhelming correlation covers up a distinct aspect of post-communist transformation: These societies also faced an equally important if less obvi-ous challenge of reconstructing state institutions and state authority. In

---

[9] Hadenius, Stig. 1985. *Swedish Politics During the 20th Century*. Boras: Swedish Institute, p. 124.

[10] Logue, John, and Einhorn, Eric. 1988. "Restraining the Governors: The Nordic Experience with Limiting the Strong State," *Scandinavian Political Studies*, 11, 1: 45–67.

[11] Ibid.

[12] The state subsidized the press, since it was seen as important to political debate (newspapers were strongly identified with political parties). A subsidy system was in place since 1971 in Sweden, for example, the result of an agreement between the Center Party and the Social Democrats. Hadenius 1985, p. 140.

turn, the timing and sequencing of these institutions heavily influenced how effectively they would constrain elite attempts to gain private benefits from both privatization and redistribution. And democracy alone was not enough to ensure that such institutions would arise; rather, robust competition, with its steady monitoring and its credible threat of replacement, generated the incentives to reconstruct the state rapidly and with constraint in mind. This further confirms that the pace or policy instruments of privatization do not alone determine privatization outcomes. The regulatory institutions that oversee and control the processes of selling off vast state holdings also play a critical role. This framework along with the structures inherited from the communist era, determined the location of opportunities and determined the location of resources available to actors intent on obtaining additional or private benefits from these transformations of property relations. Thus, commercialization in Poland meant the rise of enterprise boards, while the lack of autonomous oversight and clear property rights in the Czech Republic led to massive asset stripping.

A final surprise is that communist successor parties, if they reinvented themselves to be committed and credible democrats, could form the linchpin of a robust opposition. They were powerful critics and monitors, and their very existence served as an incentive to establish new formal institutions of state monitoring and oversight. Wherever they succeeded in reinventing themselves, they became both the chief target of blame and the key source of criticism.

Over the centuries of state development, diverse domestic and international factors have affected the formation of state institutions. As the recent episode of post-communist state reconstruction shows, however, a specific set of institutional architects can assume primacy. When political parties are the only actors with both the incentives and the capacity to exploit the state, their competition profoundly alters how the state is built, how it develops – and whose ends it serves.

A

PEAK PARTY ORGANIZATIONS IN POST-COMMUNIST DEMOCRACIES, 1990–2004

Hungary[a]	Members	Local Cells
Fidesz	5,000–15,000	325
FKGP	40,000–60,000	2,000
KDNP	10,000–28,000	885
MDF	23,000–34,000	820
MSzP	60,000–38,000	2,500
SzDSz	24,000–16,000	759

[a] Bill Lomax. 1996. "The Structure and Organization of Hungary's Political Parties," in Lewis, Paul, ed. *Party Structure and Organization in East-Central Europe*. Cheltenham: Edward Elgar; Party interviews, spring 1997. Available at http://www.Europeanforum.net.

Estonia[a]	Members	Local Cells
ERL	7,000	n/a
IL	1,400	76
K	7,937	136
KMÜ/KE	500	n/a
RE	n/a	151
RP	1,800	−100
SDE/RM	2,400	70

[a] Party websites and personal communication. Data available at http://www.keskerakond.ee, http://www.reform.ee, http://www.isamaaliit.ee, and http://www.sotsdem.ee.

Slovenia[a]	Members	Local Cells
DeSUS	26,000–36,000	150
LDS	5,300	340
Nsi	8,900	185
SDS	20,000	190
SLS+SKD	40,000	51
ZLSD	23,000–27,000	210

[a] Party websites; personal communication (April 2004); Ramet, Sabrina Petra. 1999. "Democratization in Slovenia," in Dawisha, Karen, and Parrott, Bruce, eds. *Politics, Power, and the Struggle for Democracy in South-East Europe.* Cambridge: Cambridge University Press, pp. 189–225.

Lithuania[a]	Members	Local Cells
DP	12,000	n/a
LDDP	9,000–10,000	60
LKDP	8,000–10,500	57
LSDP	600–1,500	~52 (LSDP and LDDP united in 2001)
NS	5,000	60
TS	13,000–16,000	85

[a] Krupavičius, Algis. 1998. "The Post-Communist Transition and Institutionalization of Lithuania's Parties," *Political Studies*, 46, 3: 465–91. NS was founded in 2000; data come from http://www.nsajunga.lt. Information on party cells is from party websites and private communication.

Poland[a]	Members	Local Cells
AWS	2,000,000[e]	n/a
KPN	19,000–4,000	175
PO	20,000	380
PSL	200,000[c]–100,000 (2003)	2,000
Samoobrona	93,000 (2003)	~60 [f]
SdRP-SDL	60,000–87,000 150,000 (2002–3 only)[b]	2,400
UW	22,000–16,000 (2004)	375
ZChN	8,000–6,000	26 regional[d]

[a] Party interviews, spring 2003, spring 1999, and summer 1997; *Wprost,* 21 March 1993 and 26 May 2002; PO regional webpages.

[b] Party membership rose as high as 150,000 by mid-July 2003, but a wholesale verification of members reduced the membership to 80,000 by the fall of 2003.

[c] Figures may be too high, since the party retained its pre-1989 membership rolls.

[d] No register of local organizations is available.

[e] Formal union members, not party members.

[f] Regional level. The party does not reveal data for local-level organizations.

Party Organizations in Post-Communist Democracies

Czech Rep.[a]	Members	Local Cells
ČSSD	13,000 (1996)–18,000 (2003)	1,500
KDU-ČSL	100,000 (1995)–47,000 (1999)	2,240
KSČM	350,000 (1990)–140,000 (1993)	6,900
ODA	2,000	200
ODS	22,000 (1995)–16,000 (1998)	1,400
SPR-RSČ	60,000–30,000	2,000

[a] Party interviews, spring 2004, spring 1999, and fall 1996. *Hospodarské Noviny*, 2 December 1995. Available at http://www.Europeanforum.net.

Slovakia[a]	Members	Local Cells	Central Employees
DU	5,000	200	27, of whom 7 regional
HZDS	40,000 (1994)–72,000 (2000)	2–3,000	136–166, of which 86 regional
KDH	10,000[b]	2,000	45–65, of whom 25–35 regional
SDK	114	n/a	3, all central
SDL'	45,000–18,000	2,000	29, all central
SMK	11,636		14, of whom 6 regional
SNS	2,000 (1994)–7,600 (1997)	1,500	17, of whom 7 regional
SOP	5,900		27, of whom 14 regional

[a] Party interviews, spring 2004, spring 1999, and winter 1997. Malčická, Lenka, "Vybrané aspekty financovania politických strán a hnutí v SR," manuscript, Bratislava, 2001.
[b] Large but unspecified numbers of members moved to the SDKU in 2000.

Bulgaria[a]	Members	Local Cells
BSP	330,000 (1990)–180,000 (1999)	7,892
BZnS (BANU)	n/a	n/a
DPS (MRF)	8,000	65
NDSV	22,000	294[b]
SDS (UDF)	35,000	~150

[a] Personal communication (April 2004); party websites; http://www.online.bg, accessed 13 January 2004; Freedom House. 1999. *Nations in Transit 1999.* Washington: Freedom House.
[b] Coordinators rather than organizations per se.

Latvia[a]	Members	Local Cells
DSP	800	n/a
JL	320–402	23
JP	n/a	n/a[b]
LC	400–1,300	33
LKDS	1,000	n/a
LPP	1,200	n/a
LSDSP	5,000	n/a
LVP	1,500	n/a
LZS + LZP	6,000	200
PCTVL	600	n/a
TB/LNNK	3,000	34
TP	4,000	85

[a] Plakans, Andrejs. 1999. "Democratization and Political Participation in Postcommunist Societies: The Case of Latvia," in Dawisha, Karen, and Parrott, Bruce, eds. *The Consolidation of Democracy in East-Central Europe.* Cambridge: Cambridge University Press; pp. 245–89; party websites; personal communication (April 2004); Auers, Daunis. 2003. "On Potemkin Villages and Campaign Finance Reform," 13 May. Available at http://www.policy.lv/index.php?id=102671&lang=en.

[b] The JP, DSP, and LVP were eliminated in the 1998 elections.

B

DETERMINING STATE ADMINISTRATION EMPLOYMENT AND RATE OF GROWTH

State administration consists of central and territorial offices of the national state: the employees of the ministries, regulatory and fiscal agencies, social security and labor office administration, and their territorial branches. This category excludes employees in state health care, education, and the armed forces. The data used in Chapter 4 and throughout the book were gathered from the national statistical offices in the countries under consideration.

This book relies on government statistical offices reporting of the Statistical Classification of Economic Activities in the European Community (NACE) state administration category. The NACE is used in all of the countries under consideration, and has been used consistently since 1990. The main category used and reported here is L: state administration and defense; compulsory social security. This category includes the following: administration of the state and economic and social policy of the community, general public service activities, regulation activities of state agencies, regulation and contribution to more efficient operation of business, supporting service activities for government as a whole, provision of services to the community as a whole, foreign affairs, defense activities, justice and judicial activities, public security, law and order activities, fire service activities, and compulsory social service activities. The L category excludes the soldiers and officers of the armed forces. It also explicitly excludes education and health care (reported in the M and N categories, respectively), as well as other community, social, and personal service activities (sanitation, membership organizations, media, artistic and literary activities, libraries and archives, sports arenas and recreational activities, or museums and national parks), which are reported in the O category.[1]

The advantage of using NACE categories is twofold. First, it is consistent across countries, allowing for relatively valid comparisons among cases. Second, it is also consistently used across time, so that we can more confidently trace the development of public employment over time. Its main disadvantage is that it includes services that are not directly part of the state administration – the police, civilian armed forces employees, and firefighters. As a broader measure than simply counting the ministerial offices and their territorial branches, it allows for the possibility that shifts in state administration hiring do not happen only in the central administration, but in the various auxiliary organizations and structures. In these places, hiring is at state discretion, but employers may wish to hide the particularistic nature of the hire. (In other words, it is that much easier for a party official to hire a secretary or a regional office assistant than to hire the same person at the same level in a highly visible ministry.)

Two methods of reporting the NACE categories exist: labor force survey results (which ask respondents, usually less than 1 percent of the labor force, what activity they performed in the last week) and sectoral reporting (in which enterprises and institutions report their employment levels). Where possible this appendix uses NACE L data as reported by sectors as the single measure comparable across countries. Sectoral reporting of NACE L is the one source collected most consistently across the years, allowing for far broader intracountry and intercountry comparisons over time than other measures afford us.

For Poland and Hungary, labor force surveys are used, since sectoral and labor force data were often merged. Labor force surveys tend to report a higher number of employees in the administration than sectoral reporting methods. Therefore, they would make the Polish and Hungarian figures closer to the null hypothesis: that competition does not constrain state growth. That we still see lower growth than in the other countries suggests that competition indeed holds down the true values of state administration.

Since the sector-reported NACE measure tends to be strongly correlated to other measures (see individual country reports later in this appendix for bivariate correlations of the data reported by various sources), it is very likely that the results of the analysis would be similar if other data sources

---

[1] EU List of NACE Codes. Available at http://www.europa.eu.int/comm/competition/mergers/cases/index/nace_all.html.

were used. The assumption is that the overinflation of state administration numbers due to the inclusion of auxiliary organizations or security forces is constant over time and across countries, and that the relative shifts are accurate measurements. In other words, it is unlikely that one country vastly increased its number of firefighters, for example, from year to year and relative to other countries. Where there are discrepancies within the same source, older data were used rather than subsequent revisions (which are reported in parentheses).

Using the NACE L as a single consistent measure avoids some of the problems with data on state employment: There is no widely agreed upon or clear measure of state administration employment, and this creates considerable analytical problems. International organizations, such as the World Bank, have attempted to generate comparable data.[2] However, both because data are missing and reporting standards vary, numerous codings are problematic; for example, according to the World Bank, civilian central government employment went from 64,000 in 1991–5 to 490,000 in 1996–2000 in the Czech Republic, a figure that no other source has been able to support. Moreover, in some cases, because of data limitations, different categories of employees are included in the count; again, in the World Bank study, education, health, and police forces are excluded where possible, but not consistently.

Other measures of state administration employment exist, each with specific disadvantages and benefits. First, there are country-specific measures: Several of the countries under consideration have also used narrower definitions of "state administration," broken down into central administration (ministries and branch offices), territorial administration (regional and local offices of the central state administration), and local self-government administration. While more accurately depicting the number of actual state administration employees, the main problem here is of lack of comparability. Both statistical offices and ministries of finance or interior (the main sources of such data) tend to use idiosyncratic measures that do not afford comparisons across countries. Even explicit attempts to collect data that are comparable, such as O'Dwyer (2004), have been unable to separate out the individual components of state administration employment. For example, Polish central administration includes foreign service units, such

---

[2] See World Bank. 2001. The Cross-National Data Set on Government Employment and Wages, World Bank Administrative and Civil Service Reform Project, OECD Public Management Service 2001.

as embassies and consulates, and labor offices, which its Czech and Slovak counterparts do not.[3] Moreover, there are shifts in accounting measures over time, such as the Czech shift in reporting categories in 1995–6 that otherwise would produce a false jump in central administration, or the devolution of several offices after the 1998 regional reforms in Poland. Therefore, the NACE L category is used as the most consistently measured, and most reliable, indicator.

Measuring State Administration Employment

Tables B.1 through B.4 report measures of state administration employment in four cases with the greatest diversity of data sources. Bulgaria, Estonia, Latvia, Lithuania, and Slovenia have far fewer competing sources of data. Growth rates for each period of data collection are also reported; these vary considerably largely as a function of missing year observations. Table B.5 measures state administration as a percentage of total employment and in absolute numbers.

---

[3] O'Dwyer 2004 defends the measure by arguing that there has been little growth in Czech labor office employment. However, this measure may still attribute too much growth to the Polish central administration, if labor offices were the sector responsible for Polish administrative growth. Given Poland's increasing unemployment, reaching nearly 20 percent by 2000, hiring in labor offices would have expanded considerably.

Measuring State Administration Employment

Table B.1. *State Administrative Employment and Rate of Growth, Hungary[a]*

Hungary	LFS[b]	Sectoral[c]	Other
1989	297,900		258,000[d]
1990	295,308		
1991	285,840		11,257 central administration[e]
1992	293,700		44,570 subnat'l, 38,750 local[f] 311,000
1993	299,500	108,000	
1994	320,200	105,000	
1995	318,100	102,000	147,000 central, 133,000 subnat'l[g] 316,000
1996	306,600	102,000	
1997	293,800	106,000	50,000 central, 40,000 local[h]
1998	294,000		
1999	301,900	106,000[i]	148,000 central, 158,000 subnat'l[j]
2000	299,000	111,746[k]	112,000[l]
2001	289,000		
2002	316,000		
% growth	106	104	

Notes:

[a] Bivariate Correlations: No significant correlation between the data sources.

[b] *Magyar Statisztikai Évkönyv 1998, 2002* [Hungarian Statistical Yearbook]. Budapest: KSH, 1994, 1999, 2003. (Different figures are reported in the 2003 Hungarian Statistical Yearbook from earlier editions.)

[c] Ministry of Labor reporting, Nunberg 2000, p. 280.

[d] Kézdi, Gábor. 1998. "Wages, Employment, and Incentives in the Public Sector in Hungary." Budapest Working Papers on the Labour Market, BWP 1998, 3 March.

[e] István Balázs. 1993. "The Transformation of Hungarian Public Administration," in Hesse 1993, p. 79.

[f] Ibid., p. 79.

[g] World Bank 2001.

[h] Suleiman 2003, p. 300.

[i] Gajduschek, György, and Hajnal, György. 2000. "Evaluation of the Hungarian General Civil Service Training Program." Discussion Paper No. 16, Local Government and Public Service Reform Initiative, Open Society Institute.

[j] World Bank 2001.

[k] Government of Hungary. 2000. *Governance and Public Administration in Hungary*. Budapest.

[l] Hungarian Government Information Service.

Table B.2. *State Administrative Employment and Rate of Growth, Poland*[a]

Poland	O'Dwyer[b]	LFS	Sectoral	Min. of Interior[c]	Media and Other Sources
1989		260,700	161,579	213,600	42,000 central in 1988[d]
1990	75,229	259,700	159,000[e]		
1991	93,294	273,100			53,000 central[f]
1992	104,728	296,600	158,000		
1993	115,361	336,600	129,741	238,074 (108,333 local)	
1994	133,400	375,700	133,400	268,352 (135,022 local)	
1995	141,508l	381,300	141,508	280,789 (139,295 local)	89,000 central[g]
1996	146,789	402,500	156,800	290,225 (133,369 local)	70,000 central[h]
1997	163,487	423,100	163,487	305,601 (142,114 local)	140.000 total[i]
1998	171,246	429,800	171,246	309,473 (138,227 local)	
1999	179,920	431,500	148,000[j]	306,390 (158,555 local)	
2000	178,668	492,600	130,177	305,802 (175,625 local)	105,000 civil servants[k] 164,000 central, 113,000 regional[l]
2001		525,700			110,000 central[m]
2002		522,200			
% growth	173	200	80	143	261

Notes:

[a] Bivariate Correlations: LFS and O'Dwyer: .806*; Labor Force and Ministry of Interior: .947**; O'Dwyer and Ministry of Interior: .773* (* significant at .05 level, ** significant at .01 level, two-tailed test).

[b] Central employees include those of ministries, central offices, the foreign service, and labor offices. Branch employees include those of territorial offices of the central state.

[c] Sectoral and local self-government figures. Central: ministries, foreign service offices, territorial offices of special government administration. Branch: territorial offices of the general administration (*voivodeship*, regional, auxiliary units). Local: *gminy* and *voivodeship*, and after 1998, *powiaty* and cities with rights of *powiaty*. In 2000 and afterward, labor offices are also included.

[d] Taras, Wojciech. 1993. "Changes in Polish Public Administration 1989–1992," in Hesse 1993, p. 29.

[e] Paradowska, Janina "Pełniący Obowiązki," *Polityka*, 2 June 2001.

[f] Taras 1993, p. 29.

[g] World Bank 2001.

[h] *Polityka*, 10 August 1996

[i] *Wprost*, 25 January 1998.

[j] GUS data cited by Gorzelak, Grzegorz, Jałowiecki, Bohdan, and Stec, Mirosław, eds. *Reforma Terytorialnej Organizacji Kraju: Dwa Lata Doświadczeń*. Warsaw: Scholar, 2001, p. 67.

[k] Suleiman 2003, p. 300.

[l] World Bank 2001.

[m] Paradowska 2001.

Table B.3. *State Administrative Employment and Rate of Growth, Czech Republic[a]*

Czech	O'Dwyer[b]	LFS[c]	Sectoral[d]	Min. of Finances[e]	Machaček[f]	World Bank[g]
1989			91,700			
1990			95,700			
1991			99,100			
1992			123,400			
1993	38,667	308,400	132,700	65,498	212,000	64,000 central
1994	40,088	322,400	146,300	68,134	220,000	77,000 central
1995	39,950	302,300	161,600	69,022	228,000	
1996	43,922	310,600	167,900	135,861[b]	228,000	
1997	45,334	320,600	180,100	148,479	235,000	90,000 central
1998	44,960	322,800	181,200	154, 356[i]	231,000	
1999	44,608	336,500	182,800		232,000	155,000 central[j]
2000	45,024	342,900	186,800		241,000	490,000 total
2001		340,000	193,500		245,000	
2002		325,700	193,500		245,000	
% growth	116	106	211	237	116	766

Notes:

[a] Bivariate correlations: Sectoral and O'Dwyer: .935**; Sectoral and LFS: .678*; Machaček and O'Dwyer: .857**; Sectoral and Machaček: .961**; Machaček and LFS: .663* (* significant at .05 level, **significant at .01 level, two-tailed test).

[b] Central employees include those of ministries, central offices, the foreign service, and labor offices. Branch employees include those of territorial offices of the central state.

[c] *Trh práce v České republice*, publication 3103-03, December 2003, Prague.

[d] *Časové řady základních ukazatelů statistiky práce 1948–2002* [Time-Series Indicators of Basic Labour Statistics], 2003. Prague: Czech Statistical Office. Statistics were derived from NACE (Statistical Classification of Economic Activities in the European Community).

[e] Figures for central administration. Národní Vzdělávací Fond. 1998. "Analýza veřejné správy České republiky," September. Data include central organs of the state administration, including fourteen ministries, the presidential offices, and the Supreme Court. They also include the regulatory and service arms of the state, including labor offices, financial offices, school inspectorates, and assay offices.

[f] Machaček, David. 2003. "Úředníků už je přes čtvrt milionu," *Hospodariké Noving*. Ihned.cz, 9 (October). Employees of the public administration include those employed in central administrative offices, regional and local offices (and until 2002, *okresní*), as well as financial, educational, employment, and other offices.

[g] World Bank. 2001. *Cross-National Data Set on Government Employment and Wages*. Available at http://ww1.worldbank.org/publicsector/civilservice/development.htm.

[h] The large change between the 1995 and 1996 data is due to accounting shifts. Prison and court officials, police, central state administration and territorial offices, and the ministry of defense employees were included to comply with NACE.

[i] Nunberg, Barbara. 2000. "Ready for Europe: Public Administration Reform and EU Accession in Central and Eastern Europe." World Bank Technical Paper No. 466, 2000, p. 85, citing the Czech Ministry of Labor.

[j] Národní Vzdělávací Fond 2001.

Table B.4. *State Administrative Employment and Rate of Growth, Slovakia[a]*

Slovakia	O'Dwyer[b]	LFS[c]	Sectoral	Others
1989			32,833	
1990		49,053	47,715	
1991		56,531	56,531	
1992		83,591	83,767	
1993	22,123	72,739	72,739	
1994	22,977	126,600	72,775	
1995	25,147	137,300	78,000	67,000 central[d]
1996	29,342	157,200	81,647	
1997	40,819	160,300	84,951	
1998	40,288	153,900	84,355	
1999	38,430	150,400	84,900	40,092 central[e]
2000	37,880	158,300	80,195	340,000 total[f]
2001		157,800	80,507	
2002		149,700	82,834	
% growth	171	306	252	

Notes:

[a] Bivariate correlations: Sectoral and O'Dwyer: .776*; Sectoral and LFS: .905**; LFS and O'Dwyer: .822*. (*significant at .05 level, **significant at .01 level, two-tailed test).

[b] Central: ministries, central offices, foreign service, and labor offices. Branch: branch administration of central offices and territorial administration (regional offices).

[c] *Statistická Ročenka Slovenskej Republiky.* 1993, 1996, 1999, 2002, 2003. Bratislava: Věda.

[d] World Bank 2001.

[e] INEKO for the Slovak Government. 2000. "Zaverečná správa o výsledkoch a odporučaniach audity súladu činnosti a financovania úsredných orgánov štánej správy," August, p. 2.

[f] Nižnansky, Viktor, and Knažko, Miroslav. 2001. "Public Administration," in Mesežnikov et al., p. 114.

Table B.5. *State Administration as a Percentage of Total Employment and in Absolute Numbers, 1989–2004*[a]

	Hungary		Estonia		Slovenia		Lithuania		Poland		Czech R.		Slovakia		Bulgaria		Latvia	
1989	5.8	297,900		n/a		N/a		n/a	1.6	260,700	1.7	91,729	1.4	32,833	1.3	53,270		n/a
1990	5.9	302,200	3.9	32,000	2.9	26,776		n/a	1.6	259,700	1.7	95,743	2.2	47,715	1.3	49,364	1.5	21,000
1991	6.2	285,840	3.9	31,500	3.5	25,024		n/a	1.8	273,100	3.0	99,098	2.6	56,531	1.4	50,454	1.7	23,700
1992	7.6	293,700	4.3	32,400	3.9	27,658	2.7	49,900	1.9	296,600	2.5	123,448	3.9	83,767	1.6	51,753	2.8	32,914
1993	7.8	299,500	4.9	34,500	4.3	35,022	3.4	56,600	3.3	298,400	2.7	132,675	3.4	72,739	2.1	67,146	3.5	37,332
1994	8.5	320,200	5.2	35,300	4.5	38,042	3.6	59,600	3.6	330,400	3.0	146,266	3.5	72,775	2.3	75,263	4.7	45,328
1995	8.1	318,100	5.5	34,500	4.6	40,146	4.1	67,600	2.6	384,800	3.2	161,640	3.6	78,000	2.3	76,084	5.4	57,000
1996	8.4	306,600	5.4	33,700	4.7	41,000	4.1	68,800	2.6	402,100	3.3	167,917	3.9	81,647	2.2	73,831	6.0	61,000
1997	8.0	293,800	5.3	32,300	4	36,000	4.1	69,200	2.7	423,100	3.5	180,100	3.9	84,951	2.5	78,689	6.1	63,000
1998	7.9	294,000	5.7	34,700	4.5	41,000	4.3	71,100	2.7	430,300	5.1	181,200	4.2	84,355	2.6	80,723	6.1	64,000
1999	7.9	301,900	6.0	34,600	5.5	49,000	4.4	72,400	2.8	439,500	5.5	182,800	4.2	82,102	2.9	89,959	6.3	61,490
2000	7.8	299,000	5.9	33,900	5.9	53,000	5.3	73,400	3.2	492,600	5.8	186,800	4.1	80,195	3.1	91,700	7.5	71,000
2001	7.5	289,000	5.9	34,200	5.3	48,000	5.1	67,700	3.5	525,700	6.1	193,500	4.0	80,507	5.0	95,825	7.1	68,000
2002	8.0	316,000	5.7	33,100	5.3	46,853	5.3	81,200	3.5	522,200	6.2	193,500	4.2	82,834	5.2	96,892	6.9	68,000
2003	8.7	320,900	5.8	35,700	5.7	48,085	5.7	75,800	3.7	528,000	6.4	195,154	4.2	88,334	5.5	117,445	6.9	67,000
2004	9.7	318,200	5.8	37,100	6.1	49,932	6.1	82,400	3.9	535,100	6.8	205,769	4.2	86,499	5.6	118,186	7.0	69,000
Increase (%)	167	107	149	116	210	186	211	165	244	205	400	225	300	263	431	223	467	329
Average annual growth[b]	.49	1.14		5.07		4.55		5.02		5.70		5.95		7.57		7.54		

Notes:

[a] Average number of registered employees by NACE L sector. Average state administration employment as a percentage of total employment in OECD countries: 4.2 percent. Average state administration employment as a percentage of total employment in developing countries: 1.7 percent. Schavio-Campo, Salvatore, de Tommaso, Giulio, and Mukherjee, Amitabha. 1997b. "An International Statistical Survey of Government Employment and Wages." World Bank Policy Research Working Paper No. 1806.

[b] Average annual growth: $\sum T_1 - T_0/T_0 + T_2 - T_1/T_1, \ldots + T_n - T_{n-1}/T_{n-1}/n$, where T_0 is the baseline ("previous") year, T_1 is the next year and n = number of years.

Sources: Rocznik Statystyczny. 1990–2006. Warsaw: GUS; Magyar Statisztikai Évkönyv. Budapest: KSH; Statistická Ročenka České Republiky, Prague: CSU; Časové řady základních ukazatelů statistiky práce 1948–2002 [Time-Series Indicators of Basic Labour Statistics]. 2003. Prague: Czech Statistical Office; Statistická Ročenka Slovenskej Republiky. Bratislava: Veda; Statistični Letopis. Ljubljana: Slovenian Statistical Office; Statističeski Rodišmik. Sofia: Bulgarian National Statistical Institute.

C

ANCHORING VIGNETTES

This book avoids relying on surveys of the perceptions of corruption as indices of state exploitation. Existing surveys have focused on business elites and owners rather than citizens per se (for example, both BEEPS and Transparency International [TI] surveyed only businesspeople, and TI polls only the representatives of international firms, which may face additional barriers in countries where the ways of doing business may not be familiar[1]). Others have asked the question only sporadically (for example, the New Democracies Barometer asked questions regarding bribery, but only in the Czech Republic in 1998[2]). Even where public opinion regarding state efficacy and corruption has been canvassed, the indices are problematic.[3] The respondents rely on previous survey results in formulating their opinion. Comparability across countries is severely limited. "Effectiveness," "corruption," and "legitimacy" are concepts that are difficult to measure, and the reference baselines vary enormously from country to country.

Minor corruption can be publicized to the point of creating perceptions of massive catastrophe. It is thus not surprising that as more and more international agencies began to pay attention to corruption, all the

---

[1] Sík, Endre. 2002. "The Bad, the Worse, and the Worst: Guesstimating the Level of Corruption," in Kotkin, Stephen, and Sajo, Andras. *Political Corruption: A Sceptic's Handbook*. Budapest: CEU Press, pp. 91–114.

[2] Domestic public opinion agencies have occasionally asked the question as well, but these databases are not accessible to researchers.

[3] Ades, Alberto, and Di Tella, Rafael. 1997. "The New Economics of Corruption: A Survey and Some New Results," *Political Studies*, 496–515; Treisman 2000. One exception is Lancaster, Thomas D., and Montinolla, Gabriella. 2001. "Comparative Political Corruption: Issues of Operationalization and Measurement," *Studies in Comparative International Development*. (Fall): 3–28, which relies on qualitative comparative analysis (QCA).

countries in the region received worse rankings after 1997. Such changes in perceptions of corruption and politicization may have more to do with their changed form than with any increase in actual levels. Some analysts have defended such polls by arguing that since they are expensive and yet are in high demand, the data must be valuable.[4] Yet the high prices may simply reflect the absence of other reliable measures rather than the validity of the technique.

To resolve these problems and obtain more comparable results, I use "anchoring vignettes" in the surveys.[5] These have several advantages over surveys relying on elite perceptions of corruption. First, this method resolves the crosscountry comparability by providing a comparative baseline, or anchoring. The survey questions are accompanied by a range of short, two-to-three-sentence vignettes that represent a range of scenarios that correspond to various experiences of the measured concept. Respondents' identification with a given scenario helps to anchor their survey question response, making possible valid crosssample comparisons. Respondents are asked to evaluate their personal experience with the usefulness of party affiliation and the propensity of government officials to take bribes. They then evaluate the experiences of hypothetical individuals along the same scale, so that the respondents' answers are "anchored" – given an objective baseline common to all respondents. This technique thus allows us to examine both what respondents mean by their evaluation and how they rank their evaluation ordinally.

Preparation, Administration, and Analysis of the Surveys

Survey questionnaires were translated into Bulgarian, Czech, Latvian, Polish, and Slovak, then translated back into English, in consultation with local collaborators. Pretests in both the United States and in the country cases were conducted to ensure the internal validity of the survey questions. As a result, an additional question on tax collection was eliminated; given the differences in methods of tax collection (filing individual income tax forms in Poland is universal, but in Slovakia and in the Czech Republic

---

[4] Kaufmann, Daniel, Kraay, Aart, and Zoido-Lobatón, Paolo. 1999. "Governance Matters." World Bank Policy Research Working Paper No. 2196, October. Mauro 1998. See also Ades and Di Tella 1997; Mauro, Paolo. 1998. "Corruption: Causes, Consequences, and Agenda for Further Research," *Finance and Development* (March): 11–14.

[5] Gary King developed the technique and the accompanying software. See http://gking.harvard.edu/vign.

only those who seek additional reimbursements and tax easements file), comparability was called into question.

In each country, the sample size exceeded one thousand respondents. The different collaborators used slightly different sampling methods; for example, CBOS used a three-stage probability sample of adults over eighteen, CVVM used a two-stage representative quota sample of those over fifteen, and Focus used a quota sample. Public opinion polling agencies in each country conducted the surveys.

Anchoring Vignettes: State Effectiveness and Corruption

1. [Discretionary provision of government jobs/services]

    A. Question: How important is political party affiliation in your obtaining a job in the government sector?

    Response:

      1. Essential
      2. Very important
      3. Moderately important
      4. Slightly important
      5. Unimportant

    B. Vignettes: Now please assess how important political party affiliation is for these hypothetical individuals' obtaining a job in the government sector.

    [PLEASE RANDOMIZE THE ORDER, and use same response categories as above]:

[X] wants a job as an accountant in a government office. He files the official application, which asks only for his education and experience. Although he's been active in the opposition party, no one asks him about this during the application process, and he gets the job. How important is political party affiliation in X's obtaining a job in the government sector?

[X] wants a job as an accountant in a government office. X is a member of the governing party, which gave him a recommendation for the job. He scores as well as the other candidate on the difficult qualifying exam. X gets the job. How important is political party affiliation in X's obtaining a job in the government sector?

[X] wants a job as an accountant in a government office. The job application requires five years of experience. X is less qualified than the other applicants: he has three years of experience as an accountant. But he is active in the ruling party, and he gets the job. How important is political party affiliation in X's obtaining a job in the government sector?

[X] wants a job as an accountant in a government office. Other applicants are far more qualified, but do not belong to the ruling party, and the official application asks for party affiliation. X is a long-standing governing party activist, and he gets the job. How important is political party affiliation in X's obtaining a job in the government sector?

Potential variants (not used): clerk in a court of justice, state health inspector, tax collector.

2. [Prevalence of bribery]

A. Question: How useful is it for you to make informal additional payments to government officials to obtain government services?

Response:

1. Essential
2. Very useful
3. Moderately useful
4. Slightly useful
5. Not useful

B. Vignettes: Now please assess how useful it is for these hypothetical individuals to make informal additional payments to government officials to obtain government services.
[PLEASE RANDOMIZE THE ORDER, and use same response categories as above]:

[X] needs a building permit. Informal additional payments are an important source of the local government officials' income, and X never had an application accepted without such payment. How useful is it for X to make informal additional payments to government officials to obtain government services?

[X] needs a building permit. Informal additional payments are welcomed. X usually includes an additional informal payment with his application. When he didn't, his applications were sometimes lost or greatly delayed, and he had to refile. How useful is it for X to make informal

245

additional payments to government officials to obtain government services?

[X] needs a building permit. Informal additional payments are accepted. X makes such payments, but only if he needs a permit especially quickly. How useful is it for X to make informal additional payments to government officials to obtain government services?

[X] needs a building permit. No one he knows ever made an informal additional payment. To speed up his application, he tries to pay, but the officials all refuse to accept the payment. They chastise (reprimand/criticize) him for even trying. How useful is it for X to make informal additional payments to government officials to obtain government services?

Potential variants (not used): small business license, copy of birth certificate, driver's license.

Bibliography

Ades, Alberto, and Di Tella, Rafael. 1999. "Rents, Competition, and Corruption," *American Economic Review*, 89, 4 (September): 982–93.

———. 1997. "The New Economics of Corruption: A Survey and Some New Results," *Political Studies*, 45, 3: 496–515.

———. 1995. "Competition and Corruption." Applied Economics Discussion Paper Series No. 169. Oxford University.

Ágh, Attila, ed. 1994. *The First Steps*. Budapest: Hungarian Center of Democracy Studies.

Ágh, Attila, and Kurtán, Sándor. 1996. "'Parliaments' and 'Organized Interests' in Civil Society: Local Government Legislation and Elections in Hungary (1990–1995)," in Ágh, Attila, and Ilonszki, Gabriella, eds. *Parliaments and Organized Interests: The Second Steps*. Budapest: Hungarian Center for Democracy Studies.

Ákos, Róna-Tas. 1997. *The Great Surprise of the Small Transformation*. Ann Arbor: University of Michigan Press.

Albats, Yevgenia. 2003. *The State Within a State: The KGB and Its Hold on Russia*. Ph.D. Dissertation, Harvard University.

Aldrich, John. 1995. *Why Parties?* Chicago: University of Chicago Press.

Allina-Pisano, Jessica. 2005. "Informal Politics and Challenges to Democracy: Administrative Resource in Kuchma's Ukraine." Unpublished Manuscript, Harvard University.

Amsden, Alice, Kochanowicz, Jacek, and Taylor, Lance. 1994. *The Market Meets Its Match*. Cambridge: Harvard University Press.

Ansell, Christopher, and Burris, Arthur. 1997. "Bosses of the City Unite! Labor Politics and Political Machine Consolidation, 1870–1910," *Studies in American Political Development*, 11 (Spring): 1–43.

Appel, Hilary. 2004. *A New Capitalist Order: Privatization and Ideology in Russia and Eastern Europe*. Pittsburgh: University of Pittsburgh Press.

———. 2001. "Corruption and the Collapse of the Czech Transition Miracle," *East European Politics and Societies*, 15, 3: 528–53.

Arian, Alan, and Barnes, Samuel. 1974. "The Dominant Party System: A Neglected Model of Democratic Stability," *Journal of Politics*, 36, 1: 592–614.

Auers, Daunis. 2002/2003. "Latvia's 2002 Elections: Dawn of a New Era?" *East European Constitutional Review*, 11/12, 4/1 (Fall/Winter): 106–10.

Axelrod, Robert. 1970. *Conflict of Interest*. Chicago: Markham.

Baldersheim, Harald, et al. 1996. "New Institutions of Local Government: A Comparison," in Baldersheim, Harald, Illner, Michal, Offerdal, Audun, Rose, Lawrence, and Swaniewicz, Paweł, eds. *Local Democracy and the Processes of Transformation in East-Central Europe*. Boulder: Westview Press.

Barnes, Andrew. 2003. "Comparative Theft: Context and Choice in the Hungarian Czech, and Russian Transformations 1989–2000," *East European Politics and Societies*, 17, 3: 533–65.

Bartlett, David. 1997. *The Political Economy of Dual Transformations*. Ann Arbor: University of Michigan Press.

———. 1996. "Democracy, Institutional Change, and Stabilization Policy in Hungary," *Europe-Asia Studies*, 48, 1: 47–83.

Bartolini, Stefano. 1999–2000. "Collusion, Competition, and Democracy," *Journal of Theoretical Politics*, 11, 4: 435–70; 12, 1: 33–65.

Bartolini, Stefano. 2002. "Electoral and Party Competition: Analytical Dimensions and Empirical Problems," in Gunther, Richard, Montero, Jose Ramon, and Linz, Juan, eds. *Political Parties*. Oxford: Oxford University Press, pp. 84–110.

Bartolini, Stefano, and Mair, Peter. 1990. *Identity, Competition, and Electoral Availability*. Cambridge: Cambridge University Press.

Barzelay, Michael. 1997. "Central Audit Institutions and Performance Auditing," *Governance*, 10, 3: 235–60.

Bates, Robert. 1981. *Markets and States in Tropical Africa*. Berkeley: UC Press.

Bendor, Jonathan, Glazer, A., Hammond, T. 2001. "Theories of Delegation," *Annual Review of Political Science*, 4: 235–69.

Bennett, Colin. 1997. "Understanding Ripple Effects: The Cross-National Adoption of Policy Instruments for Bureaucratic Accountability," *Governance*, 10, 3: 213–33.

Benoit, Kenneth. 2004. "Models of Electoral System Change," *Electoral Studies*, 23: 363–89.

Benoit, Kenneth, and Hayden, Jacqueline. 2004. "Institutional Change and Persistence: The Evolution of Poland's Electoral System, 1989–2001," *Journal of Politics*, 66, 2: 396–427.

Bercík, Peter, and Nemec, Juraj. 1999. "The Civil Service System of the Slovak Republic," in Verheijen, Tony, ed. *Civil Service Systems in Central and Eastern Europe*. Cheltenham: Edward Elgar, pp. 184–210.

Bernhard, Michael. 2000. "Institutional Choice After Communism," *East European Politics and Societies*, 3: 316–47.

Bielasiak, Jack. 1983. "The Party: Permanent Crisis," in Brumberg, Abraham, ed. *Poland: Genesis of a Revolution*. New York: Vintage.

Birch, Sarah. 2002. *Electoral Systems and Political Transformation in Post-Communist Europe*. London: Palgrave MacMillan.

———. 2001. "Electoral Systems and Party System Stability in Post-Communist Europe." Paper presented at American Political Science Association Annual Meeting, 30 August–2 September 2001, San Francisco.

Bibliography

Birnir, Jóhanna Kristín. 2005. "Public Venture Capital and Party Institutionalization," *Comparative Political Studies*, 38, 8 (October): 915–38.

Bruszt, Laszlo, and Stark, David. 1991. "Remaking the Political Field in Hungary: From the Politics of Confrontation to the Politics of Competition," *Journal of International Affairs*, 45, 1 (Summer): 201–45.

Brym, Robert, and Gimpelson, Vladimir. 2004. "The Size, Composition, and Dynamics of the Russian State Bureaucracy in the 1990s," *Slavic Review*, 63, 1: 90–112.

Buchanan, James, and Tullock, Gordon. 1963. *The Calculus of Consent: Logical Foundations of Constitutional Democracy*. Ann Arbor: University of Michigan Press.

Bugaric, Bojan. 2005. "The Europeanization of National Administrations in Central and Eastern Europe: Creating Formal Structures Without Substance?" Paper prepared for the Apres Enlargement Workshop, EUI, Florence, 29–30 April.

Bukowska, Xymena, and Czesnik, Mikołaj. 2002. "Analiza Treści Programów Wyborczych," in Markowski, Radoslaw, ed. *System Partyjny I Zachowania Wyborcze*. Warsaw: ISP PAN.

Bunce, Valerie. 2001. "Democratization and Economic Reform," *Annual Review of Political Science*, 4.

———. 1999. "The Political Economy of Postsocialism," *Slavic Review* 58, 4: 756–93.

Calvo, Ernesto, and Murillo, Maria Victoria. 2004. "Who Delivers? Partisan Clients in the Argentine Electoral Market," *American Journal of Political Science*, 48 (4 October): 742–57.

Carey, John. 2000. "Parchment, Equilibria, and Institutions," *Comparative Political Studies*, 33, 6/7: 735–61.

Carpenter, Daniel. 2001. *The Forging of Bureaucratic Autonomy*. Princeton: Princeton University Press.

CBOS. 2000. "Finansowanie partii politycznych." Komunikat z badań (Fall).

Cekota, Jaromir, Gönenç, Rauf, and Kwang-Yeol Yoo. 2002. "Strengthening the Management of Public Spending in Hungary," OECD Economics Department Working Paper No. 336 (30 July).

Center for Study of Democracy. 2004. Brief. Bulgaria Sofia (July). Available at http://www.csd.bg, accessed 19 November 2004.

Čigāne, Lolita. 2002. "A Reflection of the Shortcomings in Legislation on Party Financing in the 2001 Finance Declarations." Soros Foundation Latvia and Transparency International "delna," Riga Latvia (April). Available at http://www.politika.lv.

Cirtautas, Arista. 1995. "The Post-Leninist State: A Conceptual and Empirical Examination," *Communist and Post-Communist Studies*, 28, 4: 379–92.

Colazingari, Silvia, and Rose-Ackerman, Susan. 1998. "Corruption in a Paternalistic Democracy: Lessons from Italy for Latin America," *Political Science Quarterly*, 113, 3: 447–70.

Collier, David, and Levitsky, Steven. 1997. "Research Note: Democracy with Adjectives: Conceptual Innovation in Comparative Research," *World Politics*, 49, 3: 430–51.

Colomer, Josep. 1995. "Strategies and Outcomes in Eastern Europe," *Journal of Democracy*, 6, 2: 74–85.

Comisso, Ellen. 1986. "State Structures, Political Processes, and Collective Choice in CMEA States," in Comisso, Ellen, and Tyson, Laura D'Andrea, eds. *Power, Purpose, and Collective Choice: Economic Strategy in Socialist States*. Ithaca: Cornell University Press.

Coppedge, Michael. 2001. "Political Darwinism in Latin America's Lost Decade," in Larry, Diamond, and Richard, Gunther, eds. *Political Parties and Democracy*. Baltimore: Johns Hopkins Press, pp. 173–205.

———. 1993. "Parties and Society in Mexico and Venezuela: Why Competition Matters," *Comparative Political Studies*, 26, 1 (April): 253–74.

Cotta, Maurizio. 1996. "Structuring the New Party Systems after the Dictatorship," in Pridham, Geoffrey, and Lewis, Paul, eds. *Stabilising Fragile Democracies*. London: Routledge, pp. 69–99.

Crenson, Matthew, and Ginsberg, Benjamin. 2004. *Downsizing Democracy*. Baltimore: Johns Hopkins Press.

Crombrugghe, Alain de. 1997. "Wage and Pension Pressure on the Polish Budget." Report for World Bank Project RPO 678–96, Policy Research Working Paper No. 1793.

Czabański, Krzysztof. 2003. "Rywin TV." *Wprost*, 26 October.

Dallek, Robert. 1998. *Flawed Giant: Lyndon B. Johnson, 1960–1973*. New York: Oxford University Press.

De Mesquita, Bruce Bueno. 1974. "Need for Achievement and Competitiveness as Determinants of Political Party Success in Elections and Coalitions," *American Political Science Review*, 68, 3: 1207–20.

Della Porta, Donatella. 2000. "Political Parties and Corruption: 17 Hypotheses on the Interactions Between Parties and Corruption." EUI Working Papers RSC 2000/60, European University Institute, Fiesole, San Domenico, Italy.

Della Porta, Donatella, and Meny, Yves, eds. 1997. *Democracy and Corruption in Europe*. London: Pinter.

Della Porta, Donatella, and Vannucci, Alberto Vannucci. 1997. "The 'Perverse Effects' of Political Corruption," *Political Studies*, 45, 3: 516–38.

Demsetz, Harold. 1982. *Economic, Legal, and Political Dimensions of Competition*. Amsterdam: North-Holland.

Di Palma, Giuseppe. 1990. "Establishing Party Dominance," in Pempel, T. J., ed. *Uncommon Democracies: The One-Party Regimes*. Ithaca: Cornell University Press.

Diermeier, Daniel, and Merlo, Antonio. 2000. "Government Turnover in Parliamentary Democracies," *Journal of Economic Theory*, 94: 46–79.

Dnitrova, Zoya. 2002. *Financing Election Campaigns*. Unpublished Manuscript. Ljabljana: Peace Institute.

Downs, Anthony. 1957. *An Economic Theory of Democracy*. New York: Harper and Row.

Duverger, Maurice. 1965. *Political Parties*. New York: Wiley and Sons, p. 308.

Dyson, Kenneth. 1977. "Party, State, and Bureaucracy in Western Germany." Sage Professional Papers in Comparative Politics, No. 01-063. Beverly Hills: Sage.

Bibliography

East European Constitutional Review. 2001. (Winter). Available at http://www.balticsworldwide.com/wkcrier/0301_0322_99.htm, accessed February 9, 2006.

RFE/RL OMRI Daily Digest Report, 29 July 1996.

Ekiert, Grzegorz. 2001. *The State After State Socialism: Poland in Comparative Perspective*. Unpublished Manuscript. Harvard University.

Ekiert, Grzegorz, and Zielonka, Jan. 2003. "Introduction: Academic Boundaries and Path Dependencies Facing the EU's Eastward Enlargement," *East European Politics and Societies*, 17, 1 (Winter): 7–23.

Elster, Jon, Offe, Claus, and Preuss, Ulrich K. 1998. *Institutional Design in Post-Communist Societies*. Cambridge: Cambridge University Press.

Enyedi, Zsolt. 2006. "Party Politics in Post-Communist Transition," in Katz, Richard, and Crotty, William, eds. *Handbook of Party Politics*. London: Sage.

———. 2003. "Cleavage Formation in Hungary: The Role of Agency." Paper presented at the 2003 Joint Sessions of the ECPR Edinburgh.

———. 1996. "Organizing a Sub-Cultural Party in Eastern Europe," *Party Politics*, 2, 3: 377–96.

Epstein, David, and O'Halloryn, Sharyn. 1994. "Administrative Procedures, Information, and Agency Discretion," *American Journal of Political Science*, 38/3: 697–722.

European Union Commission. 2000. *Regular Report on the Czech Republic's Progress Towards Accession*. Brussels: EU.

Evans, Peter, Rueschemeyer, Dietrich, and Skocpol, Theda, eds. 1985. *Bringing the State Back In*. Cambridge: Cambridge University Press.

Eyal, Gil, Szelényi, Ivan, and Townsley, Eleanor. 1998. *Making Capitalism Without Capitalists*. London: Verso.

Fainsod, Merle. 1963. *Bureaucracy and Modernization*. Stanford: Stanford University Press.

———. 1958. *Smolensk Under Soviet Rule*. Cambridge: Harvard University Press.

———. 1953. *How Russia Is Ruled*. Cambridge: Harvard University Press.

Fearon, James. 1999. "Electoral Accountability and the Control of Politicians: Selecting Good Types Versus Sanctioning Poor Performance," in Stokes, Susan, Przeworski, Adam, and Manin, Bernard, eds. *Democracy, Accountability, and Representation*. Cambridge: Cambridge University Press.

Ferejohn, John. 1999. "Accountability and Authority: Toward a Theory of Political Accountability," in Stokes, Susan, Przeworski, Adam, and Manin, Bernard, eds. *Democracy, Accountability, and Representation*. Cambridge: Cambridge University Press, pp. 131–53.

———. 1986. "Incumbent Performance and Electoral Control," *Public Choice*, 30: 5–25.

Fidrmuc, Jan, Fidrmuc, Jarko, and Horvath, Julius. 2002. "Visegrad Economies: Growth Experience and Prospects." GDN Global Research Project: Determinants of Economic Growth.

Firmin-Sellers, Kathryn. 1995. "The Politics of Property Rights," *American Political Science Review*, 89, 4: 867–81.

Fish, M. Steven. 1998. "The Determinants of Economic Reform in the Postcommunist World," *East European Politics and Societies*, 12: 31–78.

Freedom House. 2002. *Nations in Transit, 2001*. Washington: Freedom House.

Frič, Pavol, et al. 1999. *Korupce na český způsob*. Prague: G Plus G.

Friedrich, Carl, and Brzezinski, Zbigniew. 1956. *Totalitarian Dictatorship and Autocracy*. Cambridge: Harvard University Press.

Frydman, Roman, Murphy, Kenneth, and Rapaczynski, Andrzej. 1998. *Capitalism with a Comrade's Face*. Budapest: Central European University Press.

Frye, Timothy. 2002. "The Perils of Polarization," *World Politics*, 54 (April), pp. 308–37.

———. 1997. "A Politics of Institutional Choice: Post-Communist Presidencies," *Comparative Political Studies*, 30: 523–52.

Ganev, Venelin. 2005. *Preying on the State: State Formation in Post-Communist Bulgaria (1989–1997)*. Unpublished Manuscript.

———. 2000. "Post-Communism as a Historical Episode of State Building, or Explaining the Weakness of the Post-Communist State." Paper presented at the twelfth International Conference of Europeanists Chicago, March.

Gazsó, Ferenc. 1992. "Cadre Bureaucracy and the Intelligentsia," *Journal of Communist Studies* (September): 76–90.

Geddes, Barbara. 1994. *The Politician's Dilemma*. Berkeley: University of California Press.

Geddes, Barbara, and Neto, Artur Ribeiro. 1992. "Institutional Sources of Corruption in Brazil," *Third World Quarterly*, 4: 641–2.

Gimpelson, Vladimir, and Treisman, Daniel. 2002. "Fiscal Games and Public Employment," *World Politics*, 54: 145–83.

Goetz, Klaus H. 2001. "Making Sense of Post-Communist Central Administration: Modernization Europeanization or Latinization?" *Journal of European Public Policy*, 8, 6 (December): 1032–51.

Goetz, Klaus, and Margetts, Helen. 1999. "The Solitary Center: The Core Executive in Central and Eastern Europe," *Governance*, 12, 4 (October): 425–53.

Golden, Miriam, and Chang, Eric. 2001. "Competitive Corruption: Factional Conflict and Political Malfeasance in Postwar Italian Christian Democracy," *World Politics*, 53: 588–622.

Goldsmith, Arthur. 1999. "Africa's Overgrown State Reconsidered," *World Politics*, 4: 520–46.

Government of the Czech Republic. 1998. "Programové prohlašení Vlády České Republiky" [Programmatic declaration of the Government of the Czech Republic] (27 January). Available at http://www.vlada.cz/ASC/urad/historie/vlada98/dokumenty/progrprohl.il2.htm.

Government of the Republic of Slovakia. 2001. "Správa o boji proti korupcii na Slovensku." [Report of the Slovak government]. October. Available at http://www.government.gov.sk, accessed 23 November 2002.

Grabbe, Heather. 2001. "How Does Europeanization Affect CEE Governance? Conditionality, Diffusion, and Diversity," *Journal of European Public Policy*, 8, 6 (December): 1013–31.

Greene, Kenneth. 2004. *Defeating Dominance: Opposition Party Building and Mexico's Democratization in Comparative Perspective*. Ph.D. Dissertation, University of California at Berkeley.

Gros, Daniel, and Suhcrke, Marc. 2000. "Ten Years After: What Is Special About Transition Countries?" EBRD Working Paper No. 56, August.

Grzymała-Busse, Anna. 2004. "Informal Institutions and the Post-Communist State." Paper prepared for the Conference on the Role of Ideas in Post-Communist Politics: A Re-Evaluation Havighurst Center, Luxembourg, 5–9 July.

———. 2003. "Political Competition and the Politicization of the State," *Comparative Political Studies*, 36, 10 (December): 1123–47.

———. 2002. *Redeeming the Communist Past*. Cambridge: Cambridge University Press.

Grzymała-Busse, Anna, and Innes, Abby. 2003. "Great Expectations: The EU and Domestic Political Competition in East Central Europe," *East European Politics and Societies*, 17, 1: 64–73.

Grzymała-Busse, Anna, and Jones Luong, Pauline. 2002. "Reconceptualizing the Post-Communist State," *Politics and Society*, 30, 4 (December): 529–54.

György, Istvan. 1999. "The Civil Service System of Hungary," in Verheijen, Tony, ed. *Civil Service Systems in Central and Eastern Europe*. Cheltenham: Edward Elgar: 131–58.

Habermas, Jürgen. 1975. *Legitimation Crisis*. Boston: Beacon.

Hadenius, Stig. 1985. *Swedish Politics During the 20th Century*. Boras: Swedish Institute.

Hegedüs, József. 1999. "Hungarian Local Government," in Kirchner Emil, ed., *Decentralization and Transition in the Visegrad*. Basingstoke: Macmillan.

Heidenheimer, Arnold J., Johnston, Michael, and Levine, Victor, eds. 1989. *Political Corruption*. New Brunswick: Transaction.

Hellman, Joel. 1998. "Winners Take All: The Politics of Partial Reform," *World Politics*, 50, 2 (January): 203–34.

Hellman, Joel, and Kaufmann, Daniel. 2001. "Confronting the Challenge of State Capture in Transition Economics," *Finance and Development*, 38, 3 (September).

Hellman, Joel, Jones, Geraint, and Kaufmann, Daniel. 2000. "Seize the State, Seize the Day." World Bank Policy Research Paper No. 2444.

Hendley, Katherine. 1996. *Trying to Make Law Matter*. Ann Arbor: University of Michigan Press.

Herrera, Yoshiko. 2001. "Russian Economic Reform 1991–1998," in Barany, Zoltan, and Moser, Robert, eds. *Challenges to Democratic Transition In Russia*. New York: Cambridge University Press.

Hesse, Joachim Jens. 1993. "From Transformation to Modernization: Administrative Change in Central and Eastern Europe," in idem. ed. *Administrative Transformation in Central and Eastern Europe*. Oxford: Blackwell.

Heywood, Paul. 1997. "Political Corruption: Problems and Perspectives," *Political Studies*, 45, 3: 417–35.

Hirszowicz, Maria. 1980. *The Bureaucratic Leviathan*. Oxford: Martin Robertson.

Hojnacki, William. 1996. "Politicization as a Civil Service Dilemma," in Bekke, Hans, Perry, James, and Toonen, Theo, eds. *Civil Service Systems in Comparative Perspective*. Bloomington: Indiana University Press, pp. 137–64.

Holmes, Stephen. 1996. "Cultural Legacies or State Collapse: Probing the Post-Communist Dilemma," in Mandelbaum, Michael, ed. *Postcommunism: Four Perspectives*. New York: Council on Foreign Relations.

Holmstrom, Bengt. 1982. "Managerial Incentive Problems: A Dynamic Perspective," in *Essays in Economic and Management in Honor of Lars Wahlbeck*. Stockholm: Swedish School of Economics.

Horowitz, Shale, and Petréš, Martin. 2003. "Pride and Prejudice in Prague: Understanding Early Policy Error and Belsteol Reform in Czech Economic Transition," *East European Politics and Societies*, 17, 2: 231–65.

Horráth, Tamás, ed. 2000. *Decentralization: Experiments and Reforms*. Budapest: Open Society Institute.

Hough, Jerry. 1969. *The Soviet Prefects*. Cambridge: Harvard University Press.

Hough, Jerry, and Fainsod, Merle. 1979. *How the Soviet Union Is Governed*. Cambridge: Harvard University Press.

Howard, Marc Morjé. 2003. *The Weakness of Civil Society in Post-Communist Europe*. Cambridge: Cambridge University Press.

Huber, John, and Shipan, Charles. 2002. *Deliberate Discretion?* Cambridge: Cambridge University Press.

Humphrey, Caroline. 2002. *The Unmaking of Soviet Life*. Ithaca: Cornell University Press.

Hutchcroft, Paul. 1998. *Booty Capitalism*. Ithaca: Cornell University Press.

Ichino, Nahomi. 2006. *Thugs and Voters: Political Tournaments in Nigeria*. Ph.D. Thesis Department of Political Science, Stanford University.

Ikstens, Jānis, Smilov, Daniel, and Walecki, Marcin. 2002. "Campaign Finance in Central and Eastern Europe," *IFES Reports* (April). Washington: IFES.

Ilonszki, Gabriella. 2002. "A Functional Clarification of Parliamentary Committees in Hungary, 1990–1998," in Olson, David, and Crowther, William, eds. *Committees in Post-Communist Democratic Parliaments: Comparative Institutionalization*. Columbus: Ohio State University Press, pp. 21–43.

_____. 2000. "The Second Generation Political Elite in Hungary: Partial Consolidation," in Frentzel-Zagórska, Janina, and Wasilewski, Jacek, eds. *The Second Generation of Democratic Elites in East and Central Europe*. Warsaw: PAN ISP.

_____. 1998. "Representation Deficit in a New Democracy: Theoretical Considerations and the Hungarian Case," *Communist and Post-Communist Studies*, 14: 157–70.

INEKO for the Slovak Government. 2000. "Záverečná správa o výsledkoch a odporúčaniach audity súladu činnosti a financovania úsredných orgánov štátnej správy," August.

Innes, Abby. 2002. "Party Competition in Post-Communist Europe: The Great Electoral Lottery," *Comparative Politics*, 35, 1: 85–105.

International Monetary Fund. 1999. Report on Observance of Standards and Codes, August 1999/March 2000.

Ishiyama, John. 1997. "Transitional Electoral Systems in Post-Communist Eastern Europe," *Political Science Quarterly*, 112, 1: 95–115.

Issacharoff Samuel, and Pildes, Richard. 1998. "Politics as Markets: Partisan Lock-ups of the Democratic Process," *Stanford Law Review* (February): 642–717.

Iversen, Torben, and Wren, Anne. 1998. "Equality, Employment, and Budgetary Restraint," *World Politics*, 50, 4: 507–46.

Jabłoński, A. 1998. "Europeanization of Public Administration in Central Europe: Poland in Comparative Perspective." NATO Individual Democratic Institution Research Fellowships, Final Report 1995–7.

Jackman, Robert. 1993. *Power Without Force*. Ann Arbor: University of Michigan Press.

Jacoby, Wade. 2004. *The Enlargement of the EU and NATO: Ordering from the Menu in Central Europe*. New York: Cambridge University Press.

Jarosz, Maria. 2001. *Manowce Polskiej Prywatyzacji*. Warszawa: PWN SA.

Jednotka boji proti korupci, Ministry of Interior. 2001. *Zpráva o korupci v ČR a o plnění harmonogramu opatření vládního programu boje proti korupci v ČR.*

Johns, Michael. 2003. "Do as I Say and Not as I Do: The European Union, Eastern Europe, and Minority Rights," *East European Politics and Societies*, 17, 4 (November): 682–99.

Jones Luong, Pauline. 2002. *Institutional Change and Political Continuity in Post-Soviet Central Asia: Power, Perceptions, and Pacts*. Cambridge: Cambridge University Press.

Jones Luong, Pauline, and Weinthal, Erika. 2004. "Contra Coercion: Russian Tax Reform, Exogenous Shocks and Negotiated Institutional Change," *American Political Science Review*, 98, 1: 139–52.

Jungerstam-Mulders, Susanne, ed. 2006. *Post-Communist EU Member States: Parties and Party Systems*. London: Ashgate.

Kalniņš, Valts, and Čigāne, Lolita. 2003. "On the Road Toward a More Honest Society." Policy Report, January. Available at http://www.politika.lv.

Kaminski, Antoni. 1992. *An Institutional Theory of Communist Regimes: Design, Function, and Breakdown*. San Francisco: ICS Press.

Kang, David. 2002. *Crony Capitalism: Corruption and Development in South Korea and the Philippines*. Cambridge: Cambridge University Press.

Kaplan, Karel. 1993. *Aparát ÚV KSC v letech 1948–1968*. Sesity Ústavu pro Soudobé Dějiny AV ČR Sv. 10.

———. 1987. *The Short March: The Communist Takeover of Power in Czechoslovakia, 1945–1948*. Boulder CO: Westview Press.

Karasimeonov, Georgii. 1996. "Bulgaria's New Party System," in Pridham, Geoffrey, and Lewis, Paul, eds. *Stabilizing Fragile Democracies*. London: Routledge.

Karklins, Rasma. 2002. Typology of Post-Communist Corruption, *Problems of Post-Communism*, 49 (July/August): 22–32.

Karl-Heinz, Nassmacher. 1989. "Structure and Impact of Public Subsidies to Political Parties in Europe," in Alexander, Herbert, ed. *Comparative Political Finance in the 1980s*, Cambridge: Cambridge University Press, pp. 236–67.

Katz, Richard, and Mair, Peter. 1995. "Changing Models of Party Organization and Party Democracy," *Party Politics*, 1: 5–28.

Kaufman, Daniel. 2003. "Rethinking Governance: Empirical Lessons Challenge Orthodoxy." World Bank Working Paper.

Kaufman, Daniel, Kraay, A., and Mastruzzi, M. 2005. *Governance Matters IV: Governance Indicators 1996–2004*. Washington: World Bank.

Keri, Laszlo. 1994. *Balance: The Hungarian Government 1990–1994*. Budapest: Korridor.

Kettle, Steve. 1995. "Straining at the Seams." *Transition* (April). Available at http://www.tol.cz.

King, Roswitha. 2003. "Conversations with Civil Servants: Interview Results from Estonia, Lithuania, Czech Republic and Poland." Manuscript, University of Latvia Riga.

Kiss, Csilla. 2003. "From Liberalism to Conservatism: The Federation of Young Democrats in Post-Communist Hungary," *East European Politics and Societies*, 16, 3, 739–63.

Kitschelt, Herbert. 2001. "Divergent Paths of Post-Communist Democracies," in Diamond, Larry, and Gunther, Richard, eds. *Political Parties and Democracy*. Baltimore: Johns Hopkins Press, pp. 299–323.

––––––. 2000. "Linkages Between Citizens and Politicians in Democratic Polities," *Comparative Political Studies*, 33, 6/7: 845–79.

Kitschelt, Herbert, Mansfeldová, Zdenka, Markowski, Radoslaw, and Toka, Gábor. 1999. *Post-Communist Party Systems*. Cambridge: Cambridge University Press.

Kitschelt, Herbert, and Wilkinson, Steven. Forthcoming. "Citizen-Politician Linkages: An Introduction," in Kitschelt and Wilkinson, eds. *Patrons, Clients, and Linkages*. Manuscript, Duke University.

KNAB. 2003. "Progress and Results in the Field of Corruption Prevention and Combat," Periodic Update 24 (November). Available at http://www.knab.gov.lv/ru/actual/article.php?id=18863, accessed 12 February 2004.

Knight, Jack. 1992. *Institutions and Social Conflict*. Cambridge: Cambridge University Press.

Kochanowicz, Jacek. 1994. "Reforming Weak States and Deficient Bureaucracies," in Nelson, Joan M., Kochanowicz, Jacek, Mizsei, Kalman, and Munoz, Oscar, eds. *Intricate Links: Democratization and Market Reforms in Latin America and Eastern Europe*. Washington: Overseas Development Council, pp. 194–206.

Koole, Ruud. 1996. "Cadre, Catch-all or Cartel? A Comment," *Party Politics*, 4: 507–23.

Kopecký, Petr. 2006. "Political Parties and the State in Post-Communist Europe: The Nature of the Symbiosis," *Journal of Communist Studies and Transition Politics*, 22, 3 (September): 251–73.

Kopstein, Jeff, and Reilly, David. 2000. "Geographic Diffusion and the Transformation of the Postcommunist World," *World Politics*, 53, 1: 1–37.

Körösényi, Andras. 1999. *Government and Politics in Hungary*. Budapest: CEU Press.

Krasner, Stephen. 1984. "Approaches to the State: Alternative Conceptions and Historical Dynamics," *Comparative Politics*, 16, 2 (January): 223–46.

Krašovec, Alenka. 2001. "Party and State in Democratic Slovenia," in Lewis, Paul G., ed. *Party Development and Democratic Change in Post-Communist Europe*. London: Frank Cass, pp. 93–106.

Bibliography

Krause, Kevin Deegan. 2006. *Elected Affinities*. Stanford: Stanford University Press.

Krueger, Anne. 1974. "The Political Economy of the Rent-Seeking Society," *American Economic Review*, 64, 3: 291–303.

Krupavičius, Algis. 1998. "The Post-Communist Transition and Institutionalization of Lithuania's Parties," *Political Studies*, 46, 3: 465–91.

Kunicová, Jana, and Rose-Ackerman, Susan. 2005. "Electoral Rules and Constitutional Structures as Constraints on Corruption," *British Journal of Political Science*, 35: 573–606.

Kurczewski, Jacek. 1999. "The Rule of Law in Poland," in Přibán, Jiří, and Young, James, eds. *The Rule of Law in Central Europe*. Aldershot: Ashgate.

Lancaster, Thomas D., and Montinolla, Gabriella. 2001. "Comparative Political Corruption: Issues of Operationalization and Measurement," *Studies in Comparative International Development*, 36, 3 (Fall): 3–27.

La Palombara, Joseph. 1994. "Structural and Institutional Aspects of Corruption," *Social Research*, 61, 2 (Summer): 325–50.

Laver, Michael, and Shepsle, Kenneth. 1999. "Government Accountability in Parliamentary Democracy," in Stokes, Susan, Przeworski, Adam, and Manin, Bernard, eds. *Democracy, Accountability, and Representation*. Cambridge: Cambridge University Press, pp. 279–96.

Lawson, Stephanie. 1993. "Conceptual Issues in the Comparative Study of Regime Change and Democratization," *Comparative Politics*, 25, 2 (January): 183–205.

Levi, Margaret. 1997. *Consent, Dissent, and Patriotism*. Cambridge: Cambridge University Press.

_____. 1988. *Of Rule and Revenue*. Berkeley: University of California Press.

Levite, Ariel, and Tarrow, Sidney. 1983. "The Legitimation of Excluded Parties in Dominant Party Systems," *Comparative Politics*, 15, 3 (April): 295–327.

Levitsky, Steven. 2003. *Transforming Labor-Based Parties in Latin America*. Cambridge: Cambridge University Press.

Lewanski, Rudolf. 1997. "Italian Civil Service: A Pre-Modern Bureaucracy in Transition?" Paper prepared for the Conference on Civil Service Systems in Comparative Perspective, Indiana University, 5–8 April.

Lewis, Paul, and Gortat, Radzisława. 1995. "Models of Party Development and Questions of State Dependence in Poland," *Party Politics*, 4: 599–608.

Lewis, Paul G. 2000. *Political Parties in Post-Communist Eastern Europe*. London: Routledge.

Lieven, Anatol. 1994. *The Baltic Revolution*. New Haven: Yale University Press.

Lijphart, Arendt. 1999. *Patterns of Democracy: Government Forms and Performance in Thirty Six Countries*. New Haven: Yale University Press.

_____, ed. 1992. *Parliamentary Versus Presidential Government*. Cambridge: Oxford University Press.

Lindberg, Staffan. 2004. *The Power of Elections: Democratic Participation, Competition, and Legitimacy in Africa*. Lund: Lund University.

Linek, Lukáš. 2002. "Czech Republic," *European Journal of Political Research*, 41: 931–40.

Linek, Lukáš, and Rakušanová, Petra. 2002. "Parties in the Parliament: Why, When, and How Do Parties Act in Unity?" Institute of Sociology, Czech Republic Sociological Paper No. 02:9.

Linz, Juan. 1994. "Introduction: Some Thoughts on Presidentialism in Post-Communist Europe," in Taras, Ray, ed. *Postcommunist Presidents*. Cambridge, Oxford University Press: 1–14.

Lippert, Barbara, Umbach, Gaby, and Wessels, Wolfgang. 2001. "Europeanization of CEE Executives: EU Membership Negotiations as a Shaping Power," *Journal of European Public Policy*, 8 (6 December): 980–1012.

Logue, John, and Einhorn, Eric. 1988. "Restraining the Governors: The Nordic Experience with Limiting the Strong State," *Scandinavian Political Studies*, 11, 1.

Łoś, Maria, and Zybertowicz, Andrzej. 1999. "Is Revolution a Solution?" in Krygier, Martin, and Czarnota, Adam, eds. *The Rule of Law After Communism*. Aldershot: Ashgate.

Lucking, Richard. 2003. *Civil Service Training in the Context of Public Administration Reform*. New York: United Nations Development Program.

Lupia, Arthur, and McCubbins, Matthew. 2000. "The Institutional Foundations of Political Competence," in Lupia, Arthur, McCubbins, Mathew D., and Popkin, Samuel L., eds. *Elements of Reason: Cognition, Choice, and the Bounds of Rationality*. New York: Cambridge University Press, pp. 47–66.

———. 2000. *Privatizing the Police State*. New York, St. Martins.

Luther, Kurt Richard, and Müller, Wolfgang. 1992. *Politics in Austria: Still a Case of Consociationalism?* London: Frank Cass.

Mainwaring, Scott. 1993. "Presidentialism, Multipartism, and Democracy: The Difficult Combination," *Comparative Political Studies*, 26, 2 (July): 198–228.

Mair, Peter. 1997. *Party System Change: Approaches and Interpretations*. Oxford: Clarendon Press.

———. 1995. "Political Parties, Popular Legitimacy, and Public Privilege," *West European Politics*, 18, 2 (July): 40–57.

———. 1994. "Party Organizations," in Katz, Richard, and Mair, Peter, eds. *How Parties Organize*. New York: Sage, pp. 134–57.

Majone, Giandomenico. 1994. "The Rise of the Regulatory State in Europe," *West European Politics*, 12, 3 (July): 77–101.

Malcická, Lenka. 2001. "Vybrané aspekty financovania politických strán a hnutí v SR" [Selected aspects of party and movement financing in Slovakia]. Manuscript, Bratislava. Available at http://politika.host.sk/prispevky/prispevok_malcicka_financovaniestran.htm, accessed 21 June 2001.

Malová, Darina. 1997. "The Development of Interest Representation in Slovakia After 1989," in Szomolányi, Soňa, and Gould, John, eds. *Slovakia: Problems of Democratic Consolidation*. Bratislava: Friedrich Ebert Foundation.

Mann, Michael. 1988. *States, War, and Capitalism*. Oxford: Basil Blackwell.

"Marching Backwards: Slovakia's Counterrevolution." 1995. October. Available at http://project-syndicate.org/surveys/marching_bac.php4, accessed 10 September, 2004.

Mattli, Walter, and Plümper, Thomas. 2002. "The Demand-Side Politics of EU Enlargement: Democracy and the Application for EU Membership," *Journal of European Public Policy*, 9, 4: 550–74.

Mauro, Paolo. 1998. "Corruption: Causes, Consequences, and Agenda for Further Research," *Finance and Development* (March): 11–14.

———. 1995. "Corruption and Growth," *Quarterly Journal of Economics*, 110, 3: 681–712.

McChesney, Fred. 1987. "Rent Extraction and Rent Creation in the Economic Theory of Regulation," *Journal of Legal Studies*, 16: 101–18.

McCubbins Matthew, Noll, Roger, and Weingast, Barry. 1989. "Structure and Process; Politics and Policy: Administrative Arrangements and the Political Control of Agencies," *Virginia Law Review*, 75, 2: 431–82.

———. 1987. "Administrative Procedures as Instruments of Political Control," *Economics and Organization*, 77 (March): 243–77.

McFaul, M. 1995. "State Power, Institutional Change, and the Politics of Privatization in Russia," *World Politics*, 47, 2: 210–43.

McMann, Kelly. 2003. "The Civic Realm in Kyrgyzstan: Soviet Economic Legacies and Activists' Expectations," in Jones Luong, Pauline, ed. *The Transformation of Central Asia: States and Societies from Soviet Rule to Independence*. Ithaca: Cornell University Press, pp. 213–45.

McMenamin, Iain, and Schoenman, Roger. 2004, "Political Competition: The Rule of Law and Corruption in Successful Post-Communist Countries," *Working Papers in International Studies*, 7.

Meltzer, Allan H., and Richard, Scott F. 1981. "Rational Theory of the Size of Government," *Journal of Political Economy*, 89, 5: 914–27.

Mendilow, Jonathan. 1992. "Public Party Funding and Party Transformation in Multiparty Systems," *Comparative Political Studies*, 25, 1 (April): 90–117.

Mesežnikov, Grigorij. 2002. "Domestic Politics," in Mesežnikov, Grigorij, Kollár, Miroslav, and Nicholson, Tom, eds. *Slovakia 2001*. Bratislava: Institute for Public Affairs, pp. 21–92.

———. 1997. "The Open-Ended Formation of Slovakia's Political Party System," in Szomolányi, Soňa, and John, Gould, eds. *Slovakia: Problems of Democratic Consolidation*. Bratislava: Friedrich Ebert Foundation.

Meyer-Sahling, Jan-Hinrik. 2006. "The Rise of the Partisan State? Parties, Patronage, and the Ministerial Bureaucracy in Hungary," *Journal of Communist Studies and Transition Politics*, 22, 3 (September): 274–97.

Miller, William, Grødeland, Ase, and Koshechkina, Tatyana. 2001. *A Culture of Corruption? Coping with Government in Post-Communist Europe*. Budapest: CEU Press.

Moe, Terry M. 1990. "Political Institutions: The Neglected Side of the Story," *Journal of Law, Economics and Organization*, 7: 213–53.

Moe, Terry M., and Caldwell, Michael, 1994. "The Institutional Foundations of Democratic Government: A Comparison of Presidential and Parliamentary Systems," *Journal of Institutional and Theoretical Economics*, 150/1: 171–95.

Moe, Terry, and Miller, Goney. 1983. "Bureaucrats, Legislators, and the Size of Government," *American Political Science Review*, 77: 297–323.

Montinola, Gabriella, and Jackman, Robert. 2002. "Source of Corruption: A Cross-Country Study," *British Journal of Political Science*, 32, 1 (January): 147–70.

Moravcsik, Andrew, and Vachudová, Milada Anna. 2003. "National Interests, State Power and EU Enlargement," *East European Politics and Societies*, 4, 17, 1 (Winter): 42–57.

Morlino, Leonardo. 2001. "The Three Phases of Italian Parties," in Diamond, Larry, and Gunter, Richard, eds. *Political Parties and Democracy*. Baltimore: Johns Hopkins Press, pp. 109–42.

Müller-Rommel, Ferdinand, Fettelschoss, Katja, and Harst, Philipp, 2004. "Party Government in Central East European Democracies: A Data Collection (1990–2003)," *European Journal of Political Research*, 43: 869–93.

Müller, Wolfgang. 2006. "Party Patronage and Party Colonization of the State," in Katz Richard, and Crotty, William, eds. *Handbook of Party Politic*. London: Sage, pp. 189–95.

———. 1992. "Austrian Governmental Institutions: Do They Matter?" in Luther, Kurt Richard, and Müller, Wolfgang, eds. *Politics in Austria: Still a Case of Consociationalism?* London: Frank Cass, pp. 99–131.

Munck, Gerardo, and Verkuilen, Jay. 2002. "Conceptualizing and Measuring Democracy: Evaluating Alternative Indices," *Comparative Political Studies*, 35, 1: 5–34.

Myerson, Roger. 1993. "Effectiveness of Electoral Systems for Reducing Government Corruption," *Games and Economic Behavior*, 5: 118–32.

Nassmacher, Karl-Heinz. 1989. "Structure and Impact of Public Subsidies to Political Parties in Europe," in Alexander, Herbert, ed. *Comparative Political Finance in the 1980s*. Cambridge: Cambridge University Press, pp. 236–67.

Nello, Susan Senior. 2001. "The Role of the IMF," in Zielonka, Jan, and Pravda, Alex, eds. *Democratic Consolidation in Eastern Europe. Vol. 2: International and Transnational Factors*. Oxford: Oxford University Press.

Nørgaard, Ole, Ostrovska, Ilze, and Hansen, Ole Hersted. 2000. "State of the State in Post-Communist Latvia: State Capacity and Government Effectiveness in a Newly Independent Country." Paper presented at the 2000 European Consortium for Political Research (ECPR) Joint Sessions, Copenhagen.

North, Douglass. 1990. *Institutions, Institutional Change, and Economic Performance*. Cambridge: Cambridge University Press.

———. 1981. *Structure and Change in Economic History*. New York: W. W. Norton.

North, Douglass, and Weingast, Barry. 1989. "Constitutions and Commitment: The Evolution of Institutional Governing Public Choice in Seventeenth-Century England," *Journal of Economic History*, 49, 4 (December): 803–32.

Novotný, Vít. 1999. "Deset lat po listopadu: Omězme Moc české Politické Oligarchie," *Britské Listy*, 29 November.

Nunberg, Barbara. 2000. "Ready for Europe: Public Administration Reform and European Union Accession in Central and Eastern Europe." World Bank Technical Paper No. 466. Washington: World Bank.

Bibliography

————, ed. 1999. *The State After Communism*. Washington: World Bank.

O'Dwyer, Conor. 2004. "Runaway State Building: How Political Parties Shape States in Postcommunist Eastern Europe," *World Politics*: 520–53.

————. 2003. "Expanding the Post-Communist State? A Theory and Some Empirical Evidence." Paper presented at the Annual Convention of the American Association for the Advancement of Slavic Studies (AAASS) Toronto, Canada.

————. 2002. "Civilizing the State Bureaucracy: The Unfulfilled Promise of Public Administration Reform in Poland, Slovakia, and the Czech Republic (1990–2000)." Occasional paper, Berkeley Program in Soviet and Post Soviet Studies.

OECD. 2001a. *Issues and Developments in Public Management: Czech Republic–2000.*

OECD. 2001b. *Issues and Developments in Public Management: Hungry–2000.*

Olson, David. 1998. "Party Formation and Party System Consolidation in the New Democracies of Central Europe," *Political Studies*, 46, 3: 432–64.

Olson, Mancur. 1993. "Dictatorship, Democracy and Development," *American Political Science Review*, 87 (3 September): 567–76.

O'Neil, Patrick. 1998. *Revolution from Within*. Cheltenham: Edward Elgar.

————. 1996. "Revolution from Within: Institutional Analysis, Transitions from Authoritarianisms, and the Case of Hungary," *World Politics*, 48, 4 (July): 579–603.

————. 1993. "Presidential Power in Post-Communist Europe: The Hungarian Case in Comparative Perspective," *Journal of Communist Studies*, 9, 3: 177–201.

Orenstein, Mitchell. 2001. *Out of the Red: Building Capitalism and Democracy in Postcommunist Europe*. Ann Arbor: University of Michigan Press.

Örkény, Antal, and Scheppele, Kim Lane. 1999. "Rules of Law: The Complexity of Legality in Hungary," in Krygier, Martin, and Czarnota, Adam, eds. *The Rule of Law After Communism*. Aldershot: Ashgate.

Ost, David. 1991. "Shaping a New Politics in Poland." Program on Central and Eastern Europe Working Paper Series, Center for European Studies (CES) Harvard University, No. 8.

Panków, Irena. 1991. "Przemiany środowiska społecznego Polaków w latach osiemdziesiatych," *Kultura i Społeczenstwo*, 1: 53–65.

Parlamentní Zpravodaj. 1999. "Jakě jsou klady a zapory aktualního navrhu novely zakona o politických stranach" [What are the bases for the current proposal for the novelization of the law on political parties].

Pempel, T. J. 2000. *Regime Shift: Comparative Dynamics of the Japanese Political Economy*. Ithaca: Cornell University Press.

Peltzman, Sam. 1998. *Political Participation and Government Regulation*. Chicago: University of Chicago Press.

Perkins, Doug. 1996. "Structure and Choice: The Role of Organizations, Patronage, and the Media in Party Formation," *Party Politics*, 2, 3: 355–75.

Persson, Torsten, Tabellini, and Guido. 2002. *Political Economics*. Cambridge: MIT Press.

Persson, Torsten, Tabellini, Guido, and Trebbi, Francesco. 2001. *Electoral Rules and Corruption*. Manuscript, June.

Petroff, Włodzimierz. 1996. *Finansowanie partii politycznych w postkomunistycznej Europie* [The financing of political parties in Europe]. Warsaw: Polish Parliamentary Bureau of Analyses and Expertise.

Pettai, Vello. 1997. "Political Stability Through Disenfranchisement," *Transition*, 3, 6 (4 April).

Pettai, Vello, and Kreuzer, Marcus. 2001. "Institutions and Party Development in the Baltic States," in Lewis, Paul, ed. *Party Development and Democratic Change in Post-Communist Europe*. London: Frank Cass, pp. 107–25.

PHARE and NVF. 1998. "An Analysis of Public Administration of the Czech Republic." Summary Report, Prague, September.

Piattoni, Simona. 2001. "Introduction," in Piattoni, Simona, ed. *Clientelism, Interests, and Democratic Representation*. Cambridge: Cambridge University Press, pp. 1–30.

Pierre, Jon, Svasand, Lars, and Widfeldt, Anders. 2000. "State Subsidies to Political Parties: Confronting Rhetoric with Reality," *West European Politics*, 23, 2 (July): 1–24.

Pinto-Duschinsky, Michael. 1985. "How Can Money in Politics Be Assessed?" Paper presented at the International Political Science Conference Paris.

Plakans, Andrejs. 1998. "Democratization and Political Participation in Post-Communist Societies: The Case of Latvia," in Dawish, Karen, and Parott, Bruce, eds. *The Consolidation of Democracy in East-Central Europe*. Cambridge: Cambridge University Press.

Plasser, Fritz, Ulram, Peter, and Grausgruber, Alfred. 1992. "The Decline of 'Lager Mentality' and the New Model of Electoral Competition in Austria," in Luther, Kurt Richard, and Müller, Wolfgang, eds. *Politics in Austria: Still a Case of Consociationalism?* London: Frank Cass.

Poggi, Gianfranco. 1990. *The State: Its Nature, Development, and Prospects*. Stanford: Stanford University Press.

Powell, Bingham. 2000. *Elections as Instruments of Democracy*. New Haven: Yale University Press.

Protsyk, Oleh. 2003. *Reforming Cabinets in Post-Communist Countries: Political Determinants of Cabinet Organization and Size*. Manuscript, University of Ottawa, Canada.

Przeworski, Adam. 1999. "Minimalist Conception of Democracy: A Defense," in Shapiro, Ian, and Hacker-Cordón, Casiano, eds. *Democracy's Value*. Cambridge: Cambridge University Press, pp. 23–55.

———. 1997. "The State in a Market Economy," in Nelson, Joan, Tilly, Charles, and Walker, Lee, eds. *Transforming Post-Communist Political Economies*. Washington: National Academy Press, pp. 411–31.

———. 1991. *Democracy and Market*. Cambridge: Cambridge University Press.

———. 1990. *The State and the Economy Under Capitalism*. London: Harwood Academic.

Przeworski, Adam, et al. 1995. *Sustainable Democracy*. Cambridge: Cambridge University Press.

Pujas, Véronique, and Rhodes, Martin. 1999. "Party Finance and Political Scandal in Italy, Spain, and France," *West European Politics*, 22, 3: 41–63.

Raiser, Martin, Di Tommaso, Maria, and Weeks, Melvyn. 2000. "The Measurement and Determinants of Institutional Change: Evidence from Transition Economies." EBRD Working Paper No. 60.

Reed, Quentin. 2002. "Corruption in Czech Privatization: The Dangers of 'Neo-Liberal' Privatization," in Kotkin, Stephen, and Sajos, Andras, eds. *Political Corruption: A Skeptic's Handbook*. Budapest: CEU Press, pp. 261–86.

_____. 1996. *Political Corruption, Privatization and Control in the Czech Republic.* Unpublished Doctoral Dissertation, Oxford University.

Regulski, Jerzy. 1999. "Building Democracy in Poland: The State Reform of 1998." Discussion Paper 9, Local Government and Public Service Reform Initiative. Budapest: Open Society Institute.

Remington, Thomas, and Smith, Steven. 1996. "Institutional Design, Uncertainty, and Path Dependency During Transition," *American Journal of Political Science* 40, 4: 1253–79.

Rice, Eric. 1992. "Public Administration in Post-Socialist Eastern Europe," *Public Administration Review*, 52, 2 (March/April): 116–24.

Richardson, Bradley. 2001. "Japan's '1995 System' and Beyond," in Diamond, Larry, and Gunther, Richard, eds. *Political Parties and Democracy*. Baltimore: Johns Hopkins Press, pp. 143–69.

Riker, William. 1982. *Liberalism Against Populism*. Prospect Heights: Waveland Press.

Riker, William, and Ordeshook, Peter. 1968. "A Theory of the Calculus of Voting," *American Political Science Review*, 62: 25–43.

Robinson, James, and Verdier, Therry. 2002. "The Political Economy of Clientelism." Centre for Economic Policy Discussion Paper Series No. 3205.

Roland, Gerard. 2001. "Ten Years After . . . Transition and Economics." IMF Staff Papers, No. 48. Washington: International Monetary Fund.

Róna-Tas, Ákos. 1997. *The Great Surprise of the Small Transformation*. Ann Arbor: University of Michigan Press.

Rose-Ackerman, Susan. 1999. *Corruption and Government: Causes, Consequences, and Reform*. Cambridge: Cambridge University Press.

_____. 1978. *Corruption*. New York: Academic Press.

Roubini, Nouriel, and Sachs, Jeffrey. 1989. "Government Spending and Budget Deficits in the Industrial Economies." NBER Working Papers No. 2919, National Bureau of Economic Research.

Rus, Andrej. 1996. "Quasi Privatization: From Class Struggle to a Scuffle of Small Particularisms," in Benderly, Jill, and Kraft, Evan, eds. *Independent Slovenia: Origins, Movements, Prospects*. New York: St. Martin's Press, pp. 225–50.

Rybář, Marek. 2006. "Powered by the State: The Role of Public Resources in Party-Building in Slovakia," *Journal of Communist Studies and Transition Politics*, 22, 3 (September): 320–40.

Rydlewski, Grzegorz. 2000. *Rządzenie Koalicyjne w Polsce*. Warsaw: Elipsa.

Sadurski, Wojciech, ed. 2002. *Constitutional Justice, East and West: Democratic Legitimacy and Constitutional Courts in Post-Communist Europe*. The Hague: Kluwer Law International.

Sajo, Andras. 1998a. "Corruption, Clientelism, and the Future of the Constitutional State in Eastern Europe," *East European Constitutional Review*, 7, 2. Available at http://www.law.nyu.edu/eecr/vol7num2.

———. 1998b. "How the Rule of Law Can Facilitate the Spread of Sleaze," *East European Constitutional Review*. 7, 2. Available at http://www.law.ngu.edu/eecr/vol7num 2.

Samuels, David. 2001. "Does Money Matter? Credible Commitments and Campaign Finance in New Democracies," *Comparative Politics*, 34, 1 (October): 23–42.

Sartori, Giovanni. 1976. *Parties and Party Systems: A Framework for Analysis*. Cambridge: Cambridge University Press.

Scarrow, Susan. 2002. "Parties Without Members?" in Dalton, Russell, and Wattenberg, Martin, eds. *Parties Without Partisans: Political Change in Advanced Industrial Democracies*. Oxford: Oxford University Press.

Schamis, Hector E. 2002. *Re-Forming the State: The Politics of Privatization in Latin America and Europe*. Ann Arbor: University of Michigan Press.

Schavio-Campo, Salvatore, do Tommaso, G., and Mukherjee, A. 1997a. "Government Employment and Pay in Global Perspective." Washington: World Bank Policy Research Working Paper No. 1771.

———. 1997b. "An International Statistical Survey of Government Employment and Wages." World Bank Policy Research Working Paper No. 1806.

Scheppele, Kim Lane. 2002. "Democracy by Judiciary." Paper presented at the conference. Rethinking the Rule of Law in Post-Communist Europa: Past Legacies, Institutional Innovations, and Constitutional Discourses, EUI, Florence, 22–3 February.

Scherpereel, John. 2003. "Appreciating the Third Player: The European Union and the Politics of Civil Service Reform in East Central Europe." Paper prepared for presentation at the Annual Meeting of American Political Science Association (APSA), Philadelphia, 28–31 August.

Schumpeter, Joseph. 1948. *Capitalism, Socialism, and Democracy*. Chicago: University of Chicago Press.

Scott, James. 1972. *Comparative Political Corruption*. Englewood Cliffs: Prentice Hall.

Shefter, Martin. 1994. *Political Parties and the State: The American Experience*. Princeton: Princeton University Press.

Shleifer, Andrei, and Vishny, Robert W. 1998. *The Grabbing Hand: Government Pathologies and Their Cures*. Cambridge: Harvard University Press.

———. 1993. "Corruption," *Quarterly Journal of Economics*, 108: 599–617.

SIGMA. 2002a. "Bulgaria: Public Service and the Administrative Framework: Assessment 2002."

———. 2002b. "Czech Republic: Public Service and the Administrative Framework: Assessment 2002."

———. 2002c. "Latvia: Public Service and the Administrative Framework: Assessment 2002."

———. 2002d. "Slovakia: Public Service and the Administrative Framework: Assessment 2002."

_____. 1999. Public Management Profiles of Central and East European Countries: Estonia. October.

Sikk, Allan. 2006. "From Private Organizations to Democratic Infrastructure: Political Parties and the State in Estonia," *Journal of Communist Studies and Transitional Politics*, 22, 3 (September): 341–61.

_____. 2003. "A Cartel Party System in a Post-Communist Country? The Case of Estonia." Paper prepared for the European Constitution for Political Review (ECPR) General Conference, 18–21 September, Marborg, Germany.

Sjöblom, Gunnar. 1983. "Political Change and Political Accountability: A Propositional Inventory of Causes and Effects," in Daalder, Hans, and Peter, Mair, eds. *West European Party Systems*. London: Sage.

Skach, Cindy, and Stepan, Alfred. 1993. "Constitutional Frameworks and Democratic Consolidation: Parliamentarianism Versus Presidentialism," *World Politics*, 46, 1: 1–22.

Slovak Government Information Service. 2000. "Audit súladu činností a financovania ústredných orgánov štátnej správy" [Audit of the activities and finances of the central institutions of public administration]. August. Also available at http://www.vlada.gov.sk/INFOSERVIs/.

_____. 1999. "*Analysis of the Inherited State of the Economy and Society.*"

Smith, David, Pabriks, Artis, Purs, Aldis, and Lane, Thomas. 2002. *The Baltic States*. London: Routledge.

Smith, Karen. 2001. "The Promotion of Democracy," in Zielonka, Jan, and Pravda, Alex, eds. *Democratic Consolidation in Eastern Europe. Vol. 2: International and Transnational Factors*. Oxford: Oxford University Press, pp. 31–57.

Smithey, Shannon Ishiyama, and Ishiyama, John. 2000. "Judicious Choices: Designing Courts in Post-Communist Politics," *Communist and Post-Communist Studies*, 33: 163–82.

Snipe, Arta. 2003. *Financing of Political Parites: Effectiveness of Regulation. The Latvian Example*. Master's Thesis, Riga Graduate School of Law, Riga, Latvia.

Spar, Deborah. 1994. *The Cooperative Edge: The Internal Politics of International Cartels*. Ithaca: Cornell University Press.

Spruyt, Hendrik. 1992. *The Sovereign State and Its Competitors*. Princeton: Princeton University Press.

Staniszkis, Jadwiga. 1999. *Post-Socialism*. Warsaw: PAN.

Stark, David, and Bruszt, Laszlo. 1998. *Postsocialist Pathways*. Cambridge: Cambridge University Press.

Stein, Jonathan. 1998. "Still in Bed Together." *New Presence* (January). Available at http://www.new-presence.in.

Stepan, Alfred. 1994. "Corruption in South America," in Trang, Due, ed. *Corruption and Democracy*. Budapest: CEU.

Stigler, George. 1975. *The Citizen and the State*. Chicago: University of Chicago Press.

_____. 1972. "Economic Competition and Political Competition," *Public Choice*, 13: 91–106.

Stroehlein, Andrew. 1999. "The Czech Republic 1992 to 1999," *Central Europe Review*. (13 September). Available at http://www.ce-review:org.

Strøm, Kaare. 2000. "Delegation and Accountability in Parliamentary Democracies," *European Journal of Political Research*, 37: 261–89.

———. 1990. *Minority Government and Majority Rule*. Cambridge: Cambridge University Press.

———. 1989. "Inter-Party Competition in Advanced Democracies," *Journal of Theoretical Politics*, 1, 3: 277–300.

Suleiman, Ezra N. 2003. *Dismantling Democratic States*. Princeton: Princeton University Press.

Swaniewiuz. Pawet. 2004. *Consolidation or Fragmentation?* Budapest: Open Society Institute.

Szabó, Gábor. 1993. "Administrative Transition in a Post-Communist Society: The Case of Hungary," Hesse, Joachim Jens, ed. *Administrative Transformation in Central and Eastern Europe*. Oxford: Blackwell.

Szczerbak, Aleks. 2006. "State Party Funding and Patronage in Post-1989 Poland," *Journal of Communist Studies and Transition Politics*, 22, 3 (September): 298–319.

Szelenyi, Ivan, and Szelenyi, Sonya. 1991. "The Vacuum in Hungarian Politics: Classes and Parties," *New Left Review* (May–June): 121–37.

Szoboszlai, György, 1985a. "Bureaucracy and Social Control," in Szoboszlai, György, ed. *Politics and Public Administration in Hungary*. Budapest: Akadémiai Kiadó.

———, ed. 1985b. *Politics and Public Administration in Hungary*. Budapest: Akadémiai Kiadó.

Szomolányi, Soňa. 1997. "Identifying Slovakia's Emerging Regime," in Szomolányi, Soňa, and Gould, John, eds. *Slovakia: Problems of Democratic Consolidation*. Bratislava: Friedrich Ebert Foundation, pp. 9–34.

Tarrow, Sidney. 1990. "Maintaining Hegemony in Italy: 'The Softer They Rise, the Slower They Fall,'" in Pempol, T. J., ed. *Uncommon Democracies: The One-Party Dominant Regimes*. Ithaca: Cornell University Press, pp. 306–32.

Terra, Jonathan. 2002. "Political Institutions and Post Communist Transitions." Paper prepared for the Fourth Annual Society for Comparative Research Graduate Student Retreat, Budapest, May.

Thayer, Nathaniel. 1969. *How the Conservatives Rule Japan*. Princeton: Princeton University Press.

Tilly, Charles. 1990. *Coercion, Capital, and European States*. Cambridge: Blackwell.

Tisenkopfs, Tālis, and Kalniņš, Valts. 2002. "Public Accountability Procedures in Politics in Latvia." Report, Baltic Studies Center, Riga, Latvia, February.

Todorova, Rossitsa. 2001. "EU Integration as an Agent of Public Administration Reform." Unpublished Manuscript, American University in Bulgaria.

Toonen, Theo. 1993. "Analysing Institutional Change," in Hesse, Joachim Jens, ed. *Administrative Transformation in Central and Eastern Europe*. London: Blackwell.

Torres-Bartyzel, Claudia, and Kacprowicz, Grażyna. 1999. "The National Civil Service System in Poland," in Verheijen, Tony, ed. *Civil Service Systems in Central and Eastern Europe*. Cheltenham: Edward Elgar, pp. 159–83.

Trang, Duc, ed. 1994. *Corruption and Democracy*. Budapest: CEN Press.

Treisman, Daniel. 2000. "The Causes of Corruption: A Cross-National Study," *Journal of Public Economics*, 76: 399–457.

———. 1998. "Dollars and Democratization: The Role and Power of Money in Russia's Transitional Elections," *Comparative Politics*, 31, 1 (October): 1–21.

Tullock, Gordon. 1967. "The Welfare Costs of Tariffs, Monopolies and Theft," *Western Economic Journal*, 5: 224–32.

Turner, Arthur. 1993. "Postauthoritarian Elections: Testing Expectations about 'First' Elections," *Comparative Political Studies*, 26, 3 (October): 330–49.

USAID public opinion poll. 1999. Radio Free Europe/Radio Liberty broadcast, Slovakia, 10 November.

Úsek pro Reformu Veřejné správy. [Section for the Reform of the Public Administration]. 2001. "Vybrané výstupy z projekty PHARE CZ 9808.01 Posílení institucionálních a administrativních kapacit pro implementaci *acquis communautaire*." Prague.

Vachudová, Milada Anna. 2005. *Europe Undivided: Democracy, Leverage and Integration After Communism*. Oxford and New York: Oxford University Press, ch. 1.

Vanagunas, Stan. 1997. "Civil Service Reform in the Baltics." Paper presented for conference on Civil Service Systems in Comparative Perspective, Indiana University Bloomington, 5–8 April.

Van Biezen, Ingrid. 2004. "Political Parties as Public Utilities," *Party Politics*, 10, 6: 701–22.

———. 2000. "Party Financing in New Democracies," *Party Politics*, 6, 3: 329–42.

Van Biezen, Ingrid, and Kopecký, Petr. 2001. "On the Predominance of State Money: Reassessing Party Financing in the New Democracies of Southern and Eastern Europe," *Perspectives on European Politics and Society*, 2, 3: 401–29.

Vass, László. 1994. "Changes in Hungary's Governmental System," in Ágh, Attila, ed. *The Emergence of West Central European Parliaments: The First Steps*. Budapest: Hungarian Center for Democracy Studies, pp. 186–97.

Verheijen, Tony. 2002. "The European Union and Public Administration Development in Central and Eastern Europe," in Baker, Randall, ed. *Transitions from Authoritarianism: The Role of the Bureaucracy*. London: Praeger.

———. 1999. "The Civil Service of Bulgaria: Hope on the Horizon," in Verheijen, Tony, ed. *Civil Service Systems in Central and Eastern Europe*. Cheltenham: Edward Elgar, pp. 92–130.

Vinton, Lucy. 1993. Poland's New Election Law: Fewer Parties, Same Impasse? *RFE/RL Report* (8 July): 7–17.

Vládní program boje proti korupci v Česke Republice. [Government program for the fight against corruption in the Czech Republic]. 1998. "Zpráva o korupci v České republice a možnostech účinného postupu proti tomut negativnímu společenskému jevu." [Report about corruption in the Czech Republic and the possibilities of an active approach against this negative social development], 17 February.

Vreeland, James Raymond. 2003. *The IMF and Economic Development*. Cambridge: Cambridge University Press.

Walecki, Marcin, ed. 2002. *Finansowanie Polityki*. Warsaw: Wydawnictwo Sejmowe.

Warner, Carolyn. 2001. "Mass Parties and Clientelism: France and Italy," in Piattoni, Simona, ed. *Clientelism, Interests, and Democratic Representation*. Cambridge: Cambridge University Press, pp. 122–51.

Wasilewski, Jacek, 2000. "Polish Post-Transitional Elite," in Frentzel-Zagórska, Janina, and Wasilewski, Jacek, eds. Warsaw: PAN ISP. *The Second Generation of Democratic Elites in East and Central Europe*.

Waterbury, John. 1973. "Endemic and Planned Corruption in a Monarchical Regime," *World Politics*, 25, 4 (July): 533–55.

Weber, Max. 1947. *Wirtschaft und Gesellshaft*. Tübingen: Mohr.

Weingast, Barry. 1997. "The Political Foundations of Democracy and the Rule of Law," *American Political Science Review*, 91 (June): 245–63.

Weingast, Barry, and Marshall, William. 1988. "The Industrial Organization of Congress; or, Why Legislatures, Like Firms, Are Not Organized as Markets," *Journal of Political Economy*, 96, 1: 132–63.

Winiecki, Jan. 1996. "Impediments to Institutional Change in the Former Soviet System," in Alston, Lee, et al., eds. *Empirical Studies in Institutional Change*. Cambridge: Cambridge University Press, pp. 63–91.

Wittman, Donald. 1995. *The Myth of Democratic Failure*. Chicago: University of Chicago Press.

World Bank. 1999. *Corruption in Poland: Review of Priority Areas and Proposals for Action*. Warsaw: World Bank.

Zemanovičová, Daniela, and Sičáková, Emília. 2001. "Transparency and Corruption," in Mesežnikov, Miroslav, Grigorij, Kollár, and Nicholson, Tom, eds. *Slovakia 2001*. Bratislava: Institute for Public Affairs, pp. 537–52.

Zielonka, Jan. 1994. "New Institutions in the Old East Bloc," *Journal of Democracy*, 5: 87–104.

Žižmond, Egon. 1993. "Slovenia–One Year of Independence," *Europe-Asia Studies*, 45, 5: 887–905.

Zuckerman, Alan. 1979. *The Politics of Faction: Christian Democratic Rule in Italy*. New Haven: Yale University Press.

Index

Index